A New Economic History of Argentina

Edited by

GERARDO DELLA PAOLERA
American University of Paris and Fundación PENT

ALAN M. TAYLOR
University of California, Davis, NBER, and CEPR

T0323346

CAMBRIDGE UNIVERSITY PRESS
Cambridge, New York, Melbourne, Madrid, Cape Town,
Singapore, São Paulo, Delhi, Tokyo, Mexico City

Cambridge University Press
The Edinburgh Building, Cambridge CB2 8RU, UK

Published in the United States of America by
Cambridge University Press, New York

www.cambridge.org
Information on this title: www.cambridge.org/9780521283250

© Cambridge University Press 2003 (except Spanish Language)

First published 2003
Reprinted 2005, 2007

A catalogue record for this publication is available from the British Library

ISBN 978-0-521-82247-3 Hardback
ISBN 978-0-521-28325-0 Paperback

To the memory of Carlos F. Díaz Alejandro

Contents

List of tables

List of illustrations

List of contributors

María Inés Barbero
Universidad de Buenos Aires and Universidad Nacional de General Sarmiento

Sergio Berensztein
Universidad Torcuato Di Tella

Julio Berlinski
Instituto Torcuato Di Tella and Universidad Torcuato Di Tella

Carlos G. Bózzoli
Princeton University

Gerardo della Paolera
American University of Paris and Fundación PENT

Sebastián Galiani
Universidad de San Andrés

Ezequiel Gallo
Universidad Torcuato Di Tella

Pablo Gerchunoff
Universidad Torcuato Di Tella

Maria Alejandra Irigoin
Universidad Carlos III de Madrid

Ramiro Moya
Fundación Investigaciones Económicas Latinoamericanas

Yair Mundlak
Hebrew University of Jerusalem

Leonard I. Nakamura
Federal Reserve Bank of Philadelphia

Carlos Newland
Universidad Argentina de la Empresa

Marcelo Regúnaga
Universidad de Buenos Aires

Fernando Rocchi
Universidad Torcuato Di Tella

Ricardo D. Salvatore
Universidad Torcuato Di Tella

Horacio Spector
Universidad Torcuato Di Tella

Adolfo Sturzenegger
Universidad Nacional de La Plata and Universidad Austral

Alan M. Taylor
University of California, Davis, NBER, and CEPR

Carlos E. J. M. Zarazaga
Federal Reserve Bank of Dallas

Acknowledgments

This volume represents an edited collection of some papers presented at a conference on the new economic history of Argentina, which was held at the Hotel Llao Llao in Bariloche on November 7–9, 2000.

We, the editors, thank all those involved in this project for their support and enthusiasm, which was grounded in a firm belief in the importance and relevance of economic history. We think their faith has been proved right. Between the project's inception and this book's publishing, a great deal has changed in Argentina's economy, society, and politics – though fundamentally much remains the same as ever. The disastrous events of 2001–02 boomed like yet another echo from a past defined by cycles of hope and disappointment, as seasoned observers soon realized. They were quickly joined by a new crowd of puzzled bystanders, since this was a crash heard round the world through market reactions and media spin. All gathered around the latest wreck and wondered where this country went wrong. As the book was complete long before this latest crisis, none of us knew then just how timely this project would be, but current events now jarringly remind us of the enduring puzzles of the Argentine economic story.

On behalf of all participants, the editors of this volume, who were also the conference organizers, wish to express their profound gratitude to the William and Flora Hewlett Foundation, without whose very generous lead support this conference could not have taken place. We are indebted to them and to their staff on the U.S.–Latin American Relations Program, especially the program director, David Lorey, and the foundation's envoy to the conference, Joseph Ryan. The conference also received valuable support from the Banco de la Nación Argentina and we warmly appreciate their backing for this type of basic research on the Argentine economy. Editing and preparation of the book manuscript was further assisted by a grant from the University of California at

Davis, Division of Social Sciences and Office of Research, which is gratefully acknowledged.

The academic program was enlivened when the hard work of the authors was confronted with constructive comments from a distinguished panel of discussants. For their insightful critiques, not to mention their willingness to travel to the far south, we offer our thanks to Roberto Cortés Conde, Stephen Haber, Colin Lewis, George McCandless, and Tomás Serebrisky.

This book has been greatly improved by the superb editorial and production work of Cambridge University Press, and we are especially indebted to Press editor Frank Smith, editorial assistant Barbara Chin, copy editor Jennifer Robin Collier, production editing supervisor Shari Chappell, and the anonymous referees. For his additional copyediting assistance we are deeply grateful to David Jacks.

We know that we speak for all participants when we say that our time in Bariloche was as enjoyable as an academic conference could be. The facilities and hospitality (and views) provided by the Hotel Llao Llao were, as always, world class and a smooth visit was ensured by the grace and courtesy of Maria José Miguens and the rest of the hotel staff. Most of all we must thank one key individual. The organization of an event on this scale requires a great deal of administrative effort and skill, and in that respect we owe an enormous debt to Silvana Reale, who oversaw the arrangements from start to finish with impeccable efficiency, a ruthless attention to detail, and an unflagging good humor, even when surrounded by absent-minded professors deep in Patagonia.

G. d. P. and A. M. T.
Paris and Davis, November 2002

1
Introduction

GERARDO DELLA PAOLERA
American University of Paris and Fundación PENT

ALAN M. TAYLOR
University of California, Davis, NBER, and CEPR

This book provides a collection of essays on the economic development of Argentina since the late-nineteenth century, in itself one of the most puzzling stories in the annals of modern economic history. The aim is to offer the reader access to the current state of research, focusing on long-run features of the economy, major developments in policymaking, and important shifts in institutions and ideas.

A work such as this naturally draws on many years of work by researchers in various disciplines all across the social sciences to distill the important economic dimensions of the country's history and to do so in a quantitative rather than purely qualitative way. Whereas the major works in Argentine economic history have been, up to now, centered on the historian's narrative tools of description, the insights that can be drawn from formal economic analysis remain unduly neglected, with a few illuminating exceptions.

Specifically, it was high time for a project such as this on the thirtieth anniversary of Carlos Díaz Alejandro's pathbreaking *Essays on the Economic History of the Argentine Republic* (1970). That book never claimed to be a complete economic history of Argentina, and in substance and style it was as idiosyncratic as its genius author. All the same, it remains the standard reference for those seeking a more quantitative understanding of Argentina's development. It is also much more: for Díaz Alejandro, with that elusive mix of humanistic and scientific insight, was a true pioneer of a style of economic writing for which, years later, we have coined the term *analytic narrative*. Today's economic historians aspire to the same style, one that poses questions and employs methods from the field of economics.

This certainly marks a new turn in the field of Argentine economic history, one that both complements the existing historical literature and showcases a different range of skills deployed by a new generation of scholars. These researchers have made great strides employing the techniques of new economic history to craft a more sophisticated interpretation of the past. Their craft embraces a wide range of skills: the collection of archival data familiar to the traditional historian; the use of quantitative economic models of econometric methods that is the hallmark of the cliometric movement; and the study of law, political economy, and institutions that is central to the school of new institutional economics.

Following these leads, the new economic history of Argentina encompasses more than either pure economics or history alone, and draws practitioners from all disciplines in the social sciences. We were fortunate to be able to bring together just such a diverse group of experts at a conference in November 2000 from whom we had commissioned papers that would convey the major findings emerging from this exciting new literature. This edited volume is the result, a collection that looks back on nineteenth- and twentieth-century economic history and outlines the lessons from Argentina's turbulent economic past for the issues that confront scholars, students, and policymakers today.

1.1 The Argentine puzzle

What is the puzzle of Argentine economic growth?[1] It can be neatly encapsulated by looking at the level of economic development around four benchmark dates: the year 1820, a date in the early-nineteenth century shortly after independence; the year 1870, a date in the middle of the "long-nineteenth century"; the year 1913, a date at the end of the "long-nineteenth century" and at the zenith of the *Belle Époque*; and the present, when we can use the latest cross-country evidence available. Studies of historical income allow us to address a central question in world history: is the income divergence between developing economies (the "periphery") and the developed world (the "core") a "new" phenomenon, a legacy of the industrial and postindustrial twentieth century, or does it date back to 1800 or even earlier?

Around 1800, Argentina had an income level well above that of its neighbors in the region and similar to the levels seen in Europe or the United States at that time. Coatsworth (1999) estimates Argentine per capita income at 102 percent of the U.S. level in 1800, compared to 66 percent for the region as a whole. For a broader comparison, Maddison (1995) places U.S. per capita income at $1,287 in 1820 (in 1992 international dollars, used henceforth in this section), compared to $1,228 in Western Europe, and $1,236 in the "Western offshoots" (meaning Australia, Canada, New Zealand, and the United States). This would place Argentina at about $1,300 per capita if it were still at 102 percent of

---

[1] This section draws on della Paolera and Taylor (2001).

the U.S level in 1820, and the region as a whole at roughly $900. Essentially, Argentina was a relatively rich country, but others in the region were poorer.

Despite early evidence of "Argentine exceptionalism" a new trend emerged in the mid-nineteenth century. The core economies' growth accelerated as the industrial revolution spread, but Latin America, beset by wars and economic chaos, stood still, or even fell backward. By 1870 Western European incomes had risen to $1,986 per capita, and the offshoots to $2,748. But Argentine per capita income still stood at $1,300 five decades later, and the region as a whole at about $800. Argentina was still richer than its neighbors, by roughly the same amount, but it had not kept up with the core.

It was at around this time, of course, that the postindependence wars ended and aspirations for economic development that would close this gap took shape. Remarkably, the dreams started to come true: in several Latin American countries, including Mexico and Chile, but most noticeably in Argentina, there was an acceleration in economic growth rates after 1870 that implied a convergence on the core economies. For example, from the 1880s to 1913, Argentina had an average growth rate of 5 percent per annum in output, or about half that in per capita terms. This was a stunning performance – by 1900 Argentina's income per capita had risen from about 67 percent of developed-country levels in 1870, to 90 percent in 1900, and 100 percent in 1913.

In Figure 1.1 we get a more complete picture by comparing Argentine performance to a wide sample of countries from 1820 to the present. By 1913 it must have seemed that the process of convergence was almost complete and Argentina had established a clear lead in income levels over the rest of the region.[2] These trends surely fostered the idea that Argentina had become an "advanced" economy, differentiating itself from its "backward" neighbors. The Argentine level of $3,797 in 1913 even slightly surpassed the levels in many middle-income European economies at the time, such as France ($3,452), Germany ($3,134), and Netherlands ($3,533). It was eclipsed only by the United Kingdom ($5,032) and the four Western offshoots, notably the United States ($5,307) and Australia ($5,505), and it was well above the levels in poorer Southern European countries such as Italy ($2,507) and Spain ($2,255). Argentina's 1913 income level was clearly in the world top ten, and almost the top five. Whatever its exact status in 1913, for all practical purposes Argentina was an advanced country.[3]

---

[2] In the text and figure we use a weighted average of Western Europe plus Western offshoots plus Japan (a pseudo-OECD subset) as a measure of developed-country levels of income per capita.

[3] Our modern-day perspective comes from the data of Maddison (1995), but those witness to events in this period were not unaware of Argentina's elevated status; see, for example, Mulhall (1903).

Fig. 1.1. Comparative economic development

Scale: relative to Western Europe = 1.0, in all years

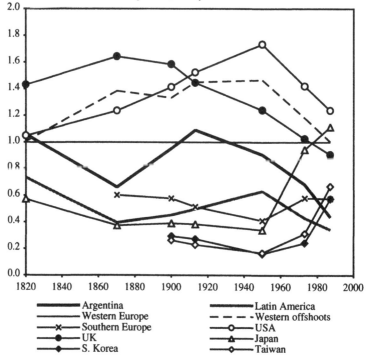

	Argentina		Latin America
	Western Europe	– – –	Western offshoots
—×—	Southern Europe	—o—	USA
—●—	UK	—△—	Japan
—◆—	S. Korea	—◇—	Taiwan

	1820	1870	1900	1913	1950	1973	1992
Argentina	1,300	1,311	2,756	3,797	4,987	7,970	7,616
Latin America (7)	900	783	1,311	1,733	3,478	5,017	5,949
Western Europe (12)	1,228	1,986	2,899	3,482	5,513	11,694	17,412
Western offshoots (4)	1,236	2,748	3,868	5,051	8,083	13,828	17,475
Southern Europe (5)	—	1,194	1,676	1,788	2,259	6,770	10,015
United States	1,287	2,457	4,096	5,307	9,573	16,607	21,558
United Kingdom	1,756	3,263	4,593	5,032	6,847	11,992	15,738
Japan	704	741	1,135	1,334	1,873	11,017	19,425
South Korea	—	—	850	948	876	2,840	10,010
Taiwan	—	—	759	794	922	3,669	11,590

Latin America (7): Argentina, Brazil, Chile, Colombia, Mexico, Peru, Venezuela.
Western Europe (12): Austria, Belgium, Denmark, Finland, France, Germany, Italy, Netherlands, Norway, Sweden, Switzerland, United Kingdom.
European New World (4, called "Western offshoots" by Maddison): Australia, Canada, New Zealand, United States.
Southern Europe (5): Greece, Ireland, Portugal, Spain, Turkey.
Notes and sources: Data in the table from Maddison (1995) in 1992 PPP-adjusted international dollars, except for the 1820 entries for Argentina and Latin America from the estimates in the text. Figure shows incomes relative to a Western Europe arithmetic average equal to 1.0. *The figure shows relative rather than absolute economic performance.*

The stage was thus set for a dramatic reversal of fortune in the twentieth century. Economic growth in Latin America lagged behind the core OECD countries, and the performance of Argentina was worse still. A regression of disturbing proportions is clearly visible in Figure 1.1. Argentina's ratio of 80 percent of OECD income levels in 1913 accords this date great historical significance as the time when Argentina was as close as it ever came to joining the "club" of core economies. Ever since, the income trend has been down and away from the OECD level, with a reversion back toward the average of Latin America as a whole. Argentina's ratio to OECD income fell to 84 percent in 1950, 65 percent in 1973, and a mere 43 percent in 1987, not so far above the regional average of 34 percent.

Argentina is therefore unique. It has nothing in common with the legions of less-developed countries that have always been relatively poor and never managed to make a transition to sustained modern economic growth. It also has little in common here with that much smaller group of poor and peripheral economies that have made a transition to developed-country status and have not, as yet, relinquished that gain.

1.2 The timing controversy

The above data leave no doubt that Argentina qualifies as the unique country in the modern era that was once relatively very rich and is now relatively poor. This fact alone tends to spark even more debate. How did this economic malaise come about? What were the causes? And, for those unsatisfied with that level of analysis, what were the causes of the causes? In the standard methodology of applied economics, changes in Argentina's economic performance can be analyzed by looking at how they have correlated with measures of economic policies, institutional change, external conditions, and a host of other variables. The main caveat is that, as the saying goes, correlation is not causation, as many of the variables that co-vary with growth are also themselves endogenous variables. These issues will be taken up in a moment, but as a start it will clear the air to ask if we can even lay down a basic timetable for Argentina's economic retardation, so that a rough timing can be established. Surprisingly, even this simple chronology has caused great controversy.

When did Argentina lose its way?[4] One traditional view places the onset of Argentine retardation after 1929, with serious divergence beginning later with the postwar autarkic policies associated with the Peronist government. Such a characterization is not at odds with the data shown above – there do appear to

---

[4] This section draws on Taylor (1992).

be marked deviations of Argentine growth from the OECD path after 1929 and more so after the Second World War. Díaz Alejandro (1970, 51–55; 1988, 232) dates the end of the *Belle Époque* as late as the onset of the Great Depression in 1929, noting that Argentine per capita income continued to converge upward on Australian levels into the 1920s. Elsewhere, he uses similar evidence on respectable growth performance relative to Australia and Canada to dismiss Di Tella and Zymelman's (1967, chaps. 2–4) thesis that Argentina experienced a "Great Delay" between 1914 and 1933, a delay they attribute to misguided policies.[5]

But were the Great Depression and the Peronist postwar period the *only* times of retardation? History need not be characterized by just one or two turning points. In defense of the early-retardation hypothesis, Di Tella can cite the precipitous decline in growth rates observed at the First World War, a retardation which has persisted to the present day. By way of explanation, he invokes the closing of the frontier, since the Pampas had become fully occupied around that time. He concludes that the extensive growth strategy had run its course:

The rate of growth of the economy, after the closing of the frontier, averaged about 3 percent per year in the interwar period, and about the same from the Second World War. But when the actual development is compared with the pre-1914 performance, or even more so with the expectations nurtured at the beginning of this century, Argentine performance looks dismal. It is this false comparison between a wrongly based projection and the actual performance that has contributed to the sense of failure which permeates the Argentines' view of themselves as a Nation. (Di Tella 1986, 122)

The possibility of a first break in the growth path circa 1913 certainly looks consistent with the data shown earlier. This year represents the point of closest convergence between Argentine and OECD per-capita income levels.

These debates matter for a very simple reason. Can all of Argentina's problems be ascribed to poor policies, that is, internal conditions? Or did external conditions, shocks in the global economy, also play a part? It was not just the Great Depression, but also the devastating recession during the First World War that encouraged Argentina and other Latin American countries to doubt the merits of an export-oriented and capital-importing strategy in an imploding global economy. Instead, these countries eventually subscribed to inward-looking economic policies and import substitution – policies later to be codified and applied by the Economic Commission for Latin America (ECLA) through the efforts of Raúl Prebisch (1984) and other structuralists. Díaz Alejandro (1970, 1974, 1978, 1984ab), in a large body of work, distinguishes between the effi-

---

[5] See also Ferrer (1967).

cacy of these "reactive" policies in the Depression years and their persistence after the Second World War that inhibited export-led growth and placed a drag on Argentine development. Clearly, then, if economic failure can be said to predate the adoption of import-substitution doctrines, the structuralist camp can evade some responsibility for decline, and some blame falls on the liberal, export-oriented policy regime prevailing until 1929 – a point lost on neither Díaz Alejandro, one of the harshest critics of structuralism, nor Di Tella, a sometime apologist for import substitution.

As noted by Taylor (1992), one's view of relative Argentine retardation depends entirely on the basis of the comparison. Australia and Canada perform dismally in the inter-war period, undergoing retardation relative to the OECD group as a whole (their ratio of income per capita relative to the OECD average fell from 1913 to 1929); in this context Argentine performance looks respectable. Furthermore, the post-1913 growth retardation was much more serious in the settler economies (ranging from 1.59 to 2.23 percentage points) than in the OECD (minus 0.25). In a sense, Díaz Alejandro is right to praise Argentina for keeping pace with the other settler economies; but keeping pace with stragglers is no great feat.[6]

Such informal empiricism has now been joined by a more formal analysis of Argentina's growth performance. In recent work, Sanz (2002) uses the econometric techniques of break-point models to investigate the existence and magnitude of structural shifts in the growth process of income per capita over more than a century of data. She found evidence of major structural breaks in the Argentine series in 1913, 1929, and 1975. In 1913 both the level and trend of real GDP per capita fell substantially, in 1929 the level fell again (only about half as much as in 1913), and in 1975 the trend fell still further.

This debate has changed perceptions about the timing question. The proposition of a single and distinct break point, a "before" and "after" dichotomy in Argentine history, may no longer be tenable. In turn, this has encouraged a more refined approach to the study of retardation over long period, encouraging a multicausal rather then monocasual perspective. The 1913 shock can be read in terms of a very open economy suffering when the external environment suddenly changes for the worse. The 1929 shock confirms the long-held view that a reactive policy stance in Argentina slowed growth in the 1930s, 1940s, and beyond. The 1975 shock reveals that the last quarter of the twentieth century of political and institutional upheaval, combined with hyperinstability in

---

[6] In fact, the settler economies were hit much harder than almost any other country by the economic shocks associated with the Great War, as seen in Maddison's data. It is striking that among the five hardest hit countries, three were settler economies.

macroeconomic affairs, took the country down an even steeper road to relative poverty.

This overview of Argentine long-run performance sets the stage for this book. The macroeconomic outcomes are clear and well known. What is less well understood are the linkages from these outcomes back to their causal origins. At the level of proximate determinants we can examine such putative correlates of growth as investment in human and physical capital, or the growth of other inputs and endowments at different times, such a natural resources and land, or the opportunities for specialization and trade. Yet factor use and accumulation is itself an endogenous outcome, depending on the incentives to accumulate, financial infrastructrure, and the discovery or appropriation of better practice technology. The ability to do all of these growth-supporting activities depends on a matrix of political and institutional qualities such as property right, rule of law, fiscal and monetary stability, and their reflection in policies, laws, norms, procedures, and so on.

One task of cutting-edge economic history is to provide what we have previously termed the kind of "thick description" that can illuminate the foundations and linkages of the growth process. In this respect our volume builds on a strong foundation of extant research on the Argentine puzzle over the last century.

1.3 The literature

The study of the economic history of Argentina has long presented a puzzle, and by generating a deep curiosity it has repeatedly attracted scholars with an interest in international affairs, economic development, trade, growth, macro-economics, and history. The puzzle is straightforward: how could a country that was once one of the richest in the world now be placed so poorly? What can we say by way of an economic accounting of that long-run divergence? And given such proximate determinants, what deeper forces – social, institutional, and political – lay deeper? Yet, when pioneering research on the Argentine economy began almost a century ago, the first scholars were not aware of the reversal of fortune that was to come.

The earliest scholarship that we can describe as economic history, as it is understood today, was the doctoral dissertation of John Williams, a student of Frank Taussig at Harvard, published in 1920. It is revealing that our earliest antecedent was a work that also confronted a puzzle and the operation of unusual institutions in the Argentine context. Williams was concerned with the strange spectacle of the 1890s – an open economy able to exchange goods and services with the rest of the world using the peculiar device of an inconvertible, that is floating, monetary standard. The book is still cited today, a seminal work that became a classic for students who wanted to understand the behavior of monetary and financial institutions, and the workings of floating exchange rates, in a small open economy.

Home-grown scholarship also dates to this era. An Argentine economist and a major policymaker from the twenties through the forties was Raúl Prebisch. His early work (1922) already demonstrated a sophisticated view of the institutional peculiarities of money and banking in a developing country that lacked mature domestic capital markets. A broader approach in the area of international affairs and internal politics is the pioneering work of Miron Burgin (1946). He analyzed the design of the Argentine Confederation and the upsurge of a federal republic, going back to the early-nineteenth century to explore the "invention" of Argentina

Work devoted to economic history was still sporadic. In 1962, Alec Ford made a very important contribution by analyzing the asymmetries between Britain and Argentina in the operation of the gold standard. In a similar vein, the work of H. S. Ferns (1973) takes off when Burgin's ends, and explores the intimate political and economic relationship with Britain. For analysis of the real economy, the most compelling studies are those by Carlos Díaz Alejandro (1970) and Roberto Cortés Conde (1979). It is striking that one of the few true microeconomic studies is the work on railroads by Colin Lewis (1983). Clearly, the program of basic research still remained fragmented: few were laboring in this field and coverage was necessarily uneven. Studies of the open economy, such as macroeconomics and trade, were more advanced, but discussion of microeconomics, such as labor markets or the history of particular sectors, was rare, as was fundamental data collection. Even so, an early textbook synthesis was attempted by Randall (1978) and the first major statistical compilation was put together by Vicente Vazquez Presedo (1971–76).

A rapid spurt of research began in the late 1980s and continues to this day. This resurgence in scholarly activity has been marked by the arrival of more formal quantitative techniques and attention to diverse aspects of the Argentine economic experience. Works by Gerardo della Paolera (1988) and Cortes Conde (1989) analyzed the linkages between exchange-rate regimes and inflation rates and the dynamics of public debt. Formal econometrics were brought to bear on sectoral equilibria in the long run, and on the history of agriculture, in the work of Domingo Cavallo and Yair Mundlak (1982; see also IEERAL 1986; Mundlak 1989). A series of papers by Alan Taylor (1992, 1997ab, 1998) has examined the demographic burden and the degree of dependence on foreign savings in the *Belle Époque*, migration and the structural change in the economy of the Pampas, ownership and tenancy in the choice of agricultural technique, and long-run integration into the world capital market. Leonard

Nakamura and Carlos Zarazaga (1999) have engaged in a pioneering archival effort to construct a historical index of stock prices to improve our knowledge of the history of Argentina's equity markets. Carlos Newland (1998, 1999) and Ricardo Salvatore (1998) have been pushing the quantitative frontier back in time through their studies of the early- to mid-nineteenth-century real economy. In that same period Maria Alejandra Irigoin (2000) has examined political economy and macroeconomic instability, an issue that was then taken up for the 1880–1935 period of the gold standard and currency board experiments by authors such as Andres Regalsky (1994) and Elias Salama (1997), and in a series of papers by della Paolera and Taylor (1999abc) culminating in their book *Straining at the Anchor* (2001). A new synthetic treatment is represented by the work of Pablo Gerchunoff and Lucas Llach (1998).

1.4 The scope of this book

As the foregoing discussion makes clear, a veritable explosion in the literature on the Argentine experience has ranged far and wide, by topic, period, and methodology. Where are we now? It is time to step back and ask what we have learned, and for that purpose a comprehensive work such as this volume has no antecedent. At the dawn of a new century, we think that students, teachers, policymakers, and the educated general reader can benefit from a coherent volume that seeks to understand the remarkable economic triumphs and tragedies of the past Argentine century for two main reasons. First, the record of Argentine economic history is so unusual in its turbulence and conflicts and promises unfulfilled that it offers an extraordinary and unparalleled laboratory for scholars of economic history, since history is the only laboratory for economic research. Second, these lessons are of great relevance for policymaking today, as economic history research can inform all areas of macro- and microeconomic policy, from money and banking to labor markets and institutions.

In the last twenty years scholars from the fields of economics, history, political science, sociology, and law have expanded our analytical views on the history of the Argentine economy. When Díaz Alejandro's seminal and still unsurpassed work was published in 1970, many of the key insights that today constitute mainstream approaches to understanding the process of sustainable economic growth were unknown – such as the new institutional economics, the design of property rights, the influence of political economy on the framing of law, the subtle linkages between capital accumulation and demography, and the dynamics of monetary and fiscal policy. Given this outpouring of new scholarship, a fresh retrospective on Argentine economic history can now include previously undeveloped approaches and so construct a more richly textured analysis to help us better understand the country's dramatic reversal of fortune.

The economic history of Argentina is particularly intriguing. While it was a "newly settled economy" like Australia and Canada, Argentina was never a formal member of the Commonwealth. This raises very important questions about the adoption and influence of various institutions – that is, the political-economy nexus – in a fledgling, independent country. Was the relationship between the government and business conducive to the development of a capitalist society? What was the influence of economic ideas on the adoption of a particular monetary standard or fiscal regime? Why did the financial system never develop into a completely mature domestic capital market? What was the tension between modernist and conservative forces with respect to the industrialization of the country? Why did a country that was once an enthusiastic participant in the nineteenth-century global economy retreat so far into autarky? Why was there so much institutional and public policy volatility in a country that was seemingly destined to join the ranks of the developed nations? When institutions did fail, why did they fail on so many dimensions, and not just one or two?

Addressing such questions requires that an economic historian's focus be sharpened and a new interdisciplinary toolkit be deployed. In contemporary analyses, ever since Díaz Alejandro, the problems caused by the chronic mis-allocation of economic resources have been well identified, but their historical origins still need to be explained by a more powerful theoretical and empirical apparatus. This volume seeks to offer new insights for the understanding of the development of Argentina, a country that appears never quite to have passed beyond the stage of being a transitional society and economy. Therefore, the lessons that can be distilled from the various chapters could prove useful not only to those concerned with this particular case of sustained failure in economic growth, but more generally to readers who are engaged with the problems of contemporary emerging-market economies.

1.5 The chapters

Some comments on the design of the volume may help the reader see the work in context. Most importantly, the book is organized by theme, rather than chronology. A progression by time would be the hallmark of almost any historical study, but the *modus operandi* of economics is to study particular mechanisms and dynamics, *even over the long run*, in a unified and systematic way, so that important breaks or structural shifts, and underlying trends, can be more clearly discerned in a common framework and through a consistent approach to the development of data and its modeling. As the last point suggests, the chapters often employ the technical apparatus of economics. Quantitative technique is central to the new economic history. To keep the book accessible to a general reader, such technical apparatus has been kept to a minimum, but even at its most dense the analysis should be understandable for those with an introductory grasp of economics.

Selecting authors with experience in particular fields of economics (for example, demography, macroeconomics, labor, trade) allows each chapter to exploit the comparative advantage of each scholar to the full, even as all contributors attempted to keep their discussion within the overall plan of the book for a coherent treatment of the entire Argentine experience. Each contribution takes as its context the existing literature and, through a process of survey, distillation, and exploration, discusses what we already know and what new research is still needed on the important historical phenomena for each topic – the central trends, the major turning points, the key policies, and the crucial political-economy problems.

Within this overall design, every chapter has its own nuances and its unique emphases on certain episodes. For example, the central debates on economic ideas in Argentina found their original expression in the late-nineteenth century, as export-oriented orthodoxy came under challenge with the rise of new urban and industrial interests manifested in new political alignments; hence the chapter on ideas takes an in-depth look at these intellectual battles. The question of how and why domestic capital markets failed was felt most acutely in the interwar period, when external finance was dramatically cut off; hence the chapter on finance emphasizes this period in its examination of equity markets. These features are apparent throughout the book, and we can comment on them as we present a brief overview of each chapter to give the reader a sense of the volume's overall structure.

In the chapter by Ricardo Salvatore and Carlos Newland, the stage is set for the rest of the volume by an examination of the early economic history of the republic, from independence in 1810 to the start of the so-called *Belle Époque* around 1870. A central theme is the growth and impact of the external sector and fluctuations in the terms of trade, features of enormous importance in a small open economy. The major sectors studied are arable and pastoral farming, whose rapid development were central to the nation building of that era. With population growth rapid, and substantial internal and external migration, demographic changes had important implications for the labor market. The authors also discuss the important outcomes, that is, income distribution and welfare, as well as some of the institutional conditions behind the development path, such as recurring monetary instability and the evolution of commercial law. Blending quantitative economic history with new institutional economics, this chapter explores the initial conditions of the economy, its institutional capacity, and the potential for sustained growth or take-off starting in the 1870s.

In Chapter 2, Gerardo della Paolera, Maria Alejandra Irigoin, and Carlos Bózzoli analyze the monetary and fiscal performance of Argentina in the long run. The study combines two distinct analytical approaches. The first, with a more classical flavor following Barro, watches key nominal and real variables determined by the design of monetary and fiscal policies and uses them to judge comparative performance. The second approach, more intertemporal in flavor, drawing on Sargent and McCallum, looks at the long-run solvency situation of the government, or transversality condition. The macroeconomic performance of different national administrations is then ranked using a database of nine core variables, from which two key indices of macroeconomic performance are distilled. The first index, the Classical Macroeconomic Pressure Index (CMPI), combines the behavior of nominal and real variables that affect the current generation of private citizens. The second index, the Fiscal Pressure Index (FPI), includes the evolution of fiscal variables that influence the set of economic possibilities for future generations of private citizens and administrators. The authors also combine both indexes to get a unified ranking. An examination of ranking reversals shows that in many historical episodes an incumbent government was "passing the buck" to the next one.

In the next chapter, Adolfo Sturzenegger and Ramiro Moya examine economic fluctuations and ask if the severity of some economic crises led to a permanent change in economic regime. They apply two approaches in their analysis of cycles. The traditional approach dates the cycles using absolute falls or recoveries in the level of economic activity and implies that a major crisis struck in years such as the Baring Crisis of 1890–91, the Great War crisis in 1914, and the Great Depression of 1930–31. The second approach is based on the difference between the level of economic activity and its long-run trend. Again the main crises revealed by this technique were as expected, except that the 1981–82 crisis looks like perhaps the worst monetary and financial crisis in Argentine economic history. One very important finding in their research is that movements in the real exchange rate, a "proxy" for the competitiveness of the real sector of the economy, tends to track movements of the nominal exchange rate in the long run, but the relationship weakens significantly along the economic cycle. The correlation became ever tighter after 1980s, suggesting that the power of active monetary policies dissipated as the Argentine economy become more dollarized.

In Chapter 4, Sebastián Galiani and Pablo Gerchunoff proffer the first comprehensive work on the labor market during the twentieth century in Argentina.

With a blend of rich synthesis and technical sophistication, the authors identify three different periods in the evolution of the Argentine labor market. First is the 1870–1940 period, which they see as a spot market period; second, the 1940–75 era defined by a modern institutional labor market; and last the 1976–2000 period, characterized as a search for a modern flexible labor market. Drawing together modern labor economics and a wealth of studies in the history of the Argentine economy, the authors analyze the impact of labor market institutions on the economic outcomes. International benchmarks deliver a clear perspective on labor market outcomes as compared to the rest of the world and, for the first time, we find a comprehensive presentation of the trends of real wages, net migration (and its relationship with internal and external conditions), income distribution, the labor supply, the composition of employment, and the level of unemployment.

In Chapter 5 Alan Taylor addresses some of the key questions in the history of Argentine capital accumulation. Why has investment, and thus growth, been so volatile? What policies have made a difference in these ups and downs? How does the pattern of domestic investment relate to national savings? When, and under what circumstances, have foreign capital inflows made a difference? What underlying variables have affected the level of investment, savings, and the current account at different times? The author characterizes the Argentine investment record in three phases. First, in the 1884–1913 period, investment demand boomed and open world markets channeled foreign savings into very productive use in the Argentine economy. Second, in the interwar period, investment demand was held back by a reliance on purely domestic savings as global capital markets seized up; growth slowed and matters were made more difficult by a fragile financial system. Third, in the postwar period, policy interventions were widespread and poorly designed, with detrimental effects on capital accumulation; high relative prices for investment goods were stimulated by tax and tariff measures and financial repression created allocation mechanisms divorced from price incentives.

Julio Berlinski writes a masterful Chapter 6 about the history of tariff and international trade for most of the twentieth century. He provides, *à la* Taussig, a long view of international trade and commercial and tariff policies based on new data collected for the 1912–99 period. His thesis is that, in spite of being a price taker in the international market for goods, Argentina conducted an endogenous commercial policy as a response to foreign shocks, such as wars and exogenous changes in the prices of exports and imports. Berlinski uses the difference between the foreign and the domestic terms of trade as an index or benchmark of active trade policies. Most notably, he also analyzes the reversal of Argentina from an open to a closed economy and discusses the static and dynamic costs of protection.

In a complementary vein, Chapter 7 by Yair Mundlak and Marcelo Regúnaga discusses how the signals given by the international economy, distorted for most of the time by interventionist policies, influenced the curious path of the first Argentine "engine of growth" – the agricultural sector. The authors show the impact of autarkic policies on the evolution of output and productivity levels for crops and livestock, input prices, average crop yields, and land prices. Policy distortions are seen as having had a major impact on the dramatic divergence of agricultural productivity levels, which fell far behind world leaders such as North America. Finally, the chapter opens a new avenue for future research on the degree to which Argentine agricultural production was cumulatively sub-optimal, as compared to a hypothetical "production possibility frontier" for the 1913–96 period.

María Inés Barbero and Fernando Rocchi, in Chapter 8, deal with the puzzling Argentine long-run phenomenon of incomplete industrialization. The truncated path to industrialization has haunted Argentine and foreign scholars for many years, and these authors provide an insightful overview of Argentine industrialization and its relationship to overarching explanations of the country's general economic decline. A careful analysis of the evolution of industrial and sectoral variables is conducted, with a special emphasis on the role of firms and incipient entrepreneurs in the process. Finally, following naturally from Berlinski's analysis of relative price signals to industry, the chapter explores how policy changes affected the evolution of industry, stepping back to see the costs and benefits of the "Argentine way" of industrialization in a broader perspective.

In Chapter 9 Leonard Nakamura and Carlos Zarazaga show that at the beginning of the twentieth century neither the Bolsa (The Buenos Aires Stock Exchange) nor the private domestic banks developed rapidly enough to fully replace the British investors as efficient channels for financing private investment. The authors discuss Argentine banking development through the lens of the stock market by examining in some detail the monthly stock returns of the banking and non-banking sectors of Argentina. They show that, judging by the behavior of bank's stock prices and returns, markets were not optimistic about the prospects of the Argentine economy after the Great War. This exposes an early "leading indicator" of the massive financial bailout of 1935, and the beginnings of Argentina's great divergence. Based on this observation, the authors discuss why it was that the stock market remained relatively small in the interwar period even when there was a renewed period of economic expansion and a strong demand for finance capital.

In the closing chapter Sergio Berensztein and Horacio Spector expand on the important institutional foundations of Argentine economic development. They focus on the relationship between government and business, with a particular emphasis on the design of law in relation to the economic system. The authors argue that from the 1860s until the early 1920s the Supreme Court of Argentina struck down economic regulations issued by the federal government or the provinces, consistently upholding laissez-faire economic principles. The thrust of their interpretations changed in the 1920s: constitutional doctrine regarding commercial activity and property rights then began to legitimize a vastly expanded role of the state in the economy. The authors analyze this transition in jurisprudence and its impact on the politics of economic regulation.

An epilogue by Gerardo della Paolera and Ezequiel Gallo concludes with some observations on the past and present following the Argentine economic crisis of 2001.

The final contribution of our volume is to present a statistical appendix, with data stored on a companion CD-ROM to this volume, offering a current database of Argentine historical statistics. Such a unified source has not previously been availably in electronic form and should prove to be of enormous value to future scholars working in the area. The compilation covers most of they key data used by authors in this volume and relies on many years of archival investigation by individual researchers to compile new series. A description of secondary sources is provided.

References

Burgin, Miron. 1946. *The Economic Aspects of Argentine Federalism, 1820–1852.* Cambridge, Mass.: Harvard University Press.

Cavallo, Domingo, and Yair Mundlak. 1982. Agriculture and Economic Growth in an Open Economy: The Case of Argentina. Research Report no. 36, International Food Policy Research Institute (December).

Coatsworth, John H. 1998. Economic and Institutional Trajectories in Pre-Modern Latin America. In *Latin America and the World Economy Since 1800*, edited by John H. Coatsworth and Alan M. Taylor. Cambridge, Mass.: Harvard University Press.

Cortés Conde, Roberto. 1979. *El progreso argentino.* Buenos Aires: Editorial Sudamericana.

Cortés Conde, Roberto. 1989. *Dinero, deuda y crisis: Evolución fiscal y monetaria en la Argentina, 1862–1890.* Buenos Aires: Editorial Sudamericana.

della Paolera, Gerardo. 1988. How the Argentine Economy Performed During the International Gold Standard: A Reexamination. Ph.D. dissertation, University of Chicago.

della Paolera, Gerardo, and Alan M. Taylor. 1999a. Economic Recovery from the Argentine Great Depression: Institutions, Expectations, and the Change of Macroeconomic Regime. *Journal of Economic History* 59 (September): 567–99.

della Paolera, Gerardo, and Alan M. Taylor. 1999b. Finance and Development in an

Emerging Market: Argentina in the Interwar Period. In *Latin America and the World Economy Since 1800*, edited by John H. Coatsworth and Alan M. Taylor. Cambridge, Mass.: Harvard University Press.

della Paolera, Gerardo, and Alan M. Taylor. 1999c. Internal Versus External Convertibility and Developing-Country Financial Crises: Lessons from the Argentine Bank Bailout of the 1930s. Working Paper Series no. 7386, National Bureau of Economic Research (October).

della Paolera, Gerardo, and Alan M. Taylor. 2001. *Straining at the Anchor: The Argentine Currency Board and the Search for Macroeconomic Stability, 1880–1935*. NBER Series on Long-Term Factors in Economic Growth. Chicago: University of Chicago Press.

Di Tella, Guido. 1986. Economic Controversies in Argentina from the 1920s to the 1940s. In *The Political Economy of Argentina 1880–1946*, edited by Guido Di Tella and D. C. M. Platt. New York: St. Martin's Press.

Di Tella, Guido, and Manuel Zymelman. 1967. *Las etapas del desarrollo económico argentino*. Buenos Aires: Editorial Universitaria de Buenos Aires.

Díaz Alejandro, Carlos F. 1974. Some Characteristics of Recent Export Expansion in Latin America. In *The International Division of Labor: Problems and Perspectives*, edited by Herbert Giersch. Tübingen: Mohr.

Díaz Alejandro, Carlos F. 1978. Delinking North and South: Unshackled or Unhinged? In *Rich and Poor Nations in the World Economy*, edited by Albert Fishlow, et al. New York: McGraw-Hill.

Díaz Alejandro, Carlos F. 1984a. The 1940s in Latin America. In *Economic Structure and Performance: Essays in Honor of Hollis B. Chenery*, edited by Moshe Syrquin, Lance Taylor, and Larry E. Westphal. Orlando, Fla.: Academic Press.

Díaz Alejandro, Carlos F. 1984b. Latin America in the 1930s. In *Latin America in the 1930s: The Role of the Periphery in World Crisis*, edited by Rosemary Thorp. New York: St. Martin's Press.

Díaz Alejandro, Carlos F. 1988. No Less Than One Hundred Years of Argentine Economic History Plus Some Comparisons. In *Trade, Development and the World Economy: Selected Essays of Carlos F. Díaz Alejandro*, edited by Andrés Velasco. Oxford: Basil Blackwell.

Díaz Alejandro, Carlos F. 1970. *Essays on the Economic History of the Argentine Republic*. New Haven, Conn.: Yale University Press.

Ferrer, Aldo. 1967. *The Argentine Economy*. Berkeley and Los Angeles: University of California Press.

Ferns, H. S. 1973. *The Argentine Republic, 1516–1971*. Newton Abbot: David & Charles.

Ford, Alec G. 1962. *The Gold Standard, 1880–1914: Britain and Argentina*. Oxford: Clarendon Press.

Gerchunoff, Pablo, and Lucas Llach. 1998. *El ciclo de la ilusión y el desencanto: Un siglo de políticas económicas argentinas*. Buenos Aires: Ariel.

IEERAL (Instituto de Estudios Económicos sobre la Realidad Argentina y Latinoamericana). 1986. Estadísticas de la evolución económica de Argentina 1913–1984. *Estudios* 9 (July/September): 103–84.

Irigoin, Maria Alejandra. 2000. Inconvertible Paper Money, Inflation and Economic Performance in Early-Nineteenth Century Argentina. *Journal of Latin American Studies* 32: 333–59.

Lewis, Colin M. 1983. *British Railways in Argentina, 1857–1914: A Case Study of Foreign Investment*. Institute of Latin American Studies Monographs 12. London: Athlone.

Maddison, Angus. 1995. *Monitoring the World Economy.* Paris: OECD.
Mundlak, Yair, Domingo Cavallo, and Roberto Domenech. 1989. Agriculture and Economic Growth in Argentina, 1913–1984. Research Report no. 76, International Food Policy Research Institute (November).
Mulhall, Michael George. 1903. *The Dictionary of Statistics.* London: G. Routledge.
Nakamura, Leonard I., and Carlos E. J. M. Zarazaga. 1999. Economic Growth in Argentina in the Period 1905–1930: Some Evidence from Stock Returns. In *Latin America and the World Economy Since 1800*, edited by John H. Coatsworth and Alan M. Taylor. Cambridge, Mass.: Harvard University Press.
Newland, Carlos. 1999. Economic Development and Population Change: Argentina, 1810–1870. In *Latin America and the World Economy Since 1800*, edited by John H. Coatsworth and Alan M. Taylor. Cambridge, Mass.: Harvard University Press.
Newland, Carlos, and Barry Poulson. 1998. Purely Animal: Pastoral Production and Early Argentine Economic Growth. *Explorations in Economic History* 35: 325–345.
Prebisch, Raúl. 1922. Anotaciones sobre nuestro medio circulante. *Revista de Ciencias Económicas* (May–June).
Prebisch, Raúl. 1984. Five Stages in My Thinking on Development. In *Pioneers in Development*, edited by Gerald M. Meier and Dudley Seers. New York: Oxford University Press.
Randall, Laura. 1978. *An Economic History of Argentina in the Twentieth Century.* New York: Columbia University Press.
Regalsky, Andrés. 1994. La evolución de la Banca Privada Nacional en Argentina (1880–1914): Una introducción a su estudio. In *La formación de los bancos centrales en España y América Latina (siglos XIX y XX)*, edited by Banco de España-Servicio de Estudios. Madrid: Banco de España.
Salama, Elias. 1997. El orden monetario Caja de Conversion–Banco de la Nación. Documentos de Seminario no. 27, Universidad Torcuato Di Tella (October).
Salvatore, Ricardo D. 1998. Heights and Welfare in Late-Colonial and Post-Independence Argentina. In *The Biological Standard of Living in Comparative Perspective*, edited by John Komlos and Joerg Baten. Stuttgart: Franz Steiner Verlag.
Sanz Villarroya, Isabel. 2002. La economía argentina en el largo plazo: 1875–1990. Ph.D. dissertation. Universidad de Alcalá de Henares.
Taylor, Alan M. 1992. External Dependence, Demographic Burdens and Argentine Economic Decline After the *Belle Époque. Journal of Economic History* 52 (December): 907–36.
Taylor, Alan M. 1997. *Latifundia* as Malefactor in Economic Development? Scale, Tenancy, and Agriculture on the Pampas, 1880–1914. *Research in Economic History* 17: 261–300.
Taylor, Alan M. 1997. Peopling the Pampa: On the Impact of Mass Migration to the River Plate, 1870–1914. *Explorations in Economic History* 34 (January): 100–132.
Taylor, Alan M. 1998. Argentina and the World Capital Market: Saving, Investment, and International Capital Mobility in the Twentieth Century. *Journal of Development Economics* 57 (October): 147–84.
Vázquez-Presedo, Vicente. 1971–76. *Estadísticas historicas argentinas.* 2 vols. Buenos Aires: Ediciones Macchi.
Williams, John H. 1920. *Argentine International Trade Under Inconvertible Paper Currency, 1880–1900.* Cambridge, Mass.: Harvard University Press.

2

Between independence and the golden age: The early Argentine economy

RICARDO D. SALVATORE
Universidad Torcuato Di Tella

CARLOS NEWLAND
Universidad Argentina de la Empresa

Until recently, our understanding of the period between 1810 and 1870 in Argentina has been rather vague and partial due to the lack of comprehensive statistical sources, the minimal economic training of historians, and the limited effort invested in quantification. During the past decade, however, new studies have begun to fill the gap in our knowledge, contributing both new information and new modes of interpretation regarding the early Argentine economy. Research on the late colonial and postindependence periods has presented us with a quite different picture of rural society: ranchers are no longer the powerful agents they were supposed to be; family farms now seem more important than before; the economy was affected by significant changes in the allocation of resources and in productivity; and population dynamics produced important transformations in labor and commodity markets. Furthermore, new studies of monetary instability, commercial law, wealth distribution, and biological welfare have illuminated aspects of the early Argentine economy hitherto unknown. In this chapter, we attempt to articulate these new findings, emphasizing those that we consider most relevant for the comprehension of economic institutions and economic performance.

Our challenge is to understand the economy of the six decades following Argentine independence. We focus in particular on the question of long-term growth, structural economic change, and the institutional factors that conditioned this evolution. By necessity, we concentrate our review on the region of Buenos Aires and the Argentine littoral. For this region, we examine the literature addressing the following central themes: (a) the growth and impact of the external sector; (b) farming and livestock-raising; (c) demographic changes and labor markets; (d) wealth distribution and welfare; and (e) money, commercial law, and government. In each of these areas, we summarize the findings of the recent literature, consider their strengths and weaknesses, and offer some new questions that we believe will stimulate further research on the performance of the Argentine economy during this formative period.

More than a simple review of the literature, this chapter tries to reframe and pose anew – in the light of current evidence – the most important questions about the early Argentine economy. The territory of economic history is still fairly undeveloped and fundamental questions remain unanswered. Questions of economic inequality, relative factor shares, the rate of economic growth, technological innovation, property rights, and resource use are in need of urgent consideration. For this reason, in our final commentary we reflect on the type of economic history that scholars have been producing and suggest some important directions for future work. We believe that the insights of the New Economic History, the New Institutional Economics, and other novel approaches can be useful in thinking about growth and welfare during this period.

2.1 The external sector

The consolidation and growth of a livestock-raising economy was based upon the abundance of fertile land, especially in the littoral provinces. The region contained vast plains with natural grazing land, sufficient rainfall distributed throughout the year, a temperate climate and, in general, relatively easy access to the rivers of the River Plate basin. During the period under consideration, an important share of exports came from cattle and sheep production. Hides, tallow, jerked beef, wool, and other livestock goods constituted the main exportable products. Agriculture apparently lacked comparative advantage vis-à-vis livestock raising. Chilean traveler Vicuña Mackenna, who visited the Pampas in 1850, pointed out that all productive activities were "purely animal."

With independence, an era in which commerce was controlled by a small group of peninsular merchants came to an end. The removal of tariff and nontariff barriers to foreign trade, and the coincidental end of the Napoleonic wars, opened up the gates of commerce in the region.[1] As a result, during the postindependence period, the River Plate economy became one of the most open economies in the world. Between 1830 and 1860, per capita exports (in silver pesos) in the Argentine Confederation were about three times as large as those of contemporary developed countries, and probably twenty-five times larger than those of today's third world countries (Newland 1998b). The combined effect of declining prices of textiles and rising prices of livestock products produced dramatic improvements in the terms of trade, which rose 377 percent between 1810 and 1825 (in local prices). The convergence between local prices and

---

[1] For a long time, however, internal customs and tolls increased the cost of transaction between Buenos Aires and the interior provinces.

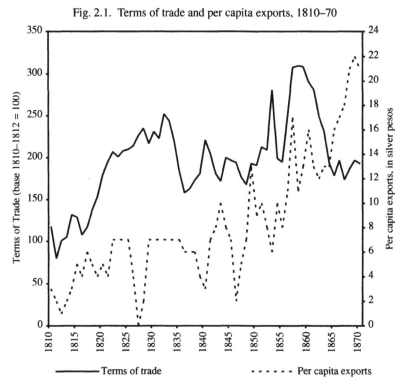

Fig. 2.1. Terms of trade and per capita exports, 1810–70

—— Terms of trade   · · · · · · Per capita exports

Source: The sources listed in Newland (1998b).

international prices (due to a sharp fall in transport and other transaction costs) stimulated the production of tradable goods, while at the same time lowering the cost of imported food and cloth (Newland and Ortiz 2001, 279). However, after 1830 and except for a short recovery during the Crimean war, the prices of Argentine exports were in decline. Hides, in particular, lost 40 percent of their value between 1830 and 1850. Yet, as import prices continued to fall at declining rate, commodity terms of trade remained basically unchanged between 1830 and 1860 (see Figure 2.1).

During the first sixty years after independence exports of livestock products grew significantly. According to one estimate based upon data produced by the Buenos Aires customs office, total exports (in silver pesos) grew at a rate of 5.5 percent a year between 1810 and 1870 (Newland 1998a). This meant an increase of 3.5 percent a year in per capita exports. The pace of export growth was not constant over this period. Exports rose 4 to 5 percent annually from 1810 to 1850 and 7 to 8 percent from 1850 to 1870 (Newland 1997, 55). It is likely, however, that the acceleration of export growth started in the 1840s. A recent independent estimate by Rosal and Schmit (2000) tends to confirm these findings: the value of the four key livestock exports grew at 4.6 percent a year during the period 1814–54.[2] This rapid growth in the leading sector of the economy was achieved mostly through the extension of the frontier and also through greater efficiency in livestock production. Of course, purely extensive growth (expansion in the use of resources) cannot explain the paradox posited by Halperin Donghi more than thirty years ago: the great boom in the ranching economy was achieved during a time (1830–50) of declining export prices.

As a result of the diversification in markets and products, Argentina managed to escape the trap of a single-staple economy and sustained its economic growth over six decades. Initially in 1822, Great Britain was the most important purchaser of Argentine products, but after 1840 other countries increased their participation – in particular, the United States, France, and Belgium. Though foreign commerce continued to be dominated by British firms, the assertion that the Argentine export sector was entirely dependent upon British markets is no longer credible. In fact, the leading consumers of Argentine goods changed over time: France in 1842, the United States and Britain in 1851, and Belgium in 1872 (Amaral 1998, 252).[3] Furthermore, the composition of exports changed in adaptation to shifting conditions in world markets. By 1820, hides claimed the largest share of the value of exports, followed at a distance by salted (jerked) beef. By 1865, on the other hand, wool was the most important export staple, followed by hides, tallow, and sheepskins. Rather than a single commodity dominating Argentine exports, there were six livestock products that claimed the bulk of export trade (Amaral 1998, 270–71).

The ranching economy seemed to have been responsive to changes in relative prices. As wool and tallow appreciated in terms of hides, producers shifted their product mix toward the new products (Salvatore 1987). The development in the 1850s of new European markets (Belgium and France) for a new product (wool) constituted a watershed in the rural economy of the Pampas (Amaral 1998, 283). Changes in land use in response to signals from external markets can explain the increase in the rate of growth of exports during the last two decades of the period under examination. For, in the absence of a transportation revolution or of major technological changes in the rural economy, the reallocation of existing resources in response to changing external markets was central to the process of growth.

---

[2] Using estimates of the CIF (cost, insurance, and freight) value of imports of Argentine products into European countries and the United States, Amaral (1998) also found a remarkable increase in livestock exports from 1820.

[3] Amaral's findings on market diversification confirm the pioneering work of Brown (1979, 79).

Domestic and international conflicts generated ups and downs in the export economy. Different authors have shown the negative impact that external blockades of the Buenos Aires port had on the export economy.[4] During the blockade of the war with Brazil of 1826–28, the French blockade of 1838–40, and the Anglo-French blockade of 1845–48, the price of exportable goods fell abruptly. Presumably, this had a negative effect on the rents of landowners and the income of livestock producers.[5] More important sources of instability to the export economy, however, were the sharp fluctuations in the value of money (and in the rate of exchange) created by a regime of fiat money that spanned most of the period covered in this chapter (1826–66). This factor added uncertainty to a sector already burdened with frequent blockades and declining export prices.

What were the welfare benefits derived from increased external trade? Did the increase in imports spell the demise of local manufactures? Did European and North American demand for leather generate a specialization in the region's economy? Undoubtedly, cheap imports of cloth and food benefited Argentine consumers. Although we know very little about the evolution of artisan crafts after independence, it is safe to assume that, because of the high costs of internal transportation, imported textiles and food only constituted a real competitive threat to producers located in the Pampas or along the Paraná River coast. It is clear also that the livestock-raising sector had a favorable impact upon tertiary activities such as commerce and transportation, and a less important yet visible effect on the secondary sector. The export economy favored the development of new industries such as meat-salting plants, tallow factories, tanneries, and wool-cleaning workshops. Though difficult to measure directly, this impact can be observed by the comparatively high rate of urbanization attained during this period (Brown 1979; Newland 1998b).

Regarding the regional impact of export growth, Brown suggested that the interior economies suffered initially (1827–33) but later recovered (1834–49) (Brown 1979, 201–223). Santa Fé, Entre Ríos, and Corrientes were allegedly the main beneficiaries of this transition. Recent research has tended to sustain this thesis. Estimates based upon internal customs demonstrate how the production of hides for exports did not originate only in Buenos Aires province: the littoral and central provinces contributed significantly to export production.[6] With respect to the growth of exports, Entre Ríos was the interior province

---

[4] Other authors have argued, instead, that exports produced in the Argentine Confederation could easily find outlets through Montevideo during times of blockade. See Brown (1979).

[5] Lacking reliable information about real wages or employment, little can be said about the effect of these blockades upon these variables.

[6] Rosal and Schmit (1995) present a good description of this process.

that experienced the most rapid growth, followed closely by Santa Fé and Corrientes. These provinces experienced significant increases in population and river trade. Córdoba, instead, showed no significant growth in exports.[7]

2.2 Livestock-raising and farming

At the time of independence, the rural economy consisted of two sectors of undeniable importance: farming and livestock raising. Farming supplied the wheat required to feed the population of the city of Buenos Aires and its hinterland. Livestock raising produced hides and jerked beef for export. The postindependence period brought about a dramatic change in relative prices, which affected the allocation of resources between these two sectors. As the price of cattle rose in relation to that of wheat (especially after 1821),[8] livestock raising started to absorb labor and capital previously invested in agriculture. Thus, a large share of the new lands opened on the southern frontier was devoted to livestock raising. As the country started to import flour from the United States and *farinha* from Brazil, agricultural producers returned to self-sufficient strategies or supplied only local markets.[9] Later, the rise in military recruitment made more pressing the problem of labor shortages, worsening the prospects for agriculture.[10]

Given that livestock raising was a capital and land intensive activity whereas agriculture was labor intensive, the most likely effect of such a shift in investment must have been an increase in the income of landowners and cattle raisers. In fact, as Amaral (1998) has pointed out, the appreciation of land was the most important trend in the expansion of the cattle-ranching economy. Apparently, the expansion of land compensated for the employment effect of the shift toward a less labor-intensive activity. Also, the state entered into competition with ranchers and farmers for scarce labor resources (by increasing military recruitment), preventing wages from falling. In the mid-1830s and then again in the 1850s, a shift toward sheep raising meant a return to labor-using techniques. Toward the end of our period, due to a worsening of the terms of trade for livestock goods, agriculture reemerged as a viable option. We know that farming

---

[7] Rosal and Schmit (2000) contributed important evidence to the question of the regional distribution of export-led growth. Their estimates of hides per capita show that Buenos Aires, Santa Fé, and Corrientes all grew at similar rate (by a factor of 2.3 to 2.5 between 1831–35 and 1840–50) while Entre Ríos grew even faster (by a factor of 3.1). Córdoba and other provinces of the interior showed no significant increase in per capita exports of hides.

[8] Garavaglia suggests that prices of cattle and wheat grew at similar rates between 1808 and 1821, but afterwards the free importation of foreign flour depressed the market for wheat while cattle prices continued to grow (Garavaglia 1999b, 286–91).

[9] It is assumed here that high transport costs act as a tariff barrier, so that the importation of flour can only outcompete flour produced within a narrow circle of Buenos Aires city.

[10] The decline in agriculture is indicated quantitatively by the fall of the proportion of *estancias* having plowing instruments and flourmills in this period.

regained its comparative advantage because in the late 1870s the Argentine littoral shipped its first exports of grain since the early postindependence period (Gallo 1983).

A recent study evaluates the impact of the dramatic change in the terms of trade upon the prices of cattle and land. Newland and Ortiz (2001), using prices estimated by Garavaglia (1995), show how the marked improvement in the price of tradable goods affected the price of factors of production in the immediate postindependence period. Both the prices of export goods and those of land and cattle grew about 350 percent between 1810 and 1825. The price of export goods, however, responded more rapidly than the price of land. For example, by 1816, while the prices of hides had risen 110 percent and those of cattle 50 percent, land still maintained its 1810 price.

Recent scholarship has revisited the question of the capital structure, profitability, and rationality of the typical cattle-ranching *estancia*. Low investment per hectare (capital was composed mostly of livestock) and relatively small labor requirements were the chief characteristics of this type of rural enterprise. According to Amaral (1998, 73), the most important changes in the capital structure of *estancias* between 1820 and 1850 were the increase in the value of land as a proportion of total capital (rising from 11 to 51 percent) and the corresponding decline in the value of cattle (falling from 66 to 24 percent). These contradictory trends illustrate the challenges confronting cattle ranchers: with declining prices for cattle and rising land prices, they still had to generate normal returns to capital. Apparently they did. The sparse evidence available speaks of relatively high (though not extraordinary) rates of return. How was this possible? In part, it was due to the natural reproduction of cattle stock in the Pampas, and in part, according to Amaral, it was due to the entrepreneurial skills of cattle ranchers.

Amaral portrays the cattle rancher as a rational agent who tried to maximize benefits in a very competitive environment. With almost no barriers to entry and relatively low capital requirements, cattle ranchers faced increasingly stiff competition in the market place. Running a successful business demanded constant fine-tuning and attention to innumerable details. Managerial skills were crucial for coordinating the many activities of a cattle ranch. Rates of return to capital were high, but so were the risks associated with production. Droughts, wild dogs, thistles, bandits, and indocile laborers conspired against the profitability of the *estancia*.[11] Business failure was an ever-present fear.

---

[11] Amaral (1998, 229) exaggerates when he suggests that rural producers enjoyed no rents, that all their net income was the return to capital and organizational skills. Although entrepreneurial skills were important for staying in the market at a time of declining prices (1830–50), increases in land values reveal that investors anticipated greater than normal returns from land.

Although the main structural features of the *estancia* remained unaltered before 1850, there were, nonetheless, some notable changes in the allocation of resources in the rural economy. One of the notable changes in the aggregate was that activities turned increasingly labor intensive as a result of a great increase in the share of wool production (Sábato 1990). In addition, ranching became more capital intensive through an increase in the number of animals per hectare (Newland and Poulson 1998). Comparing *estancias* of the period 1751–1815 with those of the period 1816–53, Garavaglia (1999) found fewer changes than continuities. Among the changes he notes are an increase in the value of cattle and land for the typical ranch and a reduction in the importance of slavery, which finally disappeared toward the end of the Rosas period.[12] Improvements on the land were also on the rise, a sign of the intensified use of resources within the ranch.

As demonstrated by Amaral (1998), however, the process of capitalization of *estancias* was not linear. The number of animals per hectare declined between 1820 and 1850, in spite of the fact that the total number of stock increased rapidly during the same period. This indicates the existence of an intermediate period – subsequent to the dramatic expansion of the Southern frontier in the mid-1830s – in which the productive process became more land intensive and less capital intensive. This intermediate period coincides with waves of crossbreeding in sheep stock, signaling the importance of these new activities in increasing the profit margins of existing *estancias*.

Was the growth of the rural economy solely extensive? Newland and Poulson (1998) have found a notable increase in the productivity of the livestock-raising sector of the Argentine littoral between 1825 and 1865. They estimate that total factor productivity (TFP) grew during this period at a rate of 2 percent a year. This evidence refutes the idea of a technologically stagnant economy. The chief candidates for this increase in productivity are crossbreeding in sheep farms, more frequent and better management of *rodeos* in cattle ranches, and forms of sharecropping and subcontracting that served to better organize available labor resources and distribute risks. Amaral is convinced as to the sources of these changes: "Production was, therefore, carried out in a more efficient way and, barring technical changes, the only factor explaining such increasing efficiency is management" (Amaral 1998, 100).

Recent scholarship has emphasized the existence of types of economic organizations other than the *estancia* that are likely to have been equally efficient. Although cattle raising remained the predominant economic activity during this

---

[12] Amaral (1998), on the other hand, comparing *estancias* of the 1820s with those of the 1850s, finds significant changes in their capital structure.

period, scholars have found a greater diversity in productive strategies than previously thought. Small-scale enterprises operating with the help of family labor also were present in the Buenos Aires countryside. They were called *pastores* or *labradores* depending on whether their predominant activity was livestock raising or farming. Quite likely, their persistence in the marketplace was highly dependent upon organizational strategies that saved capital and (remunerated) labor. Using family labor and cooperative (unremunerated) labor, peasant small farms and ranches managed to survive (Garavaglia 1999b). Also, the appreciation of wool made it possible for small producers to enter the market. Sheep farms required much less initial capital and those producers who were "rich in family labor" were better prepared to compete.[13]

2.3 Population growth, migration, and labor markets

In the absence of reliable figures of GDP growth, indicators of population change – such as rates of natural growth, interprovincial migration flows, and urbanization rates – can be used as proxies for economic development. Throughout the period 1820–70, there were major changes in these indicators (see Table 2.1). The population of the littoral region grew at an annual rate of 3.1 percent.[14] In addition to foreign immigrants, who started to arrive in the mid-1840s and grew in numbers in the 1850s and 1860s, internal migrants from the northern and central provinces comprised an important inflow to the region. The littoral provinces achieved the comparatively high rates of urbanization of 36.8 percent in 1819 and 45.7 percent in 1869. By contrast, the interior provinces grew at slower pace (2.2 percent per year) and showed a decline in their rate of urbanization (18.1 percent in 1818 and 15.9 percent in 1869). This lack of dynamism in the interior vis-à-vis Buenos Aires also can be observed in the change of occupational structures. While Buenos Aires and the littoral provinces showed an important share of the population occupied in secondary and tertiary employment, the interior retained large proportions of the population in agricultural employment (Newland 1998a).

New demographic evidence taken from local registers confirms earlier suspicions about the importance of internal migration to the growth of the littoral. In Buenos Aires (both city and countryside), demographic growth accelerated after independence between c.1815 and 1822, decelerated between 1822 and 1838, and then grew at a faster rate between 1838 and 1854. During the whole period,

---

[13] Looking at figures for animal stock, Gelman (1996) has found for the mid-1830s that sheep rapidly replaced cattle in the districts surrounding the city. Small sheep-raising farms coexisted with the large cattle *estancias*.

[14] According to Moreno and Mateo (1997), the different districts of the province of Buenos Aires grew at 3 to 4 percent a year after 1838.

Table 2.1. *Demographic and economic variables, 1820–60*

	1820	1860
Population		
Littoral	184,822	847,518
Interior	292,416	889,405
Total	477,238	1,736,923
Urbanization rate (pecent)		
Littoral	36.8	45.7
Interior	18.4	15.9
Total	25.5	30.4
Exports (silver pesos, thousands)	3,082	27,049
Terms of trade (base 1820 = 100)	100	96
Height of recruits (cm)	160	167
School enrollment rate (pecent)	49	63
Pastoral sector in the littoral (base 1820 = 100)		
Land/Labor	100	33
Capital/Labor	100	52
Capital/Land	100	156
Production	100	730
Gold ounce in paper pesos	42	401

Notes: The figures are in general decade averages. Population figures are for 1819 and 1869. The urbanization rate is defined as the share of population living in cities of over 1,000 inhabitants. Littoral includes the provinces of Buenos Aires, Santa Fé, Corrientes and Entre Ríos. Interior includes the remaining provinces. Terms of trade are in international (not local) prices. School enrollment and height of recruits refers to the population resident in the city of Buenos Aires.
Sources: Agote (1881–88); Lopez (1950); Newland (1994); Newland (1998a); Newland (1998b); Newland and Poulson (1998); Salvatore (1998).

internal migration kept the rate of population growth much higher than the natural rate – calculated at 1.3 to 1.5 percent per year (Moreno and Mateo 1997). The province showed both high birth rates and high mortality rates.[15] The uneven rhythm of growth among different districts of Buenos Aires province indicates the existence of a high degree of population mobility. Recent migrants constituted the majority of the population of the rural towns south of the Salado River. After 1822, the "new south" attracted new settlers whereas the northern districts of Buenos Aires province began to expel population. On the expanding frontier, families of four to five members – with couples sometimes forming in the migration process – settled the land (Mateo 1993).

Most authors have emphasized the crucial role of the expansion of the frontier in the growth of the region's economy. Few, however, have considered whether growth of the labor force accompanied this expansion or not. The answer to this question is not easy, for we lack estimates of both economically active

[15] In explaining high birth rates, there is the suspicion that women "married" at an earlier age than in ancient regime societies.

population and labor force participation rates. What we do know is that in the province of Buenos Aires rural population was increasing at a faster rate than urban population during the period 1815–54, thanks to the contribution of interior migrants (Moreno and Mateo 1997). This evidence indicates that the natural growth of the province was insufficient to meet the demands of an expanding agrarian frontier. Was the rural economy of the littoral characterized by persistent labor shortages? The lack of reliable estimates of rural wages makes it difficult to settle this question.

Amaral (1998) has argued that labor shortages were only a seasonal phenomenon, and presents as unfounded the claims of general labor shortages. For Buenos Aires province, Amaral estimated labor requirements based upon technical coefficients obtained from the accounts of late colonial *estancias* and then compared these estimates with a potential labor supply calculated as a fixed percentage of the active male population. Predictably, he found that the supply of labor always exceeded the demand, and that the rate of employment in rural production fluctuated between 22 and 83 percent from one season (fall) to the other (winter). If anything, this exercise shows that if one extrapolates the fluctuating labor demand of one colonial cattle ranch to the whole economy, one would find employment to be highly seasonal. But such assumptions cannot be used to reject the hypothesis of a chronic shortage of labor. First, the ranching economy constituted only part of the total demand for labor. Farming, the military, transportation, and urban crafts and services must also be considered. Second, labor requirements per unit of land must have changed over time as firms changed their product mix and adapted to new markets. Third, because labor markets were not yet fully developed in this period, it is difficult to estimate aggregate labor supply. The rate of population growth and the age structure of the population will not give us a supply function unless we can estimate what proportion of the total annual work days people (men, women, and children) were willing to work for wages (that is, the proletarianization rate).

Under these circumstances, all we can do is to characterize labor markets and ponder the difficulties facing rural entrepreneurs. Sábato (1990) has shown how the expansion of the pastoral economy in the period 1840–80 was facilitated by the diffusion of various types of sharecropping contracts. To reduce the risk involved in sheep raising as well as to minimize the problem of labor recruitment, landowners entered into partnerships with immigrant sharecroppers. Similarly, it is well known that ranchers sought laborers in the interior provinces, offering them attractive wage differentials to induce them to move. However, to the extent that *arribeños* found greater levels of income and personal safety in Buenos Aires province, they continued to migrate South. This fact reflects what is perhaps the most important aspect of rural labor markets – the temporal and spatial mobility of the workforce.

Salvatore (1991, 1993) has argued that workforce mobility was crucial to the functioning and efficiency of the postindependence rural economy. Short-term, unwritten contracts were the norm in the labor market, workers often abandoned their jobs earlier than agreed upon, and the authorities had neither the intention nor the muscle to prosecute and arrest them. High rates of labor turnover in cattle ranches attest to the existence of ample freedom of entry and exit from jobs. Protection contracts offered by ranchers to fugitives of the law were not easy to sustain in the context of recurrent military drafts and constant prosecution of deserters, draft dodgers, and other delinquents by judicial authorities. From the workers' perspective, it was convenient to be constantly on the move if they wanted to avoid military drafts; by moving from one *partido* to the next, peons minimized the possibility of being "taxed" with military duties.

Ranchers were unable to retain workers against their will. Instead of peonage or other forms of coercive measures, it was the economic incentives that attracted laborers to farms and ranches. They could only bargain with them, offering them higher wages, additional rations (meat, sugar, tobacco, and *yerba*), and, on occasion, the possibility of bringing their families into the ranch. Those peons who stayed longer with a given *patrón* could aspire to some extra benefits, including the possibility of becoming a foreman and, if proven reliable, a share of the annual production of yearlings. Hence, it was not unusual for a foreman to become a small *criador* (cattle or sheep raiser).

Information about wage incentives and employment opportunities in Buenos Aires province apparently reached the interior provinces. Migrants from Córdoba, Santiago del Estero, San Luis, and Tucumán knew exactly where they were going when they joined a troop of ox-carts in their towns of origin. Extant *filiaciones* (military or judicial interrogations of traveling rural workers) reveal that wage differentials and employment opportunities were important to their decision to emigrate. In addition, these sources reveal that this migration was temporary. Northern migrants wanted to earn money and return to their provinces within a year or two.[16] Migrants from the interior constituted a labor force that was very malleable; indeed, they were considered *peones para todo servicio*. They could tend cattle, till the land, cut and twist leather, slaughter cattle, or wash wool (Salvatore 1993).

Yet, in spite of the malleability of labor and the high mobility of the workforce, the rural economy suffered from localized labor shortages. The disper-

---

[16] Migrants received support from relatives already residing in Buenos Aires province who provided them with fresh horses, food, and information about labor market conditions and politics.

sion of production, imperfect information about jobs, and the risks associated with military recruitment contributed to this outcome.[17] In local circumstances and in the short-run, an undetermined proportion of rural producers could not find (at the current wage rate) enough laborers to round up cattle, send them to market, or slaughter them. Consequently, actual output remained below its potential level. Crucial evidence in support of this thesis can be found in the information on wages. The daily wage of a laborer (calculated over a month) was several times higher than that afforded to monthly peons. In this context of a highly mobile workforce, motivated by aversion to military service and by the prevalence of short-term contracts, certain locations received fewer laborers than required even if they offered higher wages than average. Though ranchers had great incentives to hire monthly peons, frequently they had to settle for more expensive day laborers. State press gangs (*levas*) heightened the risk of an abrupt termination of a work contract. Hence, workers-on-the-move preferred daily contracts with higher wages to the relative security of a somewhat more permanent job. Though it is possible to argue that some peons accepted lower wages in exchange for job security, the high premium paid for casual laborers speaks of localized and temporary labor shortages. As the average length of the contract of a permanent worker was just three months, job security remained elusive in the Pampas.

2.4 Distribution: Wealth and biological welfare

In the absence of reliable series about income, wages, and consumer prices, it is difficult to assess the impact of postindependence economic growth upon different social groups. Did independence increase economic opportunities for the poor? Did the transition only serve to facilitate the reproduction of a mercantile-administrative elite? Was the consolidation of a livestock-producing economy accompanied by a rapid concentration of wealth in the hands of a relatively small landowning class?

These questions, though implicit in much of the period's historiography, are still in need of examination. For we can no longer take for granted the traditional view of a rent-seeking economy dominated by a few land-owning families. Recent work has tried to fill this vacuum by contributing new evidence and models. Work on the rent-to-wage ratio, the distribution of wealth, and the evolution of stature are beginning to throw new light on the question of distribution.

---

[17] This notion should not be confused with an overemployment of labor or the equally unsound notion of high activity rates.

2.4.1 Rent and the profit-wage ratio

Newland and Ortiz (2001) have recently postulated that the postindependence shock in the terms of trade (1810–25) must have increased the ratio between returns to capital-land and wages. They used a Heckscher-Ohlin model of trade in an open economy with three sectors (exportables, importables, and nontradables) and two factors (land/capital and labor).

To show the result, the authors assume a fixed endowment of factors (not an unrealistic assumption, before 1820, in regard to land), so that resources moved from the import-competing activity (farming) to the export activity (livestock raising). As livestock raising, the less labor-intensive activity, became more profitable, it started to draw capital resources away from agriculture. The labor liberated from agriculture found fewer opportunities for employment, and as the use of land intensified, its price rose relative to wages.

In a three-sector model with free mobility of resources, the external shock to relative prices (an improvement in the terms of trade) tends to produce deterioration in the distribution of income: returns to capital and land increase relative to wages.[18] This analytical result needs to be corroborated by more historical evidence and perhaps be modified to account for additional facts.

While there are strong indications that the cost of capital went up during 1810–25, it is less clear that wages fell in significant proportion. Perhaps farms operating with family labor (a factor not contemplated in this model) did not liberate as much labor as expected. The sons of farmers could not move so freely in search for higher wages. Lower prices for agricultural goods (wheat, for instance) must have reduced the income per head of a typical farm. But farmers could compensate this loss by also producing exportable goods.[19]

2.4.2 Wealth

Using probate inventories, Johnson (1994) has estimated the evolution of the distribution of wealth in three time periods: 1800, 1829–30, and 1855–56. His estimated Gini coefficients are: 0.71 for 1800; 0.63 for 1829–30; and 0.73 for 1855–56.[20] In the late colonial period, Johnson found a high degree of

---

[18] The model actually predicts an initial increase in nominal wages in the export sector and a decline in wages in the import-competitive and nontradable sectors.

[19] Nutrition conditions remained stable between 1810–14 and 1820–24. This situation was related to the fall in the price of imported foodstuffs (such as flour, oil, and wine) and to the adjustments of farmers to the new conditions of relative prices. They changed their product mix so as to maintain prior levels of income.

[20] Whereas in his original 1994 article Johnson estimated the Gini coefficients to be 0.61 for 1829–30 and 0.80 for 1855–56, the author has recently reestimated these values, adjusting for age and wealth bias in the probate sample (Johnson 2000).

wealth inequality, similar to the situation of plantation economies (such as the antebellum American South). In the immediate postindependence period, he found that wealth inequality was in decline. Wealth was redistributed away from commercial and government elites towards skilled workers and other middling groups. Finally, according to Johnson's estimates, the Rosas administration was a time of increasing inequality. Rosas' policy of distributing lands among allies and friends, the expansion of the grazing sector, and the reinvestment of rural profits into urban land and commerce served to recreate a wealthy elite. Hence, the author concludes that "the transition from a commercial- and public-sector dominated economy of 1800 to the grazing economy of 1855 was accomplished at a substantial cost in terms of social justice" (Johnson 1994).

Johnson's estimates suffer from various shortcomings. First, the different composition of the samples (1800 urban only; 1829–30 and 1855–56 both rural and urban) conspires against the comparability of the first two Gini coefficients. Second and perhaps more important, probate records capture only the higher strata of society. As the cost of wills was high, people with fewer assets did not go to the public notary to have their wills drafted. Many died intestate, among them small-scale cattle and sheep raisers, farmers, military officers, and small, rural merchants. Thus, a large number of proprietors – those in the lower and middle trenches of the Lorenz curve – never had their property registered. Third, it is unclear how the distribution of wealth related to the functional distribution of income, unless we take for granted the assumption that the appreciation of land (increasing rents) was not matched by rising wages and benefits. Impressionistic evidence tends to portray the Rosas period as a time of social equalization. Was this only a perception disseminated by federalist propaganda or was it consistent with a trend in the distribution of income?

Against Johnson's view of a U-shaped evolution of inequality, Garavaglia (1999) found a sustained, long-term increase in the concentration of productive capital. Between 1751–1815 and 1816–53 the typical *estancia* grew larger in terms of land and cattle. In addition, the accumulation strategies of proprietors and nonproprietors of land differed. While proprietors and nonproprietors increased their sheep stocks in almost the same proportions (118 percent compared with 110 percent), proprietors increased their cattle stock twice as much as nonproprietors (67 percent compared with 32 percent).[21]

While Garavaglia presents this concentration in the property of cattle stock as a sign of increasing economic and social inequality, a different interpretation is possible. At a time in which relative prices were shifting in favor of sheep, small

---

[21] Also important, nonproprietors experienced a reduction of 23 percent in their stock of oxen, a strong indication that they were abandoning farming.

producers (generally nonproprietors) were responding more rapidly to market changes, reallocating their limited capital and resources into assets with higher returns (sheep). Producers with extended land holdings (usually proprietors) were trying instead to stock their lands with both cattle and sheep.[22] The differential accessibility to land resources of proprietors and nonproprietors resulted in distinct accumulation strategies.

The concentration of the cattle stock in fewer hands should not be read as a symptom of the increasing domination of the *hacendado* class. Rather, it seems to be the case that, in a context of shifting relative prices, small-scale producers were taking the most rational path in order to survive in a competitive market. With limited land and capital resources, and with a nontrivial opportunity cost for their labor, they had to concentrate their efforts on sheep raising, the most labor intensive and profitable activity per hectare.

On the other hand, it should be stressed that the transition from a mixed (farm and livestock) strategy to one concentrated in the production of livestock goods must have affected the food security of small-scale producers. The drastic reduction in the number of draft animals meant an abandonment of the cultivation of wheat and, consequently, an increased dependence on the market for the provision of bread and flour.

Exercises in the comparative statics of distribution of wealth or cattle are misleading if we do not take into account the dynamic of income distribution. Against the traditional story of a landowning class with a concentrated and large share of the wealth, land, and cattle of Buenos Aires province run recurrent stories of upward social mobility. As noted earlier, during the postindependence period it was possible for a peon to move up to the position of ranch foreman and, from that position, accumulate a small herd of cattle and horses. Complementing the pay of foremen with a proportion of the calves and mares of the year seems to have been an extended practice.

Over many years migrants from the northern provinces continued to come to Buenos Aires province, risking apprehension by the army, simply because the opportunities for individual and family improvement were ample. If this was true for an important proportion of wage earners and migrants, then postindependence society was much more economically open and egalitarian than is often assumed.

---

[22] When the data are broken down by region, it becomes clear that survival in this competitive economy – under a process of land concentration – implied the adoption of a distinct capital strategy. In the newly opened areas of the southern frontier (Garavaglia's "South 1"), nonproprietors had reduced over the long run their stocks of cattle 10 percent and increased their stocks of sheep 88 percent. Proprietors in the South had during this long period of time increased their cattle stocks by 83 percent, while increasing their stocks of sheep by 34 percent.

2.4.3 *Stature*

The use of average heights as a measure of biological well-being is by now a standard procedure in economic history. As a residual between a person's production of energy (food intake) and the claims against this energy for body maintenance, fighting disease, and work, stature represents a robust indication of biological well-being. Recent estimates by Salvatore (1998) based upon army recruits born between 1780 and 1840 have demonstrated the existence of two distinct trends in the evolution of stature. The late colonial period – particularly between 1790 and 1810 – was characterized by an absolute decline in average heights (see Figure 2.2: average heights refer to birth cohorts). This trend was reversed in the postindependence period when average heights rose significantly, first recovering from the deterioration of the late colonial period and then reaching a new plateau during the 1810s and 1820s. After a short decline in 1825–29, there was an acceleration of stature growth in the 1830s.

The decline in well-being in the late colonial period was related to the interruption of trade caused by the Napoleonic wars (as imports constituted an important part of popular consumption during this period) and to the disruption of the mining economy of Alto Perú. Height evidence makes it clear that lower-income groups suffered a serious deterioration in nutrition and health. High prices of food that were due to tariff barriers and high transportation costs may have been responsible for this. Johnson (1990) estimated that between 1795 and 1808 the consumer price index rose from 109 to 173. The rise in consumer prices eroded all gains in nominal wages, so that real wages fell in the last decade of the colonial regime. Furthermore, in the 1803–05 period the colonial crisis was compounded by severe harvest failures (the results of a generalized drought) that generated dramatic increases in the price of food. Not surprisingly, the crude death rate between 1788–94 and 1802–10 rose from twenty-four per thousand to thirty-four per thousand (Johnson 1990). Undoubtedly, the late colonial period was one of increasing social inequality and declining well-being for the lower classes.

The rise in average stature after 1810 seems remarkable during a time in which the wars of independence were taking resources (men, horses, and food) away from the peasant economy. Average heights show an even more impressive performance during the 1830s, a period marked by civil wars. How can we explain these apparent paradoxes? Free trade had a salutary effect on the nutritional status of the population, particularly during the first opening of trade in 1809–22. The liberalization of trade reduced significantly the cost of imported food (flour, olive oil, wine, sugar, manioc flour, and other dried goods). Cheaper textiles imported from Britain made it possible for lower-class groups

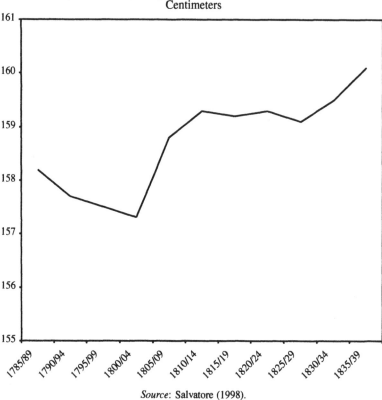

Fig. 2.2. Average height of Argentine soldiers, 1785–1839
Centimeters

Source: Salvatore (1998).

to have more than a single change of clothes, thus improving their hygiene. In addition, with the shift from wheat to livestock, the economy produced a greater volume of calories than before. The increased exports of hides, tallow, and grease created a surplus of beef for internal consumption. A diet richer in protein benefited the growth of children. Also, wars created conditions under which more people had access to meat consumption. Postindependence armies incorporated itinerant laborers, youths, and ex-slaves under the flag, promising them food rations (meat, sugar, and *yerba*). Later, the Rosas state extended the provision of meat rations to the families of veterans.

Was the increase in net nutrition the result of rising income and employment?[23] The expansion of the cattle frontier after 1825 required a growing

---

[23] As noted before, Newland and Ortiz (2001) have suggested that the postindependence trade shock produced a relative deterioration of wages. If this was so, there must have been other sources of improved biological well-being.

workforce. With greater productivity caused by specialization and the shift from farming to livestock raising, nominal wages in the export sector must have risen. And even when inflation eroded nominal wages (for the periods 1826–28 and 1840–66), it is possible that workers managed to increase their nonmonetary income. Through itinerant work, state transfers, and direct appropriation of food, peons, soldiers, and poor women found ways to increase their real income. Changing relations of power (citizens in arms and a proto-populist state) made meat available to the lower classes. In addition, after 1830 there was some improvement in public health. The movement of population out of the city and into the countryside, together with Rosas' campaigns of vaccination against smallpox, must have contributed to the overall increase in health. There was, however, a short span of time during the postindependence period in which biological welfare declined. This was the Cisplatine war (1825–28), when inflationary policies coincided with forced military recruitment to generate a situation of food shortage. Wartime recruitment efforts drove peasants off the land, leaving their crops un-harvested. As a consequence, the price of wheat rose substantially.

2.5 Money, mercantile law, and government

Institutions have an undeniable effect on economic growth: as they limit or enhance the choices open to economic agents, increase the availability of information, ameliorate open social conflict, and make possible the reduction of transaction costs, institutions can affect the performance of a given economy. In relation to the period under consideration, recent work has reopened a series of interesting and important questions relating to inflationary financing, commercial law, and the stalemate in national (constitutional) organization. For example: Did the transition from "anarchy" to "order" under an authoritarian republic favor the expansion of the market economy? Could a loose federation of semi-autonomous provinces generate enough stability and order to protect private property and promote economic growth? Was a corporate, noncodified, and traditional legal system able to ensure private contracts? How was it possible for the economy to grow in the context of inflationary public financing? Operating under severe institutional constraints – political dictatorship, nonconstitutional federation, traditional legal order, inflationary financing – the export bonanza of the postindependence period appears even more remarkable.

According to Adelman (1999), the postindependence transition generated a regime of "quasi-law," that is, a situation in which the executive ruled mostly by decree and the political organization of the country was not sustained by a constitution. A loose federation enforced by occasional shows of force served to maintain social and political order. During the period 1835–52 Governor Rosas was able to provide protection to property owners and free trade to merchants (especially to *porteño* merchants), but only if these groups granted him unquestioned political authority. In exchange for political support, Rosas granted merchants the adjudication of their own property disputes. The Tribunal Comercial, a new corporate body which replaced the colonial Consulado, came to enforce the rule of "relational property," a sort of consensus "in which good faith, reputation, and mutual respect bound the behavior of disputants" (Adelman 1999, 246).

By simply enforcing existing legislation, Rosas provided greater protection to property rights in land and cattle than was previously granted. Still, in the absence of a constitutional agreement and a reliable justice system, the actual enforcement of private contracts was perpetually at risk.[24] Moreover, the Tribunal Comercial favored the interests of the commercial community over the letter of private contracts. This regime of quasi-law and corporate commercial settlement of property disputes proved insufficient, in the end, to guarantee a regime of absolute private property. After the fall of Rosas, the very bonanza of foreign trade made legal uncertainty an even greater problem for the mercantile class. Hence, merchants strove to create a new legal basis for the enforcement of contracts.[25] During the 1840s and 1850s, Adelman argues, there occurred a remarkable change in legal practices concerning property. The Tribunal Comercial ceased to defend corporate interests and relational property and started to privilege individual property rights and a formal reading of contractual obligations. As a result, "the jural language of amity and corporate reciprocity gave way to individual adversarial litigation" (Adelman 1999, 233). Debts began to be honored according to the specifications of private contracts. More importantly, in order to enforce private contracts judges were willing to send people who did not comply with their financial obligations to debtors' prison. Finally, merchants had secured the promises of early postindependence liberalism – the private, legal autonomy for capital.

The postindependence period also brought about much instability to government finances, particularly in Buenos Aires province (Cortés Conde 1997). Monetary policy and public financing were important for the overall economic

---

[24] Adelman (1999, 131–32) writes: "Herein lay the ambiguity of Rosas' cronyism for the Buenos Aires elite. On the one hand, he was the handmaiden for a reconstituted elite that identified with private property holdings and market competition whose business relied increasingly on private contracts. Merchants and their landed cousins thrived on Rosas's preservation of Buenos Aires' grip on Atlantic trade; private capital needed to preserve the political power of the regional capital. On the other hand, by ruling through quasi-law, he did not create public institutions of governance to allow property owners to contract under stable and credible conditions."

[25] In 1859 a Commercial Code was enacted in the province of Buenos Aires. When this code turned national in 1862, the old Tribunal Comercial ceased to operate.

Fig. 2.3. Currency depreciation, 1826–65

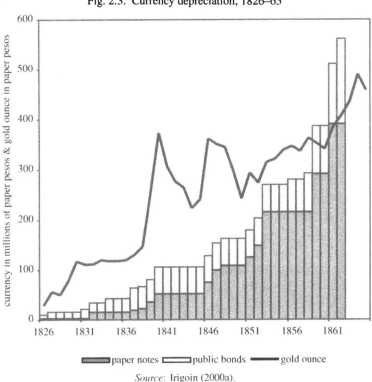

Source: Irigoin (2000a).

performance of the economy. During a period of inconvertible paper money (1826–67) inflationary financing shaped the conditions in which investment and saving decisions were made and, consequently, influenced the rate of growth of the export economy (Amaral 1988). To the political uncertainty created by the civil wars the government added economic uncertainty about the future value of the currency, generating a situation that discouraged long-term investment and technological change. Rather than responding passively to the dictates of Rosas, economic agents anticipated in the gold market the fiscal policies of the state (buying gold and selling pesos), thereby conditioning to an extent the government's room for maneuver (Irigoin 2000a). Every issue of inconvertible paper money produced an increase in the premium on gold, depreciation of the local currency, and change in the relative prices of exports and imports.

Though the paper currency depreciated during most of this period, there were some instances of grave monetary instability (see Figure 2.3). The first corresponded to the period 1826–28, when the war with Brazil pushed the government into huge fiscal deficits financed by the issue of inconvertible notes. A second instance of high inflation occurred in 1838–51 after an experiment of financing public deficits with issues of bonds reached a point of saturation and the government started to finance its wars with issues of inconvertible paper money. By contrast, the early 1830s and the period 1852–67 were periods of relative monetary stability (Irigoin 2000a). When inflation was high, people tried to protect their assets by changing the composition of their capital. Merchants hoarded gold and purchased land; people with liquid capital invested in land and livestock. Not by coincidence, periods of expansion in the sale of public lands coincided with periods of increased monetary instability. Thus, an increased preference for illiquid assets and a preference for short-term contracts were the common symptoms of inflationary financing (Irigoin 2000b).[26]

Inflationary financing contained an implicit subsidy towards export producers and merchants. The whole postindependence period was characterized by a tax structure that favored livestock exports at the expense of imports bought by consumers. This tax structure changed only when the elite decided to attack the problem of monetary instability. In the late 1850s and early 1860s a new governing coalition was able to raise taxes on exports while reducing taxes on imports (Irigoin 2000b, 289ff). With an improvement in finances, the government was able to reduce dramatically the fluctuation in the value of money, which made economic decisions more predictable. Finally, the constitutional arrangement of 1860, combined with the financial reforms of the late 1850s, prepared the terrain for the return of foreign investment.

2.6 An agenda

In spite of the progress made in the last decade or so in our understanding of the early Argentine economy, there still remain core problems to be addressed with the help of quantitative methods and rigorous economic theory. Among these problems, some seem especially relevant.

First, we need estimates of income per capita and real wages to complement our understanding of welfare during this period. Existing price indexes do not represent adequately either the evolution of the cost of living or the implicit prices of aggregate production. Since we can no longer equate export growth with economic growth, we need estimates of domestic aggregate production. We lack estimates on GDP before 1875. Intuitively, transportation, commerce,

---

[26] Extrapolating from this monetary and financial evidence, Irigoin (2000ab) suggests that the economic growth of the period of inflationary financing (1838–1852) was suboptimal. That is, in the absence of such inflationary expectations, economic agents would not have allocated so much of their funds to land and livestock raising, and would have invested instead in agriculture and craft industries.

and services must have been important in the early Argentine economy, yet we cannot evaluate the contribution of each sector. We assume that livestock and farming (and defense) must have claimed a large share of the workforce, but we cannot provide figures to support this intuition. The same could be said about the functional distribution of income: until we construct reliable estimates of wages, interest, and rent, crucial questions will remain unanswered.

A second problem is the question of the relative efficiency of small-scale production. Underscoring much of the work of Garavaglia, Gelman, and collaborators is the idea that small-scale producers (both farmers and cattle raisers) were able to survive, during a period of increasing concentration of wealth, due to their comparative efficiency vis-à-vis the great *estancias*. So far, no study has demonstrated this crucial assumption. Did the labor savings made by family units compensate for the greater access to credit and markets enjoyed by large *estancias*? How did these two types of firms respond to state taxation? Were small-scale producers better prepared to minimize the loss of production due to theft? Did the fuzzy borders of property and the wandering of cattle play in favor of small-scale producers? To answer these questions, we need solid quantitative evidence about comparative returns to capital of large and small firms, about the allocation of factors under different conditions of accessibility to land and credit, and about the relative ability of small and large firms to avoid taxation and combat theft of produce.

Third, the question of the extension of markets during this period demands immediate attention. Was economic growth driven by external demand as conventional wisdom has traditionally asserted? Were internal markets an important factor in the expansion of production? What was the degree of integration of the early Argentine economy? Was the "revival of internal commerce" related to a reduction in transportation costs? These questions regarding the extension of markets should be reexamined taking into consideration the crucial importance of transportation costs, urbanization, and specialization. If the revival of farming in Buenos Aires province was related to the emergence of towns generating food deficits, we need to be able to show a correlation between urban density and agricultural production. But it is also important to include some hypothesis about the evolution of overland transportation costs during this period. It is difficult to envision market-widening economic growth without some reduction in transportation costs. The revival of commerce between Buenos Aires and the interior noticed by Brown must have had at its root an improvement in the frequency, reliability, and cost of transportation.

The issue of labor markets provides a fourth set of important questions that remain unanswered. Did migratory flows from the interior compensate and finally solve the chronic shortage of labor emphasized by contemporary observers? Was there a change in the rate of natural population growth and, if so, what were its causes? Can we estimate reliably the activity rates for men and women during this period? To provide answers to these questions we need to make substantial progress in historical demography. We still lack reliable indicators about crude birth and death rates, mean age of marriage, and fertility, and we know practically nothing about the growth of the workforce or the evolution of participation rates. A rise of capitalism in the Pampas would have depended crucially upon the formation of labor markets. Was there a commercialization of the rural population (an increase in the share of population living off wage earnings)? If so, when did it happen?

Finally, the survival or demise of self-sufficient farming during the livestock export bonanza is of immense importance for the economic history of this early period. In order to characterize better the nature of the postindependence economy, we need to understand this question, both in the littoral and in the interior. Did rural districts far from the city of Buenos Aires integrate into urban markets or did they retreat into self-sufficient production? Did the increased importation of grain and flour from the United States and Brazil drive market farming units far from cities? Did the reallocation of resources to sheep raising entail a parallel abandonment of grain production? The question of the decline of agriculture (between 1820 and 1860) requires work on relative prices (agriculture versus livestock raising), comparative cost structures, and the relative access of farmers and ranchers to credit and labor. To understand the economic sustainability of this type of activity more fully, we also need more information about profit rates and a more reliable estimation of real interest rates.

These are all important issues in the history of the early Argentine (or *bonaerense*) economy that we need to address. New findings about the social and demographic composition of rural towns, about the persistence of farming and wheat production, and about changes in the composition of productive capital in ranches and farms has added to our understanding of the rural economy in the late colonial and early independence periods. But we need to go beyond this type of inquiry and ask central questions about the profitability, sustainability, performance, and institutional makeup of this early economy. Once we agree that there was wheat farming, and that small-scale family firms constituted the majority of producers in the Pampas, the types of questions posed by the fields of New Economic History and New Institutional History are necessarily the next step. Combining quantitative estimates with economic modeling or, at least, the enunciation of clear hypotheses about the alternative paths under examination seems to be a condition for further progress in our knowledge about the postindependence economy.

Counterfactual hypotheses can also help the economic historians advance our comprehension of important debates. Irigoin (2000ab) suggests that an economy without such great monetary instability would have produced a more balanced mix between farming and livestock raising. This type of exercise is worth pursuing, for it could demonstrate the relevance of inflationary expectations in the general performance of the postindependence economy and contribute explanations to the puzzle about the decline of farming. Similarly, the issue of land concentration could be reexamined with the help of a counterfactual exercise.

Rather than concentrating on microdemographic studies of localities, we need aggregate indicators for population growth, labor force participation, wages and income, interest rates, and rents. Recent studies have emphasized correctly the importance of regional differentiation in Buenos Aires province and within the Argentine Confederation. What we need now is to reexamine the question of regional integration in terms of price differentials and the evolution of transportation costs. From an economic perspective, the expansion of markets and the evolution of productivity appear to be central questions. By contrast, the study of social codes and relationships within rural communities can only marginally illuminate questions of economic development. Scholars need to understand that the very nature of the rural economy of the Pampas is at stake. The problem is no longer a question of social types ("peasant" versus "*gaucho*" and "*labrador*" versus "*estanciero*") or about the combination between ideal types ("*ancien régime*" versus "market economy"). Rather, the new schema refers to the dynamic of a complex economy operating under severe constraints: labor and credit shortages, massive and recurrent military recruitment, differential taxation, inflation, and unstable government coalitions.

An illumination of this complexity requires renewed efforts in quantification and in the construction of analytical models. We need to find a way to isolate the contributions of the various pieces of this puzzle (law, inflation, taxes, labor, markets, migration, etc.) to economic growth and, at the same time, relate them to the inherited visions of the society and economy of the Pampas. Economic performance, the role of institutions, and the question of distribution should be at the center of this new research agenda. We argue for a greater integration of economic history and sociodemographic studies as a means to avoid false dichotomies and exclusionary research agendas. Clearly, a better comprehension of the microdynamic of rural towns and small regions helps us visualize the constraints and choices facing economic and social agents. Yet, economic theories and quantification (on a scale larger than the isolated village) should be the bases for a new understanding of the early Argentine economy as a whole. The period between independence and the golden age presents economic historians with fascinating lessons and challenges for the future.

References

Adelman, Jeremy. 1999. *Republic of Capital: Buenos Aires and the Legal Transforma-tion of the Atlantic World*. Stanford: Stanford University Press.

Agote, Pedro. 1881–88. *Informe del Presidente del Crédito Público sobre la deuda pública, bancos y emisiones de papel moneda y acuñacion de monedas de la República Argentina*. 5 vols. Buenos Aires: Crédito Público.

Amaral, Samuel. 1988. El descubrimiento de la financiación inflacionaria: Buenos Aires, 1790–1830. *Investigaciones y Ensayos* 37: 379–417.

———. 1998. *The Rise of Capitalism on the Pampas: The Estancias of Buenos Aires, 1785–1870*. Cambridge: Cambridge University Press.

Barba, Fernando Enrique. 1999. *Aproximación al estudio de los precios y salarios en Buenos Aires desde fines del siglo XVIII hasta 1860*. La Plata: Editorial de la Universidad Nacional de la Plata.

Brown, Jonathan C. 1979. *A Socioeconomic History of Argentina, 1776–1860*. Cambridge: Cambridge University Press.

Cortés Conde, Roberto. 1997. *La economía argentina en el largo plazo: Ensayos de historia económica de los siglos XIX y XX*. Buenos Aires: Editioral Sudamerica.

Johnson, Lyman L. 1990. The Price History of Buenos Aires during the Viceregal Period. In *Essays on the Price History of Eighteenth-Century Latin America*, edited by L. L. Johnson and E. Tandeter. Albuquerque, N.M.: University of New Mexico Press.

———. 1994. Distribution of Wealth in Nineteenth-Century Buenos Aires Province: The Issue of Social Justice in a Changing Economy. In *The Political Economy of Spanish America in the Age of Revolution, 1750–1850*, edited by K. J. Andrien and L. L. Johnson. Albuquerque, N.M.: University of New Mexico Press.

———. 2000. The Pampa Transformed: Measuring Economic Growth and Wealth Inequality in the Rosas Period. University of North Carolina, Charlotte. Photocopy.

Gallo, Ezequiel. 1983. *La Pampa gringa: la colonización agrícola en Santa Fe (1870–1895)*. Buenos Aires: Editorial Sudamericana.

Garavaglia, Juan Carlos. 1995. Precios de los productos rurales y precios de la tierra en la campaña de Buenos Aires: 1750–1826. *Boletín del Instituto de Historia Argentina y Americana Dr. Emilio Ravignani* 11: 65–112.

———. 1999a. Un siglo de estancias en la campaña de Buenos Aires: 1751 a 1853. *Hispanic American Historical Review* 79 (4): 702–34.

———. 1999b. *Pastores y labradores de Buenos Aires*. Buenos Aires: Ediciones de la Flor.

Garavaglia, Juan Carlos, and Jorge Gelman. 1995. Rural History of the Río de la Plata, 1600–1850. *Latin American Research Review* 30 (3): 75–105.

Gelman, Jorge. 1996. Unos números sorprendentes: Cambio y continuidad en el mundo agrario bonaerense durante la primera mitad del siglo XIX. *Anuario IEHS* (Tandil, Argentina: Universidad Nacional del Centro de la Provincia de Buenos Aires, Facultad de Ciencias Humanas, Instituto de Estudios Histórico-Sociales) 11: 123–45.

Irigoin, Maria Alejandra. 2000a. Inconvertible Paper Money, Inflation and Economic Performance in Early-Nineteenth-Century Argentina. *Journal of Latin American Studies* 32: 333–59.

Irigoin, Maria Alejandra. 2000b. Finance, Politics and Economics in Buenos Aires 1820s–1860s: The Political Economy of Currency Stabilisation. Ph.D. dissertation, Department of Economic History, London School of Economics.

Lopez, Juan S. 1950. La estatura masculina en la ciudad de Buenos Aires. *Anales del Instituto Etnico Nacional* 3: 113–38.

Mateo, José. 1993. Migrar y volver a migrar: Los campesinos agricultores de la frontera bonaerense a principios del siglo XIX. In *Población, sociedad, familia y migraciones en el espacio rioplatense, siglos XVIII y XIX*, edited by J. C. Garavaglia and J. L. Moreno. Buenos Aires: Cántaro.

Moreno, José Luis, and José Antonio Mateo. 1997. El 'descubrimiento' de la demografía histórica en la historia económica y social. *Anuario IEHS* (Tandil, Argentina: Universidad Nacional del Centro de la Provincia de Buenos Aires, Facultad de Ciencias Humanas, Instituto de Estudios Histórico-Sociales) 12: 35–55.

Newland, Carlos. 1994. The Crowding Out Effect in Education: The Case of Buenos Aires in the Nineteenth Century. *Education Economics* 2 (3): 277–86.

———. 1998a. Economic Development and Population Change: Argentina, 1810–1870. In *Latin America and the World Economy Since 1800*, edited by J. H. Coatsworth and A. M. Taylor. Cambridge, Mass.: Harvard University Press.

———. 1998b. Exports and Terms of Trade in Argentina, 1811–1870. *Bulletin of Latin American Research* 17 (3): 409–16.

Newland, Carlos, and Barry Poulson. 1998. Purely Animal: Pastoral Production and Early Argentine Economic Growth. *Explorations in Economic History* 35: 325–345.

Newland, Carlos, and Javier Ortiz. 2001. The Economic Consequences of Argentine Independence. *Cuadernos de Economía* 38: 275–90.

Rosal, Miguel and Roberto Schmit. 1995. Las exportaciones del litoral argentino al puerto de Buenos Aires entre 1783 y 1850. *Revista de Historia Económica* 13 (3): 581–607.

———. 2000. Las exportaciones pecuarias rioplatenses (1768–1854). Photocopy.

Sábato, Hilda. 1990. *Agrarian Capitalism and the World Market: Buenos Aires in the Pastoral Age, 1840–1890*. Albuquerque, N.M.: University of New Mexico Press.

Salvatore, Ricardo D. 1987. Class Struggle and International Trade: Rio de la Plata's Commerce and the Atlantic Proletariat 1780–1850. Ph.D. dissertation, University of Texas at Austin.

———. 1991. Autocratic State and Labor Control in the Argentine Pampas: Buenos Aires, 1829–1852. *Peasant Studies* 18 (4): 251–78.

———. 1993. El mercado de trabajo en la campaña bonaerense (1820–1860): Ocho inferencias a partir de narrativas militares. In *La problemática agraria: Nuevas aproximaciones*, edited by M. Bonaudo and A. Pucciarelli. Buenos Aires: Centro Editor de América Latina.

———. 1998. Heights and Welfare in Late-Colonial and Postindependence Argentina. In *The Biological Standard of Living in Comparative Perspective*, edited by J. Komlos and J. Baten. Stuttgart: Franz Steiner Verlag.

3

Passing the buck: Monetary and fiscal policies

GERARDO DELLA PAOLERA
American University of Paris and Fundación PENT

MARIA ALEJANDRA IRIGOIN
Universidad Carlos III de Madrid

CARLOS G. BÓZZOLI
Princeton University

In search of a more satisfactory approach to assess the performance of the Argentine economy over the last century and a half, this chapter considers the outcomes of monetary and fiscal policymaking and the reaction of the public, as well as the constraints thereon. In particular, we place new emphasis on the so-called transversality condition – the long-run, intertemporal budget constraint of the government that places bounds on public finance policy choices.

In the long run, macroeconomic policy choice can be viewed as a game between past, present, and future generations of political rulers and economic agents. Like any other player in this game, a current government takes decisions subject to a set of bestowed restrictions, and will, in turn, bestow new restrictions on the next generation of government. It is here that the intertemporal fiscal constraints matter.

In this conception, policymaking is not a static game in which current payoffs are only affected by today's decisions. As Thomas Sargent (1986, 21) has shown, it is a dynamic game "that requires time to complete and whose current score depends on past actions of the various players." This claim is extremely important for the intellectual flavor of this chapter. Restrictions faced by each administration are heavily determined by the concurrent reaction of their constituency and by the results of similar interactions in preceding periods.

Given these constraints, a comprehensive historical analysis of the economic performance of Argentina at any point in time necessarily has to consider the burdens "inherited" from previous periods. This does not imply a causal ordering; rather, it is truly the case that *history matters*. Each period is the result of an allocation process determined by government choices and agents' preferences. Over time, each period acts as a link in a chain of outcomes where decisions are

Comments from conference participants improved this chapter. The suggestions from Colin Lewis and Alan Taylor were particularly helpful. The authors are solely responsible for remaining errors.

taken that are conditional on past outcomes and expectations about the future. This path dependence helps to frame conceptually the choice set and link the decision making of both rulers and agents throughout time.

Of course, this process "is not a story of inevitability in which the past neatly predicts the future."[1] Nor is this a story of good or bad policymakers. This study does not assume a particular utility function in the ruler, because the data in use constitute a reduced-form expression of the interaction between government and public. Furthermore, the government's preferences need not be either time invariant, or identical to those of the government's constituency, or even reflect a common or unified constituency over time.[2] We present only a forward-looking assessment of the macroeconomic results in this interaction, and do not attempt to explain the underlying process that gave birth to each outcome.[3]

In short, the aim of this chapter is to analyze the macroeconomic performance of Argentina in the long run. The database used for this purpose is an annualized series of macroeconomic and fiscal indicators built from different sources. It is the first attempt to develop a database of nine core variables that covers the entire period under study, and these 150 years of macroeconomic history are organized according to the governing national administrations. We begin with a section that stresses the contribution this analysis makes to the literature on Argentine economic history. The next section presents our methodology. Two indices are built to rate the macroeconomic outcomes during each administration. The first combines the behavior of nominal and real variables that affect the current generation of economic agents. The second includes the evolution of fiscal variables that embody intertemporal linkages by conditioning the set of choices available to future generations, both agents and rulers. Both sets of indicators are used to rank particular governments. We then compare the two rankings and seek to identify the underlying factors in the historical process. The conclusion reexamines the main features of the Argentine economy in the long run in light of this new analytical framework.

---

[1] On path dependence see David (1997). The same idea has been used by Douglass North (1990, 98–99) to explain the path-dependent pattern of institutional evolution: "At every step along the way there were choices, both political and economic, that provided real alternatives." Mokyr (1990, 163–65) has stressed the path dependent nature of technological change.

[2] Recent literature on the political economy of government behavior is vast and varied. For a survey see Persson and Tabellini (2000). Ljunqvist and Sargent (2000) extend the relevant fiscal and monetary theory. Alesina and Perotti (1995) also provide a good survey on the political economy of budget deficits.

[3] However, our annual data set could permit us to unveil the driving forces in an evolving macroeconomic situation. By focusing on the indicators selected for this chapter it would be possible to identify the causality underpinning particular changes in the historical process.

3.1 The contribution to the literature

This particular view of the economic performance of Argentina is original and more amenable to historical analysis when compared with the existing body of literature. Our recent research on monetary, financial, and fiscal problems in the nineteenth century is changing the agenda for the study of macroeconomic history, and the current contribution follows in that trend. Overall, the century now appears to have been an unending process of searching for macroeconomic stability. Following the seminal works of Williams (1920) and Ford (1962) on the gold standard, della Paolera (1988) discussed the issues of public debt management, inflation, and the exchange-rate regime, emphasizing the linkages between monetary and fiscal policies in an intertemporal, open-economy framework. Recently, Irigoin (2000a) has offered a reinterpretation of the economic performance of Argentina in the earlier part of the nineteenth century by examining the effects of monetary instability and the inflationary finance of fiscal deficits.[4]

Yet the most reputed historical works on the Argentine economy in the twentieth century have produced assessments that only account for the results of decisions taken unilaterally by rulers. In this view, the by-product of different governments' economic policies ultimately explains the history of the Argentine economy.[5] We argue that this conventional view, which has characterized economic and political realms as unrelated, has been prone to isolate and evaluate the performance of different administrations at each point in time. As a result, the success (or failure) of a particular economic policy has been interpreted without reference to the constraints received from the past and the limitations that were bequeathed to the future. Consistent with the high degree of ideological "noise" that prevails in the economic analysis of past and present events in Argentine history, the traditional literature has tended to disregard the intertemporal constraints that are always in operation.[6] In contrast, we empha-

---

[4] Cortés Conde (1989) followed a similar approach to produce a thorough account of the fiscal and financial situation for the period 1860–90. However, his institutional analysis is organized by separated terms of government, assuming each administration faced a discrete and separable set of policy choices and acted in isolation from the public and from past economic choices. Other scholars have also recently been interested in the topic, e.g., Bordo and Végh (1998) and della Paolera and Taylor (2001). See also Bordo and Capie (1993).

[5] See the various chapters in the edited volumes by Di Tella and Platt (1986) and Di Tella and Dornbusch (1989). See also Gerchunoff and Llach (1998); Mallon and Sorrouille (1975); Rapoport (1984); Garcia Vazquez (1995); Sourrouille and Lucángeli (1983); Llach (1984); and O'Connell (1984).

[6] This was also noted by Carlos Díaz Alejandro (1970): "The primacy of economics over politics and [more importantly the] de-ideologizing of issues of political economy into questions of output and efficiency [contributed to the] social basis for productivity-enhancing politics." Similarly, de-ideologization helps to explain the "exceptional speed and stability of European economic growth in the 1950s and 1960s." It is true that "one must take into account the equally

size the tradeoff between current sets of choices for macroeconomic policies and their impact on framing the feasible alternatives for subsequent generations.

This analysis is dynamic rather than static because we conceive of macroeconomic performance in the long run as a continuum of mutually interdependent interactions. To explore the intuition of this concept, consider an example: think of an administration that keeps inflation low while implementing an expansionary fiscal policy by increasing government debt. A static analysis of policymaking would only consider macro-outcome variables such as present inflation or activity growth rates. Instead, our approach also takes into account the fact that a low inflation and high deficit scenario is unsustainable in the long run since future generations would have to pay for the cost of today's decisions – in this case by having to service the accumulated public debt.

As a result, by way of applying a degree of consistency to the historical analysis, our approach internalizes the costs arising from the decisions of present generations that are passed on to subsequent ones. Because no administration sets out from exactly the same initial situation, it is never feasible to compare just the results of each government's relative success with contemporaneous economic policymaking. Hence, we do not judge the decisions taken by a government while in office, but only the relative outcomes bequeathed at the end of its mandate conditional upon the situation they inherited at the start.

3.2 The methodology

3.2.1 The intervals

To organize the analysis, we identified discrete intervals according to the terms of all national administrations from 1853 to 1999. This classification of each government is made irrespective of the nature of the political regime from which it emerged. Up to 1930 Argentina had enjoyed a seventy-year period of institutional stability within a representative political system in which governments were appointed by suffrage.[7] In September 1930 constitutional order was discontinued for the first time in the political history of the country. This happened again in 1943, 1955, 1962, 1966, and 1976. For our purposes, each of these years are treated as a change of political regime. Elected governments reappeared in 1931, 1946, 1958, 1964, 1973, and 1983. From 1983 until the present, democratically appointed governments have ruled the country without

exceptional circumstances whereby a number of factors affecting the production system and the macroeconomic structures were allowed to interact with singularly apt institutional arrangements in the international economy and in the individual countries" (Crafts and Toniolo 1996, 22–23).

[7] However, in practice the ballot was a restricted exercise until 1916. Only in 1912 did the Electoral Law grant and guarantee a universal franchise for male citizens.

interruption. This has been the longest span of time during which representative political institutions have stood in place without interruption and no political party has been banned since the inception of universal suffrage in 1916.[8]

According to constitutional rules enacted in the early 1850s, the length of a presidential term was set at six years with no provision for a second term.[9] Twice, in 1949 and 1994, this constitutional provision was changed and the presidential term reduced to four years. On both occasions it resulted in the re-election of the person that was currently in office.[10] Therefore, the two subsequent presidencies of Juan Domingo Perón (1946–51 and 1952–55) and Carlos Menem (1990–95 and 1996–99) are identified as separate terms of administration in our analysis.

For convenience, we label the years of each term of an administration according to the name of the president. This convention does not necessarily coincide with the date in which the person was elected or effectively took office. Our method assigns years according to whether the incumbent or incoming government ruled for the larger part of the year. On four occasions the president died in office and was replaced by the vice-president following the constitutional order of succession. In these cases, we indicate both names on the ticket: they were Luis Sáenz Peña/José E. Uriburu (1893–98), Roque Sáenz Peña/Victorino de la Plaza (1911–16), Roberto Ortiz/Ramón Castillo (1938–42), and Perón, who was succeeded by his wife Isabel Perón (1973–75).[11]

In addition, certain major break points in the political and economic history of the country have been distinguished and are treated separately. Following the crisis in 1890, Vice President Carlos Pellegrini (1891–92) took over after Miguel Juárez Celman resigned, and completed the mandated term. This was the first political consequence of a major financial and economic crisis earlier that year. Since Pellegrini's leadership in resolving the crisis was crucial, the discontinuity merits consideration as a distinct interval in our classification. In

---

[8] From 1930 to 1946, and from 1955 to 1972, the current major political parties, the *radicales* and *peronistas*, were banned from electoral competition. The Argentine political system has been again strained at the end of 2001, when five presidents served in the space of two weeks. That episode would be a challenge for our classification system, but it is so recent as to lie outside the sample period of our study, which concludes with the second Menem administration of 1996–99.

[9] Because we are using the Governor of Buenos Aires province as the head of a proxy national administration for 1853–62, it is worth remembering that the provincial constitution in 1854 ruled out a second term, but the mandate was set to a three-year term.

[10] The reformed constitution of 1949 was amended in 1956 restoring six-year terms and again ruling out reelection.

[11] In 1973 there were two consecutive elections. In March President Campora won under the appeal of *Campora al gobierno, Perón al poder* ("Campora for president, power for Perón"). He and the vice-president resigned and, by virtue of the *Ley de Acefalia*, a new election was held in September, which Perón won in a landslide with 62 percent of the votes.

1930 General José F. Uriburu led a coup against the ruling President Hipólito Yrigoyen, leader of the Radical Party, setting the stage for a series of military coups that deposed democratically elected civilian governments. Elections were reinstated in the following year, but by then the *Radicales* were banned from the contest. This ban was in effect until 1946.

In subsequent years, every military regime has been considered a distinct interval, with the exception of the periods 1962–63 and 1967–72. In 1962, the ruling president Arturo Frondizi was overthrown by another military coup. The Peronist party, which had been banned seven years earlier following the overthrow of Perón, was allowed to participate in provincial elections and won an overwhelming victory. This led to the suspension of the election procedures for selecting a president, and for two years the senator José Guido, a puppet of the military, acted as a surrogate president. From 1967 to 1972 three generals alternated in office. Social turmoil and growing political violence resulted in Juan Carlos Onganía's resignation. From 1970, Roberto Levingston and Alejandro Lanusse ruled while a process took shape for restoring elections, now with the legal inclusion of the Peronist Party. The shift in the army toward the restoration of civilian rule justifies a separate treatment for the different periods.

As a result of this classification, a sequence of 150 years of macroeconomic performance was aggregated into thirty-three intervals associated with different "administrations." These administrations will now be ranked on a scale according to the relative improvement in macroeconomic performance during their term. In our long-run analytical perspective, the best outcome (position one) should be the closest to the theoretically desirable one. For instance, the lowering of the inflation rate is assessed as a good indicator because by reducing a distortion on cash holdings it helps intermediate economic transactions. Likewise, a lower level of debt means – other things being equal – a lower expected level of the tax burden on future income. Thus, by lowering distortions on the economy, such changes would enhance the outlook for future investment, production, and consumption.

3.2.2 The indices

To rank the macroeconomic performance of different administrations we propose two indices. The Classical Macroeconomic Pressure Index aggregates the outcomes for classical indicator variables; we include here inflation, devaluation, and interest rates, together with annual estimates of changes in the level of economic activity (output growth). The Fiscal Pressure Index is constructed quite differently by introducing key fiscal time series that introduce intertemporal constraints which reflect the burden of debt financing; we include here the ratios of public debt to GDP and to exports, the ratio of primary deficit to revenues and debt service, and the real interest rate faced by Argentina (a proxy for country risk) adjusted by the increase in the level of activity (an adjustment to control for the explosiveness of debt-GDP ratios). Both indices aggregate annual data in each of the thirty-three intervals corresponding to every administration, either national (after 1862) or for the province of Buenos Aires (before 1862).[12] As mentioned, the values are assigned each year according to the person who was in office the longest in the respective year. Finally, both indices were combined into a third index, the Overall Index, to offer a "compromise" economic scoreboard of the different administrations.

3.2.2.1 The Classical Macroeconomic Pressure Index (CMPI)

The rationale for building a macroeconomic pressure index is to rank the improvements that occurred during a particular administration in key nominal and real macroeconomic variables. It is important for the reader to note that our conception of the CMPI measures the results of these variables compared to their levels under the previous administration (the "bequest received") . Thus the CMPI is more of a *comparative* index than a *situational* index.

The CMPI has been built on four indicators – the inflation rate, the devaluation rate, the interest rate, and the growth rate of economic activity – as follows:

(i) The inflation rate is usually linked to the government's high-powered money policy and the expectations of agents about its future rate of expansion (Sargent 1986). It sheds light on the results of one of the sources of revenue that Argentine governments have repeatedly used: the inflationary tax or seigniorage (Amaral 1988, Irigoin 2000a, and della Paolera and Taylor 2001);[13]

(ii) The devaluation rate is another way of measuring changes in nominal

---

[12] Data for 1853 to 1862 only refer to the situation in the province of Buenos Aires. The share of the province in the national economy makes the proxy acceptable. In 1860 Buenos Aires furnished 82 percent of total export value, and the trend matches the national values thereafter. By 1864, Buenos Aires's share in national public finances amounted to 73 percent of total ordinary revenues and 75 percent of total expenditure at the national Treasury. Its native population represented 30 percent of all Argentineans, though 82 percent of resident foreigners were living in the province by 1869, in advance of the waves of mass migration that were to follow. See *Censo Nacional de Población*, 1869 Table 6, page 20. Finally, after 1862, the fourteen provinces that form the territory of present-day Argentina united in a federal state under a leadership and institutional structure drawn from Buenos Aires. The then *bonaerense* governor, Mitre, was duly elected as the first Argentine constitutional president.

[13] The inflation rate is measured as continuously compounded, that is, given price level in year t (P_t) and the price level in the precedent year t-1 (P_{t-1}), the continuously compounded inflation rate observed in year t is defined as $\ln(P_t/P_{t-1})$, where ln is the natural logarithm function. This measure prevents the inflation rate from fluctuating widely during hyperinflation periods and

values in the economy. In particular it is a very important indicator of the willingness of a government to stabilize the external value of the domestic currency. Devaluation is often associated with balance of payments crises (Eichengreen, Rose, and Wyplosz 1996) and fiscal crises (della Paolera 1994). It also plays a part in recurrent episodes of political instability (Irigoin and Salazar 2000).[14]

(iii) The real interest rate on hard currency is a proxy for country risk fluctuations and tightness in the credit market. In a country with long periods of financial repression and credit rationing, the interest rate in the domestic credit market is not a useful measure of credit-market tightness. Thus, an estimate of the costs of borrowing in international credit markets seems a better alternative;

(iv) The growth rate on economic activity indicates the influence of the incumbent administration on the changing pace of economic development. Since the population growth rate sometimes fluctuates in response to immigration and demographic change, the rate of growth is computed from the per capita level of activity.[15]

Table 3.1 displays *contemporaneous* macroeconomic performance during different political administrations according to these measures. While interesting and highly informative, this information alone could be misleading for our ranking of the administration outcomes. The assessment of an administration will be flawed if the crucial conditions inherited from its predecessor are neglected. For instance, by purely contemporaneous macroeconomic performance standards, one of the most highly regarded Argentine presidents, Pellegrini, would have ranked as one of the worst chief executives in the country's history (Gallo 1997).

Table 3.2 depicts for all administrations their *comparative* macroeconomic performance, following Barro (1996).[16] With four standardised measures of outcome innovations for each year, the Classical Macroeconomic Pressure In-

having excessive influence in the CMPI. Also, this measure of inflation rate can be described as the (first order) logarithmic difference of the price level.

[14] Devaluation is also measured as a continuously compounded rate.

[15] Since data on labor is not available through the entire sample, it is impossible to accurately measure activity per worker.

[16] Barro (1996, chap. 3) expands on Okun's "misery index" as a measure to assess macroeconomic performance. To isolate each administration he uses the changes in inflation, unemployment, interest rate, and the shortfall of economic activity. The difference with our index is not only due to the variables chosen. The CMPI also differs on the assignation of percentiles to the outcome innovations. Given the fact that inflation is more volatile and has a very different distributional shape than activity growth, a sum of outcome innovations would give too much weight to changes in inflation and too little weight to activity growth. Thus, to make a representative index we use percentiles to overcome this problem.

Table 3.1. *Contemporaneous macroeconomic performance*

Term	Chief of administration	Average over term (percent)			
		Inflation rate	Devaluation rate	Interest rate	Activity growth rate
1853	Alsina	14.11	14.11	15.19	-17.53
1854/56	Obligado	3.19	3.19	14.10	7.15
1857/59	Alsina	0.53	0.53	15.72	-4.82
1860/68	Mitre	1.68	2.08	12.70	7.43
1869/74	Sarmiento	4.33	0.00	8.63	2.30
1875/80	Avellaneda	10.01	2.24	10.02	5.19
1881/86	Roca	-2.94	3.25	7.22	8.08
1887/90	Juárez Celman	12.06	15.46	8.79	5.40
1891/92	Pellegrini	10.86	12.15	9.72	-4.43
1893/98	Sáenz Peña, L./Uriburu, J. E.	-1.23	-4.12	8.22	0.72
1899/04	Roca	-1.72	-1.76	7.32	3.82
1905/10	Quintana/Figueroa Alcorta	4.97	0.04	5.50	2.43
1911/16	Sáenz Peña, R./de la Plaza	3.71	0.06	3.73	-3.99
1917/22	Yrigoyen	1.03	2.70	5.08	3.10
1923/28	De Alvear	0.09	-2.72	8.63	2.94
1929/30	Yrigoyen	-3.67	7.47	8.77	-2.45
1931	Uriburu, J. F.	-3.31	23.26	8.72	-9.22
1932/37	Justo	3.98	-0.62	6.02	1.88
1938/42	Ortiz/Castillo	4.52	4.55	2.09	0.77
1943/45	Ramirez/Farrell	5.57	-1.46	0.52	0.77
1946/51	Perón	20.93	31.58	-0.02	2.72
1952/55	Perón II	10.25	7.19	-1.25	0.89
1956/57	Aramburu	20.93	1.64	-0.49	2.21
1958/61	Frondizi	34.67	20.15	0.46	2.31
1962/63	Guido	26.05	24.42	2.89	-2.41
1964/66	Illia	22.84	22.50	4.39	6.42
1967/69	Onganía	11.59	9.24	7.64	4.93
1970/72	Levingston/Lanusse	37.01	40.28	5.48	3.37
1973/75	Perón III	70.83	79.67	2.44	2.35
1976/83	Videla/Viola/Galtieri/Bignone	108.58	94.51	5.15	0.03
1984/89	Alfonsín	178.76	181.46	17.38	-1.96
1990/95	Menem	53.35	33.73	14.26	3.09
1996/99	Menem II	-0.60	0.00	9.75	2.31

Notes and sources: See text and Appendices.

dex is calculated as a simple average of the standardised variables for the respective period of each administration.[17] Thus, a chief of the executive who
ranks above the fiftieth percentile is better than the median administration in
terms of macroperformance.

Indeed, initial conditions matter if we are to accurately evaluate the result
of the interaction between government and economic agents' decisions during
a particular administration. Therefore, our Classical Macroeconomic Pressure
Index has been adapted to account for the conditions that exist when each
administration takes office. Each variable has been adjusted by the "legacy
component" received from the previous administration as follows: the values
within the term have been subtracted from the last annual observation of the
variable for the preceding administration. The resulting difference is a measure
of "outcome innovation" – which we think yields a more accurate ranking of
the changes, positive or negative, in key variables.

To compare different outcome innovations, a ranking of the national administrations has been organised for each variable. We assigned each observed outcome innovation a percentile by comparing it with similar innovations across all
years for which information is available. The highest percentile corresponds
to the best innovation or improvement (lowest inflation innovation, highest
activity-growth innovation, and so on) and the lowest one reflects the worst.
This exercise provides some interesting details on the performance of various
administrations.

In 1931, during Uriburu's year in office, the interest rate on hard currency
was 8.72 percent, as can be seen on the column corresponding to average interest rate in Table 3.1. The legacy component, in this case the interest rate
in the last year of the second Irigoyen term (1930), was 8.70 percent.[18] The
outcome innovation for the interest rate in that administration is consequently
0.02 percent, which ranks the Uriburu administration outcome with respect to
interest rates at the 40th percentile, worse than the *median* innovation (the 50th
percentile). In the case of Nicolás Avellaneda's administration (1875–80), inflation innovation is found by comparing actual inflation to the legacy value,
that is, the inflation rate in the last year of Domingo Sarmiento's administration.

Another important example is provided by the analysis of the administrations
of Adolfo Alsina and Pastor Obligado. The real dimension of their performance
is apparent when we include the legacy component. Alsina was elected gov-

---

[17] It is worth remembering that the results in the tables only show average values for each term of
administration. Data are available per year upon request.

[18] The legacy component for each government can be inferred by subtracting the innovation component from the average value of the variable considered in each administration. Further details
about index construction can be found in Appendix A.

Table 3.2. *Comparative macroeconomic performance*

Term	Chief of administration	Average innovation (percent)			
		Inflation rate	Devalua-tion rate	Interest rate	Activity growth rate
1853	Alsina	20.91	20.91	0.00	-43.42
1854/56	Obligado	-10.92	-10.92	-1.09	24.68
1857/59	Alsina	-1.63	-1.63	-0.01	-12.54
1860/68	Mitre	4.80	5.19	-4.70	8.13
1869/74	Sarmiento	3.34	0.00	-3.93	8.96
1875/80	Avellaneda	9.16	2.24	2.20	27.33
1881/86	Roca	-48.32	14.01	-0.71	3.88
1887/90	Juárez Celman	9.01	14.01	0.93	8.42
1891/92	Pellegrini	-23.06	-23.85	-0.62	3.30
1893/98	Sáenz Peña, L./Uriburu, J. E.	21.51	8.70	-0.93	-4.77
1899/04	Roca	2.01	10.66	-0.55	-1.66
1905/10	Quintana/Figueroa Alcorta	2.63	0.13	-0.55	-5.88
1911/16	Sáenz Peña, R./de la Plaza	-4.06	-0.20	-1.38	-6.07
1917/22	Yrigoyen	-11.25	4.01	3.34	7.89
1923/28	De Alvear	9.48	9.60	0.40	-2.03
1929/30	Yrigoyen	-4.69	7.62	0.30	-5.75
1931	Uriburu, J. F.	0.95	9.68	0.02	-2.46
1932/37	Justo	7.29	-23.88	-2.70	11.10
1938/42	Ortiz/Castillo	-8.70	12.35	-2.77	-4.74
1943/45	Ramirez/Farrell	-1.18	-2.01	-0.27	1.31
1946/51	Perón	9.71	31.13	-1.01	7.65
1952/55	Perón II	-30.83	-42.06	0.51	-0.91
1956/57	Aramburu	10.18	-28.25	0.39	-2.94
1958/61	Frondizi	12.02	18.39	1.04	-1.13
1962/63	Guido	11.26	23.81	1.00	-9.20
1964/66	Illia	1.87	27.14	1.75	9.23
1967/69	Onganía	-11.75	-8.99	0.11	4.57
1970/72	Levingston/Lanusse	30.27	40.20	-2.38	-4.98
1973/75	Perón III	17.73	60.39	-1.97	0.75
1976/83	Videla/Viola/Galtieri/Bignone	-39.96	-81.35	4.00	1.15
1984/89	Alfonsín	13.42	47.80	2.81	-4.16
1990/95	Menem	-342.83	-409.31	-9.18	10.73
1996/99	Menem II	-4.25	-0.20	-6.36	6.49

Notes and sources: See text and Appendices.

ernor of Buenos Aires by the provincial chambers that were restored after the collapse of General Juan Manuel de Rosas' twenty-year autocratic rule. However, because of prevailing political instability, Alsina could not complete his mandate. In 1853 Buenos Aires seceded from the rest of the Confederation – the latter led by General Justo José Urquiza who had defeated Rosas and with that relinquished his base of power in Buenos Aires. Buenos Aires seceded to maintain its monopolies on custom revenues and the seigniorage provided by the only existing bank.[19]

In 1854, Obligado was elected to be the first constitutional governor of the province. During his term a process of dramatic institutional changes occurred with the emergence of a political market place and substantive fiscal and financial reforms. A mix of taxation reform (which lowered taxes on consumers and expanded the fiscal base to include exporters, who were formerly free of duty), a reorganisation of public expenditure management (on a more rational basis and controlled by public officials), and a tight control over the administration's financial and monetary policy (by both the legislature and "the market") rendered extraordinary results. Economic uncertainty arising from political arbitrariness was reduced while an unprecedented balance in the fiscal accounts and a virtuous monetary policy tended to diminish inflationary expectations. Increasing stability in financial and monetary events led to the restoration of external credit in 1857 and the restoration of convertibility in 1866.[20]

Table 3.1 shows how inflation subsided and the level of economic activity recovered during Obligado's term. However, the picture better captures the real changes in the economy when we include the legacy component as in Table 3.2. Here, the reduction in the inflation rate looks even more impressive. The interest rate was also lowered, and the rate of activity growth recovered notably. These achievements of the Obligado administration are outstanding and strongly contrast with the situation that had prevailed during the previous three decades of inconvertibility and inflationary finance.

3.2.2.2 The Fiscal Pressure Index (FPI)

For a small, open economy like Argentina's, the management of public debt matters, and substantially so. Debt management should be conducted so as to avoid unbearable pressure on the fiscal arithmetic of the forthcoming govern-

---

[19] Both had been fundamental in the fiscal and monetary policies of Buenos Aires that had established the province's leadership in the region. Rosas is now remembered for arbitrary rule and recourse to inflation taxes to fund fiscal deficits. These inflationary policies did not start with him, they went back to the 1820s. In any event, the legacy of the formative years of the Argentine state and market were dramatically shaped by fiscal deficit, the curtailment of external borrowing, the exhaustion of domestic credit and, ultimately, inflationary finance.

[20] See Irigoin and Salazar (2000).

ment. The Fiscal Pressure Index (FPI) augments the estimates from the CMPI by adding the fiscal policy dimension. This allows us to incorporate pressures emerging via the intertemporal budget constraint of a government, which is also known as the "transversality condition" in macroeconomics.

The FPI permits a closer characterization of the economic scorecards of the different administrations. That is, monetary and fiscal policy must be coordinated to obtain an intertemporally consistent outcome. In the case of a mature economy, the CMPI is quite adequate for the task of comparing different administrations in terms of their overall management. However, the CMPI is, we think, quite insufficient to satisfactorily assess the economic history of Argentina, a peripheral economy with an imperfect and small domestic capital market and recurrent macroeconomic crises. The Ricardian equivalence proposition – which asserts the irrelevance of the debt level for a given level of government expenditures – is not an adequate representation for an economy with incomplete information and debt ceilings. A long history of financial crises in Argentina, each one temporarily curtailing the government's ability to finance deficits through debt issue, underscores the fact that fiscal solvency does indeed matter.

The aim of the Fiscal Pressure Index is to rank administrations in their efforts to cope with the intertemporal solvency constraint. Given a government decision on current expenses, the incumbent administration has to decide how to fund them by choosing a combination of taxes, money base expansion, and new debt issues. The particular mix that is chosen matters. An accurate assessment of macroeconomic management has to consider the intertemporal effects of present decisions on net debt issues and the primary deficit. These decisions certainly will affect present outcomes (e.g., inflation and devaluation rates, or activity growth). But they also have a strong impact on future restrictions on macroeconomic policymaking (e.g., country risk, the burden of future debt servicing, and the possibility of an eventual future debt ceiling).

The new index has been constructed to rank administrations while correcting for changes in the intertemporal solvency situation. The Fiscal Pressure Index allows us to characterize the fiscal legacy handed down. High indebtedness or an unbalanced budget is a hot potato passed to succeeding administrations; the opposite situation is a "positive externality" that future generations of both policymakers and economic agents will inherit.

The Fiscal Pressure Index is based on the following first-order difference equation linking the debt-to-GDP ratio at a given point in time (t) to its previous ($t - 1$) value and the primary fiscal result, assuming for simplicity a Ricardian regime (where debt payments and primary deficit are entirely bond financed) and that bonds possess a one-period maturity (see *inter alia* della Paolera and Taylor 2001):

$$\frac{B_t}{Y_t} = \frac{1+r_t}{1+g_t}\frac{B_{t-1}}{Y_{t-1}} + \frac{DEF_t}{Y_t},$$

where: B_t is national government debt measured in real terms, in period t; Y_t is real GDP measured in period t; $1+r_t$ is the one-period real gross interest rate between time $t-1$ and t; and $1+g_t$ is the growth rate of the activity level between time $t-1$ and t, that is Y_t/Y_{t-1}.

The first order difference equation on B/Y sheds light on the dynamic determinants of the government debt burden. On the one hand, low growth or high interest rates push the ratio B/Y up, so that $(1+r)/(1+g)$ can be seen as an amplifying factor that determines the future debt-to-GDP ratio given its initial value. Hence, the loss of credibility on future debt payments (an increase in r) or a poor growth performance (a fall in g) will result in a higher debt burden in the future. The primary fiscal result also directly affects the ratio of debt-to-GDP passed on to the next administration. *Ceteris paribus*, the higher the fiscal deficit, the higher is the need for issuing bonds. Ultimately, this will increase the ratio of debt to GDP that subsequent policymakers will have to face in the future.

The Fiscal Pressure Index therefore aggregates five indicators:

  (i) the ratio of government debt to GDP as a measure of the debt burden relative to real activity;
 (ii) the ratio of government debt to exports estimates the debt burden on the capacity of the economy that would allow a government to repay its obligations;
(iii) the ratio of the primary fiscal result to total government revenues, which discounts the amount of debt services bequeathed from previous administrations – it is a net measure of the management ability of an administration on fiscal issues;
 (iv) the ratio of the primary fiscal result to debt servicing, stressing the available resources to service the public debt. It expresses the relation between the results of ordinary revenues minus current expenditure and the amount needed to effectively service the debt; the lower the ratio the more gloomy would be the outlook for debt fulfillment and, hence, for borrowing in the future;
  (v) the ratio of the gross interest rate on hard currency to the growth rate of activity, $(1+r)/(1+g)$, which shows the factor by which the debt-to-GDP ratio would increase if the fiscal primary deficit were nil. It allows

for market sensitivity to the actions taken by administrators in office the expectations on future decisions about debt management.

To characterize key features of the components of the Fiscal Pressure Index, Table 3.3 presents the average value of the variables for each administration considered in the time span of the study. Next, in a similar fashion to the method used for the CMPI, "legacy components" (or the "initial conditions" for the five indicators) are computed to obtain the innovations or improvements for each year and variable in the FPI. For each variable, each observed "outcome innovation" is assigned a percentile by comparing it with similar innovations across all years for which information is available. The highest percentile corresponds to the best innovation (greatest reduction in debt burden, or greatest improvement in the fiscal situation) and the lowest one reflects the worst. With these new standardized time series for outcome innovations, the Fiscal Pressure Index is calculated as a simple average of the five components for the respective period of each administration. Thus, a chief of the executive that ranks above the fiftieth percentile is better than the median administration in terms of fiscal performance.

3.3 The results

3.3.1 The Classical Macroeconomic Pressure Index (CMPI)

To compare macroeconomic improvements over the last 150 years of Argentina's history, Figure 3.1 ranks the 33 identified administrations according to the CMPI over the period. On this basis, it looks as if the best macroeconomic performance in the history of the Argentine economy was near the very end, the six years associated with the first term of Menem (1990–95). Why? There was a drastic change in the monetary regime during his tenure as a result of the inception of the Convertibility Law in 1991 and the establishment of the independent Central Bank. The latter acted as a quasi-currency board, creating a virtual dollar exchange standard, and had rapid success in cutting the inflation and devaluation rates.

This macroeconomic situation, measured by the CMPI, has no equivalent in Argentine macroeconomic history over the 150 years considered here. Menem had inherited high inflation (or hyperinflation) from his predecessor Raúl Alfonsín (1984–89), whose departure was so hasty that he even arranged to advance the balloting to elect his successor in violation of the constitution.[21] Yet one might still be inclined to say that achieving *disinflation* after a time of exorbitant rates of inflation should not be taken alone as evidence of heroic policymaking

---

[21] Incidentally, Alfonsín's term ranks twenty-sixth in the classification of all thirty-three terms.

Table 3.3. *Contemporaneous fiscal performance*

Term	Chief of administration	Debt/ GDP	Debt/ exports	Primary result/ revenue	Primary result/ debt service	$\frac{(1+r)}{(1+g)}$
		Average over term (percent)				
1853	Alsina	60.1	130.1	-121.0	-406.7	133.7
1854/56	Obligado	49.7	111.1	2.7	11.2	104.0
1857/59	Alsina	59.1	121.3	-33.1	-260.6	117.5
1860/68	Mitre	69.8	148.9	-3.7	-20.6	102.3
1869/74	Sarmiento	80.6	186.2	-11.1	-18.0	105.2
1875/80	Avellaneda	68.7	174.0	3.6	8.1	102.6
1881/86	Roca	58.3	181.0	-25.2	-72.8	97.6
1887/90	Juárez Celman	82.0	281.4	-13.0	-91.5	100.7
1891/92	Pellegrini	124.7	366.9	-1.5	6.4	112.1
1893/98	Sáenz Peña, L./Uriburu, J. E.	110.2	384.9	-9.5	-20.7	104.4
1899/04	Roca	93.1	240.2	35.9	85.2	101.4
1905/10	Quintana/Figueroa Alcorta	54.2	122.3	2.2	2.5	98.6
1911/16	Sáenz Peña, R./de la Plaza	57.4	122.9	-14.3	-51.9	104.3
1917/22	Yrigoyen	54.0	78.5	4.3	18.9	100.3
1923/28	De Alvear	49.5	91.6	1.8	12.3	102.5
1929/30	Yrigoyen	52.1	135.8	-12.5	-35.1	108.7
1931	Uriburu, J. F.	42.7	131.9	3.4	9.7	116.8
1932/37	Justo	52.1	281.8	7.1	16.7	102.5
1938/42	Ortiz/Castillo	54.4	390.5	-21.3	-105.8	99.7
1943/45	Ramirez/Farrell	56.7	392.9	-51.1	-210.7	98.5
1946/51	Perón	36.6	175.4	-32.1	-315.6	95.4
1952/55	Perón II	36.1	209.4	-32.9	-312.6	96.2
1956/57	Aramburu	32.1	222.3	-42.4	-359.5	95.7
1958/61	Frondizi	20.1	209.6	-40.6	-528.1	97.0
1962/63	Guido	16.4	168.4	-27.5	-328.7	103.8
1964/66	Illia	14.4	169.1	-25.8	-268.2	97.0
1967/69	Onganía	11.8	177.0	-10.9	-129.2	101.2
1970/72	Levingston/Lanusse	11.4	154.3	-14.8	-113.5	100.5
1973/75	Perón III	14.1	138.5	-69.3	-286.2	98.5
1976/83	Videla/Viola/Galtieri/Bignone	24.5	276.3	-36.3	-153.3	103.8
1984/89	Alfonsín	66.0	656.6	-17.5	-126.8	118.4
1990/95	Menem	42.0	624.7	3.6	32.6	109.8
1996/99	Menem II	38.1	438.8	3.0	6.9	106.2

Notes and sources: See text and Appendices.

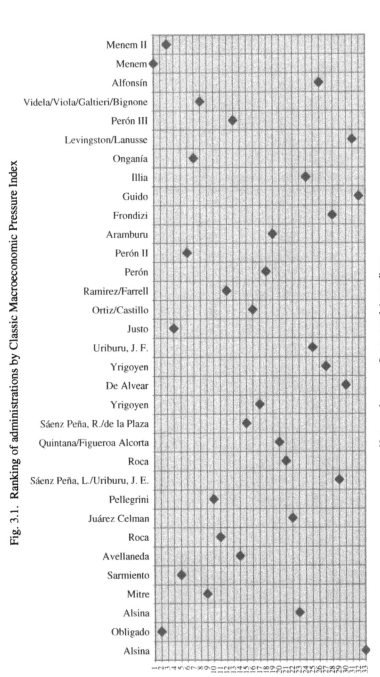

Fig. 3.1. Ranking of administrations by Classic Macroeconomic Pressure Index

Notes and sources: See text and Appendices.

skill. However, a particularly salient aspect of President Menem's first term in power is that Argentina achieved more than in previous short-run programs of stabilization. A drastic change of monetary regime achieved stability after the extreme hyperinflationary experiences of 1989–90. A considerable reduction in country risk and the return to sustained activity growth after almost twenty years of stagnation could still justify Menem's position at the head of the rankings. Furthermore, macroeconomic stability and a decent economic performance continued throughout his second presidency (1995–99), which stands in third place according to the CMPI.

Proceeding in descending order, the second best outcome came at the very beginning of the 150-year period under analysis. In the period 1854–57 the fruits of major institutional reforms allowed a substantial change in expectations about the chronic insolvency of the state. The recourse to inflation tax disappeared and the costs of exercising power and political strife were curtailed dramatically; this allowed for high rates of economic growth. These achievements look even more impressive when compared with the inherited situation. Although technically attained by preceding governments, a definitive change in the macroeconomic situation was put firmly in place.[22] Considering that the second interval associated with Alsina falls in twenty-third place, the sudden slowdown in economic growth deserves an explanation. In fact, 1859 and 1861 were years of warfare when Buenos Aires' army clashed with the other provinces' confederation army. Currency issues to fund the war disrupted the rate of recovery of both the inflation and the interest rates, but these effects did not last long.

The early 1930s in Argentina are another interesting case. According to the rankings, the years associated with General Agustín Justo's administration (1932–38) had the fourth best macroeconomic indicators. A combination of greater exchange rate stability after the demise of the gold standard in 1931–32 and the recovery of growth after the Great Depression of 1930–32 justifies the position in the rankings. This is an interesting finding because it suggests that, at least through the lenses of the CMPI, Justo's presidency in the interwar period was one of the most successful of the entire twentieth century until the hyperinflation of the late 1980s. Remarkably, Argentina recovered from the

---

[22] Among many other existing institutions, the single bank of issue was reformed and its management was made independent of the government. Monetary policy was thereafter a matter of bargaining between administrations, the legislature, and the merchants on the board of the bank. The institution regained the favor of the public and greatly expanded its business of discounting commercial bills. Deposits grew at an unprecedented rate, both in paper (i.e., inconvertible) and metallic currency, demonstrating the greater confidence placed in the institution. Interests rate diminished substantially and credit reappeared and was readily available to the public. Formal sources of credit resulted in lower interest rates while greater monetary stability was conducive to greater activity growth. See Irigoin (2000a).

effects of the Great Depression in spite of the relative decline of the United Kingdom.[23] The years 1933–44 are a period in the economic history of the country that surely deserves further research .[24]

We might also consider Sarmiento's tenure (1869–74), when Argentina enjoyed six years on an uninterrupted gold standard regime with a hard peso (*peso fuerte*) quoted at a fixed rate of twenty-five paper pesos. The devaluation rate was zero, nominal interest rates converged for the first time to North American levels, and the expansion of economic activity was unparalleled.[25] These facts also justify the inclusion of Sarmiento's administration as one of the best five as assessed by the CMPI.

So much for the top five; what about the bottom of the rankings? The worst times for the Argentine economy – measured by substantial inflation rates and interest rates and by a shortfall in economic activity growth – correspond, perhaps not surprisingly, with times of severe political instability. The first mandate of Alsina was a replay of conditions first seen forty years earlier – a failure to organize the state and polity after independence. As mentioned above, inflationary tax was the ultimate means to meet excessive expenditure that was most often a result of civil war. Economic uncertainty caused by political instability or discretionary rulers explains the abysmal rate of economic activity of the early 1850s. Other times of economic malaise are associated with the 1962–63 and 1970–72 intervals.[26] These were the years of greatest political instability in the last century. An increasing rate of inflation and more pronounced rates of devaluation, plus a substantial reduction in the levels of activity, both contemporaneous and adjusted for the legacy component, mark these as the darkest years in the performance of the Argentine economy.

The incorporation of initial conditions, or legacy components, seems to make a difference in our rankings, and some findings here seem quite notable. Again, for most historians, the role of Pellegrini (1891–92) in alleviating the 1890s crisis has secured his prominent and revered place in the annals of history. However, the outcome of his mandate looks dire if we consider only the contemporaneous data as depicted in Table 3.1. Only when adjusted for the legacy he inherited can his administration be viewed much more favorably, as in Table 3.2. In 1890, tumultuous macroeconomic shocks following the Baring crash

[23] See della Paolera and Taylor (2001).

[24] See, however, O'Connell (1984) and Llach (1984).

[25] See della Paolera and Taylor (2001, 43).

[26] It should be mentioned that these rankings are based on averages in each administration. A year-by-year ranking, not reported in this chapter, also highlights some other crucial periods of instability. Examples include the first year of hyperinflation in 1989, the transition to democracy in 1983, and the last and agitated year of the mandate of Isabel Perón in 1975, previous to the *coup d'état*.

spelled the demise of the financial system and, fiscally, the collapse of the national administration. Even so, Pellegrini still ranks tenth among thirty-three administrations. This is a decidedly better performance than his predecessor, Juárez Celman (1887–90) who ranks twenty-second, highlighting the fact that Pellegrini inherited an extraordinarily bad macroeconomic situation.

3.3.2 The Fiscal Pressure Index (FPI)

Using a procedure similar to that employed to calculate the CMPI, the results of the Fiscal Pressure Index are charted in Figure 3.2. We now find that the fiscal and financial history of Argentina over 150 years shows a quite different ordering of intervals when ranked by the FPI.

As further evidence of the extraordinary success of the 1854–57 reforms, Obligado's administration now leads the ranking. As shown in Table 3.3, the performance of the fiscal indicators during Obligado's administration was extraordinary. The ratio of debt to GDP and to exports was reduced at the same time as unprecedented balance was brought to the fiscal accounts.[27] The Baring loan of 1824 was renegotiated in 1856, renewing access to foreign borrowing for the first time since the default on this loan in 1827. Similarly, public credit in the domestic market was restored in 1856 with the launch of the first series of public bonds since 1840, the year in which conventional means of financing the deficit were exhausted under Rosas' regime.[28]

The second administration of Julio A. Roca (1899–04) stands second in the rankings. This administration was clearly in favor of restoring the gold standard and achieved extraordinary results in Argentina's fiscal position. The relative performance in debt reduction as measured by the ratio of debt to GDP and an extraordinary average surplus for the treasury explain Roca's success at the turn of the twentieth century. The third-best administration in the FPI rankings is the one associated with Menem's first term (1990–95), putting him slightly ahead of President Juan Perón's first term in office (1946–51).

One of the most impressive fiscal performances took place during Avellaneda's administration (1875–80), which ranks fifth overall. In these years, the

---

[27] The Treasury showed an unprecedented trend towards balancing its budget – a feat not managed since 1810. Other achievements were the drafting and constructive redrafting of the Budget Law in congress, marking a consensus for the first time in decades. Furthermore, a bicameral committee annually audited the final accounting of the budget as mandated by the law.

[28] The main engineer of the reforms conducting these outstanding outcomes was de La Riestra, who was minister in charge of provincial finances from 1855 to 1861 and worked in several of the administrations listed in the tables. He was the main advisor for macroeconomic policy to President Mitre (1862–68) and was back in office throughout the presidency of Avellaneda (1875–80).

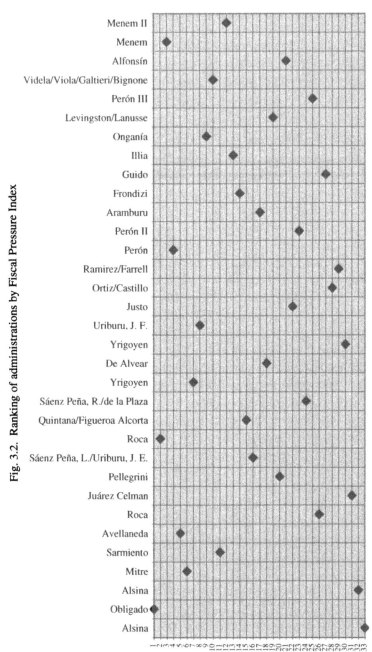

Fig. 3.2. Ranking of administrations by Fiscal Pressure Index

Notes and sources: See text and Appendices.

government redressed problems associated with the fiscally overheated economy that had developed during the preceding administration, a hot potato left behind by the departing president. The ratio of debt to GDP fell by around 10 percent from the average levels it had reached during Sarmiento's term (1869–74). As a result of virtuous fiscal policy during Avellanda's mandate, high indebtedness was reduced while a significant reduction in country risk came about after the crisis of 1876. Avellaneda passed on to his successor, Roca (1881–86), a much more manageable economic environment.

Similarly, there are some intervals of interests in the twentieth century that rank surprisingly well compared to conventional wisdom. Notably, Yrigoyen's first mandate (1917–22) appears close to the top. A mild surplus in the primary fiscal results following a recovery after the First World War, together with a reduction in the relative rate of indebtedness, puts Yrigoyen in seventh place. The first term of Menem (1990–95) shows substantial gains in fiscal performance, though its FPI ranking is not as high as its CMPI ranking. A notable improvement in revenues plus a reduction in the debt-to-GDP ratio stand out in these years. His second mandate, though, does not show comparable achievements: it falls to twelfth position as a result of increasing debt-to-GDP ratios from 1997 and no major improvements in the fiscal accounts.

At the other end of the rankings, the provincial administrations led by Alsina (1853 and 1857–59), which coincided with the secession of Buenos Aires, show an extremely poor performance. Efforts to fund extraordinary expenditure on the internecine conflict with the Confederation (a war between Buenos Aires and the rest of the provinces), made the fiscal deficit skyrocket. The final battles in the civil wars occurred in 1859–61 and soured the achievements obtained during Obligado's (1854–56) term in office. Not surprisingly, one of the worst times in the country's history, according to the FPI, is the period (1887–90) associated with Juárez Celman. A substantial increase in the ratio of debt to GDP toward the end of his tenure and an increasing weakness in the fiscal situation over the years was fatal for the political survival of Juárez Celman and almost as unhealthy for the country as whole, and this was the mess inherited by Pellegrini.

Table 3.4 displays the comparative positions of each Administration ranked by the CMPI, the FPI, and the average position derived from the two rankings.[29] There are some notable reversals in the respective rankings that are worth describing in detail. They reflect the occurrence of certain short-run monetary

---

[29] The average position is calculated by ranking the simple average of the CMPI and FPI for each administration.

and fiscal policies that could not be expected to remain consistent in the long run.

First, from 1860 until the 1890 crisis, there is a noticeable alternation of administrations in both rankings. This stresses the importance of the legacy effect as an intertemporal linkage between subsequent governments. In other words, a relative (and short-lived) amelioration in one of the indices is achieved at the expense of a worse performance in the other index as the hot potato is passed.

The pair of presidents Sarmiento (1869–74) and Avellaneda (1875–80) offers a good example. Sarmiento ranks fairly well at fifth place according to the CMPI; however, the FPI ranks him eleventh. This difference in the rankings of Sarmiento's term is explained by a favorable macroeconomic environment (a fixed exchange rate regime and the convergence of interest rate with international levels) on the one hand and an explosion in the ratio of debt to GDP on the other hand. In 1870, total debt amounted to 48 million gold pesos. A year later, it had increased almost twofold. Sarmiento's administration generated growth, but at a price.

This phenomenal expansion in the ratio of debt to GDP could hardly be disregarded by his successor, Avellaneda. He ranks only fourteenth in the CMPI, in part because of tough actions needed to get the debt under control. In the middle of his term (1876) convertibility was once again suspended. The inflation rate rose to almost 20 percent in the following year. However, the ratio of debt to GDP plummeted. Avellaneda's administration was the first to deliver a balance in the fiscal accounts since the mid-1850s. This explains his outstanding position, according to the FPI, at fifth all time. He ranks only seventh on the overall index, but Sarmiento ranks only tenth overall.

Nevertheless, according to this last ranking, the decades of the 1860s and 1880s experienced the most favorable performance of the economy overall, setting the stage for the so-called Golden Age of Argentine history. Up to the late 1880s, the rankings still show an alternation in the relative position of administrations. This indicates the possible existence of a stop-and-go dynamic, a feature common even in later periods of Argentine economic historiography (Cortés Conde 1997). Thus, we may consider this to have been a very long-run characteristic of the country's economic performance.

Until 1887, administrations had somehow managed to overcome the intertemporal solvency constraint. They had succeeded at passing the buck to the following government. Over these years, beyond the alternations, we also see a gradual deterioration in the trend of the overall index, which may explain the extent of the crisis that Argentina finally suffered in 1890. All the same, between 1853 and the 1930s, fiscal instability was a transitory phenomenon.

Table 3.4. *Comparative ranking of Argentine administrations, 1853–1999*

Term	Chief of administration	Rank		
		CMPI	FPI	Overall index
1853	Alsina	33	33	33
1854/56	Obligado	2	1	2
1857/59	Alsina	23	32	31
1860/68	Mitre	9	6	3
1869/74	Sarmiento	5	11	10
1875/80	Avellaneda	14	5	7
1881/86	Roca	11	26	16
1887/90	Juárez Celman	22	31	29
1891/92	Pellegrini	10	20	14
1893/98	Sáenz Peña, L./Uriburu, J. E.	29	16	25
1899/04	Roca	21	2	5
1905/10	Quintana/Figueroa Alcorta	20	15	17
1911/16	Sáenz Peña, R./de la Plaza	15	24	21
1917/22	Yrigoyen	17	7	11
1923/28	De Alvear	30	18	27
1929/30	Yrigoyen	27	30	30
1931	Uriburu, J. F.	25	8	15
1932/37	Justo	4	22	12
1938/42	Ortiz/Castillo	16	28	24
1943/45	Ramirez/Farrell	12	29	22
1946/51	Perón	18	4	8
1952/55	Perón II	6	23	13
1956/57	Aramburu	19	17	18
1958/61	Frondizi	28	14	23
1962/63	Guido	32	27	32
1964/66	Illia	24	13	19
1967/69	Onganía	7	9	6
1970/72	Levingston/Lanusse	31	19	28
1973/75	Perón III	13	25	20
1976/83	Videla/Viola/Galtieri/Bignone	8	10	9
1984/89	Alfonsín	26	21	26
1990/95	Menem	1	3	1
1996/99	Menem II	3	12	4

Notes and sources: CMPI = Classic Macroeconomic Pressure Index. FPI = Fiscal Pressure Index. See Tables 3.1–3.3, text, and Appendices.

Because of the relatively balanced budget in the long run, and fairly frequent access to international capital markets, governments had some room for maneuver. Expansionary policies (deficits) were feasible in some administrations, and were considered an occasional but expected phenomena, reflecting the belief that economic growth would in the long run generate the resources to pay today's bills. This explains the outcomes during the Sarmiento and Juárez Celman regimes. The disequilibrium (assessed by deterioration in the FPI) was corrected in the subsequent administrations. Avellaneda's and Pellegrini's terms emphasized fiscal equilibrium and debt repayment rather than expansive demand policies.

After 1914 the policy context changed dramatically. There was now limited access to the international capital markets (Taylor 1992, 1994). After heavy fiscal imbalances began in the 1940s monetary expansion became the crucial link between chronic deficits and nominal instability.[30] As shown in Tables 3 and 4, only those administrations that tried to reduce the fiscal gap improved both their FPI and CMPI outcomes, and they are the ones that appear higher in the rankings. For example, Onganía, with his finance minister Adalbert Krieger Vasena, succeeded – if only briefly – in improving Argentina's fiscal position in the period 1967–69. This helped reduce monetary expansion and, hence, annual inflation rates into single digits in 1969. This explains the favorable position assigned to this administration. But few postwar administrations had such success: corrections in fiscal disequilibrium became very rare until the 1990s, so that stabilization attempts tended to collapse shortly after being implemented. The lesson from the second half of the twentieth century is that fiscal discipline is the *sine qua non* condition for achieving nominal stability.

3.4 Conclusions

According to the Overall Index displayed in Table 3.4, the five most successful periods in the macroeconomic history of Argentina are the episodes associated with Menem's two mandates (1990–95 and 1996–99), Roca's second term (1899–1904), and years of the Obligado (1854–56) and Bartolomé Mitre (1860–68) administrations. It is worth noting that all of these five periods share one important institutional commonality: they each featured the establishment of, or convergence toward, a convertible monetary regime. This chapter thus offers one very striking finding; namely, that a good position in the macroeconomic

---

[30] An exception occurred in the late 1970s and early 1980s, when the government's external debt grew at rates approaching 50 percent per year. This abrupt issue of liabilities ended in severe capital flight, default on obligations, and the inability to access international credit markets during the 1980s.

Fig. 3.3. Ratio of primary result (net of interest) to fiscal revenues

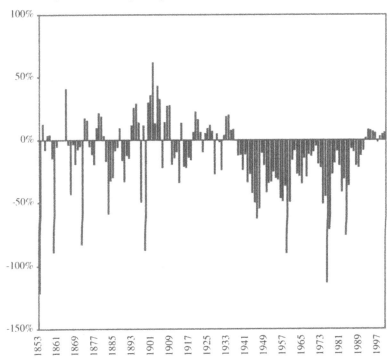

Notes and sources: No data are available for the period 1861–63. See text and Appendix B.

rankings is definitively associated with a hard or strong currency regime. More-over, a sound currency plan has proved sustainable in the immediate future only on those occasions when it has been associated with a sound fiscal situation. The above-mentioned intervals are also clear benchmarks in the history of Argentina's fiscal performance, as shown in Figure 3.3 containing the ratio of primary results to fiscal revenues from the mid-nineteenth century to recent years.

Although Argentina's first experience with a convertible monetary regime since independence officially occurred solely in 1867, the process of stabilization had already started in 1854. This trend toward greater macroeconomic stability was temporarily interrupted in the later years of the 1850s. The combination of warfare and currency issues during Alsina's second term (1857–59) was a clear manifestation of the devastating effects of civil war, and they affected the path to economic recovery so adversely that the second Alsina term is at the bottom of the rankings. Fortunately, this was a short-lived discontinuity between the administrations of Obligado and Mitre, which rank as the second and third best periods, respectively.

The period 1854–57 was a crucial turning point for the treasury, with the reduction of chronic imbalances that manifested the ongoing economic costs of independence and delays in the process of nation building. Recall that in 1854, the only existing financial institution – and the single bank of issue – was reformed, granting to its managers independence from government financial needs. Henceforth, Argentina pursued a virtuous monetary policy for some time. From 1899 during Roca's second presidency, the treasury enjoyed outstanding primary surpluses for six years in a row. This outcome was truly extraordinary in relation to the entire fiscal record from the country's 150 years of public finances. Thereafter, the budget was balanced on average and showed no significant shortfalls until the early 1930s.

After five years of fiscal bonanza following the recovery from the Great Depression, a dramatic and persistent string of deficits was re-inaugurated in 1936. We can note here that the central bank had just been created the year before. Not only was fiscal deficit the rule for more than fifty years until the 1990s, but it also reached substantial levels at times. In 1945, 1958, 1975–6, and 1983 the disparity between revenues and expenditure represented over 60 percent of total revenues. This trend only reversed in 1991 when the primary results turned positive. Although they were smaller in comparison with previous episodes, the surplus was steady. Once again, as part of the reforms introduced in the 1990s, the management of the central bank became autonomous from the government. A new charter established the bank as an independent authority in monetary policymaking.[31]

The relation between the institutional reforms in monetary authority and the shifts in the fiscal position of Argentina are apparent in Figure 3.4. The figure displays the evolution of the ratios of primary results to fiscal revenues and of the inflation tax to GDP. As mentioned before, fiscal disequilibrium was a transitory phenomenon from the 1850s to the 1930s, when budget deficit came to rule Argentine public finances. As was the case prior to the 1850s, currency issue was the ultimate recourse taken to meet the fiscal gap. This was the result of the government's capacity to influence the authorities in charge of monetary policymaking. Eventually, excessive monetary expansion led to inflation and allowed the government to repudiate some of its liabilities. Because inflation diminished the real value of money, the monetization of the fiscal deficit acted as a progressive expropriation of domestic currency held by private agents, i.e., it

---

[31] In 2001 this charter was *de facto* amended and modified by one of its architects, minister of finance Domingo Cavallo, terminating the bank's brief period of autonomy.

Fig. 3.4. Fiscal imbalance and inflation tax: A link between CMPI and FPI?

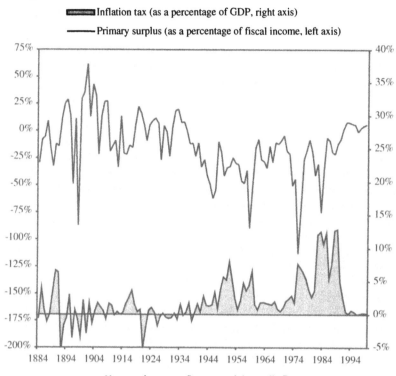

Inflation tax (as a percentage of GDP, right axis)

—— Primary surplus (as a percentage of fiscal income, left axis)

Notes and sources: See text and Appendix B.

acted as an inflation tax. This permanent erosion in the purchasing power of the public's cash holdings had dramatic consequences. Over time, this repeatedly used device reached extreme proportions: on a percentage basis, increases in the fiscal deficit were often met one-for-one with increases in inflation tax.[32]

The use of monetization to finance persistent fiscal deficits was one of the main problems of the Argentine economy in the second half of the twentieth century. At different points in time, several programs sought to break this pattern. Success was always ephemeral. Some of these measures achieved a reduction in the inflation rate that lasted for several months or for a few years;

[32] For example, as explained in Appendix C, by using a narrow definition of cash in the hands of the public, between 1960 and 1990 the inflation tax yielded $175 billion, and with the same figure exceeding $300 billion if we consider a broader definition of currency (M1). These figures are even greater than the outstanding public debt today ($125 billion) and represent more than 3 times the present annual fiscal revenues ($50 billion). Thus, given the magnitude of the fiscal disequilibrium this repeated recourse to inflation tax to fund deficit dramatically affected the nominal and real variables expressed in the Classical Macroeconomic Index.

but soon, the fiscal scenario was repeated, and all stabilization plans ended in failure. These attempts usually began in periods of contraction in economic activity and soon afterwards they gave rise to demand booms that faded away when inflation accelerated again. Short-lived recoveries did not evolve into sustained growth because the fundamental problems underlying the fiscal problem remained unsolved. In the long run these failed stabilization attempts underline an incongruity between nominal stability and fiscal disequilibrium that was always, until the 1990s, ultimately solved in favor of maintaining the imbalances. Thus, the economy returned, again and again, to a path of increasing rates of inflation until it reached levels that brought about the need to try another round of stabilization.

For more than half a century governments made frequent recourse either to printing money or to trying other, more sophisticated means of expanding the money supply to resolve fiscal deficits, e.g., rediscounting facilities to private banks that fostered artificial credit expansion. All such policies resulted in high levels of inflation. Moreover, positive rates of inflation persisted in every year from 1940. This process reached a dramatic peak during the hyperinflation of 1989–90 when inflation rates neared 200 percent per month.

This pattern changed in 1991 once the mechanism was truly exhausted. In fact, by 1989–90 Argentines were reducing their real cash holdings, marking the start of a complete demonetization of the economy. Contemporary balance sheets of the Argentine central bank reveal the dramatic drop in cash available for transactions. Notes and coins in the hands of the public represented less than 2 percent of GDP. This is the ultimate example of the complex interaction between government choices and agents' preferences: a massive substitution of currency had occurred. This causes us to question the conventional interpretation of the economic history of Argentina as a mere reflection of economic policy, and it is one of the main features of the analysis developed in this chapter.

In 1991, the monetary discipline of the Convertibility Law curtailed the scope for fiscal imbalances. Because every increase in the stock of currency could only arise from an equivalent increase in the country's reserves, the new regime sought to tie the government's hands, preventing the expansion of unbacked money as a means to fund the deficit. Subsequently, there were only two alternatives: a reduction in the fiscal imbalance or its funding through debt issue. The alternative chosen in the 1990s was a mixed policy, and it signified a dramatic change in regime. Although in 1991, as mentioned before, the government achieved an unusual primary fiscal surplus that it maintained throughout the decade, it was insufficient to pay for the interest on the debt. Hence, debt increased, although until 1997 it grew at a slower rate than that of the economy. Thus, debt to GDP and debt to export ratios diminished during the majority of

Fig. 3.5. Ratio of debt service to government revenues, 1853–1999

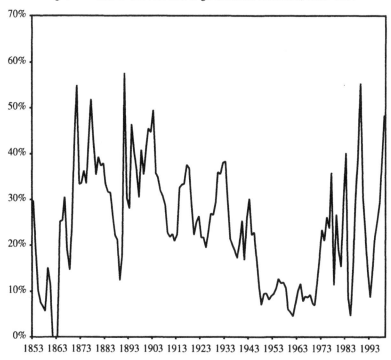

Notes and sources: No data are available for the period 1861–63. See text and Appendix B.

the 1990s. As a result of relatively greater economic growth, greater fiscal discipline, and a virtuous monetary policy, country risk was reduced substantially as compared to the 1980s. In other words, the burden of the debt appeared to be alleviated, at least in the short run.

The situation changed dramatically after 1997 when debt ratios started to increase. Within the framework of lower economic growth, the increase of debt services without a matching surplus in primary results penalized the strategy of rolling over. Since 1993, the service of amortization and interest has reached extremely high levels as shown in Figure 3.5. By 2001, more than half of government revenues were committed to servicing the debt, a situation comparable to the one faced by Juárez Celman's administration (1886–90). Furthermore, the cost of using debt instruments to maintain actual fiscal imbalances proved increasingly dangerous, reaching prohibitive levels. Argentina seems to be approaching a new turning point in its economic history. The discipline imposed by the Convertibility Law ended in the months of December 2001 and January

2002 when the new Argentine authorities decided to devalue and default on both the internal and external public debt.

The problem of macroeconomic policymaking is yet again at center stage for Argentina. Can consistent policies be designed and implemented? Or will stablilizations alternate with crises, a stop-and-go cycle that has been so destructive over time? This chapter offers some historical perspective. We have considered the performance of the Argentine economy for the last 150 years by analyzing the relationship between nominal, real, and fiscal indicators. The indices presented are reduced forms for the interaction between government choices and agents' preferences over time. Since history really does matter, this interaction implies a strong path dependency linking past and present.

The inexorable intertemporal restriction – that is, how the fiscal deficit is financed over time – is today strongly conditioned by the path-dependent nature of Argentine economic history. Previous outcomes of the interaction between economic policy and public reaction have narrowed the choice set for decisionmakers when searching for ways to fund the deficit. There are almost no degrees of freedom left and woe to any administration that ignores the fiscal foundations of the economy. In a country that was once rich and proud, there is no longer time for fiscal illusion.

The once-abundant economic rents of Argentina have been consumed bit by bit during the twentieth century, and this of necessity prompts society to take more seriously the simple but ill-understood phenomenon of economic scarcity. How are Argentines going to cope with scarcity? Can they develop credible institutions for the purpose of dealing with a real, hard budget constraint? We have an intuition that a new constitutional and fiscal design could help the country escape the trap of discretionary rulers and diminish the incentives for opportunistic administrators to pass the buck.

Appendix A: Methodology

Both the Classical Macroeconomic and Fiscal Pressure indices can be interpreted as a summary of variables that reflect the outcome of the interplay between policymakers and agents over time relative to the initial conditions inherited. Thus, they are not "situation indices," but instead are "relative indices" in the sense that they reflect innovations instead of the compiling of the results of current and previous interactions between the government and the private sector.

The procedure to obtain both indices can be summarized as follows. First, time series of key macroeconomic variables are selected as primary components of both indices. These are observed at annual frequency from 1853 to 1999. These variables are summarized in Table 3.5. Second, each year is assigned to an administration (the chief of the executive branch of the national government after 1862 or the chief of the executive branch of Buenos Aires province before 1862) that ruled during the majority of the year. In this case, the period 1853–1999 was divided into thirty-three administrations. Let k

Table 3.5. *Index components*

Classic Macroeconomic Pressure Index	Fiscal Pressure Index
1. Inflation rate[1]	1. Debt to activity ratio
2. Devaluation rate	2. Debt to export ratio
3. Real interest rate[1]	3. Ratio of primary result of central government to total revenues[2]
4. Activity growth rate	4. Ratio of primary result of central government to debt servicing[2]
	5. Real interest rate adjusted by growth of activity, $(1+r)/(1+g)$

[1] Some observations are based on proxies. See Appendix B for further details.
[2] Observations are missing for the period 1861–63. See Appendices A and B for further details.

denote an administration (or interval), that is $k \in K = \{1, 2, \ldots, 33\}$, and let $t \in T$, the set of all years between 1853 and 1999. Then, according to the previously detailed administration assignment rule, each year $t \in T$ is assigned an element of $k \in K$. For each k there is a set A_k whose elements are the years in which administration k ruled. For example, the elements of A_2 are the years when the second administration (Obligado's) ruled: hence, $A_2 = \{1854, 1855, 1856\}$.

Third, let X_{jt} be the value observed at time $t \in T$ for the variable $j \in J$, the latter considered as primary component (e.g., inflation rate, activity growth, debt to export, etc.) of either the classic macroeconomic index or the fiscal pressure index. Now, for each variable $j \in J$ and administration $k \in K$ an inherited or "legacy component" level of the considered variable is computed. This number is the value observed in the last year of the previous administration and is labeled $X_{jk}(-1)$. Note that the value $X_{jk}(-1)$ is repeated in all the years of an uninterrupted administration, that is holding k and j fixed $X_{jk}(-1) = X_{jtk}(-1)$ for all $t \in (T \cap A_k)$. The sequence of $X_{jtk}(-1)$ (holding j fixed and $t \in (T \cap A_k)$) can be regarded as the previous administration's legacy for variable X_j. Hence, X_{jt} can be decomposed as the sum of two components:

$$X_{jt} = X_{jt}(-1) + x_{jt},$$

where: $X_{jt}(-1)$ is the legacy component, that is, the initial conditions for variable j inherited from previous administration; and $x_{jt} = X_{jt} - X_{jt}(-1)$ the innovation component, also the "outcome innovation" for administration ruling in year t. The innovation component can be regarded as the improvement over the "legacy component" or "initial condition" inherited from the previous administration, as defined above. Thus, the innovation component is the desired time series in order to build a *relative* index, because it corrects for initial conditions.

Fourth, the sequence of outcome innovations, namely $x_{jt} = X_{jt} - X_{jt}(-1)$, is computed and then sorted so that the best year of macroeconomic management is listed at the top of the rank according to indicator x_{jt}. For example, let $x_{jt} = X_{jt} - X_{jt}(-1)$, $t \in T$ be the sequence of outcome innovations for the inflation rate. Since higher innovations in inflation are associated with worse outcomes, the sequence x_{jt} will be sorted in ascendant order and at the top of the ranking will be the year with the lowest value of x_{jt} (lowest inflation innovation). In other cases, such as activity growth innovation, the sorting will be descending: the higher is the growth innovation, the better the position in the ranking.

Table 3.6. *Sorting of innovation index components*

Innovation component	Sort
Inflation rate	Ascending
Devaluation rate	Ascending
Real interest rate	Ascending
Activity growth rate	Descending
Debt to activity ratio	Ascending
Debt to export ratio	Ascending
Ratio of primary result of central government to total revenues	Descending
Ratio of primary result of central government to debt servicing	Descending
Real interest rate adjusted by growth of activity, $(1 + r)/(1 + g)$	Ascending

Table 3.6 summarizes the sort ordering used to construct the percentile rank table of for each policy innovation variable.

Finally, given these positions for each year and each variable (measured by its outcome innovation component) we define a relative index for the positions of each variable in the following manner. For a certain variable j (e.g., the policy innovation of the inflation rate) each year with available observations is assigned a relative position in the [0, 1] segment, using the position in the ranking. The year ranked as number one will be assigned number one and the year with the lowest position will be assigned number zero. The rest of the years will get the corresponding percentile fraction according to the position in the ranking according to the following formula:

$$R_{jt} = (O_j - o_{jt})/O_j,$$

where: o_{jt} is the position in the ranking of the policy innovation for variable j in period t (using the ordering shown in Table 3.6); and O_j is the total number of observations ranked for policy innovation x_{jt}.

To sum up, for each variable, this method considers its innovation component (the difference between actual outcomes and initial conditions), and then standardizes the innovation component in the [0, 1] interval using a percentile ranking method. The higher the value in this relative index, the better the management situation of the incumbent government as measured by the variable considered.

The Classic Macroeconomic Index for an administration is the average of four relative indices (in the [0, 1] range) over all years of the term of that administration. These indices are based on the four primary components of the Classical Macroeconomic Index mentioned above: inflation, devaluation, and interest rates together with activity growth.

The Fiscal Pressure Index for an administration is the average of five relative over all years of the term of that administration. One caveat should be made: there are no available observations for the following ratios in the 1861–63 period (Mitre Administration): primary result of central government to total revenues, and primary result of central government to debt servicing. If one were to compute the average based on the other three available policy innovations, this would create distortions in the evolution of the index for that year because of variable omission. To reduce partially this risk, interpolated values for both relative (those based on primary result of central government to total revenues and primary result of central government to debt servicing) were calculated by assuming a constant growth rate for each index in the 1861–63 period. The values of the relative indices for years other than the above-mentioned period are left unchanged.[33] This procedure corrects for spurious level changes in the Fiscal Pressure Index that might arise if the latter were calculated only on the levels of the three relative indices mentioned above. However, given the constant-rate-change hypothesis used to interpolate, the actual volatility of the Fiscal Pressure Index during these years can be underestimated. The effect on the average value of the Fiscal Pressure Index for the Mitre administration (1860–68) is roughly nil because this average is based on forty-five observations (nine years of government with five variables per year), of which only six have been interpolated.

Appendix B: Data sources and methodology

Inflation rates

1853–65: Annual devaluation rates (Irigoin 2000a and Cortés Conde 1989).

1866–79: Implicit export prices growth (Diéguez 1972) converted to paper pesos using exchange rates (Cortés Conde 1989).

1880–84: Based on a price index constructed by Cortés Conde (1989, 210–11).

1885–1939: della Paolera and Ortiz (1995).

1939–49: Simple average between CPI and WPI inflation from *Revista Económica*, Banco Central de la Republica Argentina (BCRA), several issues; *Anuario Estadístico de la República Argentina*, several issues; and *Statistical Yearbook of the League of the Nations*, several issues.

1949–99: Simple average between CPI and WPI inflation, from *Boletin Techint*, several issues, and DATAFIEL (database of Fundacion de Investigaciones Economicas Latinoamericanas, FIEL).

Devaluation rates

Based on the devaluation rate of paper money to gold (until 1938) and to U.S. dollar (since 1939):

1822–63: Irigoin (2000a).

1864–84: Cortés Conde (1989).

1885–1938: della Paolera and Ortiz (1995).

1939–46: End of year quotation from *Revista Económica*, BCRA, several issues.

1947–59: End of year quotation, *Boletín Techint*, several issues.

1960–89: Average of December quotations from Ruíz (1990).

1990–99: Average of December quotations from DATAFIEL.

Note: When necessary, the assumed conversion factor between *pesos fuertes* and gold pesos considered was unity.

Interest rates

1853–63: Least squares interpolation using observed discount rates on hard currency for the period 1850–80 and long-term yield on specified issues of public bonds (*fondos públicos*) denominated on hard currency for the period 1864–80 (Cortés Conde 1989). The estimated relation for the 1864–80 period is $i_t = 1.3909 d_t + 0.0046$, where i_t is the

---

[33] Note that these completed relative indices no longer have the interpretation of percentile ranks. However, the difference is minimal, since interpolation was done on only three of almost ninety observations.

long-term yield on *fondos públicos* and d_t is the discount rate of Banco de la Provincia de Buenos Aires.

1864–82: Long-term yield on specified issues of *fondos públicos* denominated on hard currency (Cortés Conde 1989).

1883–1913: della Paolera (1988). Cortés Conde (1989) and della Paolera (1988) have coincident values in the 1883–84 period, thus there is no spurious level change when changing from one source to the other.

1914–26: From della Paolera and Ortiz (1995), subtracting expected inflation rate. della Paolera (1988) and della Paolera and Ortiz (1995) have coincident values in the 1884–1913 period, thus there is no spurious level change when changing from one source to the other.

From 1945 to the end of the 1980s: Real interest rates were almost always negative (with a few exceptions, such as the financial liberalization experiment in late 1970s or during the late 1960s), because of financial repression. We constructed time series that reflect the cost of foreign debt (in real terms) following the methodology of Rodriguez (1986) and subtracting U.S. expected inflation rate, and with balance of payments data from Balboa (1972) and Oficina de Estudios para la Colaboración Económica Internacional (OECEI) from 1926 to 1969. To avoid changes in 1926, the real interest rate calculated from della Paolera and Ortiz (1995) was given decreasing weight in the period 1926–40. Thus, only estimates based on Balboa and OECEI 1940–69 are reported for the 1940–69 period. Further information on external debt were constructed from IEERAL (1986) and Avramovic (1964).

1970–81: Rodriguez (1986).

1981–94: We constructed a new monthly database for the *bonos externos* (BONEX) using information on term structure of T-bills to approximate the expected interest yield (the coupon rate was not fixed). Weights on different issues of BONEX were used to avoid excessive fluctuations in the duration of the bonds in the portfolio.

1994–99: Average stripped yield of Argentine Foreign Bonds provided by J. P. Morgan (EMBI and EMBI+).

Note: in all cases, the expected inflation rate was computed as the trend of inflation rate using Hodrick–Prescott Filter (the relevant smoothing parameter was set at 100, given the frequency of the data).

Exports and imports

1853–61: Observations in some years based on statistics included in Irigoin (2000a) for the 1822–61 period. Missing observations were replaced with interpolations made with most adjacent available data and assuming constant growth rates for both imports and exports separately.

1862–82: della Paolera and Taylor (2001).

1883: Vázquez-Presedo (1971–76) coincident in overlapping years with della Paolera (1988).

1884–1899: della Paolera (1988).

1900–99: Gerchunoff and Llach (1998) and *Informe Económico*, Ministerio de Economía, several issues.

GDP (activity)

Growth rates based on:

1853–75: Export plus imports in gold pesos.

1876–84: Cortés Conde (1997) index of GDP.

1885–1993: della Paolera and Ortiz (1995).

1994–99: *Informe Económico*, Ministerio de Economía, several issues.

Because the della Paolera and Ortiz (1995) source extends to 1993, the constructed index based on the previous sources was denominated in gold pesos using the value of the constructed index in 1986, GDP at 1986 prices (in australes), and the exchange rate index in 1986. These two last series are based on della Paolera and Ortiz while the first is constructed on growth rates from different sources mentioned above. Growth rates from 1994 to 1999 are based on GDP at constant 1993 prices.

Note that for the 1853–75 period this index assumes that the exports plus imports ratio to GDP remains constant.

Fiscal revenues, total expenditures, and deficit

1853–60: Irigoin (2000a).

1862: Cortés Conde (1997).

1864–83: Cortés Conde (1989).

1884–89: Weighted average of Cortés Conde (1989) and della Paolera and Ortiz (1995). Weights for 1884 are 1/7 for the latter data and 6/7 for the former. The weights for della Paolera and Ortiz (1995) increase linearly in 1/7 per year, thus weighting 7/7 = 1 in 1890. Weights for Cortés Conde are the difference between 1 and the weights for della Paolera and Ortiz (1995).

1890–1940: della Paolera and Ortiz (1995).

1940–99: Combines data from della Paolera and Ortiz (1995) for 1940–71, FIEL (1987) for the period 1960–85 (primary deficit), IDB Database for the period 1980–94 (primary deficit), and Ministerio de Economía, which covers 1987–91 and 1993–99 (primary deficit). Information in overlapping periods is a weighted average of sources, to avoid sudden changes in values.

Debt servicing

1853–60: Irigoin (2000a).

1864–75: Cortés Conde (1989).

1876–89: Based on Cortés Conde (1989) and Vázquez-Presedo (1971–76), with linear increasing weights for the latter in the same manner that was done for revenues and expenditures in the 1884–89 period (see above).

1890–1914: Vázquez-Presedo (1971–76).

1915–70: Garcia Vizcaíno (1972).

1971–77: From FIEL (1987) and *Anuario Estadístico* (INDEC), several issues.

1978–85: From FIEL (1987) and *Memoria Anual*, BCRA, several issues.

1986: From *Memoria Anual* 1986, BCRA, and IDB database.

1987–91): From IDB database and Ministerio de Economía.

1992–99: Dal Din and Lopez Isnardi (1998) and Ministerio de Economía.

Internal and external debt

1853–70: Own calculations based on Irigoin (2000a), Burgin (1971), Agote (1881–88).

1870–1909: Coincident data based on Chiaramonte (1971) and Vázquez-Presedo (1971–76).

1910–14: Weighted average from Vázquez-Presedo (1971–76) and Cottely (1981, converted to gold pesos). The latter labels this particular series Deuda en Circulación. Weighted average was based on linear increasing weight for Cottely's data in this period.

1915–40: Cottely (1981), converted to gold pesos.

1940–99): Own calculations based on Vázquez-Presedo (1971–76); *Boletin Estadístico*, BCRA, several issues; Dornbusch and de Pablo (1988); IEERAL (1986); Dal Din and Lopez Isnardi (1998); and Ministerio de Economía.

Population Growth

Used to calculate the increase in per capita GDP/ACTIVITY levels. Based on Cottely (1981) for the period before 1950. For the 1853–1864 period the assumed rate of population growth is the average for this variable over the years 1865–69. Penn World Tables data is used for the period 1950–74. Instituto Nacional de Estadística y Censos (INDEC) estimates are used from 1975.

Appendix C: The intratemporal budget constraint of the government

The interaction between debt, inflation, and deficits over the long run can be addressed through the introduction of a simple tool, the intratemporal budget constraint of the government.[34] Over the last 150 years, and despite the heterogeneity of fiscal-monetary regimes, the national government had to obey in every moment a golden rule, the so-called intratemporal budget constraint. This simple constraint will us help to understand the mechanics of deficit financing under different regimes and their consequences for the evolution of money supply, inflation, and debt.[35]

To simplify, assume that government debt consists of one-period bonds, that is, bonds that mature one period after being issued. Thus, the intratemporal budget constraint in period t is:

$$G_t = T_t + [B_t - (1 + r_t)B_{t-1}] + [M_t - M_{t-1}]/P_t,$$

where G_t is real government expenditures (the term real means that the considered nominal variable was divided by a representative price index; then real expenditure can be seen as the expenditure measured in terms of goods rather than money; this helps to differentiate fluctuations in the level of nominal expenditures caused by inflation from other types of movements). In addition, T_t is real government tax revenues; B_t is the real value of debt at the end of period t (in this case, the income from bonds issued in period t); $B_{t-1}(1 + r_t)$ is the real value of debt at the end of previous period plus real interest income earned between period $t - 1$ and t; M_t is the nominal stock of currency in period t (similar for M_{t-1}); and P_t is the price level index in period t (similar for P_{t-1}).

Note that $[B_t - (1 + r_t)B_{t-1}]$ represents the net borrowing of the government in period t and $[M_t - M_{t-1}]/P_t$ are real resources raised from money issuing at period t. The last expression is known seigniorage or real revenue of money issue.

---

[34] An *intra*temporal restriction links variables observed in a determined period, characterizing the inherent restriction for that period. An *inter*temporal restriction links variables observed in many periods, and is therefore quite different.

[35] An excellent reference that addresses this issue in depth is Sargent (1986), especially chapters 1, 2, and 5.

The interpretation of the intratemporal government restriction is simple: current expenditures are financed by a combination of (1) tax revenues in the same period, (2) net borrowing, and (3) money issue.

Rearranging the restriction, we obtain the following expression:

$$G_t - T_t = [B_t - (1 + r_t)B_{t-1}] + [M_t - M_{t-1}]/P_t.$$

The above equation means that primary deficit $G_t - T_t$ must financed via net borrowing and/or seigniorage (money increase). Eventually, excessive money expansion will lead to inflation, thus allowing the government partially to repudiate part of its liabilities because inflation will erode the real value of money, a nominal liability of the government.

Noting that

$$[M_t - M_{t-1}]/P_t = M_t/P_t - [(M_{t-1}/P_{t-1})(P_{t-1}/P_t)],$$

and defining $m_t = M_t/P_t$, the amount of currency in real terms held by the public at the end of period t (similarly for m_{t-1}), and $(1 + \pi_t) = P_t/P_{t-1}$, one plus the rate of inflation between $t - 1$ and t, we conclude that

$$[M_t - M_{t-1}]/P_t = m_t - [m_{t-1}/(1 + \pi_t)] = m_t - m_{t-1} + m_{t-1}[\pi_t/(1 + \pi_t)].$$

Then we know that the real resources raised from money issuing at period t, $[M_t - M_{t-1}]/P_t$ can be decomposed into $m_t - m_{t-1}$, that is, the increase in money demand from the public, and $m_{t-1}[\pi_t/(1 + \pi_t)]$, that is, the real amount eroded by price increase between $t - 1$ and t. The expression $m_{t-1}[\pi_t/(1 + \pi_t)]$ is usually labeled "inflationary tax", and $[\pi_t/(1 + \pi_t)]$ is the "tax rate" on real balances held by the public. The inflationary tax is not necessarily the revenue arising from money printing, but is a good measure to evaluate the erosion on real money holdings. Note that money is indeed a liability of the government, hence the inflation tax can be seen as a tax on a subset of government creditors – those who hold money. Thus, through inflation, the government diminish the amount of liabilities to the private sector. In this interpretation, inflation can be seen as a partial default on monetary liabilities.

Two remarks about the sources used to construct the series of Inflation Tax must be made. First, to compute the evolution of inflation tax as displayed in Figure 3.4, a time series of real cash holdings and real GDP is obtained, considering $M = M0 = $ currency in the hands of public plus vault cash. The database used in Figure 3.4 is from della Paolera and Ortiz (1995), completed with information from the Ministerio de Economía (*Informe Económico*, several issues). The results are based on annual observations.

Second, to calculate the amount of inflation tax between 1960 and 1990, monthly series were used to get higher accuracy. Two different series, cash in the hands of public and M1, were used as a proxy for M. The primary source was the Banco Central de la República Argentina and the price index used was the CPI provided by Instituto Nacional de Estadística y Censos. Given the above definitions, and considering all monthly observations as a sequence from $t = 1, \ldots, t_{max}$, the inflation tax at prices of time T totalizes

$$P_T \sum_{t=1}^{t_{max}} m_{t-1} \frac{\pi_t}{1 + \pi_t}.$$

References

Agote, Pedro. 1881–88. *Informe del Presidente del Crédito Público sobre la deuda pública, bancos y emisiones de papel moneda y acuñacion de monedas de la República Argentina*. 5 vols. Buenos Aires: Crédito Público.

Alesina, Alberto, and Roberto Perotti. 1995. The Political Economy of Budget Deficits. *IMF Staff Papers* 42 (1): 1–31.

Amaral, Samuel. 1988. El descubrimiento de la financiación inflacionaria: Buenos Aires, 1790–1830. *Investigaciones y Ensayos* 37. Buenos Aires: Academia Nacional de Historia.

Avramovic, Dragoslav. 1964. *Economic Growth and External Debt*. Baltimore, Md.: Johns Hopkins Press.

Balboa, Manuel. 1972. La evolución del balance de pagos de la Republica Argentina, 1913–1950. *Desarrollo Económico* 12 (45): 153–72.

Barro, Robert J. 1996. *Getting it Right: Markets and Choices in a Free Society*. Cambridge, Mass.: MIT Press.

Bordo, Michael D., and Forrest Capie. 1993. Introduction. In *Monetary Regimes in Transition*, edited by Michael D. Bordo and Forrest Capie. Cambridge: Cambridge University Press.

Bordo, Michael D., and Carlos A. Végh. 1998. What if Alexander Hamilton Had Been Argentinean? A Comparison of the Early Monetary Experiences of Argentina and the United States. Working Paper Series no. 6862 (December), National Bureau of Economic Research.

Burgin, Miron. 1946. *The Economic Aspects of Argentine Federalism, 1820–1852*. Cambridge, Mass.: Harvard University Press.

Chiaramonte, José Carlos. 1971. *Nacionalismo y liberalismo económicos en Argentina, 1860–1880, Biblioteca Dimensión argentina*. Buenos Aires: Solar/Hachette.

Cortés Conde, Roberto. 1989. *Dinero, deuda y crisis: evolución fiscal y monetaria en la Argentina, 1862–1890*. Buenos Aires: Editorial Sudamericana.

———. 1997. *La economía argentina en el largo plazo: Ensayos de historia económica de los siglos XIX y XX*. Buenos Aires: Editorial Sudamerica.

Cottely, Esteban. 1981. Características basicas de la gestion fiscal en la Argentina. *Boletín Techint* 223.

Crafts, N. F. R., and Gianni Toniolo. 1996. *Economic Growth in Europe Since 1945*. Cambridge: Cambridge University Press.

Dal Din, C., and N. López Isnardi. 1998. La deuda pública argentina, 1990–1997. Documento de trabajo no. 56 (June), Fundación de Investigaciones Económicas Latinoamericanas.

David, Paul. 1997. Path Dependence and the Quest for Historical Economics: One More Chorus on the Ballad of QWERTY. Discussion Papers in Economic and Social History no. 20 (November), Oxford University.

della Paolera, Gerardo. 1988. How the Argentine Economy Performed During the International Gold Standard: A Reexamination. Ph.D. dissertation, University of Chicago.

———. 1994. Experimentos monetarios y bancarios en Argentina: 1861–1930. *Revista de Historia Económica* 12 (3): 539–90.

della Paolera, Gerardo, and Javier Ortiz. 1995. Dinero, intermediación financiera y nivel de actividad en 110 años de historia económica argentina. Documentos de Trabajo no. 36 (December), Universidad Torcuato Di Tella.

della Paolera, Gerardo, and Alan M. Taylor. 2001. *Straining at the Anchor: The Argentine Currency Board and the Search for Macroeconomic Stability, 1880–1935*. Chicago: University of Chicago Press.

Di Tella, Guido, and Rudiger Dornbusch. 1989. *The Political Economy of Argentina, 1946–83*. Basingstoke: Macmillan.

Di Tella, Guido, and D. C. M. Platt. 1986. *The Political Economy of Argentina, 1880–1946*. New York: St. Martin's Press.

Díaz Alejandro, Carlos F. 1970. *Essays on the Economic History of the Argentine Republic*. New Haven, Conn.: Yale University Press.

Dornbusch, Rudiger, and Juan Carlos de Pablo. 1988. *Deuda externa e inestabilidad macroeconómica en la Argentina*. Buenos Aires: Editorial Sudamericana.

Eichengreen, Barry, Andrew K. Rose, and Charles Wyplosz. 1996. Contagious Currency Crises. Working Paper Series no. 5681 (July), National Bureau of Economic Research.

FIEL (Fundación de Investigaciones Económicas Latinoamericanas, Buenos Aires). 1987. *El gasto público en la Argentina, 1960–1985*. Buenos Aires, Argentina: La Fundación.

Ford, Alec G. 1962. *The Gold Standard, 1880–1914: Britain and Argentina*. Oxford: Clarendon Press.

García Vázquez, Enrique. 1995. *La política económica argentina en los últimos cincuenta años*. Buenos Aires: Ediciones Macchi.

García Vizcaíno, José. 1972. *La deuda pública nacional*. Buenos Aires: Editorial Universitaria de Buenos Aires.

Gerchunoff, Pablo, and Lucas Llach. 1998. *El ciclo de la ilusión y el desencanto: Un siglo de políticas económicas argentinas*. Buenos Aires: Ariel.

IEERAL (Instituto de Estudios Económicos sobre la Realidad Argentina y Latinoamericana). 1986. Estadísticas de la evolución económica de Argentina 1913–1984. *Estudios* 9 (39): 103–84.

Irigoin, Maria Alejandra. 2000a. Finance, Politics and Economics in Buenos Aires 1820s–1860s: The Political Economy of Currency Stabilisation. Ph.D. dissertation, Department of Economic History, London School of Economics.

———. 2000b. Inconvertible Paper Money, Inflation and Economic Performance in Early Nineteenth Century Argentina. *Journal of Latin American Studies* 32: 333–59.

Irigoin, Maria Alejandra, and E. Salazar. 2000. Linking Political Events and Economic Uncertainty: An Examination of the Volatility in the Buenos Aires Paper Peso Rate of Exchange, 1826–1866. Paper presented to the 2d LACLIO Conference, Stanford University (November).

Ljungqvist, Lars, and Thomas J. Sargent. 2000. *Recursive Macroeconomic Theory*. Cambridge, Mass.: MIT Press.

Llach, Juan José. 1984. El plan Pinedo de 1949, su significado histórico y los márgenes de la economía política del Peronismo. *Desarrollo Económico* 23 (92): 515–558.

Mallon, Richard D., and Juan V. Sourrouille. 1975. *Economic Policymaking in a Conflict Society: The Argentine Case*. Cambridge, Mass.: Harvard University Press.

O'Connell, Arturo. 1984. La Argentina en la Depresion: Los problemas de una economía abierta. *Desarrollo Económico* 23: 479–514.

Oficina de Estudios para la Colaboración Económica Internacional. 1966. *Argentina económica y financiera*. Buenos Aires: Fiat Concord.

Persson, Torsten, and Guido E. Tabellini. 2000. *Political Economics: Explaining Economic Policy*. Cambridge, Mass.: MIT Press.

Rapoport, Mario. 1984. *De Pellegrini a Martínez de Hoz: El modelo liberal*. Buenos Aires: Centro Editor de América Latina.

Rodriguez, Carlos. 1986. La deuda externa argentina. Working Paper no. 54 (December), Centro de Estudios Macroeconómicos de Argentina.

Ruíz, Jorge. 1990. *Dólar libre 1960–1989 día por día*. Unigraphic SRL Editores.

Sargent, Thomas J. 1986. *Rational Expectations and Inflation.* New York: Harper & Row.

Sourrouille, Juan V., and Jorge Lucángeli. 1983. *Política económica y procesos de desarrollo: La experiencia argentina entre 1976 y 1981. Estudios e informes de la CEPAL* 27. Santiago de Chile: United Nations.

Taylor, Alan M. 1992. External Dependence, Demographic Burdens and Argentine Economic Decline After the *Belle Époque. Journal of Economic History* 52 (4): 907–36.

———. 1994. Tres fases del crecimiento económico argentino. *Revista de Historia Económica* 12 (3): 649–83.

Vázquez-Presedo, Vicente. 1971–76. *Estadísticas historicas argentinas.* 2 vols. Buenos Aires: Ediciones Macchi.

Williams, John H. 1920. *Argentine International Trade Under Inconvertible Paper Currency, 1880–1900.* Cambridge, Mass.: Harvard University Press.

4

Economic cycles

ADOLFO STURZENEGGER
Universidad Nacional de La Plata and Universidad Austral

RAMIRO MOYA
Fundación Investigaciones Económicas Latinoamericanas

Argentina's economic history is rich in contrast. It was once one of the most open in the world in terms of the flows of goods, services, and factors; soon thereafter it became almost closed to international trade for many decades. It was also one of the most promising countries in terms of economic growth by the end of the nineteenth century, comparable only to the United States, Canada, and Australia; eighty or so years later, however, it had became apparent that initial conditions are not enough to guarantee continued development. In macroeconomic terms, Argentina was one of the most stable and conservative countries until the Great Depression, after which it turned into one of the most unstable, and experienced one of the highest inflation rates.

In this chapter we study the business cycle of Argentina, or the short-run macroeconomic fluctuations of the economy, over the period 1884 to 1990. We start in 1884 because data is limited for earlier years, and we end in 1990 since a major macroeconomic reform in that year suggests a natural break.

This period of study provides a laboratory for reviewing the cyclical behavior of the economy in long-run series. In this work it will be shown that, just like the experience of other countries after the Second World War when the economic environment changed, increases in the volatility and persistence of major nominal variables (monetary aggregates, prices, inflation, nominal exchange rate) became noticeable. We also see in the Argentine data other typical changes: some reduction in the volatility of GDP and consumption, and anomalous investment behavior over historically exceptional periods.

Still, maybe the most substantive and striking fact is seen in the behavior of nominal variables that cast doubts on monetary neutrality in the short term. Specifically, the nominal exchange rate seems to move *pari passu* with the real exchange rate, as in other countries, challenging the theories of the real business

We especially thank Pablo Alvarez for comments and statistical support, and conference participants for their suggestions.

cycle (RBC) school, which state that the real exchange rate should move only on account of any changes in the fundamental real conditions in the economy. However, the reason that changes in the real exchange rate scarcely show any relation with the GDP cycle is also a puzzle, leaving open the question of what might be behind this asynchronicity. Other facts tend to agree with certain tenets of the RBC school, such as the countercyclical pattern of prices and the strong procyclical pattern of the real wage. Is there a basis here for a simple, general theory of cycles for Argentina? Obviously, the behavior of the real exchange rate makes doubtful even the more basic formulations of the RBC theory for the Argentine economy.

We claim that some of these unusual findings can be reconciled with a theory of "stop-and-go" cycles based on strong, contractionary devaluations and recoveries via expansive demand-driven policies.[1] For example, history shows that devaluations were used to solve balance of payments problems through an increase in tradable prices that, in turn, caused a fall in real wages and in the real money supply. This policy of exchange rate devaluation was against all priors in that it was decidedly contractionary and not at all expansionary, as in the simple Mundell-Fleming theory. Some of these patterns will be noted in this chapter.

But first, we will begin by trying to simply identify the business cycle. The next section starts with a more traditional approach to business cycle study, letting the data speak through a simple analysis. We will then use the more modern method of detrending each economic series (with the bandpass filter) to isolate trend and cyclical components in macroeconomic time series. This will be helpful for our goal of identifying important cyclical regularities in Argentine macroeconomic history.

4.1 Characterizing the economic cycle

The proper way to identify and characterize economic cycles, and to describe them, has always been a controversial matter in the economic literature. The empirical approach of Burns and Mitchell (1946) attempted to analyze, through detailed measurements of the behavior of certain economic variables and their relation to GDP, changes over the phases of the typical cycle. This approach was criticized for its lack of methodological rigor, and critics labeled it "measurements without theory" (Koopmans 1947). However, as argued by Kydland and Prescott (1990), the "facts" revealed by such studies are an important part of scientific research.

---

[1] See Diaz Alejandro (1963, 1966) for a classic treatment of the contractionary effects of devaluation in Argentina; see Brodersohn (1974) as an example of a stop-and-go cycle.

More recently, the definition by Lucas (1977) of cycles as deviations of real Gross National Product around its trend spurred a further effort to isolate the trend component of all economic variables. Also, according to this conception, the study of cycles must consist of the analysis of the cyclical regularities in the comovements, volatilities, and persistence of all the key, detrended aggregate variables of the economy.

Bridging the strictly empirical approach and the definition by Lucas, in this study two definitions were chosen to characterize the Argentine economic cycle. One is the so-called traditional method, in the spirit of Burns and Mitchell; the second, from the definition of a long-run trend, involves filtering of macroeconomic time series and formal quantitative analysis.[2]

4.2 Economic cycles in the traditional approach

The traditional approach considers an economic contraction to be an absolute decline in GDP, and an expansion to be an increase in the same aggregate. The concept of long-run trend is absent from this first definition. There are two reasons that lead us to implement it all the same. Firstly, it allows a quite clear characterization of what constitutes an economic crisis or downturn, that is, when GDP recedes in absolute terms. Secondly, the extant literature in Argentine economic history generally tends to define the movements of the economy in this way. For example, this is the methodology used by Di Tella and Zymmelman (1967, 1973) in their studies of cycles in Argentine history.[3]

Figure 4.1 shows the annual variation in the GDP growth rate in Argentina between 1885 and 1990. This information allows us to summarize the cycles by their length (annual duration) and their depth. A review of this figure and Table 4.1 allows us to observe the following historical characteristics:[4]

(i) Over the period of 106 years that are covered, positive GDP growth rates are evident in 80 years (or 75 percent of the sample), implying that negative growth rates in the same variable occur in the remaining 26 years.

(ii) Twenty GDP expansion phases and nineteen contraction phases occurred during the period from 1885 to 1990

(iii) Expansions averaged 4.3 years in duration, while contractions lasted

---

[2] As detailed below, the filter used corresponds to that originally used by Baxter and King (1999).

[3] Additionally, even when the economic cycle was not the main issue, almost every historical study of Argentina has attempted to define cycles and crises in terms of variations in GDP. See, for example, Di Tella and Dornbusch (1989) and Gerchunoff and Llach (1998).

[4] For more details, see also Table 4.10 in the Appendix.

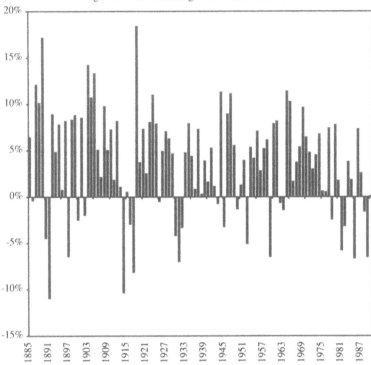

Fig. 4.1. GDP annual growth rate, 1885–1990

Notes and sources: See text and Appendix 1.

1.4 years. Therefore, a complete cycle of contraction and expansion averaged 5.7 years.

(iv) The annual growth rate of GDP during an expansion averaged 6.1 percent, while contractions gave rise to average annual declines of 4.0 percent. During the typical complete cycle there was an average annual growth rate of 3.6 percent.

(v) During contractions, growth rates were less uniform than during expansions (according to a simple dispersion measure).

(vi) The longest period of contraction corresponded to the years of the Great Depression, during which time GDP receded in three consecutive years for a cumulative fall of 13.8 percent.

(vii) The longest period of expansion was from 1964 through 1977, a total of fourteen uninterrupted years of economic growth.[5] The annual average

---

[5] By filtering the GDP series – that is, by isolating the cycle from the long-term trend – the duration of this economic expansion period is reduced.

Table 4.1. *Expansions and contractions, traditional measure, 1885–1990*

	Expansions	Contractions	Entire period
Number of years	80	26	106
Phases	20	19	39
Average phase (years)	4.3	1.4	2.8
Annual growth rate[1]	6.1%	-4.0%	3.6%
Dispersion[2]	54.2%	70.0%	156.0%

[1] Simple average of annual growth rates. [2] Standard deviation of annual growth rates divided by simple average of annual growth rates.
Sources: See appendix.

GDP growth rate was 5.4 percent, for a cumulative increase of 107.6 percent. Another significant period of expansion was from 1903 to 1913 when the average annual growth was 7 percent and the cumulative figure was 111.2 percent.

(viii) The longest cycle (from one peak to the next) lasted from 1962 until 1977 (16 years) and achieved 103.4 percent cumulative growth. The shortest contraction and expansion periods lasted only one year and occurred in 1900–01 and 1943–44.

(ix) The most serious crisis (contraction) in terms of the year-to-year fall in the average annual GDP growth rate occurred during 1914 when the rate declined 10.3 percent. The most intense expansion, also in terms of the annual growth rate, occurred between 1887 and 1889 when GDP increased 13.1 percent annually and totaled 44 percent in only three years.

Table 4.2 summarizes the main contraction and expansion periods. If cycles are outlined by contractions – what we will call crises – the next logical question is: What brought about these collapses in output?[6]

4.3 On the origins of the cycles

Throughout Argentine history, the causes of economic crisis have not always been economic in nature. Other factors have been both domestic and external in origin, and most notable among external factors were the two world wars. At the risk of oversimplification, Table 4.3 lists the likely propagators of the main episodes of economic crisis. Likewise, it proposes hypothetical policy responses that *could have* helped overcome each crisis. It should be noted

[6] This does not mean that it should be accepted that the economy has a natural tendency to grow – as unfortunately was seen in Argentina in the 1980s.

Table 4.2. *Main contractions and expansions, 1884–1990*

	Period	Years	Annual growth (%)	Cumulative growth (%)
Longest contraction	1930–32	3	-4.8	-13.8
Longest expansion	1964–77	14	5.4	107.6
Shortest contraction[1]	1886, 1897, 1900,1902, 1914, 1925, 1943, 1945, 1949, 1952, 1959, 1978, 1985	1	-3.5	—
Shortest expansion[1,2]	1901, 1915, 1944	1	6.8	—
Longest cycle[3]	1962–77	16	4.8	103.4
Shortest cycle[3]	1900–01	2	5.8	5.8
	1914–15	2	-9.8	-14.8
	1943–44	2	10.5	10.5
Deepest contraction[4]	1914	1	-10.3	—
Strongest expansion[4]	1887–89	3	13.1	44.5

[1]Simple average growth rate. [2]Excluding 1884 and 1990 (the first and last years in the sample). [3]From peak to peak. [4]Measured by annual growth rate.
Sources: See appendix.

that some of the less important periods of contraction have not been included. There are some common patterns among the different crises, and in fact, external factors (e.g., the balance of payments) were the main causes of these crises in all cases, with recent exceptions in 1978, 1985, and 1988–89.

Crises brought about largely by problems with the current account occurred in 1897, 1952, and 1959; those related primarily to the capital account occurred in 1890–91 and 1981–82; and those related to problems on both sides of the balance of payments occurred in 1914, 1916–17, 1930–32, and 1962–63.

To overcome almost all crises it proved necessary to induce some explicit readjustment to the nominal exchange rate or to the monetary arrangements in force (e.g., the annulment of the currency board), with exceptions in 1897, 1916–17, and 1952.[7]

From 1952 onward crises also originated in problems with inflation. This fact is key to an understanding of what happened during postwar cycles in Argentina, a point that will be discussed later. As a consequence, from that year on all crises, without exception, were overcome in conjunction with stabilization

---

[7] The 1952 stabilization plan did not include an explicit devaluation, although the change in export taxes involved an improvement of the prices received by exporters.

Table 4.3. *Main economic crises and their features*

Year(s)	Origins	Causes	Economic policies
1890–91	Domestic	Fiscal imbalances and fragility in financial system.	A commitment to apply solid fiscal and monetary policies was assumed. A currency board was legislated in 1890. The old financial system was replaced.
1897	Domestic	Bad crop.	Episodic shock: no relevant economic policy intervention was applied.
1914	External and domestic	Capital outflow and bad crop.	The currency board system was suspended to avoid a money contraction, although there was no monetary expansion due to the currency board.
1916–17	External	Imports for industrial production were almost impossible. Also, capital outflow caused by the World War.	Episodic shock: no relevant economic policy intervention was applied.
1930–32	External	International trade fell dramatically. Argentina's TOT fell and deficits in the balance of trade required an adjustment in domestic absorption. Capital outflows were also encouraged by a tighter monetary policy in the United States.	The currency board was suspended in 1929, although the government tried to manage the ER until 1931. Exchange control was then applied. Other measures included loans to banks in trouble, the creation of the Central Bank, and an increase in external tariffs, and wider government intervention in many markets.
1945	External	Fall in TOT and difficulties in importing capital goods.	No specific public policy was applied inmediately.
1949	Domestic	Bad crop and difficulties in importing (financial constraint).	Devaluation. External credit was taken in 1950.
1952	Domestic and external	Bad crop (strong drought) and fall in TOT.	A plan to reduce domestic absorption and to avoid a new balance of trade crisis was launched. Public investment and money growth were cut. Other administrative measures were taken in order to incentive exports and discourage imports. Also internal prices paid by IAPI to agricultural producers were increased. In 1953 the crop was excellent.

Table 4.3. (Continued)

Year(s)	Origins	Causes	Economic policies
1959	Domestic	Fiscal and trade imbalances. Inflation rate was high. A new stabilization plan was launched. It included a tighter monetary policy, a cut in public expenditures, and increases in taxes and utility prices.	As a consequence of the stabilization plan, fiscal and trade imbalances were solved. This prompted economic growth inmediately.
1978	Domestic	Tight monetary policy and appreciation of real exchange rate. Real interest rate went up.	At the end of 1978 a new estabilization plan was launched. It included an pre-announced rate of devaluation.
1981–82	Domestic and External	The credibility plan launched in 1978 failed. Capital outflow came as a consequence. Political climate was very rare. The Malvinas war also affected the economy significantly.	Since 1982 economic policies had no clear goals. There was chaos in the economy.
1985	Domestic	The economy entered a hyperinflation. A devaluation and tighter fiscal and monetary policies came as a consequence.	A new stabilization plan (the Austral) was launched in mid-1985. This included a devaluation, a correction in utility prices, and a credible mechanism to stop "inertial" inflation. As a consequence, internal demand (consumption) recovered inmediately.
1988–89	Domestic	High fiscal deficit brought about a potencially high monetary expansion. Confidence crisis and capital outflow caused hyperinflation.	A new estabilization plan was launched in 1989. Planned structural reforms to public sector gave credibility to this plan. Devaluation was included.

Sources: Cortés Conde (1989), Díaz Alejandro (1970), Di Tella and Dornbusch (1989), Di Tella and Zymelman (1967, 1973), Gerchunoff and Llach (1998).

plans. The 1978 crisis was the only one in which a fall in GDP was intentionally implemented by the government through a monetary contraction that was meant to stop inflation.

In more general terms, we can also observe remarkable differences among cycles, both before and after World War II. The first major difference is that crises before the Great War were more serious. In this regard, the most important collapses in GDP in Argentine history correspond to the 1890–91 crisis if the fall is calculated in terms of the cumulative rate of decline, and the 1914 crisis if measured in annual rates.

A second difference between both periods is of a more qualitative nature. Before World War II, external factors prevailed as the main causes of crisis, while after World War II causes were almost exclusively domestic. Perhaps this distinction is suggestive of an explanation for the varying degree in the severity of crises over time. A third difference, which might supplement any explanation for differences in severity between the pre- and post-war periods, is that during the latter period there was greater macroeconomic activism through fiscal, monetary, or exchange rate adjustments.

These numerous observations can now be contrasted with a more modern approach to economic cycles, which in fact leads to similar conclusions. It will show that GDP tended to be less volatile after 1945 than before, and that the increase in volatility and correlation between nominal variables (e.g., the nominal exchange rate) and GDP indicates a higher level of policy activism after World War II.

4.4 Economic cycles as deviations around the trend

From the time series it is apparent that GDP shows some volatility throughout history. However, without statistical refinements it is very difficult to differentiate between the influence of the long-run growth trend, cyclical movements, and movements coming from temporary or irregular factors. In the most recent literature, at least three methodologies have been used to eliminate the trend component of GDP and, thus, to isolate both regular cyclical behavior and (in a residual) the irregular components.

By assuming that GDP is stationary in first difference, as was thought by Nelson and Plosser (1982), the most natural way to isolate the trend is to work with the differenced series that, when expressed in natural logarithms, turns into an annual percentage rate of change. Problems with this adjustment are that it does not eliminate, but rather exaggerates, the irregular component; it creates phase distortion; and it prevents isolation of the main component of interest – the cyclical one.

A second filter, used widely in the literature on economic cycles, is the one developed by Hodrick and Prescott (1997). This represents a substantial improvement from the use of the first difference, as it reduces the noise caused by the irregular components of the series. However, the problem remains that a large portion of the high-frequency fluctuations (e.g., for periods shorter than six quarters) still passes through the filter, depending on the cycle definition. This leads, for example, to higher GDP volatility and a less persistent series (Baxter and King 1999). The advantage of using this filter is that it is well known and has been used in a number of studies on cycles, allowing comparisons to be drawn among them. We count here the works by Backus and Kehoe (1992), Backus, Kehoe, and Kydland (1995), and Hodrick and Prescott (1997) on the United States and other countries, and Carrera, Féliz, and Panigo (1996) and Kydland and Zarazaga (1997) on Argentina.

A third filter, which avoids some of the aforementioned problems, was developed by Baxter and King (1999). Their bandpass filter is based on a centered moving average of a certain length (twelve quarters or three years) with weights that are selected in order to minimize the squared difference between the optimal filter (which eliminates all low and high frequencies, depending on the cycle definition adopted) and the approximate filter for finite samples. This filter has been used, for example, by Stock and Watson (1998) for U.S. macroeconomic time series and by Basu and Taylor (1999) for a historical comparison among countries.

For this chapter, the Baxter-King filter has been used for annual series. Our choice of a three-year moving average explains the loss of the first three observations, but not the last three, as data is available for the post-1990 period.[8] Figure 4.2 shows the behavior of the GDP when filtered in order to isolate the cyclical component.[9] The series shows a larger number of phase changes than does the unfiltered GDP series, provided it is accepted that a reduction (or expansion) in economic activity of only one year constitutes a phase. In general, the main contractions match those found with the unfiltered GDP series, though if the rate of GDP reduction is considered, the ranking of crises by magnitude is altered. Here, the 1914 crisis is not the most dramatic in terms of annual GDP fall, but rather the one of 1890–91 becomes the most serious crisis with a 10.5

---

[8] The parameters used are the same as those suggested by the authors for annual series: the high frequency threshold is two years, the low frequency threshold is eight years and the moving average is three years, so the filter is BP(2,8,3).

[9] The figures in Appendix 2 show GDP at an annual frequency filtered by the above three methodologies. The series derived from the bandpass filter stand out in relation to the other two in a number of ways, namely their lower volatility (with this contrast being greater before 1945), greater persistence vis-à-vis the first difference filter, and lower persistence vis-à-vis the Hodrick-Prescott series.

Fig. 4.2. Filtered GDP, Baxter-King BP(2,8,3) filter
Deviation from trend

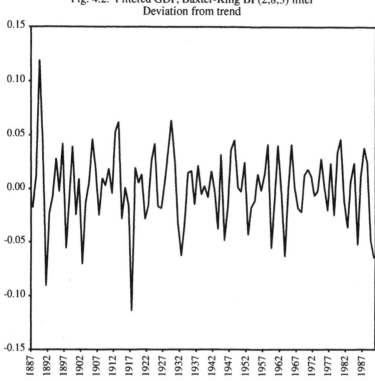

Notes and sources: See text and Appendix 1.

percent annual rate of decline. Other years that saw significant declines in GDP were 1897 (–9.8 percent), 1902 (–8 percent), 1914 (–9.1 percent), 1945 (–8.1 percent), and 1959 (–9.7 percent). Expansions also follow almost the same pattern as detected in the unfiltered GDP analysis, though again the ordering of expansions by GDP growth rate is different. In fact, the most vigorous growth corresponded not to the one detected in 1887–89, but the one of 1918 with a 13.3 percent rate of increase. Other pronounced periods of expansion occurred in the years 1944 (7 percent) and 1887–89 (6.9 percent annually).

The two methods of characterizing cycles are therefore in general agreement. The cyclical regularities are discussed in greater detail in the following two sections using the filtered GDP series.

4.4.1 Cyclical regularities of the main macroeconomic variables

In this subsection, we follow Lucas (1977) and consider economic cycles as deviations of real GNP on its long-run trend. According to this concept, the study of cyclical regularities involves the analysis of the comovements of economic variables in the cycle. The purpose of this section is not to characterize the "typical" Argentine cycle in theory, but to make an empirical contribution through the description of the behavior of economic aggregates in order to arrive at some stylized facts. This kind of presentation follows the work by authors such as Backus and Kehoe (1992) and Cooley (1995) for the OECD countries, Stock and Watson (1998) for the United States, and Kydland and Zarazaga (1997) for Argentina.

A question has emerged in business cycle studies as to whether economic fluctuations have turned less volatile in recent years. This volatility reduction may correspond to the increase in the share of services in GDP (especially the government sector), to the extension of institutions which operate as "automatic stabilizers" (e.g., unemployment insurance), to the lower intensity and frequency of financial crises, or to better handling of governments' macroeconomic policies (Zarnowitz 1992). A simple way to determine whether volatility has increased is to look at the temporal evolution of the standard deviation of key macroeconomic aggregates.

A second question to be answered is, according to our definition of the cycle, what relation exists between a given variable and the cycle – that is, does it move procyclically, acyclically, or countercyclically? The usual way to measure the comovement of a variable is to look at its correlation with the closest measure of aggregate activity, GDP. A third question concerns changes in an important property of macroeconomic series, that of persistence. This tends to be measured in terms of first order autocorrelation.

The cyclical behavior of variables can be analyzed by considering Argentine economic history as being divided into two major stages, one corresponding to the years prior to the end of World War II (up to 1945) and another corresponding to the postwar years. This division coincides to a certain extent with an important change in Argentine economic conditions – that from markets relatively open to international trade, labor, and capital markets, toward a more autarkic environment.[10] It also matches periodizations used in studies of other countries

---

[10] Some studies consider that Argentine policy choices initiated the import substitution process during the years of the Great Depression (Diaz Alejandro 1970). It has also been claimed, however, that external conditions (the disruption of international trade caused by the Great Depression and World War II) generated this process "naturally". What is somewhat agreed upon among different authors is that the process of import substitution and greater autarky of the Argentine economy was explicitly encouraged starting with the policies applied by General Perón (1946–55).

in which cyclical variables are analyzed by separating the postwar period from the prewar period. Thus, for example, Basu and Taylor (1999) envision four stages according to the monetary arrangement of countries from 1870, one of them being the era of the Bretton Woods agreement (1945–70). Backus and Kehoe (1992) divide their cross-country study into the prewar (before 1914), interwar (1920–39), and postwar (after 1945) periods.[11]

4.4.1.1 Cyclical behavior of GDP, components of the aggregate demand, and the labor market

Table 4.4 shows a reduction in standard deviation for Argentine GDP in the postwar period (1945–90), but this fact is not so striking given that the years covered by the interwar period and World War II are also years of low volatility.[12] If these years are set aside, the fall in volatility is more pronounced, with a drop of about one-third between 1884–1919 and 1945–1990.[13] It is also interesting to note that the low persistence shown by GDP may indicate a high degree of price flexibility, high enough to avoid any real effects from monetary expansion. In other words, high persistence tends to be associated with a nonneutral effect of money, as price rigidity should cause expansions in aggregate demand to produce lasting effects in GDP deviations around the trend. However, as will be noted later, movements in the nominal exchange rate track changes in real exchange rates, implying price rigidity rather than flexibility. Thus, evidence of low persistence casts doubts on the usual interpretation of this indicator from the statistical and theoretical points of view, as noted by Romer (1996).

Consumption shows a somewhat constant volatility between the two major periods. However, in and of itself, its volatility is 60 percent higher than that of GDP. This result may seem surprising since no theory of consumption – not even those assuming that current consumption depends on current income – states that the volatility of consumption should be *higher* than that of income. However, the result is not unusual: a high volatility pattern in consumption has also been detected in countries as diverse as Japan, Norway, Sweden, and, after 1945, Great Britain (Backus and Kehoe 1992). Likewise for the case of

---

[11] Appendix 3 also examines the same variables considered in this section, but according to a different division of history based on the periods 1884–1914, 1914–19, 1919–39, 1939–45, and 1945–90.

[12] See Appendix 2 for the details.

[13] It should be noted that the GDP series for the earliest years of the sample naturally shows a higher volatility as a result of the large share of agricultural and primary products in output. Indeed, there could be a sectoral bias in the calculated GDP before World War II that would make the series show a figmentary change in volatility. For the United States, this effect was highlighted by Romer (1986).

Table 4.4. *Cyclical behavior of GDP, aggregate demand components, labor productivity, employment, and real wages, 1887–1990*
Deviation from trend

		1887–1990	1887–1945	1945–1990
log GDP	Standard Dev.	0.035	0.038	0.031
	Obs. Number	104	59	46
	Persistence	0.060	0.071	-0.002
log CONS	Standard Dev.	0.044	0.050	0.042
	Obs. Number	75	30	46
	Output corr.	0.702	0.537	0.863
	Persistence	0.100	-0.034	0.173
log INV	Standard Dev.	0.126	0.146	0.106
	Obs. Number	88	43	46
	Output corr.	0.605	0.481	0.789
	Persistence	0.274	0.404	0.069
log IMPORT	Standard Dev.	0.151	0.138	0.166
	Obs. Number	75	30	46
	Output corr.	0.595	0.464	0.710
	Persistence	0.359	0.516	0.346
log EXPORT	Standard Dev.	0.105	0.119	0.094
	Obs. Number	75	30	46
	Output corr.	0.191	0.500	-0.090
	Persistence	-0.202	-0.277	-0.127
B. of Trade	Standard Dev.	0.191	0.178	0.204
	Obs. Number	75	30	46
	Output corr.	-0.365	-0.023	-0.620
	Persistence	0.144	0.089	0.170
log Labor Prod.	Standard Dev.	0.031	0.033	0.030
	Obs. Number	75	30	46
	Output corr.	0.946	0.983	0.918
	Persistence	0.056	0.031	0.030
log EMPLOY	Standard Dev.	0.010	0.007	0.012
	Obs. Number	66	30	37
	Output corr.	0.335	0.378	0.341
	Persistence	0.044	0.206	0.004
log dWR	Standard Dev.	0.089	0.050	0.111
	Obs. Number	65	29	37
	Output corr.	0.324	-0.076	0.574
	Persistence	-0.080	-0.343	-0.053
log WR	Standard Dev.	0.055	0.017	0.072
	Obs. Number	66	30	37
	Output corr.	0.339	0.208	0.467
	Persistence	0.214	0.064	0.217

Notes: The variables GDP, CONS (consumption), INV (investment), IMPORT (imports), EXPORT (exports), B. of Trade (Balance of Trade = log(EXPORT) – log(IMPORT)), Labor Prod. (average labor productivity), EMPLOY (employment) and WR are in levels, while dWR (real wage) is shown as a rate of change (log difference). All variables were computed using the Baxter-King bandpass filter.
Sources: See Appendix 1.

Argentina, Kydland and Zarazaga (1997) found the same result with quarterly data.

This high volatility of consumption in relation to GDP could be explained by the construction of the consumption aggregate: it includes durable goods and changes in stocks, which implies higher volatility. In fact, for the United States, Stock and Watson (1998) reported that the consumption of services was considerably less volatile (and also less procyclical) than the consumption of durable goods – a finding consistent with the smoothing of consumption implied by the permanent-income hypothesis. The procyclicality of consumption has also increased during the postwar period, with less smoothing of consumption evident in more recent years.[14]

Investment shows a volatility reduction of one-third for the postwar period. Another finding, which is also remarked upon in other cycle studies (e.g., Basu and Taylor 1999), is that investment volatility is about 3.5 times the size of that for GDP. Even though the standard deviation between the two selected periods shows some stability, the widening in a larger number of substages demonstrates great variability in this indicator. What should be expected according to the economic theory of investment behavior? If there is a possibility to distribute risk, consumption stability should be higher in times of greater openness to capital flows, but in such a case, investment stability will be adversely affected since a positive productivity shock would attract external savings and magnify the investment boom.

In contrast, in an autarkic economy, since there must be equality between saving and investment, there should be more stability in investment vis-à-vis GDP. However, as noted in the experience of other countries, the question remains: Why was investment more volatile in closed-economy periods such as 1919–39 and 1939–45, when its standard deviation was between 4.5 and 5 times that of GDP? As noted by Basu and Taylor (1999), it may be that the Great Depression experience is not fully explained by conventional business cycle theories, and such an explanation would have to consider neglected factors such as deflation and its effect on debts. It should also be stated that investment volatility was slightly higher before 1914 than in the postwar years, in accordance with what should be expected in a more open economy versus a more closed one (although the difference is not substantial). The cross-correlation of investment

---

[14] This result is also consistent with income changes having a permanent nature and, therefore, consumption responding more closely to income. Thus, it must be assumed that a correlation increase means that income shocks have taken on more of a permanent nature during the postwar period than in the previous years, though inherently this is difficult to demonstrate.

with GDP, which is relatively high, would also indicate behavior of a quite autarkic economy in both periods, but even more so after 1945.[15]

As regards imports, there is a slight volatility increase after 1945. Exports, in contrast, show a lower volatility during the postwar period.[16] Given the decreasing weight of agricultural products in total exports, volatility should be lower in external sales. Indeed, what is remarkable in foreign trade is the substantial increase in import procyclicality after the war and the increasing acyclicality of exports after 1945. In the case of imports, it should be noted that the increasing share of capital and intermediate goods, and the decreasing share of consumption goods, in total imports can explain the increase in procyclicality after the Second World War. Finally, the persistence measure has declined during the postwar period for both imports and exports.[17]

As a consequence of this import and export behavior, the balance of trade shows a higher volatility after World War II, though not substantially so. The most significant change is in its relationship with the cycle: having been acyclical before 1945, it became highly countercyclical in the postwar years. The main explanation lies in a higher import correlation with the GDP cycle and the acyclicality of exports.

Employment behavior is procyclical throughout the whole sample, although the correlation is very low. Employment volatility is lower than that of GDP (after 1945 it represents half its standard deviation), which would indicate relatively low variability throughout the entire economic cycle.[18]

Real wages show a significant volatility increase after World War II, and a standard deviation indicator four times as great as previously. In turn, this made real wage volatility turn from half to twice that of GDP. Procyclicality and persistence also increased substantially. The high correlation to the cycle is remarkable in relation to other countries' experiences. This procyclical behavior of real wages is consistent with most theories of economic cycles in which consumers optimize their choice between leisure and consumption.[19] However, for Keynesian theories, the real wage should be countercyclical because

[15] However, it should be pointed out that if consumption was more volatile than the GDP because it includes durables goods consumption, then investment should be less volatile relative to GDP, *ceteris paribus*. The procyclicality of comovements would be changed too – rising for consumption and falling for investment.

[16] These results should be read carefully as both series begin in 1916 (after being filtered) and results are strongly influenced by the period between the wars.

[17] The high import procyclicality and the low connection of exports with the cycle are also consistent with the results found by Stock and Watson (1998) for the United States.

[18] It is important to point out that the employment series is a poor proxy: it originally was constructed based on population growth, so this could attenuate the cyclical behavior of the series artificially.

[19] A high cyclical correlation was also found for postwar Argentina by Basu and Taylor (1999).

the nominal wage is fixed (following Keynes' own theory in 1936) or, at the best, acyclical (as in the theory of efficient wages).[20]

4.4.1.2 Cyclical behavior of fiscal surplus and of nominal variables

As shown in Table 4.5, the volatility of the fiscal surplus almost doubled over the 1945–90 period. The variable also shows a low correlation with the economic cycle and low persistence. The lower correlation with the GDP cycle in the early years can be explained by the fact that governments were then fiscally very conservative. After World War II, the fiscal surplus showed no relationship with GDP, as government revenue and expenditure were both procyclical. In particular, public expenditure grew, pushing aggregate demand in the expansion phases, and remained constant in nominal terms during downturns but fell in real terms because recessions in Argentina came with high inflation rates.

As noted for other countries by Backus and Kehoe (1992), nominal variables show an increase in volatility in the postwar period, including both the monetary base and M2. The monetary base showed low persistence and scarcely any correlation with GDP between 1884 and 1945, but from 1945 on, it was notably countercyclical and more persistent. The M2 aggregate also turned from being procyclical to countercyclical. The finding of countercyclical monetary variables has also been reported by Kydland and Zarazaga (1997) for the quarterly series of Argentina.

The countercyclical behavior of the monetary aggregates is a result different from that seen in many other countries. For example, the seminal work by Kydland and Prescott (1990) finds that monetary aggregates are generally procyclical, or acyclical at best (as is the case of M1). One of the reasons, as argued by Kydland and Zarazaga, is that while postwar Argentine monetary policy does not have the same significance as that of the rest of the OECD countries, it has responded more to finance the treasury deficit than to affect the money supply via open-market transactions. That is, if the fiscal deficit had a tendency to increase during recessions (a result only found very weakly in this study), it would be expected that the monetary supply will be countercyclical and not procyclical because of fiscal financing through the printing of money.

Another argument, as also shown by Kydland and Zarazaga (1997), is that the financial repression prevailing during the postwar period caused the emergence of a parallel financial system that drew resources from the regulated system (as can be seen in the monetary series). However, there is no evidence that this behavior tended to change with the cycle, and this strange regularity should lead to further research. Still our preferred explanation leans toward the idea

---

[20] For example, Akerlof and Yellen (1985).

Table 4.5. *Cyclical behavior of fiscal surplus, coefficient of openness, and nominal variables (monetary base, M2, nominal exchange rate, and international reserves), 1887–1990*
Deviation from trend

		1887–1990	1887–1945	1945–1990
Fiscal Surplus	Standard Dev.	0.012	0.008	0.014
	Obs. Number	75	30	46
	Output corr.	0.134	0.160	0.164
	Persistence	0.087	-0.012	0.111
Coef. Openness	Standard Dev.	0.0266	0.0371	0.0174
	Obs. Number	75	30	46
	Output corr.	0.287	0.364	0.247
	Persistence	0.041	0.000	0.219
log dM0	Standard Dev.	0.2291	0.0634	0.3392
	Obs. Number	104	59	46
	Output corr.	-0.264	0.100	-0.484
	Persistence	0.343	0.095	0.354
log dM2	Standard Dev.	0.2103	0.0815	0.3039
	Obs. Number	104	59	46
	Output corr.	-0.080	0.528	-0.371
	Persistence	0.361	0.127	0.384
log dER	Standard Dev.	0.2720	0.0667	0.4041
	Obs. Number	104	59	46
	Output corr.	-0.373	-0.375	-0.553
	Persistence	0.312	0.205	0.314
log dRESERV	Standard Dev.	0.3167	0.1876	0.3750
	Obs. Number	73	28	46
	Output corr.	0.075	0.290	-0.008
	Persistence	0.059	0.312	0.026

Notes: The variables Fiscal Surplus (as a percent of GDP) and Coef. Openness (EX-PORT+IMPORT/GDP) are in levels, while dM0 (nominal monetary base), dM2 (nominal M2), dER (nominal exchange rate) and dRESERV (international reserves at Central Bank) are in rates of change. All variables were computed using the Baxter-King bandpass filter.
Sources: See Appendix 1.

of inflationary recessions that tended to increase nominal quantities (including money) above their trend, and noninflationary expansions that tended to reduce them.

The volatility of the nominal exchange rate also increased in the postwar period.[21] This variable was always countercyclical, but it became even more so after 1945. This result indicates that recessions came with depreciated exchange rates and that expansions were periods of stable exchange rates. This behavior

---

[21] The exchange rate is defined as pesos per U.S. dollar. An increase in the exchange rate corresponds to a depreciation, and a decrease to an appreciation.

is the same as that noted for price levels (see below), showing that devaluations tended to be contemporaneous with the more inflationary periods.

International reserves, in turn, were also volatile in the postwar period. They had no relation with the cycle after 1945, but they did before that year when they showed a slightly procyclical behavior. This last fact is evidence of an economy that experienced booms and busts with classical gold standard adjustment at the turn of century and before the 1930s. After those years, reserves tended to be acyclical because capital and goods flows tended to move with no clear pattern; for example, sometimes the start of recessions were coincidental with balance of trade deficits (implying depleted reserves) that would be mitigated by foreign aid (rebuilding the stock of reserves).

4.4.1.3 Behavior of inflation and of internal and external prices

Table 4.6 shows the behavior of prices. According to some studies of other countries (e.g., Backus and Kehoe 1992), the levels of both internal prices and inflation rates had a tendency to increase in their volatility in the postwar period.

The Argentine case is not an exception as inflation rates show an increase not only in averages but also in volatility. In fact, the standard deviation of inflation measured by the wholesale price index was four times as high after as it was before the war, while that of retail prices was over six times as high. Also, having had a low correlation with GDP before 1945, inflation in the postwar period had a significantly countercyclical relation to the GDP cycle.

The levels of internal prices also showed an upswing in volatility after the Second World War; they were also countercyclical, and showed increased persistence levels. In these series our finding for quarterly series in Argentina is the same as that of Kydland and Zarazaga (1997). Our results are also in agreement with the findings for the leading developed countries, which were pointed out for the United States by Kydland and Prescott (1990). These results are consistent with an RBC theory in which real shocks dominate fluctuations and lead to a prediction of a countercyclical price pattern, a result not sustained by traditional Keynesian and monetary theories.

However, the countercyclicality of prices is also tightly related to so-called stop-and-go cycles that were very common after the Second World War in the Argentine economy (Brodersohn 1974). Hence, this result must be considered together with the finding of countercyclicality in the nominal exchange rate. The economy used to grow while being pushed by demand-driven policies (fiscal and monetary) as imports followed GDP growth, implying an increase in the balance of trade deficit. This deficit, when it reached a point of financial unsustainability, was resolved through a huge devaluation that caused higher inflation in tradable goods, which resulted in a fall in real wages and real money

Table 4.6. *Cyclical behavior of inflation rates, import and export prices, and terms of trade, 1887–1990*

Deviation from trend

		1887–1990	1887–1945	1945–1990
log dWPI	Standard Dev.	0.280	0.096	0.407
	Obs. Number	103	58	46
	Output corr.	-0.333	-0.137	-0.538
	Persistence	0.256	-0.266	0.295
log dCPI	Standard Dev.	0.288	0.064	0.395
	Obs. Number	88	43	46
	Output corr.	-0.355	0.122	-0.540
	Persistence	0.327	-0.389	0.345
log WPI	Standard Dev.	0.266	0.073	0.394
	Obs. Number	104	59	46
	Output corr.	-0.354	-0.333	-0.525
	Persistence	0.348	0.154	0.357
log CPI	Standard Dev.	0.271	0.047	0.376
	Obs. Number	89	44	46
	Output corr.	-0.308	0.157	-0.480
	Persistence	0.341	0.092	0.342
log IMPPRIC	Standard Dev.	0.245	0.385	0.059
	Obs. Number	75	30	46
	Output corr.	0.046	0.034	0.135
	Persistence	-0.285	-0.299	0.110
log EXPPRIC	Standard Dev.	0.098	0.123	0.082
	Obs. Number	75	30	46
	Output corr.	0.255	0.251	0.315
	Persistence	0.332	0.386	0.279
log TOT	Standard Dev.	0.077	0.096	0.071
	Obs. Number	75	30	46
	Output corr.	0.172	0.174	0.252
	Persistence	0.000	0.003	0.067

Notes: The variables dWPI and dCPI show inflation rates (log differences) while log WPI and log CPI show price levels. IMPPRIC and EXPPRIC are import and export prices respectively. TOT is the terms of trade. All variables were computed using the Baxter-King bandpass filter.
Sources: See Appendix 1.

balances. The economy was then put in recession because aggregate demand had fallen, but the improved balance of trade set the stage for recovery.

Argentina is a small country compared to the rest of the world and was, before World War II, very open to the flow of goods and services from other countries. Over the 1913–39 period, the trade ratio (measured by the sum of exports and imports as a share of GDP) was 55 percent. The policy of import substitution implemented later decreased this ratio to average levels of only 21 percent in the period 1945–90. The data also show that import and export prices were relatively less volatile after 1945 than before that year. As they are implicit prices of actual traded amounts (i.e., total value divided by quantity), there could be some bias if external sales and purchases changed substantially from one period to another.[22]

The Argentine terms of trade, like those of the OECD countries studied by Backus, Kehoe, and Kydland (1995), showed a relatively high volatility with respect to GDP, and a ratio of around 2.5 in both periods.[23] It may be more interesting to note that the terms of trade show a very low correlation with the economic cycle in the two periods under consideration. With the prewar economy so open to trade with the rest of the world, it should be expected that changes in its terms of trade would have effects on the GDP cycle by increasing the level of activity when the terms of trade are high and by reducing them when the terms are low. This result could imply that the terms of trade did not influence the cyclical evolution of the economy; or, that attempts made to isolate the economy from changes in the terms of trade were successful. That is, if government policy was to reduce the effect on domestic prices of an increase in grain prices in foreign markets and local supply could have not responded to that increase, the effect on production could have been slight. In Sturzenegger (1990) it was noted that government trade policy intended to isolate the effect of changes in export prices on the income received by farmers, which could resolve this puzzling disconnect between terms of trade and real output.

4.4.1.4 Behavior of real monetary aggregates, interest rate, and real exchange rate

We next examine the behavior of various monetary variables, interest rates, and real and nominal exchange rates in Table 4.7. The real monetary base shows a low correlation with GDP. The volatility of both the real monetary base and the real M2 aggregate increases after 1945. The real M2 aggregate shows a high correlation with the cycle. This result is not in itself compelling evidence of the nonneutrality of money since – as is pointed out insistently by RBC theorists – it does not imply causality. The real interest rate also shows a sustained increase in volatility and a low correlation with GDP. Again, it can be asked if this supports money nonneutrality, or whether should it be understood as an endogenous response to changes in the conditions of the real economy.

[22] In the chapter by Berlinsky in this volume we find that for imports the change has been substantial. In fact, consumption goods that in 1900 accounted for almost 40 percent of all imports, by the 1950s and later, except in a few years, never accounted for more than 10 percent of total imports. Offsetting this change, intermediate goods (excluding fuels) saw a rise in their share of imports.

[23] Also, although they are not strictly comparable under the different filters used, the volatility of the terms of trade in developed countries was, for the 1970–90 period, about half that found in this study for Argentina, except for Japan, where the standard deviation of the terms of trade was very similar.

Table 4.7. *Cyclical behavior of real exchange rate, real monetary aggregates, and real interest rate, 1887–1990*

Deviation from trend

		1887–1990	1887–1945	1945–1990
log ERR	Standard Dev.	0.151	0.068	0.201
	Obs. Number	89	44	46
	Output corr.	-0.172	-0.167	-0.204
	Persistence	0.147	-0.161	0.179
log MOR	Standard Dev.	0.151	0.073	0.199
	Obs. Number	89	44	46
	Output corr.	0.079	0.128	0.092
	Persistence	0.076	-0.012	0.079
log M2R	Standard Dev.	0.093	0.055	0.118
	Obs. Number	89	44	46
	Output corr.	0.500	0.456	0.589
	Persistence	0.058	0.058	0.052
log ERR1	Standard Dev.	0.116	0.059	0.162
	Obs. Number	104	59	46
	Output corr.	-0.033	0.080	-0.104
	Persistence	0.128	0.033	0.145
log MOR1	Standard Dev.	0.128	0.084	0.168
	Obs. Number	104	59	46
	Output corr.	0.264	0.363	0.253
	Persistence	0.009	-0.100	0.048
log M2R1	Standard Dev.	0.125	0.112	0.141
	Obs. Number	104	59	46
	Output corr.	0.618	0.604	0.666
	Persistence	0.084	0.039	0.123
IRR	Standard Dev.	0.336	0.132	0.449
	Obs. Number	88	43	46
	Output corr.	-0.004	-0.057	0.044
	Persistence	0.150	-0.014	0.151
IRR1	Standard Dev.	0.290	0.125	0.414
	Obs. Number	104	59	46
	Output corr.	0.072	0.124	0.106
	Persistence	0.124	0.185	0.109

Notes: The variables ERR, MOR, M2R, and IRR show real exchange rate (log(ER) + log(GDP deflator for USA) - log (CPI)), real monetary base, real M2, and real interest rate (paid on deposits). All variables were adjusted by CPI except ERR1, MOR1, M2R1, and IRR1, where WPI was used instead. All variables were computed using the Baxter-King bandpass filter.
Sources: See Appendix 1.

This impasse has led some authors to look for more convincing evidence of money neutrality in the behavior of real and nominal exchange rates. We also believe that the questions must be resolved in a wider context that also explains other behaviors, such as that noted in the real exchange rate. The cyclical behavior of the real exchange rate also shows a substantial increase

Fig. 4.3. Cyclical behavior of the real exchange rate (RER) and nominal exchange
rate (ER)

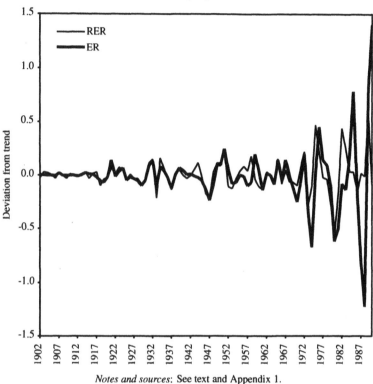

Notes and sources: See text and Appendix 1.

in volatility after the war. This behavior is matched by higher volatility in the
nominal exchange rate. In fact, as noted in Figure 4.3, the variables tend to
move together, a common observation for open economies.

Is this evidence of money nonneutrality? If money were neutral, the real
exchange rate would move in response to changes in the fundamental conditions of economy; that is, it would be determined on the "real side" (e.g., as a
result of changes in relative productivities). In contrast, the nominal exchange
rate should move in response to the conditions on the "monetary side" of the
economy. What can be seen from the evidence on Argentine history is that the
real exchange rate moves in step with fluctuations in the nominal exchange rate;
that is, *a priori* there seems to be evidence of nonneutrality in the short run.[24]

---

[24] These results, partially confirming money nonneutrality, are shown for a group of countries,
including Argentina, in Basu and Taylor (1999). For more evidence on the connection between
nominal and real exchange rate see Frankel and Rose (1995).

This result does not seem to be consistent with the predictions of simple new classical or RBC theories in which the real exchange rate is entirely determined on the real side of the economy. Instead, it seems to be more consistent with theories at the Keynesian-monetarist nexus (e.g., Friedman 1968) that posit money nonneutrality in the short run.

However, we must also note that the very low contemporary correlation between the real exchange rate and the GDP cycle seems to show that changes in relative prices do not affect the real economy in any important way.[25] There is some indication that changes in the real exchange rate have a positive effect on the balance of trade surplus with a one period lag, but not on the level of economic activity. This problem might be resolved by the fact that an increase in economic activity leads, at a later stage, to a balance of trade deterioration that eventually must be corrected by a contraction in the economy and a change in the exchange rate.[26] This scenario fits well with our stop-and-go view and is also manifest in the slight negative correlation between the real exchange rate and GDP. However, the hypothesis deserves even further research because the low correlation is still striking.

4.4.2 Argentina and the world cycle

We have examined the cycle in the Argentine economy over the very long run, from the late nineteenth century to the 1990s. At the outset we suspected that, in the earliest years we are considering, the integration of the domestic economy with international flows of goods, services, and factors caused a closer relationship between cycles in Argentina and the rest of the world. One question, then, is whether this pattern has persisted. The correlations of Argentine GDP with the GDPs of the United States, the United Kingdom, Australia, Canada, and Brazil are shown in Table 4.8.[27] The Argentine cycle was most akin to Brazil's in the 1887–1990 period as a whole, although the correlation is relatively low.

What of changes in international synchronization? The Argentine cycle stands out as initially correlated with that of the United Kingdom, as in the years 1887–1914. The First World War witnessed a cyclical response similar to

---

[25] This result was also noticed by Baxter and Stockman (1989) for a number of countries.

[26] An approximation with 4 lags resulted from the Granger causality test, which (at the 5 percent significance level) rejected the hypothesis that the real exchange rate does not cause the balance of trade; we also rejected the hypothesis that the balance of trade is not caused by the GDP. However, the hypothesis that GDP is not caused by the real exchange rate is only rejected at a 28 percent significance level.

[27] Data from all theses countries have been taken from Maddison (1995) and filtered by the bandpass method. Except for Brazil, whose series began in 1900, the other countries have a span of data comparable to the Argentine series (1887–1990).

Table 4.8. *GDP correlations with foreign countries, deviation from trend,*
1887–1990

	U.S.A.	U.K.	Canada	Australia	Brazil
1887–1990	0.079	0.161	0.071	0.074	0.201
1887–1945	0.143	0.210	0.105	0.142	0.261
1945–1990	-0.223	0.044	-0.044	-0.110	0.172
1887–1914	-0.006	0.273	-0.016	0.222	0.091
1914–1919	0.305	0.044	-0.542	-0.573	-0.844
1919–1939	0.648	0.620	0.676	0.218	0.640
1939–1945	-0.215	0.030	0.082	-0.025	0.449
1945–1990	-0.223	0.044	-0.044	-0.110	0.172

Notes and sources: See text and Appendix 1.

that of the United States and opposite to that of Brazil, Australia, and Canada. During the years between the wars (1919–39), Argentine GDP followed the cyclical behavior of all countries (except Australia). World War II drove the Argentine cycle in a similar way to that of Brazil, and slightly counter to that of the United States. It was in the postwar period, however, that the Argentine cycle found itself in a pattern unlike any other, although it did again behave counter to that of the United States. In these cross-correlations, it is clear that the Argentine cyclical pattern, except for certain stages (namely, the world wars and the Great Depression), had a tendency to move quite independently, even during periods of relative openness to external flows of goods, services, and factors.

It can also be noted that the Argentine cycle's volatility was higher than that of almost all the other countries, especially after World War II, as shown in Table 4.9. Substantial differences exist between Argentine cycles and those of the United Kingdom, Australia, and Brazil, whereas the volatility in Argentina is similar to that in the United States. This result is surprising as there are no strong correlations with any other country's cycle; thus, it is important to determine which factors explain this similarity between Argentine and U.S. volatility. Further investigation of this result is beyond the scope of this work.

4.5 Conclusions

In this paper we have tried to analyze how business cycles behaved throughout Argentine history. Our first approach, a more traditional one, showed that major crises happened in early years (1914, 1890, and the 1930s) and that they were related mainly to external factors. The import substitution process undertaken after the 1930s was associated with a quite different cycle, one more related to activist macroeconomic policies, and coterminous with higher (and sometimes

Table 4.9. *GDP relative volatility versus foreign countries, deviation from trend, 1887–1990*

Argentina = 1

	U.S.A.	U.K.	Canada	Australia	Brazil
1887–1990	1.089	0.602	0.910	0.749	0.643
1887–1945	1.194	0.638	1.044	0.833	0.652
1945–1990	0.923	0.498	0.500	0.514	0.656
1887–1914	0.799	0.389	0.705	0.799	0.591
1914–1919	0.921	0.645	1.073	0.650	0.456
1919–1939	1.554	0.927	1.670	0.870	0.910
1939–1945	2.820	1.119	1.514	1.554	0.766
1945–1990	0.923	0.498	0.500	0.514	0.656

Notes and sources: See text and Appendix 1.

unusually high) inflation rates. This last factor is crucial to our understanding of how the Argentine economy performed subsequently.

Our second approach, using more formal quantitative techniques, exposed certain regularities that are explained by no single economic theory. For example, RBC theory can explain some of the countercyclical price patterns, but Keynesian and monetarist theories fit better the real and nominal exchange rate movements. Even so, we are hard pressed to explain the unusually low correlation between the real exchange rate and GDP. For now, it should be noted that we did not set out to promote any one theory, but simply to report the main empirical results. Future research will be directed to resolving these puzzles.

We do claim that, in the postwar period, many of the stylized facts seem to fit quite well with what we call a stop-and-go cycle story in which devaluations are contractionary in countries such as Argentina because both export supply and import demand appear unresponsive to movements in the exchange rate. If we assume that this is the case and take into account the facts that imports grew faster than GDP and that both were highly correlated, we find that booms are associated with a negative balance of trade and stability in prices, while recessions involve high inflation and an improving balance of trade as large devaluations set in at the end of a booming phase. This type of story, though conjectural, can perhaps better explain some of the unusual and persistent features of postwar Argentine macroeconomic fluctuations that we have uncovered.

Appendix 1: Data description

This study uses intensively the databases published in Gerchunoff and Llach (1998) (henceforth G-L), della Paolera and Ortiz (1995) (henceforth DP-O), IEERAL (1986), and Maddison (1995). In detail, the sources used are:

Real GDP of Argentina: 1913–1990, G-L, at 1996 constant prices; 1884–1913, DP-O.

Consumption: G-L at 1996 constant prices.
Investment: G-L at 1996 constant prices.
Import and Export: G-L at 1996 constant prices.
Total Employment: IEERAL (1986).
Average Real Wage: IEERAL (1986) at 1960 constant prices.
Consumer Price Index, Wholesale Price Index, and U.S. GDP deflator: G-L.
Import Price, Export Price, and Term of Trade: G-L.
Fiscal Surplus: G-L, percent of GDP.
Monetary Base (M0), M2, and the International Reserves: DP-O.
Nominal Exchange Rate: DP-O.
Domestic Pasive Interest Rate: DP-O.
Real GDP of Australia, Brazil, Canada, United Kingdom, and United States: Maddison (1995).

Appendix 2: Comparison of filters

Figures 4.4 and 4.5 show the results of using different filters on the Argentine GDP series.

Appendix 3: Cyclical regularities: an alternative historical division

Tables 4.10–4.14 show the cyclical behavior of key macroeconomic variables.

Table 4.10. *GDP cycles*

Period	Phase	Duration	Annual change (%)	Cumulative change (%)	GDP per capita, annual change (%)	Cycle length (peak to peak)
1885	E	1	6.4	6.4	3.2	
1886	C	1	-0.4	-0.4	-3.4	
1887–89	E	3	13.1	44.5	9.7	4
1890–91	C	2	-7.7	-14.9	-10.5	
1892–96	E	5	6.0	34.0	2.8	7
1897	C	1	-6.4	-6.4	-9.6	
1898–99	E	2	8.6	17.8	4.8	3
1900	C	1	-2.5	-2.5	-5.9	
1901	E	1	8.5	8.5	4.8	2
1902	C	1	-2.0	-2.0	-5.4	
1903–13	E	11	7.0	111.2	3.3	12
1914	C	1	-10.3	-10.3	-13.4	
1915	E	1	0.5	0.5	-1.6	2
1916–17	C	2	-5.6	-10.8	-7.5	
1918–24	E	7	8.3	74.6	6.0	9
1925	C	1	-0.5	-0.5	-2.6	
1926–29	E	4	5.7	24.7	3.5	5
1930–32	C	3	-4.8	-13.8	-6.8	
1933–42	E	10	3.7	43.5	1.5	13
1943	C	1	-0.7	-0.7	-2.8	
1944	E	1	11.3	11.3	8.9	2
1945	C	1	-3.2	-3.2	-5.2	
1946–48	E	3	8.5	27.7	6.3	4
1949	C	1	-1.3	-1.3	-3.1	
1950–51	E	2	2.6	5.2	0.8	3
1952	C	1	-5.0	-5.0	-6.7	
1953–58	E	6	5.1	34.6	3.2	7
1959	C	1	-6.5	-6.5	-8.1	
1960–61	E	2	8.0	16.7	6.2	3
1962–63	C	2	-1.0	-2.0	-2.5	
1964–77	E	14	5.4	107.6	3.6	16
1978	C	1	-2.4	-2.4	-4.2	
1979–80	E	2	4.7	9.6	2.8	3
1981–82	C	2	-4.5	-8.7	-5.9	
1983–84	E	2	2.8	5.6	1.2	4
1985	C	1	-6.6	-6.6	-8.0	
1986–87	E	2	4.9	10.1	3.4	3
1988–89	C	2	-4.1	-8.0	-5.5	
1990	E	1	0.1	0.1	-1.4	
1884–1990		106	3.4	3480.8	1.1	5.7

Notes: E = expansion, C = contraction.
Sources: See text and Appendix 1.

Table 4.11. *Cyclical behavior of GDP, aggregate demand components, labor productivity, employment, and real wages, 1887–1990*

Deviation from trend

		1887–1914	1914–1919	1919–1939	1939–1945	1945–1990
log GDP	Standard Dev.	0.043	0.048	0.029	0.028	0.031
	Obs. Number	28	6	21	7	46
	Persistence	0.038	-0.288	0.369	-0.785	0.037
log CONS	Standard Dev.	—	0.015	0.054	0.046	0.042
	Obs. Number	0	4	21	7	46
	Output corr.	—	0.095	0.562	0.961	0.863
	Persistence	—	-0.460	0.059	-0.658	0.225
log INV	Standard Dev.	0.123	0.104	0.150	0.124	0.106
	Obs. Number	12	6	21	7	46
	Output corr.	0.369	0.025	0.738	-0.563	0.789
	Persistence	0.103	0.211	0.385	-0.128	0.034
log IMPORT	Standard Dev.	—	0.099	0.112	0.170	0.166
	Obs. Number	0	4	21	7	46
	Output corr.	—	-0.272	0.721	0.430	0.710
	Persistence	—	-0.114	0.311	0.757	0.290
log EXPORT	Standard Dev.	—	0.193	0.120	0.058	0.094
	Obs. Number	0	4	21	7	46
	Output corr.	—	0.919	0.268	0.455	-0.090
	Persistence	—	-0.312	-0.401	-0.270	-0.123
B. of Trade	Standard Dev.	—	0.211	0.168	0.170	0.204
	Obs. Number	0	4	21	7	46
	Output corr.	—	0.968	-0.288	-0.276	-0.620
	Persistence	—	-0.061	-0.105	0.638	0.170
log Labor Prod.	Standard Dev.	—	0.063	0.026	0.029	0.030
	Obs. Number	0	4	21	7	46
	Output corr.	—	0.995	0.967	0.999	0.918
	Persistence	—	-0.244	0.322	-0.754	0.070
log EMPLOY	Standard Dev.	—	0.007	0.008	0.001	0.012
	Obs. Number	0	4	21	7	37
	Output corr.	—	-0.332	0.516	-0.429	0.341
	Persistence	—	0.782	0.154	0.170	0.004
log dWR	Standard Dev.	—	0.056	0.050	0.054	0.111
	Obs. Number	0	3	21	7	37
	Output corr.	—	0.010	-0.145	0.595	0.574
	Persistence	—	-1.000	-0.435	-0.295	-0.041
log WR	Standard Dev.	—	0.023	0.014	0.019	0.072
	Obs. Number	0	4	21	7	37
	Output corr.	—	0.259	-0.177	0.700	0.467
	Persistence	—	0.511	-0.108	-0.111	0.220

Notes: The variables GDP, CONS (consumption), INV (investment), IMPORT (imports), EXPORT (exports), B. of Trade (Balance of Trade = log(EXPORT) – log(IMPORT)), Labor Prod. (average labor productivity), EMPLOY (employment), and WR are in levels, while dWR (real wage) is shown as a rate of change (log difference). All variables were computed using the Baxter-King bandpass filter.

Sources: See Appendix 1.

Table 4.12. *Cyclical behavior of fiscal surplus, coefficient of openness, and nominal variables (monetary base, M2, nominal exchange rate, and international reserves), 1887–1990*

Deviation from trend

		1887–1914	1914–1919	1919–1939	1939–1945	1945–1990
Fiscal Surplus	Standard Dev.	—	0.005	0.008	0.007	0.014
	Obs. Number	0	4	21	7	46
	Output corr.	—	0.819	0.012	0.268	0.164
	Persistence	—	-0.119	-0.067	0.286	0.103
Coef. Openness	Standard Dev.	—	0.0476	0.0372	0.0167	0.0174
	Obs. Number	0	4	21	7	46
	Output corr.	—	0.209	0.386	0.273	0.247
	Persistence	—	-0.481	-0.136	0.562	0.156
log dMO	Standard Dev.	0.0611	0.0525	0.0689	0.0447	0.3392
	Obs. Number	28	6	21	7	46
	Output corr.	0.085	0.503	-0.056	0.341	-0.484
	Persistence	0.162	-0.597	-0.021	-0.152	0.355
log dM2	Standard Dev.	0.1103	0.0827	0.0376	0.0264	0.3039
	Obs. Number	28	6	21	7	46
	Output corr.	0.562	0.501	0.553	0.337	-0.371
	Persistence	0.063	0.486	0.334	0.012	0.385
log dER	Standard Dev.	0.0706	0.0364	0.0757	0.0397	0.4041
	Obs. Number	28	6	21	7	46
	Output corr.	-0.509	-0.227	-0.397	0.341	-0.553
	Persistence	0.334	0.939	-0.007	0.877	0.314
log dRESERV	Standard Dev.	—	0.0576	0.2046	0.1322	0.3750
	Obs. Number	0	2	21	7	46
	Output corr.	—	1.000	0.424	-0.441	-0.008
	Persistence	—	—	0.282	0.793	0.022

Notes: The variables Fiscal Surplus (as a percent of GDP) and Coef. Openness (EX-PORT+IMPORT/GDP) are in levels, while dMO (nominal monetary base), dM2 (nominal M2), dER (nominal exchange rate) and dRESERV (international reserves at Central Bank) are in rates of change. All variables were computed using the Baxter-King bandpass filter.
Sources: See Appendix 1.

Table 4.13. *Cyclical behavior of inflation rates, import and export prices, and terms of trade, 1887–1990*

Deviation from trend

		1887–1914	1914–1919	1919–1939	1939–1945	1945–1990
log dWPI	Standard Dev.	0.122	0.049	0.069	0.066	0.407
	Obs. Number	27	6	21	7	46
	Output corr.	-0.245	-0.790	0.456	-0.097	-0.538
	Persistence	-0.282	0.123	-0.183	-0.665	0.295
log dCPI	Standard Dev.	0.031	0.088	0.079	0.049	0.395
	Obs. Number	12	6	21	7	46
	Output corr.	0.497	-0.114	0.322	-0.597	-0.540
	Persistence	-0.221	-0.465	-0.407	-0.435	0.346
log WPI	Standard Dev.	0.091	0.068	0.056	0.045	0.394
	Obs. Number	28	6	21	7	46
	Output corr.	-0.563	-0.140	0.363	-0.286	-0.525
	Persistence	0.121	0.756	0.157	-0.176	0.357
log CPI	Standard Dev.	0.023	0.067	0.053	0.037	0.376
	Obs. Number	13	6	21	7	46
	Output corr.	-0.066	0.307	0.289	-0.374	-0.480
	Persistence	-0.109	0.143	0.038	0.118	0.342
log IMPPRIC	Standard Dev.	—	0.139	0.444	0.777	0.059
	Obs. Number	0	4	21	7	46
	Output corr.	—	0.612	0.045	-0.102	0.135
	Persistence	—	0.157	-0.503	-0.707	0.111
log EXPPRIC	Standard Dev.	—	0.122	0.132	0.088	0.082
	Obs. Number	0	4	21	7	46
	Output corr.	—	-0.067	0.523	0.100	0.315
	Persistence	—	0.203	0.336	0.396	0.252
log TOT	Standard Dev.	—	0.118	0.092	0.099	0.071
	Obs. Number	0	4	21	7	46
	Output corr.	—	-0.788	0.528	0.358	0.252
	Persistence	—	-0.789	0.105	0.377	-0.008

Notes: The variables dWPI and dCPI show inflation rates (log differences) while log WPI and log CPI show price levels. IMPPRIC and EXPPRIC are import and export prices respectively. TOT is the terms of trade. All variables were computed using the Baxter-King bandpass filter.
Sources: See Appendix 1.

Adolfo Sturzenegger and Ramiro Moya

Table 4.14. *Cyclical behavior of real exchange rate, real monetary aggregates, and real interest rate, 1887–1990*

Deviation from trend

		1887–1914	1914–1919	1919–1939	1939–1945	1945–1990
log ERR	Standard Dev.	0.022	0.050	0.090	0.051	0.201
	Obs. Number	13	6	21	7	46
	Output corr.	-0.111	-0.729	-0.235	0.347	-0.204
	Persistence	-0.324	-0.133	-0.214	0.065	0.181
log MOR	Standard Dev.	0.058	0.079	0.082	0.058	0.199
	Obs. Number	13	6	21	7	46
	Output corr.	0.723	0.075	-0.236	0.506	0.092
	Persistence	-0.251	0.240	-0.028	-0.234	0.082
log M2R	Standard Dev.	0.076	0.049	0.045	0.053	0.118
	Obs. Number	13	6	21	7	46
	Output corr.	0.760	0.430	0.118	0.431	0.589
	Persistence	0.215	-0.077	-0.212	0.091	0.057
log ERR1	Standard Dev.	0.045	0.052	0.084	0.047	0.162
	Obs. Number	28	6	21	7	46
	Output corr.	0.374	-0.127	-0.308	0.358	-0.104
	Persistence	-0.029	0.805	0.021	-0.359	0.145
log MOR1	Standard Dev.	0.085	0.093	0.088	0.063	0.168
	Obs. Number	28	6	21	7	46
	Output corr.	0.666	0.385	-0.274	0.448	0.253
	Persistence	-0.253	0.226	-0.011	-0.675	0.042
log M2R1	Standard Dev.	0.155	0.055	0.047	0.048	0.141
	Obs. Number	28	6	21	7	46
	Output corr.	0.731	0.918	0.013	0.456	0.666
	Persistence	0.043	-0.473	0.174	-0.792	0.123
IRR	Standard Dev.	0.040	0.065	0.164	0.160	0.449
	Obs. Number	12	6	21	7	46
	Output corr.	0.014	-0.295	-0.232	0.529	0.044
	Persistence	-0.037	0.022	-0.123	0.731	0.143
IRR1	Standard Dev.	0.081	0.063	0.159	0.189	0.414
	Obs. Number	28	6	21	7	46
	Output corr.	0.399	0.170	-0.268	0.442	0.106
	Persistence	0.012	0.728	0.034	0.891	0.094

Notes: The variables ERR, MOR, M2R, and IRR show real exchange rate (log(ER) + log(GDP deflator for USA) - log (CPI)), real monetary base, real M2, and real interest rate (paid on deposits). All variables were adjusted by CPI except ERR1, MOR1, M2R1 and IRR1, where WPI was used instead. All variables were computed using the Baxter-King bandpass filter.
Sources: See Appendix 1.

Fig. 4.4. Filtered GDP: First difference and Baxter-King filters

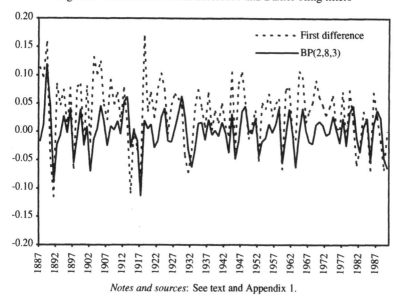

Notes and sources: See text and Appendix 1.

Fig. 4.5. Filtered GDP: Hodrick-Prescott and Baxter-King filters

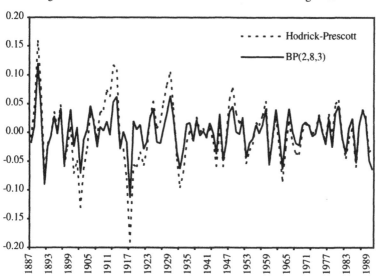

Notes and sources: Hodrick-Prescott penalty parameter $\lambda = 100$. See text and Appendix 1

References

Akerlof, George A., and Janet L. Yellen. 1985. A Near-Rational Model of the Business Cycle, with Wage and Price Intertia. *Quarterly Journal of Economics* 100 (5): 823–38.
Backus, David K., and Patrick J. Kehoe. 1992. International Evidence on the Historical Properties of Business Cycles. *American Economic Review* 82 (4): 864–88.
Backus, David K., Patrick J. Kehoe, and Finn E. Kydland. 1995. International Business Cycles: Theory and Evidence. In *Frontiers of Business Cycle Research*, edited by T. F. Cooley. Princeton: Princeton University Press.
Basu, Susanto, and Alan M. Taylor. 1999. International Business Cycles in Historical Perspective. *Journal of Economic Perspectives* 13 (2): 45–68.
Baxter, Marianne, and Robert G. King. 1999. Measuring Business Cycles: Approximate Band-Pass Filters for Economic Time Series. *Review of Economics and Statistics* 81 (4): 575–93.
Baxter, Marianne, and Alan C. Stockman. 1989. Business Cycles and the Exchange-Rate Regime: Some International Evidence. *Journal of Monetary Economics* 23 (3): 377–400.
Brodersohn, Mario S. 1974. Política económica de corto plazo, crecimiento e inflación en la Argentina, 1950–1972. In *Problemas económicos argentinos*, edited by M. S. Brodersohn. Buenos Aires: Ediciones Macchi.
Burns, Arthur F., and Wesley Clair Mitchell. 1946. *Measuring Business Cycles*. New York: National Bureau of Economic Research.
Carrera, Jorge, Mariano Féliz, and Demian Panigo. 1996. Ciclo económico en Argentina y Brasil. *Anales de la Asociación Argentina de Economía Política*, XXXI Reunión Anual, vol. 6.
Cooley, Thomas F., ed. 1995. *Frontiers of Business Cycle Research*. Princeton: Princeton University Press.
Cortés Conde, Roberto. 1989. *Dinero, deuda y crisis: Evolución fiscal y monetaria en la Argentina, 1862–1890*. Buenos Aires: Editorial Sudamericana.
della Paolera, Gerardo, and Javier Ortiz. 1995. Dinero, intermediación financiera y nivel de actividad en 110 años de historia económica argentina. Documentos de Trabajo 36, Universidad Torcuato Di Tella (December).
Díaz Alejandro, Carlos F. 1963. A Note on the Impact of Devaluation and the Redistributive Effect. *Journal of Political Economy* 71 (6): 577–80.
———. 1966. *Devaluación de la tasa de cambio en un país semi-industrializado: La experiencia de la Argentina, 1955–1961*. Buenos Aires: Editorial del Instituto.
———. 1970. *Essays on the Economic History of the Argentine Republic*. New Haven, Conn.: Yale University Press.
Di Tella, Guido, and Rudiger Dornbusch. 1989. *The Political Economy of Argentina, 1946–83*. Basingstoke: Macmillan.
Di Tella, Guido, and Manuel Zymelman. 1967. *Las etapas del desarrollo económico argentino*. Buenos Aires: Editorial Universitaria de Buenos Aires.
———. 1973. *Loc ciclos económicos argentinos*. Buenos Aires: Editorial Paidós.
Frankel, Jeffrey A., and Andrew K. Rose. 1995. Empirical Research on Nominal Exchange Rates. In *Handbook of International Economics*, edited by G. Grossman and K. Rogoff. Amsterdam: North Holland.
Friedman, Milton. 1968. The Role of Monetary Policy. *American Economic Review* 58 (1): 1–17.
Gerchunoff, Pablo, and Lucas Llach. 1998. *El ciclo de la ilusión y el desencanto: Un siglo de políticas económicas argentinas*. Buenos Aires: Ariel.

Hodrick, Robert J., and Edward C. Prescott. 1997. Postwar U.S. Business Cycles: An Empirical Investigation. *Journal of Money, Credit, and Banking* 29 (1): 1–16.

IEERAL (Instituto de Estudios Económicos sobre la Realidad Argentina y Latinoamericana). 1986. Estadísticas de la evolución económica de Argentina 1913–1984. *Estudios* 9 (39): 103–84.

Koopmans, Tjalling C. 1947. Measurement Without Theory. *Review of Economic Statistics* 29 (3): 161–72.

Kydland, Finn E., and Edward C. Prescott. 1990. Business Cycles: Real Facts and a Monetary Myth. *Federal Reserve Bank of Minneapolis Quarterly Review* 14: 3–18.

Kydland, Finn E., and Carlos E. J. M. Zarazaga. 1997. Is the Business Cycle of Argentina "Different"? *Federal Reserve Bank of Dallas Economic Review*, 4th Quarter, 21–36.

Lucas, Jr., Robert E. 1977. Understanding Business Cycles. *Journal of Monetary Economics* 5 (Supplement): 7–29.

Maddison, Angus. 1995. *Monitoring the World Economy*. Paris: OECD.

Nelson, Charles R., and Charles I. Plosser. 1982. Trends and Random Walks in Macroeconomic Time Series: Some Evidence and Implications. *Journal of Monetary Economics* 10 (2): 139–62.

Romer, Christina D. 1986. The Prewar Business Cycle Reconsidered: New Estimates of Gross National Product, 1869–1908. *Journal of Political Economy* 97 (1): 1–37.

Stock, James H., and Mark W. Watson. 1998. Business Cycle Fluctuations in U.S. Macroeconomic Time Series. Working Paper Series no. 6528 (April), National Bureau of Economic Research.

Sturzenegger, Adolfo. 1990. El caso argentino. In *Economía política de las intervenciones de precios agrícolas en América Latina,* edited by A. O. Krueger, M. W. Schiff, and A. Valdés. San Francisco: Banco Mundial, Centro Internacional para el Desarrollo Económico afiliado al Instituto de Estudios Contemporáneos.

Zarnowitz, Victor. 1992. *Business Cycles: Theory, History, Indicators, and Forecasting*. Chicago: University of Chicago Press.

5

The labor market

SEBASTIÁN GALIANI
Universidad de San Andrés

PABLO GERCHUNOFF
Universidad Torcuato Di Tella

The study of the Argentine labor market, as would be the case for any labor market during the last century, reveals a substantial transformation. Its organization has become significantly more complex. The labor market has evolved from one in which wages were entirely determined by the business cycle, there was little human capital specific to any given firm, and both hiring and firing costs were negligible (i.e., an approximation of a spot market) to one characterized by both explicit and implicit long-term commitments between firms and workers.

In the United States, this transition occurred between the 1940s and 1950s, when a market based on contracts almost completely replaced the earlier market type, which lacked such long-term commitments between workers and firms (see Goldin 2000). In this chapter, we also date the Argentine transition to the years of the 1940s and 1950s.[1] Moreover, we suggest that the most important developments of the Argentine labor market are rooted in the fundamental changes that have taken place in the way the economy of the country has integrated with the rest of the world during the past century.

Even though the labor market of the postindustrial revolution era has never been strictly a spot market, the argument is, essentially, that in the labor market prior to the early-twentieth century workers faced considerable job insecurity and widely fluctuating wages over the business cycle, invested little in human capital, and were disciplined by negative incentives. In contrast, the labor market of the post-World War II era is characterized by greater job security,

---

[1] If a modern labor market is defined as a labor market in which trade rules are based on a contractual system, and, perhaps, on a well-developed system of collective bargaining, then all developed countries achieved the transition to a modern labor market immediately after World War II. Without a doubt, this transition was initiated at different points in time and in different ways across countries. For example, the Argentine transition was considerably more abrupt than the U.S. transition, although, at least in terms of collective action, the Argentine transformation was more deeply rooted.

contracted wage arrangements, internal labor markets, firm-related benefits, investment in firm-specific human capital, and discipline by positive incentives (Doeringer and Piore 1971). In essence, the modern form of employment is characterized by job attachment (Parsons 1986).

Comparable to other labor markets during the last century, the Argentine experience also reveals that the period under study witnessed large gains in the absolute levels of wages and leisure. Additionally, the composition of the labor force has shifted considerably, and employees, to a large extent, gained job rights and employment security. However, during the last decade, job stability has deteriorated substantially in Argentina (see Galiani 2002; Galiani and Hopenhayn 2003).[2]

The development of a modern labor market in Argentina by no means implies that most workers participated in it. In developing countries, the era of modern labor markets has also been a period of dual (urban) labor markets, a phenomenon that has been accentuated in the last twenty years instead of reversed.

Most of the important changes we observe in the structure of the labor market are a reflection of the evolution and change of its institutions. Consequently, the study of the development of the labor market is, to a large extent, the study of the evolution of labor market institutions. In this chapter, we provide an integrated interpretation of the evolution of the Argentine labor market.

It needs to be underlined at the outset that the institutional development of an economy both affects and is affected by the working of the economic system. Trade unions provide a good illustration of this relationship. The standard view of trade unions is that they are organizations whose purpose is to improve the material welfare of their members, principally by raising members' wages above the competitive wage level. But what are the conditions under which unions achieve their target? For trade unions to exist as viable organizations, they must be able to capture some economic surplus. In noncompetitive industries in which firms are making extraordinary profits, unions with sufficient power can obtain higher wages without threatening the viability of the firm. Thus, one would expect a higher probability of union organization in noncompetitive industries than in competitive product markets.[3]

Likewise, consider a highly open economy that possesses comparative advantage in the production of primary goods. In that economy, the scope for

---

[2] Although it frequently has been asserted that globalization has undermined job stability ubiquitously, there is not substantial evidence in favor of this hypothesis in developed countries (cf. Burgess and Rees 1996 and Farber 1998).

[3] Historically, U.S. employers were expeditious to suppress emerging unions, whereas British employers accepted unions. This difference of attitude was due to the fact that U.S. employers faced greater competitive pressures than did British employers (see Booth 1995).

trade unions would be limited. The opposite would be the case in an extremely closed economy in which several manufacturing sectors extract rents because of the existing level of tariffs and nontariff protection (and perhaps also from government subsidies).[4]

Thus, labor market institutions do not develop in isolation. In turn, *ceteris paribus*, they may significantly affect several important economic variables (e.g., income distribution and unemployment);[5] but it is also worth noting that, at least in the long run, they would not affect other variables (e.g., real wages) that are ultimately determined by the long-term performance of the economy.

We identify three periods in the evolution of the Argentine labor market: (1) the period of spot markets from 1870 to 1929, (2) the period of modern, institutional markets from 1943 to 1975, and (3) the period of transition toward modern, flexible labor markets from 1976 to 2000.[6] Although these periods do not necessarily coincide with the phases of Argentine economic growth, they do match with the phases of integration into, and isolation from, world factor and goods markets.[7]

5.1 The spot market era

Argentina possesses definite comparative advantages in agriculture. The country is endowed with a vast amount of highly fertile land. During the second half of the nineteenth century, there was an intense process of colonization of the territory in the form of *latifundia* (Adelman 1994). The sharp increase in the disposability of land induced an expansion in livestock raising, primarily because it was not labor intensive at a time when labor was a scarce resource.[8]

---

[4] It may be useful to consider an economy populated by agents that have preferences of the Dixit-Stiglitz type, in which domestic firms' share in the industry total output is higher the more closed is the economy.

[5] Thus, labor market institutions crucially depend on the prevailing preferences on the distribution of outcomes in society.

[6] We have chosen these phases in order to account for different labor market processes and not necessarily because of the realization of breaks at the boundary dates of any of these periods. We have in mind models of development that shape these processes, and hence, strictly speaking, we are dating latent processes. In any case, singling out a particular date is a convention and not something prone to instigate too much opposition.

[7] The Atlantic economy has witnessed three periods since the mid-nineteenth century: the late-nineteenth-century *Belle Époque*, the dark ages between 1914 and 1950, and the late-twentieth-century renaissance. The first and last epochs were ones of convergence and globalization; the middle epoch was one of divergence and global devolution (see O'Rourke and Williamson 1999). Only the U.S. labor market has matched the late evolution of the Atlantic economy; both European and Argentine labor markets have had a longer period of modern institutional (or rigid) labor markets than the U.S.

[8] See Sábato (1985) for an excellent description of the Argentine labor market during the period 1850–70.

Table 5.1. *Living standards, 1870–1913*

Country	Real wages (G.B. 1905 = 100)		GDP per capita (1990 US$)	
	1870	1913	1870	1913
European periphery	31	72	1,478	2,599
Ireland	49	90	—	—
Italy	26	55	1,467	2,507
Spain	30	39	1,367	2,255
European industrial core	58	86	2,414	4,101
France	50	66	1,858	3,452
Great Britain	67	98	3,263	5,023
Europe	43	77	1,878	3,242
New World	88	139	1,986	3,932
Argentina	61	92	1,311	3,797
Australia	127	128	3,801	5,505
Brazil	39	87	740	839
Canada	99	219	1,620	4,213
United States	115	169	2,457	5,307

Notes and sources: Wage data are taken from O'Rourke and Williamson (1997). GDP per capita data are taken from Maddison (1995).

The period from 1870 to 1914 was one of free trade and market integration.[9] For instance, this period involved the most extensive real-wage convergence that the Atlantic economy has ever seen (O'Rourke and Williamson 1999). The dramatic decline in transport costs across the late-nineteenth century led to a trade boom and commodity price convergence internationally. In Argentina, the scarcity of labor and abundance of land, relative to Europe, induced a high marginal product of labor. The wage differential between Argentina and some European countries attracted a colossal flow of overseas immigrants that constituted Argentina's main labor force. A similar process also induced a massive flow of capital into the country. Table 5.1 illustrates the phenomenal wage differences in favor of Argentina compared to several European countries. It also illustrates the catch up of Argentina to the levels attained by Australia and US during the period 1870–1913.[10]

The growth of the labor force was essential for the expansion of agriculture from the beginning of this century. The area of land under cultivation doubled between 1900 and 1905, and again between 1905 and 1915. The area of the humid Pampas being exploited grew from 5 million hectares in 1895 to 25

[9] If the World War I period is not considered, this is a period of both absolute and comparatively rapid economic growth – although it is worth noting that there is not agreement about the phases of Argentine economic growth (see Díaz-Alejandro 1988 and Di Tella and Zymelman 1967).

[10] The segmented international labor market of this era affected Argentina, which drew most of its migrants from relatively low-wage areas of Europe, principally Italy and Spain (Taylor 1994).

million hectares in 1930, a level that has remained virtually unchanged ever since.[11]

Until the beginning of the twentieth century, Argentina suffered an acute scarcity of labor. It was not until immigrants substantially increased labor supply and growth slowed down that this scarcity was overcome. Labor demand was highly seasonal. Arable agriculture needed two types of workers: one willing to work intermittently (during seasons of peak demand) and another willing to work year round (Adelman 1994). During the period 1870–1914, there were also intense internal migrations as a response to differential local labor market conditions (cf. Córtes Conde 1982). This search behavior provides evidence of the existence of an integrated internal labor market during this period characterized by flows that were due not only to overseas immigration, but also to the lack of human capital in the labor force and the specific characteristics of the productive system.

There is a serious problem in identifying the sector of employment for 25 to 40 percent of the working population in the first three national censuses. Interestingly enough, the main signal we should extract from this statistical nuisance is that workers, in the main, lacked any specialization and were highly mobile between the primary and secondary sectors of the economy.

Real wages were also extremely volatile during this period. Córtes Conde (1979) presents two important series for the period 1882–1912, one for unskilled workers and the other for the workers of the Bagley firm (a large industrial producer of processed foods such as biscuits and crackers). Figure 5.1 shows the annual variability of the monthly series of wages together with the variability of real gross domestic output per capita. The figures are striking: real wages change from one year to the next by as much as thirty percent in any direction. Although it is likely that there is considerable noise in these series, especially

---

[11] It is useful to consider the Ricardian model to understand the rapid growth of the country and its development during the late-nineteenth century. At the heart of the Ricardian system is the notion that economic growth must slow down, owing to the scarcity of natural resources. The system can be outlined by supposing that the whole economy consists of a giant farm engaged in producing wheat by applying homogenous doses of "capital-and-labor" to a fixed supply of land subject to diminishing returns. As less productive land is incorporated to production, output still increases but at a diminishing rate, implying that output per capita decreases.

Thus, a progressive extension (until exhaustion) of the agricultural frontier would induce a period of rapid growth, necessarily followed by a slow down, such as we have observed in Argentina during this period. Of course, this story could have been different if the world factor markets did not collapse after the crisis of 1929. Thus, for example, during the 1920s industrialization developed at a fast pace, and it is not really possible to argue that it accelerated during the 1930s, a period often considered to be the takeoff of industrialization in Argentina (see Gutierrez and Korol 1988 and Villanueva 1972). Hence, a growing and relatively more efficient industrial sector could have mustered a high and sustainable growth rate of output per capita based on technological innovation. Certainly, developments in the labor market could have been different as a result.

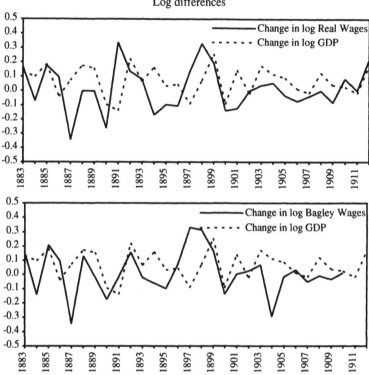

Fig. 5.1. Real wages and GDP per capita variability
Log differences

Sources: Unskilled real wages and Bagley real wages are taken from Córtes Conde (1979). Real GDP is taken from Córtes Conde (1997) and population is taken from Recchini de Lattes and Lattes (1975).

at the beginning of the period, wages were extremely volatile compared to the period of institutional or contractual labor markets.

Thus, we have some evidence that supports the assertion that the labor market before the 1930s was a spot – or more precisely, noncontractually based – labor market; this was especially so before World War I. Likewise, even during the 1920s, the industrial employment relationships were not contractually based, although industrialization had started to take off. Labor law was virtually nonexistent at both individual and collective levels. It was civil and commercial law that almost exclusively regulated labor relations during the whole period.[12]

[12] The history of the industrial relations of the meat industry in Argentina have, perhaps not surprisingly, a parallel with the development of the labor market of the manufacturing sector, although the meat industry expanded relatively earlier than the rest of the manufacturing sector. Lobato (1998) carefully documents the evolution of labor relations in the meat industry in

Table 5.2. *New World immigration rates by decade*
Per 1,000 mean population

Country	1851–60	1861–70	1871–80	1881–90	1891–1900	1901–10
Argentina	38.5	99.1	117.0	221.7	163.9	291.8
Brazil	—	—	20.4	41.1	72.3	33.8
Canada	99.2	83.2	54.8	78.4	48.8	167.6
US	92.8	64.9	54.6	85.8	53.0	102.0

Source: Ferenczi and Willcox (1929).

5.1.1 The age of mass migration: The composition of the labor force

About 60 million Europeans set sail for the resource-abundant and labor-scarce New World during the century following 1820. Although three-fifths of them arrived on the shores of the United States, Argentina was among the main recipient countries, especially after 1870 (Table 5.2).

Until well into the nineteenth century, the cost of such a move was simply too high to be afforded by free migrants. However, declining costs of passage and augmented family resources would change these conditions throughout the century. Hatton and Williamson (1998) conduct an empirical analysis of the

Berisso, Buenos Aires between 1907 and 1970. From its beginning to its decline, *Frigoríficos, Swift and Armour*, were the mayor employers of Berisso: in 1907, Swift alone had 3,000 employees. However, the number of workers fluctuated widely each day (for example, during a random month in 1915, the number of employees at Swift fluctuated nonmonotonically between 3,190 and 4,070). During this period, the labor market of the meat industry resembled a spot market. The manager of personnel chose among workers at the door to the *frigorífique* where many workers waited in line for "…you, you, and you." Between 1907 and 1930, 80 percent of the workers of Swift had completed employment spells of less than a year, even though many of them had worked for the firm in several prior years. From the stories collected in Lobato (1998), we infer that workers could be fired for any reason and be recalled back, even during the same month.

The relationship between the workers and the *frigorífique* was plagued with conflicts. Among them, the argument over the extension of the working day predominated in the first decades of the century, while wages were the main conflict during the collective bargaining era. Additionally, workers strove for better working conditions: an infirmary was built in 1912 and a new medical service was opened in 1936. The dining room dates from the 1920s and the kindergarten from the 1940s. However, in both the social and productive spaces, hierarchies among laborers were well defined, and it was only during the 1940s that most workers got access to these benefits.

During the 1940s, workers also battled for wage stability. Workers' performance was measured by outcome and, hence, their remuneration was highly volatile. In 1944, the government established a minimum payment scheme: every worker had to receive a minimum payment of 60 hours every two weeks, regardless of the time they worked during that period. Thus, the flexibility of labor relations in the industry was seriously broken.

The 1960s were a period of severe conflicts between workers and the *frigoríficos*. During the first five years of the decade, the motive of conflict was wages. During the last part of the decade, the industry entered a nonreversible decline; workers bargained over employment, opposing suspensions and layouts. By then, the industry trade union was powerful (by way of example, the strike of 1961 lasted 100 days). In 1969 Armour closed its doors. A year later, the multinational company that administered Swift went bankrupt, and Swift was then run by the Argentine state. Ten years later, Swift also closed its doors.

determinants of emigration during the period 1860–1913 by pooling decadal data from twelve European countries. They find that the main variable in explaining European emigration rates during the period considered is the ratio of home- to recipient-country wages, as previously suggested by several other studies.[13]

Figure 5.2 shows net immigration by year between 1870 and 1935. Net immigration was particularly high between 1880 and 1890 and between 1905 and 1915. The distinction between gross and net migration becomes increasingly important as return migration also accelerated from the beginning of the twentieth century. Between 1857 and 1924, return migration from Argentina (by Italians and Spaniards) was 47 percent of the gross inflow. The high return migration rate among Italians represented a growing trend toward temporary, and often seasonal, migration (Hatton and Williamson 1998).

Typically, migrants brought with them both very high labor force participation rates and very low dependency burdens. Thus, although they were unskilled and frequently obtained employment in slow-growth sectors, they contributed to a period of substantial growth in the country. In particular, they favored a dramatic expansion in the agricultural sector.[14]

Although immigrants filled the labor force in a period characterized by scarce labor, there are always some who claim that immigrants caused conditions to deteriorate in domestic labor markets. However, the empirical evidence is contrary to this view: the impact of immigrants on the domestic labor markets is usually negligible (Abowd and Freeman 1991; Friedberg and Hunt 1995). This result is the consequence of the endogeneity of the immigrants' flows. Workers migrate to places where labor demand is buoyant. Thus, it is not surprising that they diminish neither the actual wages of domestic workers nor their employment prospects. However, this is not to say that, *ceteris paribus*, wages would be unaltered if migration were restricted. Taylor (1997) calibrates a general equilibrium model to estimate the impact on wages of the massive flow of immigration to Argentina up to the World War I. His calibration suggests that the flow of immigration would have reduced real wages in Argentina by approximately twenty percent in comparison to the wages that would have prevailed if immigration had not taken place.

[13] However, this model does not explain the timing of movements, but instead just conditions on the (endogenous) wage differential between the country of origin and destination. The authors also find that emigration was positively affected by the rate of natural increase lagged twenty years, and that there is strong evidence of persistence in emigration rates as reflected in two variables: the emigration rate in the previous decade and the stock of previous emigrants living abroad.

[14] Immigrant labor was mobile. They displayed scant concern for long-term commitments that would impede their mobility. This coincided with the kind of labor force required in Argentina during this period (Adelman 1994).

Fig. 5.2. Net immigration

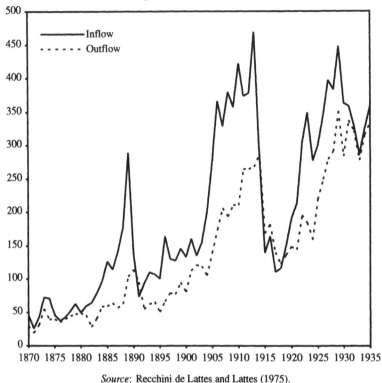

Source: Recchini de Lattes and Lattes (1975).

In any event, real wages increased during this period: between 1883 and 1911, real wages increased approximately one percent per year (Córtes Conde 1979). However, there is not doubt that the flow of immigration to Argentina, or for that matter to the entirety of the New World, had a profound distributive impact. Landlords gained since decreasing labor scarcity raised the land-labor ratio. Capitalists also gained for a similar reason. Williamson (2002) estimates a two hundred percent increase in the land-labor ratio in Argentina between 1880 and 1914. O'Rourke, Taylor, and Williamson (1996) document an eighty percent fall in the ratio of wages to land rents from 1870 to 1910.

5.1.2 Labor relations and trade unions before 1930

The Argentine syndical movement surged during the last two decades of the nineteenth century. However, prior to the 1920s, the role of trade unions was limited. Most of them were craft unions with no formal legal status and were confined exclusively to the state of Buenos Aires. Moreover, during most of this period unions were ideologically divided (Matsushita 1983).[15] There were three prevailing ideological currents among unions: anarchism, socialism, and syndicalism. Although the anarchist strain emerged early on as the predominant ideology, it lost influence after 1910.

The expansion of the economy and the development of some large unions led to the growth of syndicalism. In addition, the empowerment of this syndical current was supported by the intervention of the government between 1916 and 1922. From then, the state became a key player in the relationship between capital and labor. The intervention of the state was decisive at that time. Most employers refused to negotiate with unions unless forced to do so, while unions found it extremely difficult to shut down a plant's operations. Consequently, only the government could apply the necessary coercion to induce negotiation between firms and unions (Torre 1990 and Horowitz 1990).

It was only in 1930 that a confederation of unions was formed, La Confederación General del Trabajo (CGT). Although the socialist unions had more affiliates than the syndicalist unions, the latter group imposed its orientation on the association. In spite of the fact that the majority of union members belonged to the CGT's constituent organizations, the role of the confederation did not increase markedly until the 1940s. In particular, union power decreased significantly after the crisis of 1929. Thus, although a new model of industrialization in Argentina was emerging, which for the first time allowed some scope for the development of unions, the economic crisis delayed this process for several years.

5.2 The period of modern, institutional markets

During the period we refer to as the era of the modern, institutional (or rigid) market, labor relations became contractual, both explicitly and implicitly, at the collective and individual levels. Several circumstances converged in the development of a contractual labor market in Argentina after the recovery from the deep crisis of the early 1930s.

First, after the collapse of world trade, the country based its recovery on the growth of the manufacturing sector. From the early 1940s, the manufacturing and industrial sectors developed under the protection of an inward-looking, import-substitution strategy.[16] The development of a manufacturing sector in a

---

[15] In addition, workers were divided by cultural differences.

[16] It is worth noting that this period may itself be divided into three subperiods. A first period of mild, general industrial protection mainly was achieved through commercial and exchange rate policies and extended into the early 1940s. A second period of high levels of industrial

noncompetitive environment favored the development of powerful trade unions. Additionally, state enterprises spread through the whole economy, empowering unions. The government also considerably expanded its weight in the economy by providing long-term employment relationships.

Second, a prolabor government also favored the development of unions and established a legal system of collective and individual labor legislation during the 1940s and early 1950s (see Appendix). Additionally, during this period, the government not only favored prolabor legislation but also enforced it. Hence, unions obtained the necessary bargaining power needed for their growth.

It is important to note that labor legislation was not limited to the laws of collective organization and bargaining, although these laws remain of prime importance in understanding the historical relationship between law and labor overall. The individual labor legislation was substantial and constitutive of the set of property rights that workers own in their jobs. In particular, it is a mistake to treat the laws of collective activity in isolation from the legal system of individual employment relationships. The latter shapes the space in which collective action operates. The individual labor legislation passed during the 1940s and early 1950s was also decidedly prolabor.

Third, with the expansion of the manufacturing sector, the skill content of jobs increased substantially, especially during the period of development of the heavy industries when the degree of specificity in human capital increased substantially as well. This characteristic of the productive system increased the necessity of both explicit and implicit employment contracts to define and regulate the employment relationship. The labor force also increased in terms of other forms of human capital, especially from the 1950s.

Finally, among the other factors that contributed to the power of the Argentine syndical movement – even up to the present day – the most important was the right granted to unions to administrate the workers' national health insurance system. This characteristic is unique to the Argentine syndical movement, and certainly, it has provided the unions with a considerable and enduring amount of power.

Nevertheless, we shall highlight here a different characteristic of the modern labor market period – the recurrent intervention of the state in the system of industrial relations. The Argentine state has retained the power to interfere in syndical life, a power that has been exercised frequently. What is more,

protection in which the light manufacturing sectors were heavily promoted concurrently with redistributive polices that stimulated the domestic market spanned the first Peronist government. The final period was one in which the heavy manufacturing sectors were resolutely promoted coupled with the development of extensive infrastructure projects (cf. Díaz Alejandro 1970 and Gerchunoff and Llach 1998).

every time the constitutional order has been disrupted, collective bargaining and other labor rights were suppressed. Additionally, under civilian as well as military regimes, wages were determined by the government instead of by collective bargaining. Thus, the deep transformation of the system of labor relations initiated between the 1940s and early 1950s was as unstable as was the economy and its political institutions.[17]

5.2.1 How have unions developed?

The Argentine labor movement is the most important syndical movement of the New World. What are the causes of this phenomenon? One way to answer this question is through an analytical comparison of Argentine union expansion with the development of other trade union movements. This question is intimately related to yet another question: why did some labor movements enjoy remarkable growth in the postwar period while others withered?

Trade unions had become key players in the economies of Europe and North America by 1950. In developed countries, unions organized between one-third and two-thirds of all workers. Forty years later, things had changed markedly. Some syndical movements had grown to the point where they organized virtually the entire labor market, while others represented only a small fraction of workers left in the traditional manufacturing sectors.

Western (1997) presents strong evidence showing that labor movements grew more when they were institutionally insulated from the market forces that drive up competition among workers. Thus, although the reason trade unions developed during the autarkic period of world trade may be clear, the reason we have observed divergent trends in unionization between the 1950s and 1980s is not so evident. Western identifies three conditions essential to union growth that might explain this divergence across developed countries. His historical evidence suggests that union movements have grown where unions control unemployment benefits, where the labor market is centrally organized, and where social democratic parties with close ties to organized labor have been in power.

Labor market centralization promotes the growth of organized labor by reducing employer opposition. In most developed countries, centralization was established in the early 1950s and largely survived until the early 1980s. In Argentina, as in Germany, Australia, New Zealand, and Britain, centralization is of the middle-density type: labor relations are characterized by multi-employer agreements at the industry level with large industrial unions.

---

[17] Furthermore, constitutional governments also controlled unions through political power, and hence, restrained the unions' capacity for bargaining and demand. This was particularly true during the Peronist governments between 1946 and 1955 (Doyon 1984).

The control of the unemployment insurance system boosts unionization by giving unions control over labor market competition from unemployed workers and by maintaining contact between workers and unions during spells of unemployment. In Argentina the unemployment insurance system was developed only during the 1990s, and it is not under the control of unions. However, along similar lines, we argue that the Argentine unions have had an even more powerful resource to sustain their growth, the administration of the workers' health insurance system. This system was originally developed through collective bargaining at the end of the 1950s. Employers agreed to contribute to the funding of the system while unions imposed statutory contributions from their members. During the early 1960s, the government created by law health insurance systems for some industries and some state government employees. Finally, in 1970, there was established a mandatory system for all workers that is financed by the contributions of both employers and employees, irrespective of whether or not the latter are union members, and that is administered by the signatory union in the collective bargaining in that industry. The administration of the system, in addition to providing unions with substantial financial resources, has provided a means to maintain union density at high levels, especially in industries in which direct control of affiliation by the syndicate is too costly, as is the case in industries in which the average size of firms is small (e.g., the trade sector).[18]

The histories of unions and political parties are closely intertwined. However, the link between them is more complicated than it might first appear. Econometric evidence for the effects of prolabor parties on union growth is often weak (see, for example, Booth 1983). Western (1997) argues that this is so because political parties often influence union growth through key events, such as a change in labor law or an intervention in collective bargaining.

In Argentina, the rise of Perón, first as secretary of labor in 1943 and then as president in 1946, substantially influenced the growth of unions, mainly through Perón's passage of prolabor legislation. It is true that, as first stated by Portantiero and Murmis (1971), unions were developing before 1943, and collective bargaining had also been on the rise since 1936 (cf. Gaudio and Pilone 1983 and 1984). Indeed, Ashenfelter and Pencavel (1969) argued that trade union legislation is largely a reflection of the general climate of opinion. However, the prolabor legislation and the state support of unions during the period 1943–55 were further stimuli that foster labor movement growth. Indeed, the Peronist period was a major watershed in the labor history of Argentina (Horowitz 1990). The state shifted the balance between labor and capital in

----

[18] Union members have always been granted privileged attention in the system over nonmembers.

Table 5.3. *Union affiliation during the Peronist period*

Year	1936	1946	1948	1950	1954
Total affiliation	369,969	877,333	1,532,925	1,992,404	2,256,580
Union density (%)	10	22	40	49	49

Notes: Union density rate is total union affiliation divided by total nonagricultural employment.
Sources: Total affiliation is taken from Doyon (1975) and Horowitz (1990). Total nonagricultural employment is taken from IEERAL (1986).

favor of the former, and this action had a noticeable short-term impact, as the share of labor in national income abruptly increased eight percentage points toward the end of the 1940s, as well shall see below.

The growth of union density during the 1940s, although it is likely overestimated, is impressive and of an order of magnitude that is beyond any doubt (see Table 5.3). The union density rate in Britain and the United States in 1935 was 25 and 7 percent, respectively. It was 39 and 23 percent in 1945, while it was 44 and 25 percent in 1955. U.S. union density peaked in 1945 while Britain's density peaked in 1980 with a rate of 53 percent. Argentina's rates seem to have stabilized around 45 percent up until the early 1990s when they dipped below 40 percent. Britain's rates have also decreased since the early 1980s, and they were approximately 40 percent by the early 1990s. Thus, Britain and Argentina show similar union density rates since the 1940s.

5.2.2 *Business cycles and real wages during the era of rigid, modern labor markets*

Although both real wages and output appear to have been less volatile during the period 1930–75 than they had been previously, there are certain characteristics that deserve further consideration. During this period, if we leave aside a few exceptional years, real wages never varied more than five percent from one year to the next (with the downward variation rarely approaching this level); normally, they changed even less than that. However, it is not obvious from the rough data whether or not real wages were less sensitive to output during this period.[19]

To further explore the issue of wage persistence, we condition (linearly) the logarithm of the real wage on its lagged value, the logarithm of gross domestic product per capita, the change in the inflation rate, and its lagged valued. We estimate this regression equation for the periods 1913–29 and 1930–73.

[19] Obviously, the reading of the evidence crucially depends on the underlying view of the business cycle: if it is believed that nominal (as opposed to real) variables determine output, it may be argued that it is the increased rigidity of nominal wages that made output less volatile.

Table 5.4. *Aggregate wage equations*

Dependent variable: logarithm of the average real wages at prices of 1960 (log w_t)

	1913–29	1930–73
log $Prod_t$	1.06* (0.296)	0.18* (0.078)
log w_{t-1}	0.217 (0.228)	0.848* (0.091)
$\Delta \Pi_t$	-0.00396* (0.0011)	-0.00177 * (0.00036
$\Delta \Pi_{t-1}$	0.00252* (0.001125)	0.00118* (0.00033)
Constant	Yes	Yes
R^2	0.92	0.94
Specification tests:		
First-order autocorrelation	$F(1, 9) = 1.054$ (0.33)	$F(1, 37) = 0.093$ (0.76)
ARCH	$F(1, 8) = 0.67$ (0.44)	$F(1, 36) = 0.167$ (0.68)
RESET	$F(1, 9) = 1.56$ (0.24)	$F(1, 37) = 0.107$ (0.745)
Observations	15	45

Notes: * Statistically different from 0 at the 0.05 level of significance. w_t is the real average wage from IEERAL (1986), $Prod_t$ is GDP per capita at prices of 1990 from Maddison (1995). Π_t is the inflation rate. Standard errors are robust to departure from homoskedasticity. The regression for the period 1930–73 includes a dummy variable for the year 1946 and a dummy variable for the year 1947. If these (Peronist) dummies are not included, the estimated model is similar (coefficients and standard errors are almost the same) but the overall stability of the model is lost.

All the coefficients have the expected sign and are statistically significant at the 5 percent level, with the exception of the lagged dependent variable in the regression function for the period 1913–29 (Table 5.4). These results show that wages became much more persistent (rigid) during the institutional labor market period than they were during the previous spot market period. As wages became substantially more persistent, they were affected substantially less by changes in output.[20]

5.3 The search for a modern, flexible labor market

Since the late 1940s, the Argentine economy has operated under high inflation rates. Real wages are likely to be more flexible in an inflationary and volatile environment than in a stable economy. However, during the period in which the economy operated under the regime of high inflation (Frenkel 1979), wages were indexed to the past level of inflation – the period of adjustment being

[20] As shown, we ran a set of specification tests. We tested the null hypothesis of no first-order residual autocorrelation, the null of no first-order autocorrelated squared errors, and the null hypothesis of correct specification of the original model against the alternative that powers of the predicted value of the dependent variable have been omitted in the specification of the model (the RESET test). For both specifications reported in Table 5.4, we do not reject the null hypotheses of these tests at the conventional level of statistical significance (the statistics and the *p*-values are reported in Table 5.4). Additionally, a graphical analysis, based on recursive estimation of the models, shows that the null hypothesis of constancy of the parameters of the empirical models reveals no problems.

reduced, the higher the volatility of the inflationary process (cf. Frenkel 1984; Heymann and Leijonhufvud 1995). Thus, wage flexibility was mainly achieved through recurrent episodes with a blunt acceleration in inflation. These types of episodes, in conjunction with state intervention in the wage determination process, are capable of providing huge levels of real wage flexibility.[21]

By the early 1970s, it was clear that the strategy of inward-looking import substitution adopted during the early 1940s could not be sustained any longer. The economy needed to recover full access to world markets for capital and goods to restore a process of economic growth.[22] Additionally, in 1975, inflation reached an unprecedented level of almost two hundred percent. What is more, public perspectives on inflation were now hostile. Argentines had had enough; inflation had to be eliminated. This mood notwithstanding, it was clear that any attempt to stabilize prices would face a hurdle in the labor market.[23] The bargaining structure of Argentina was extremely inflationary. Strong unions in an extremely closed economy without any bargaining coordination is a recipe for competitive behavior between unions, leapfrogging wage demands, and, ultimately, higher unemployment rates as attempts are made to suppress inflationary pressures.[24]

This period may be characterized as one in which economic and labor market policies sought to provide the labor market with a higher degree of institutional flexibility; ultimately, this was a development achieved mainly, but not solely, in the 1990s. Interestingly enough, the main strategy adopted during this period to reduce wage pressure and discipline unions has been the increase of product market competition through trade liberalization.[25]

The military government that took power in 1976 established as its main economic goal the reduction of inflation. To achieve a successful stabilization of prices the government had to eliminate its chronic fiscal deficit. However,

---

[21] State intervention in wage determination was a characteristic of the modern era until the 1990s when price stability was finally achieved. This shows that the modern era was, perhaps, not that modern after all.

[22] The development of trading institutions in the 1950s and 1960s laid the ground for a massive growth in the global economy. World trade was further liberalized in 1973.

[23] We are not arguing that high inflation was the result of wage pushes. What we are arguing is that if money growth were suppressed, wage demands still would have been inconsistent with price stability.

[24] However, highly centralized wage bargaining systems may overcome some of the externalities generated by decentralized collective bargaining and moderate wage pressure. The problem for the fully unionized economy is the potential fragility of the coordination element. Coordination has elements of instability for all the usual reasons displayed in standard oligopoly models (see Nickell and Layard 2000).

[25] The military governments that ruled the country between 1976 and 1983 attempted to discipline unions by temporarily suppressing collective bargaining and some other syndical rights – an illegitimate and myopic strategy that did not work in the end.

in a highly inflationary economy, the fiscal deficit itself may be considered an endogenous variable. Lurking beneath the disorder in public finances, one typically finds a system of institutions unable to resolve conflicts that revolve chiefly around the distribution of income (Heymann and Leijonhufvud 1995; Mallon and Sourrouille 1975).[26]

Therefore, a necessary condition to stabilize prices in Argentina was the elimination of the high level of wage pressure, which was prevalent at even low unemployment levels and which reflected the struggle between workers and firms (and amongst workers) for their share in the distribution of income (Canitrot 1975; Mallon and Sourrouille, 1975).

In a closed economy, it may be the case that a fully decentralized bargaining system reduces wage demands in comparison to a system of bargaining at the industry level. This follows because, in a closed economy, the relevant elasticity of labor demand taken into account in wage bargaining is lower at the industry level than at the firm level. Conversely, in an open economy, a country's share of any industrial market is quite small. Thus, industry-wide bargaining may be only slightly more harmful than fully decentralized bargaining (see Layard, Nickell, and Jackman 1991).

Only as late as 2000 was there a serious attempt to decentralize the collective bargaining system within the boundaries of constitutional law. Otherwise, the *only* powerful reform implemented to weaken union power during the last three decades has been the increase in product market competition. The most prominent reforms of the modern period, a massive privatization program and a wide-ranging trade liberalization process, were implemented at the beginning of the 1990s and have considerably reduced the power of unions. Certainly, these policies were not implemented explicitly to reduce the power of unions, but they contributed to the achievement of that goal.

The debate on labor market reform has been at the center of the discussion on economic policy since the beginning of the 1990s, and the debate has intensified with the increase in the unemployment rate observed during the last few years. The debate revolves around the decentralization of the collective bargaining system and the reduction of the high dismissal costs prevalent in Argentina. At the beginning of the 1990s, the reforms introduced a wide menu of fixed-term contracts of employment. However, the reforms were later undone – a process that reflected dissatisfaction with the results.

---

[26] As part of the macroeconomic program of the military government a wide although gradual program of trade liberalization was implemented. The program itself was used as an instrument to reduce inflation, and the timing of tariff reduction was accelerated at the end of the 1970s when the stabilization program was not producing sufficient gains in reducing inflation (see Canitrot 1980 and 1981).

5.3.1 Labor market institutions

In this subsection we study the main Argentine labor market institutions by relying on a series of cross-country comparisons.[27] The institutions we consider are trade unions and the structure of wage bargaining, employment protection, and the treatment of the unemployed.

Most workers in the OECD outside the United States have their wages determined by collective agreements that are negotiated at the plant, firm, industry, or even national level. In the first two columns of Table 5.5 we show the percentage of employees who belong to a trade union and an indicator of the percentage of workers covered by collective agreements (3 means over 70 percent, 2 means 25 to 70 percent, and 1 means under 25 percent).

The main point that emerges here is that even if the number of union members is very low, as in France and Spain, it is still possible for most workers to have their wages set by union agreements. This occurs because, within firms, nonunion workers typically get the union negotiated rate and because, in many countries, union rates of pay are legally extended to cover nonunion firms (collective agreements have effects *erga omnes*). In Argentina around 45 percent of employees belong to a union and half of all employees are covered. The latter places Argentina somewhere in the spectrum between Europe and the United States. Not surprisingly, most of the covered workers in Argentina work in large firms; workers in small firms (fewer than 25 workers) are typically not represented by a union.[28]

An important aspect of union-based pay bargaining is the extent to which unions and/or firms coordinate their wage determination activities. For example, in both Germany and Japan, employers' associations are actively involved in the preparation for wage bargaining even when the bargaining itself ostensibly occurs at the level of the individual firm (cf. Nickell and Layard 2000). Columns 3 and 4 of Table 5.5 present indices of union coordination and employer coordination. The coordination indices go from a low of 1 to a high of 3. The most coordinated economies are those of Scandinavia and Austria, followed by continental Europe and Japan. The Anglo-Saxon economies, including Ireland, exhibit little or no coordination, despite having quite high levels of union density and coverage in some cases.

Turning to Argentina, it is found that most workers whose pay is covered by a collective agreement have their wages determined, at least initially, by industry-wide bargains struck between a national industry union and one or more employer federations. Further wage agreements may be struck at lower

---

[27] This subsection is based on Galiani and Nickell (1999).
[28] The data are from the Household Survey Supplement of 1990.

Table 5.5. *Trade unions and wage bargaining in the late 80s and early 90s*

	Union Density (%)	Union Coverage Index	Union Coordi- nation	Employer Coordi- nation	Employment Protection Ranking
Austria	46.2	3	3	3	16
Belgium	51.2	3	2	2	17
Denmark	71.4	3	3	3	5
Finland	72.0	3	2	3	10
France	9.8	3	2	2	14
Germany (West)	32.9	3	2	3	15
Ireland	49.7	3	1	1	12
Italy	38.8	3	2	2	20
Netherlands	25.5	3	2	2	9
Norway	56.0	3	3	3	11
Portugal	31.8	3	2	2	18
Spain	11.0	3	2	1	19
Sweden	82.5	3	3	3	13
Switzerland	26.6	2	1	3	6
U.K.	39.1	2	1	1	7
Canada	35.8	2	1	1	3
U.S.	15.6	1	1	1	1
Japan	25.4	2	2	2	8
Australia	40.4	3	2	1	4
New Zealand	44.8	2	1	1	2
Argentina	45.0	2	2	1	10

Notes: Union density is trade union members as a percentage of all wage/salary earners. Union coverage is an index, 3 = over 70% covered, 2 = 25–70%, 1= under 25%. Union and Employer coordination in wage bargaining is an index with 3 = high, 2 = middle, 1 = low.
Sources: Nickell and Layard (2000) and Galiani and Nickell (1999).

levels right down to the firm level using the industry-wide agreement as a basis. There is no evidence of any coordination of bargaining across industries, nor is there any coordination in the timing of the separate bargains.

In the last column of Table 5.5 we present an overall ranking of employment protection derived by the OECD along with an estimate of Argentina's final position. Note that in this ranking, a higher number means a stricter system. Argentina has a relatively generous system of severance pay. On the other hand, the actual procedures (for example, the notice period) are straightforward. Overall, Argentina lies about half way up the OECD ranking, well below the strict systems of Southern Europe but offering more legal job security than is standard in North America.

Lastly, turning to the unemployment benefit system, the important issues are the amount of benefit and the length of time for which the benefit is available. The Argentine system is relatively generous, but of a fixed term (it lasts at most

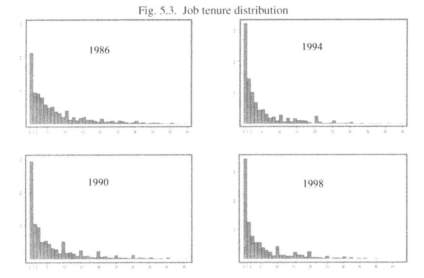

Fig. 5.3. Job tenure distribution

Notes and Sources: Histograms show tenure in years on the horizontal axis and fraction of years (frequency) on the vertical axis, using 45 accumulating intervals. Data are from the permanent household survey of Greater Buenos Aires. See Galiani (2002).

a year) and with minimal coverage (around 5 percent of the unemployed) as a result of the restrictive rules on entitlement.[29]

5.3.2 Job stability

Finally, we analyze the recent evolution of job stability.[30] Figure 5.3 shows the empirical probability distribution of reported tenure for the years 1986, 1990, 1994, and 1998. The rough shape of these distributions are similar: the highest proportion of workers are reporting tenure in the range 0–1 years with this proportion declining nearly monotonically for subsequent years. The empirical distributions of 1994 and 1998 have significantly shifted mass to the left in comparison to the distribution of 1986.

We pursue our analysis by evaluating the change in the one-year conditional retention rates. The overall retention rate did not change significantly between

---

[29] Indeed, the requirements are strict but every unionized worker with some tenure qualifies. For that reason, coverage was higher in 1993 when the manufacturing sector was shedding labor. However, as the unemployment inflow has become dominated by employees ending fix-term contracts and self-employers, the coverage of the system has been reduced to minimum levels.

[30] The empirical results of this subsection are taken from Galiani (2002).

1986 and 1990, when it decreased 1 percentage point, while between 1986 and 1998 the same statistic decreased 5.5 percentage points.

The one-year retention rate in the first year of tenure decreased 12 percentage points between 1986 and 1998. We find evidence that the unskilled group has been the one that suffered most. Notwithstanding, the semiskilled group has also been severely affected. Certainly, the contrast in the changes observed for Argentina with those for the United States is impressive. In the United States, the one-year retention rate of the first year of tenure did not change noticeably in recent decades (Diebold, Neumark, and Polsky 1997).

Overall, workers gained job stability during the century; however, that stability has dissipated for unskilled workers during the last two decades while the labor market has searched for a more flexible organization. Only skilled workers have retained the same level of job stability during the last two decades.

5.4 Labor market performance over the century

In this section we present some of the most important changes in the labor market over the century. In turn, we present long-term trends in labor supply, its composition, employment and its sectoral distribution, wages and productivity, income distribution, human capital, and unemployment.

5.4.1 Population

The Argentine population grew at extremely high rates up to World War I (Table 5.6). It is clear that rates of population growth decreased substantially between the census of 1914 and the census of 1947; the turning point occurred, most likely, during the 1920s. These initial high rates of population growth coincided with even higher rates of growth of the nonnative population as a result of the enormous flows of immigrants that the country received between 1870 and 1914. For example, the annual rate of growth in the nonnative population was approximately 5 percent between the first and third censuses and was close to 0 percent between 1914 and 1947.

Table 5.6 shows the increase in the immigrant population, mainly from southern Europe, as a share of total population up to 1914, at which time it was 30 percent of the total population. Between 1896 and 1914, the growth in the immigrant population directly contributed 35 percent of the increase in total population.[31] After World War I, overseas immigration decreased, and it has been losing weight in the share of total population ever since. Total nonnative

---

[31] Of course, this is just a lower bound estimate of the total impact of immigration on population growth (see Taylor 1994).

Table 5.6. *Population and its origins*

	1869	1895	1914	1947	1960	1970	1980	1991
Total population (million)	1.737	3.955	7.885	15.984	20.011	23.390	27.947	32.616
Immigrants in total population (%)	12.1	25.5	30.3	15.2	13.0	9.5	6.8	5.0
Immigrants by origin (%):								
Border countries	19.7	11.5	8.6	12.9	17.9	24.2	39.6	50.2
Rest of the world	80.3	88.5	91.4	87.1	82.1	75.8	60.4	49.8
Spain	20.2	22.3	38.5	35.3	33.5	30.7	32.5	—
Italy	42.3	55.3	43.1	37.0	41.1	38.0	42.5	—
Others	37.6	22.4	18.4	27.7	25.4	31.3	25.0	—

Source: Recchini de Lattes and Lattes (1975) and authors' calculations based on national censuses of population.

population itself decreased substantially in share of total population during the rest of the century, and in 1991 it was only 5 percent of total population. Since 1914, the annual rate of growth of border immigrants has always been positive and was particularly high between 1947 and 1960 (Marshal and Orlansky 1983) and between 1970 and 1980.[32]

Migration also took place within the country among the native population. Internal migration was at its highest between the censuses of 1947 and 1960. Additionally, during this period migration was almost unidirectional, from the north of the country to the growing manufacturing district of Buenos Aires.

5.4.2 Labor force composition and its evolution

It is extremely difficult to determine the level of labor force participation consistently for the past 100 years. The modern definition of the labor force took form with the 1940 federal population census in the United States and is defined as the sum of all individuals (over a given age) working plus those actively seeking work during a specific period of time. In Argentina, however, the modern definition of the labor force was adopted only in 1970. Nevertheless, Recchini de Lattes and Lattes (1975) present estimates of the labor force for certain census years from 1947. In Table 5.7, we extend these figures to the latest census.

Several important trends are represented by Table 5.7, which summarizes changes in the demographic composition of the labor force over the past one hundred years. The proportion of female workers in the labor force increased from 26 percent in 1947 to 33.2 percent in 1991. Thus, male participation in the labor force decreased from approximately 54 to 48.5 percent. These

---

[32] Of the 110,000 nonnative residents in the census of 1980 that did not live in the country before 1976, over 90 percent of them were borders immigrants.

Table 5.7. *Labor force participation rates by sex and age group*

Percent

Males	1869	1896	1914	1947	1960	1970	1980	1991
10–14	44.4	39.1	34.5	25.3	18.4	11.5	6.4	3.0
15–19	89.8	80.6	76.0	72.5	75.5	62.2	47.5	40.8
20–24	95.3	94.3	93.1	90.1	93.5	87.4	79.1	75.4
25–29	96.8	95.9	95.8	96.6	97.6	96.7	95.6	88.9
30–34	96.8	96.8	97.0	97.6	98.5	98.2	97.8	91.8
35–39	96.6	97.1	97.4	98.0	98.4	98.5	98.6	92.8
40–44	96.0	96.5	96.9	97.7	97.2	97.8	98.4	91.9
45–49	95.4	96.0	96.3	96.8	95.2	95.8	96.4	90.6
50–54	94.4	93.7	93.8	95.3	91.6	91.7	91.8	86.3
55–59	92.9	91.3	90.9	91.9	81.5	80.4	79.2	78.7
60–64	90.6	88.0	86.5	84.5	66.4	57.2	47.5	59.1
65–69	86.9	82.7	78.9	71.0	47.1	39.0	31.3	37.5
70–74	79.3	78.2	72.9	54.8	37.5	27.1	18.0	24.7
74+	67.3	78.2	72.9	54.8	37.5	27.1	8.3	12.8
All	86.0	84.8	83.4	82.0	78.7	73.2	68.8	63.4
Females	1869	1896	1914	1947	1960	1970	1980	1991
10–14	—	—	—	9.1	7.2	6.2	5.2	4.7
15–19	—	—	—	30.0	34.8	31.9	29.1	23.5
20–24	—	—	—	34.4	40.1 '	44.2	48.4	45.1
25–29	—	—	—	27.1	29.6	36.6	40.4	50.2
30–34	—	—	—	23.0	24.5	31.8	36.5	49.9
35–39	—	—	—	21.5	22.7	29.3	36.5	50.4
40–44	—	—	—	20.4	21.6	27.1	34.6	51.1
45–49	—	—	—	19.4	19.5	25.2	31.7	49.4
50–54	—	—	—	17.7	15.5	22.1	27.6	42.9
55–59	—	—	—	15.3	12.1	16.2	22.1	32.5
60–64	—	—	—	13.0	9.1	10.3	15.6	20.9
65–69	—	—	—	10.1	7.0	6.8	6.7	13.4
70–74	—	—	—	7.5	5.0	4.4	4.1	8.4
74+	—	—	—	6.0	3.3	2.3	1.5	4.4
All	—	—	—	26.0	21.6	24.3	27.1	33.2

Notes: Labor force participation rates are not strictly comparable among Censuses, especially, before 1947. For this reason, we do not present the female participation rates before 1947 since the figures from these Censuses result in severely biased estimates of the Labor participation rates. In any case, they are not available for the 1914 census. The labor force participation of the age group 10–14 is estimated since 1970 (see Recchini de Lattes and Lattes 1975).

Source: Recchini de Lattes and Lattes (1975) and authors' calculations based on censuses.

figures, however, mask disparate trends. A clearer account of the forces at work is gained through a look at the labor force trends of middle-aged groups. Between 1947 and 1991, the female labor force participation rate of the age group 25–50 approximately doubled (e.g., it increased from 23 to 49.9 percent for age group 30–34) while the male labor force rate decreased slightly for the same age group (by approximately 5 percentage points).

Table 5.8. *Comparative labor force statistics*

	Women's participation rate, 1993 (%) (1)	Early retirement index (%) (2)	Self employment share of total employment, 1990 (%) (3)	Annual hours worked per worker, 1992 (4)
Austria	58.7	60	6.7	1,610
Belgium	55.2	65	14.3	1,580
Denmark	78.3	31	6.8	1,510
Finland	70.0	55	8.8	1,768
France	59.0	54	9.1	1,654
Germany	55.2	42	8.0	1,610
Ireland	46.1	35	12.8	1,720
Italy	43.3	64	22.2	1,730
Netherlands	56.0	54	8.1	1,510
Norway	70.8	27	6.1	1,437
Portugal	62.0	33	15.9	2,004
Spain	43.0	38	17.5	1,815
Sweden	75.8	25	7.1	1,485
Switzerland	67.6	18	—	1,637
U.K.	65.3	32	12.4	1,720
Canada	67.7	35	7.5	1,714
U.S.	69.0	32	7.7	1,919
Japan	61.8	17	11.6	1,965
Australia	62.3	37	12.5	1,850
New Zealand	63.2	43	14.7	1,812
Argentina	39.7	27	21.4	2,059

Notes: (1) OECD Employment outlook (1996), table K, p.197. Female labor force divided by female working population (15–64) in 1993. West Germany is for 1990. Argentina: Household survey, May 1997. (2) OECD Employment outlook (1996), table B, p.188. Defined as (100 percent participation rate in 1990 for males aged 55–64) Argentina: Household survey, May 1997. (3) OECD Jobs Study (1994), table 6.8. Percentage share of self-employment in total employment in the non-agricultural sector. Argentina: Household survey, May 1997. (4) OECD Employment outlook (1996), table C, p. 190. Average annual hours worked per employee (1992). Argentina: Household survey, May 1997.
Source: Nickell and Layard (2000) and Galiani and Nickell (1999).

Column 1 of Table 5.8 compares female labor force participation rates in developed countries to that of Argentina in 1993. This cross-country comparison shows that female participation rates in Argentina are still well below those of the developed countries, even Italy and Spain.[33] In the remaining columns, we report a number of different aspects of labor input, most of which are self-explanatory.

[33] The female labor force participation rate in Argentina reported in Table 5.9 is above the one reported in Table 5.8 for 1991 because the former is the participation rate of densely populated urban areas only while the census figure covers the whole country. Similarly, these statistics differ because Table 5.9 only covers the population of Greater Buenos Aires, which is the area densely populated area.

Table 5.9. *Labor force participation rates*
Household survey data (Greater Buenos Aires) in percent

	Standard measures			Excluding students		
	All	Males	Females	All	Males	Females
1974[1]	62.2	88.1	38.9	—	—	—
1980	61.2	85.4	38.7	61.3	90.0	37.7
1981	59.9	83.7	38.1	59.8	88.4	36.6
1982	59.9	83.9	38.7	61.2	88.7	39.0
1984	60.7	84.0	39.2	62.3	89.4	39.4
1985	60.3	83.3	39.1	62.2	89.5	39.8
1986	62.3	84.4	42.8	63.6	90.2	43.0
1987	62.4	84.2	42.9	63.9	89.7	43.2
1988	62.9	83.6	44.2	66.1	90.2	45.4
1989	63.1	83.6	44.2	67.7	90.7	46.5
1990	63.9	84.1	45.2	68.7	91.8	47.7
1991	63.3	83.7	44.4	68.5	91.7	46.9
1992	64.5	84.5	46.0	70.0	92.3	49.5
1993	65.7	84.1	48.6	71.3	91.9	52.2
1994	65.9	84.1	48.8	72.0	92.3	52.6
1995	67.5	84.1	51.8	73.4	92.5	55.3
1996	68.1	84.8	52.3	73.8	92.6	55.8
1997	67.5	83.5	52.2	73.2	92.2	55.3
1998	67.3	83.5	52.4	74.1	93.0	56.5

Notes: All statistics are calculated for the age group 15–64. [1]The statistics for 1974 were obtained from INDEC press reports and correspond to the age group 15–69.
Source: Galiani (2002).

Column 1 in Table 5.9 shows that the participation rates for the 15–64 age group appear to have declined until the mid-1980s when they began climbing upward, particularly during the 1990s. However, a different picture emerges if the indicator excludes (from both the numerator and the denominator) those individuals attending a school or college. After taking into account the negative effect on labor supply produced by longer periods of education, participation rates have increased steadily since the early 1980s (see column 4). The female labor force grew in importance throughout the period: with or without correction for school attendance, the raw data indicate that the participation rate for the 15–64 age group rose from less than 40 percent in the early 1980s to more than 52 percent by the late 1990s.

Thus, for the central age groups, the rates of female labor force participation increased substantially during the second part of the century while the rates of male labor force participation decreased slightly. Additionally, labor force participation was reduced at both tails of the age distribution as a result of the rise of earlier retirement and the increase in educational attainment levels. Still, the participation of males in the age group 15–64 is relatively high in Argentina

Table 5.10. *Employment sectoral distribution*
Percent

	1895	1914	1947	1960	1970	1991
Primary sector	34.9	26.8	27.2	20.3	16.7	11.5
Secondary sector	29.8	35.6	29.7	35.4	33.8	25.1
Manufacturing	27.1	31.3	25.0	27.8	23.9	17.5
Construction	2.6	3.9	4.2	6.4	8.7	6.8
Electricity, gas and water	0.1	0.4	0.5	1.3	1.2	0.9
Tertiary (service) sector	35.4	37.6	43.1	44.3	49.5	63.3
Trade and Finances	13.3	16.2	14.0	13.5	16.7	26.1
Transport and Communications	3.8	3.4	6.1	7.8	6.85	5.2
Other Services	18.4	18.0	23.1	23.0	25.9	32.0

Notes and sources: Authors' calculations based on censuses.

(column 2 in Table 5.9). Similar trends have been observed in most developed countries during this century.

Finally, we consider the evolution of work hours per week, which decreased considerably at the beginning of the century. From the late 1920s to the early 1940s, the average number of hours per week in industry decreased from fifty to forty-six, close to the legal maximum. Presently, the average number of hours per week effectively worked is approximately forty-two (2,059 per year), which is well above that of the developed countries (see column 4, Table 5.8).

5.4.3 Employment structure

The relative decline of agriculture and rise of the tertiary (service) sector can be seen in Table 5.10, which presents the sectoral distribution of the labor force. Employment in the primary sector constituted 35 percent of total employment at the end of the nineteenth century, and during the past one hundred years decreased to approximately 10 percent. Starting in the 1960s, employment in the manufacturing sector also declined from a relatively high level apparent since the beginning of the twentieth century. Nevertheless, the data before 1947 are not very reliable. Finally, the proportion of employment in the tertiary sector doubled during the past one hundred years. The trends in employment distribution in Argentina are similar to the trends observed in all developed countries during this century.

5.4.4 Earnings and productivity

In the long run, wages are determined by productivity. However, in the short run, wages may respond to other factors. Real annual wages almost tripled during

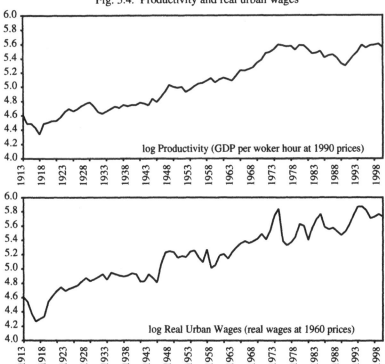

Fig. 5.4. Productivity and real urban wages

Notes and Sources: Wages are taken from Véganzonès and Winograd (1997) up to 1990, and this
series is continued until 1999 by applying the rate of growth of average wages estimated from the
household survey for Greater Buenos Aires. GDP and employment are taken from IEERAL
(1986) up to 1984, and these series are continued until 1999 by applying the rates of growth of
GDP (at prices of 1986) taken from CEPAL and total urban employment estimated from the
household survey. Average hours per week are estimated by fitting a time trend to the available
information through the century.

the century. A similar trend exists for productivity (see Figure 5.4). However,
the growth of both series has not been smooth, as both are nonstationary and
cointegrated (i.e., they have a long-run elasticity equal to one; see Figure 5.5).
By taking into account the change in hours worked through the century, it is
possible to obtain a unit elasticity of real wages to labor productivity. Thus,
the fitted values of the real wage shown in Figure 5.5 may be considered the
equilibrium path of real wages.

As such, Figure 5.5 is very informative. Notice that wages always revert
to their (stochastic) equilibrium path, which is determined by labor productivity. However, there were several salient deviations during the century as
a result of diverse economic phenomena. First, after the crisis of 1929, real

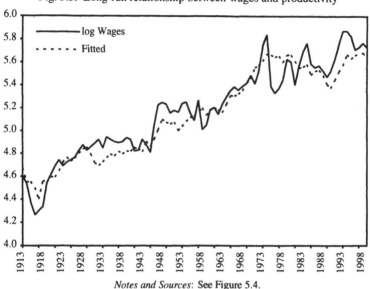

Fig. 5.5. Long-run relationship between wages and productivity

Notes and Sources: See Figure 5.4.

wages were above their long-run trend but seem to have converged to it relatively fast, especially after 1932. It is worth noting that this was a period of
price deflation. Second, during the first Peronist government, wages increased
abruptly to unsustainable levels in terms of labor productivity, and also adjusted
downward abruptly twice during this period, in 1950 and in 1955 after Perón
fell from power. Rather similar episodes took place at the end of the Peronist
governments of the early 1970s and in 1984. In all these cases, the downward
adjustment of wages was preceded by a strong devaluation of the Argentine
currency. Finally, also during the early 1990s, real wages rose well above their
long-run trend; however, on this occasion, the currency was not devalued, but
real wages finally did start to converge to trend after unemployment soared in
1995 and remained well above 10 percent during the rest of the decade.

5.4.5 *Labor productivity growth and its sources*

The most utilized decomposition of labor productivity is one that divides it into
two sources. One is the increase in productivity attributable to the enlargement
of the stock of tangible capital that is available to aid each worker, or the
contribution of the growth in capital intensity. The other element is the residual
of the increase in labor productivity not attributable to tangible capital, or the

Table 5.11. *Sources of labor productivity growth*

Period	Labor productivity growth rate	Percentage of labor productivity growth due to capital intensity growth	Percentage of labor productivity growth due to crude TFP growth
1900–92	1.3	37	63
1900–29	1.4	19	81
1930–43	0.7	−34	134
1944–80	1.8	52	48
1981–92	−0.1	30	70
1993–97	3.0	40	60

Notes and sources: Authors' calculations based on equation 2.4 and Table 2.5 in Véganzonès and Winograd (1997). Except: 1993–97 based on Kydland and Zarazaga (2000) and equation 2.4 in Véganzonès and Winograd (1997).

crude total factor productivity (TFP), denoted A. Thus, the growth rate of real output per unit of labor input can be expressed as

$$(Y^* - L^*) = A^* + \theta(K^* - L^*),$$

where Y stands for output, L for labor, and K for tangible capital stock, the asterisk denotes the per annum rate of increase, and the coefficient θ is the elasticity of output with respect to capital.

On average, labor productivity grew 1.3 percent per year during the period 1900–1992. Sixty-three percent of the rise of labor productivity is accounted by the increase in total factor productivity and, hence, the remaining 37 percent is due to the growth in capital per worker (see Table 5.11). Labor productivity growth accelerated during the 1990s when both the stock of capital per worker and total factor productivity grew at a higher rate.

More generally, for the period as a whole, total factor productivity accounts for roughly one-fourth of Argentina's growth – slightly less than capital, which accounts for 33 percent, and less still than labor, which accounts for the remaining 42 percent of Argentine growth (see Véganzonès and Winograd 1997).[34]

Labor productivity growth varied from period to period. Between 1944 and 1980 there was substantial growth of which roughly 50 percent is accounted for by the increase in total factor productivity and 50 percent by the growth in capital per worker. It also grew at a high rate between 1900 and 1930. Interestingly, labor productivity grew less during the period 1900 to 1930 than between 1944 and 1980 even though GDP grew more during the former period. Two factors contribute to this phenomenon: labor grew at a rate of 2.6 percent per year

[34] For a more detailed study of growth accounting in Argentina for the period 1950–2000 see Hopenhayn and Neumeyer (2001).

Table 5.12. *Population by education level*

Percent

Year	No education	Primary	Secondary	Higher
1910	25.0	63.0	11.0	0.5
1930	22.0	69.0	8.0	0.7
1947	13.6	77.4	7.8	1.2
1960	9.5	71.0	16.0	3.5
1970	5.7	69.0	20.5	4.7
1980	2.9	65.0	25.1	7.1
1991	2.1	54.8	31.7	11.4

Source: Véganzonès and Winograd (1997).

Table 5.13. *Enrollment rates*

Percent

Year	Primary	Secondary	Higher
1895	30	—	—
1914	59	—	—
1960	98	27	11
1970	99	45	15
1980	99	56	22
1990	99	72	38

Source: Véganzonès and Winograd (1997).

during the period 1900 to 1930 compared to 1.6 percent per year between 1944 and 1980, while the stock of capital grew at a rate of 3.5 percent per year during the former period compared to 4.7 percent per year during the latter period. Finally, labor productivity slipped during the 1980s when neither the capital stock nor total factor productivity increased.

5.4.6 Education and human capital

The progress of labor across the twentieth century is closely associated with educational advances. The virtual elimination of child labor, the rise of the female labor force, the rise in real wages, and the evolution of various modern labor market institutions can all be related to educational progress (see Goldin 2000). Mean years of schooling by birth cohort increased quite steadily for both males and females across the century (see Tables 5.12 and 5.13).

5.4.7 Income distribution

The share of labor in national income prior to the 1940s used to be around 40 percent. During the first Peronist government (1946–52) it increased to 50.9

Fig. 5.6. Labor's share in national income

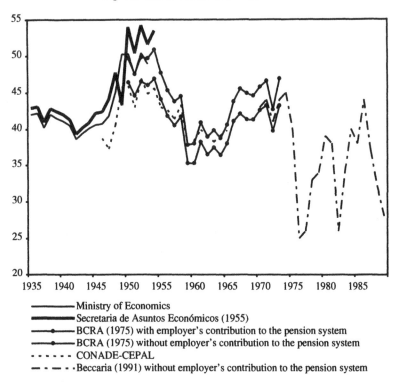

──────Ministry of Economics
━━━━━Secretaria de Asuntos Económicos (1955)
──●──BCRA (1975) with employer's contribution to the pension system
──●──BCRA (1975) without employer's contribution to the pension system
· · · · · · CONADE-CEPAL
─ · ─ · ·Beccaria (1991) without employer's contribution to the pension system

Sources: Ministry of Economics; CONADE-CEPAL (1965); De Pablo (1979); Beccaria (1991).

percent as shown in Figure 5.6.[35] After 1954, however, the share of labor in income returned to the levels seen in the more distant past. It recovered again during the1960s and early 1970s, but had an impressive fall in 1976 to its minimum as a result of the blunt adjustment imposed by the military government. Since then, it has fluctuated widely around 35 percent.

The rise in the income share of labor during the first Peronist government was clearly unsustainable. Additionally, its reversion to the trend illustrates the impossibility of fundamentally altering income distribution through redistributive policies. It is interesting to notice that the government increased the share of labor through several policies (e.g., thirteen salary, paid vacations, and higher real wages), but after a few years the share of labor in income returned

---

[35] The figure of 50.9 percent includes employers' contribution to the social security system; it was 46.9 percent excluding them.

Table 5.14. *Income distribution, employees by decile*
Percent

Year	Decile									
	1	2	3	4	5	6	7	8	9	10
1953	2.7	4.7	5.8	6.9	7.8	9.1	10.5	12.0	14.9	25.6
1959	2.8	5.0	6.0	6.7	8.0	8.9	10.2	12.0	14.7	25.5
1961	2.4	4.5	5.6	6.5	7.9	9.0	10.5	11.9	14.8	27.0
1974	2.4	4.8	6.2	7.0	8.0	9.0	10.5	12.2	14.7	25.2
1980	2.9	4.5	5.3	6.3	7.1	8.1	9.5	11.6	14.8	29.8
1985	2.8	4.5	5.6	6.4	7.3	8.5	9.7	11.6	15.1	28.6
1989	2.0	3.6	4.5	5.4	6.4	7.4	8.9	11.4	16.2	34.2
1993	2.7	4.3	5.4	6.1	7.2	8.3	9.6	11.5	15.1	29.9
1999	2.0	3.8	5.0	5.9	7.1	8.3	9.6	11.7	15.7	31.0

Sources: For 1953, 1959, and 1961, authors' calculations based on CEPAL (1959). Since 1974, authors' calculations based on the household survey data tapes for Greater Buenos Aires.

to its previous level. A similar experiment, although one more immediately costly to workers, was the wage policy of the Peronist governments of the early 1970s. Both episodes ended in a balance of payment crisis (see Gerchunoff and Llach 1998). Thus, the Peronist strategy of altering the distribution of income by arbitrarily raising real wages (without accompanying increases in productivity) was condemned to failure since, in the long run, real wages are ultimately determined by the performance of the economy. Therefore, these episodes can also be understood as illustrations of the weakness of populist policies.

Table 5.14 shows the distribution of wages since the early 1950s. Here we consider the distribution of income among workers instead of between capital and labor. The first salient feature is that the distribution of wages was almost invariant until the mid-1970s. It has clearly worsened since 1974, as wages have become more unequally distributed. Until 1974, only the workers in the first decile of the distribution lost out while the workers in the third decile apparently gained at their expense. Comparing the wage distributions of 1974 and the late 1990s, however, almost all deciles lost, save the workers in the ninth and tenth deciles.[36]

Turning to the evolution of the wage structure during the last two decades, we have to content ourselves with data only from the greater Buenos Aires area, the main urban agglomerate. We sought to emphasize the wage differentials induced by educational attainment levels, and for this purpose, we delineated three skill groups: unskilled (those individuals who never completed high school), semiskilled (those who have completed high school) and skilled workers (those who have completed a tertiary degree). We excluded the self-employed, owner-

---

[36] For example, the Lorenz curve of 1974 stochastically dominates the Lorenz curve of 1999.

Table 5.15. *Fitted time trends by schooling group*
Fitted variable: wage premia by schooling group (base category: unskilled workers)

	Semi-skilled group		Skilled group	
Period	Males	Females	Males	Females
1980–98	-2.11***	-3.37***	0.23	-3.41***
	(0.54)	(0.50)	(1.20)	(1.37)
1990–98	0.25	-0.38	10.1****	6.7**
	(1.03)	(1.21)	(1.47)	(2.2)

Notes: The time trend takes the values $t = 1, 2, 3, 6, 7, \ldots, 19$. *** indicates the coefficient is statistically different from zero at the one percent significance level. ** indicates the coefficient is statistically different from zero at the five percent significance level. We report the statistical significance of the fitted trends only as informative measures.
Source: Galiani (2002).

managers, and unpaid workers because we were only interested in changes in the actual wage structure. The results of the estimation of the wage premia (relative to the unskilled) are shown in Table 5.15.

For the whole period, the main change in the wage structure is that the semiskilled group's wages deteriorated relative to the unskilled group's wages. Additionally, the unskilled group did not see its wages deteriorate relative to those of skilled workers: the male skilled wage premium was 228 percent in 1980, 156 percent in 1991, and 211 percent in 1998, while the male semiskilled wage premium was 87, 44, and 48 percent, respectively. Nevertheless, if the analysis is restricted to the evolution of wages during the 1990s, we see a somewhat different picture. The wages of the semiskilled group did not deteriorate relative to the unskilled group wages, while both unskilled and semiskilled wages deteriorated relative to skilled wages. Indeed, the skilled-unskilled wage premium increased substantially during the 1990s. In order to quantify the magnitude of these trends we fit a constant and a linear time trend to the wage premium [for those skill groups plotted in Figure 5.7. The coefficient associated with the time trend measures the percentage change per year in the respective wage premium. Table 5.15 shows the results.

We find significant negative trends for the female wage premia for both schooling groups. However, for the tertiary group, the trend is not statistically significant when we discard the first two years. We also find a negative trend in the male secondary school wage premium. Finally, there is no statistically significant trend in the male tertiary degree group wage premium.

Thus, even though there is no significant tendency in the male college wage premium for the whole period, since the beginning of 1990 we do find a significant positive trend. In particular, the estimated coefficient for this period implies that the male college wage premium rose 10 percentage points per year

Fig. 5.7. Wage premia
Percent

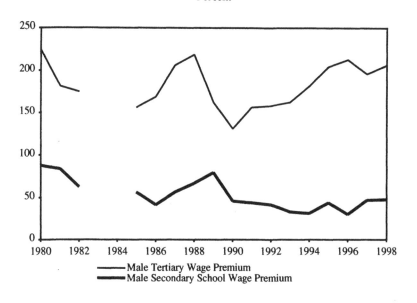

Male Tertiary Wage Premium
Male Secondary School Wage Premium

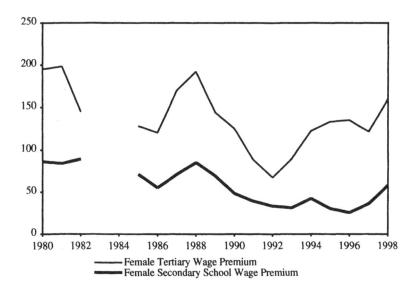

Female Tertiary Wage Premium
Female Secondary School Wage Premium

Source: Galiani (2002).

during the1990s. The female college wage premium behavior illustrates even more strongly the change in the wage structure that occurred during the 1990s. For the secondary school group we find, consistent with what we see in Figure 5.7, that its wage premium with respect to the incomplete secondary group has not changed during the 1990s, although it has been declining during the whole 1980–98 period.

5.4.8 Unemployment

Unemployment was not among the main concerns of policymakers before the late 1990s, when it came to be considered one of the most serious economic problems. Unfortunately, the time series only begins in 1963, and hence, we cannot make meaningful comparisons before that year.[37]

It is generally thought that unemployment was quite low before World War I because of the large-scale immigration and high rates of growth of real wages. However, the country went through severe crises during the twentieth century, which may have been followed by sharp increases in the unemployment rate. This seems to have been the case at the beginning of World War I (Ernesto Tornquist & Co., Ltd., 1919), but not as a result of the crisis of 1929, during which the rate was never above 10 percent.

There is no information available on unemployment during the period of industrialization even though some signs suggest low unemployment rates (cf. Véganzonès and Winograd 1997). At the beginning of the 1960s, unemployment was around 8 percent, but it decreased rapidly to less than 5 percent where it stayed until the mid-1980s when it edged toward 7 percent. Not until the mid-1990s did unemployment increase to two-digit levels, where it has remained ever since; that sharp rise is clearly illustrated in Figure 5.8.

After a successful stabilization program at the beginning of the 1990s, GDP growth increased significantly and total employment rose steadily until mid-1993 (see Table 5.16). At this point unemployment started to rise (see Figure 5.9d). During the second half of 1994, the economy slowed down (see Figure 5.9c) and unemployment increased from 10 to 12.2 percent. Although the economy was already in a mild recession at this point, conditions worsened substantially after the devaluation of the Mexican peso in December 1994. Domestic demand and GDP contracted abruptly, the latter declining by nearly 5

---

[37] Unemployment is measured through representative household surveys. Thus, it is a statistical construction of the second half of the century. Bunge (1928) and the Ministry of Labor (Comité Nacional de Geografía, 1941) developed an occupation index for the period 1914 to 1940 for Buenos Aires, which was used to estimate unemployment rates during that period. However, these estimates of unemployment are not comparable to any statistic derived from a modern household survey.

Fig. 5.8. Urban unemployment rates
Percent

Source: Authors' calculations based on household surveys.

percent in 1995 (Figures 5.9a and 5.9c).[38] The consequences of this shock for unemployment were dramatic. With the labor force continuing to expand and employment falling sharply along with aggregate demand, unemployment rose by over 6 percentage points in 6 months (see Figures 5.9b and 5.9d).[39]

The recession was short despite its severity. The economy soon recovered and, between 1996 and 1998, both output and employment grew rapidly and unemployment declined substantially. However, at the beginning of 1999, the Brazilian currency underwent a strong depreciation. The Argentine economy contracted 4 percent in 1999, and unemployment increased again. Thus, unemployment was well above its equilibrium level during the 1990s, mainly as a result of a combination of macroeconomic shocks and labor shedding in the

[38] The sharpening of the contraction is shown by the fact that between the last quarter of 1994 and the third quarter of 1995 domestic demand decreased 14 percent, investment fell 30 percent, and GDP decreased 10 percent.

[39] Indeed, the labor force grew fast during the whole period.

Table 5.16. *Change in employment*

Thousands

	87–88	88–89	89–90	90–91	91–92	92–93	93–94	94–95	95–96	96–97	97–98
Manufacturing	-7.3	-36.5	-43.6	-0.2	52.9	-41.7	-78.6	-95.9	-17.6	78.9	-8.4
Electricity, gas & water	2.3	-3.2	12.8	8.8	-3.0	-16.4	-2.6	4.6	-2.5	-2.8	-5.1
Construction	30.3	-49.8	-32.9	50.0	7.7	-16.0	20.6	-10.2	11.3	62.3	38.9
Trade	39.5	-4.3	-1.1	85.3	61.6	21.4	13.0	-27.6	33.6	-27.6	58.1
Transport & communications	18.9	37.8	-19.3	-27.0	8.4	54.3	32.6	2.8	4.5	22.5	42.4
Finance	-0.5	5.8	-21.9	28.0	5.6	4.0	53.4	18.4	21.2	43.1	44.5
Community services	1.3	-1.5	49.3	-13.1	5.0	51.7	-83.1	45.7	-29.7	216.4	222.5
Total change	84.5	-51.6	-56.7	126.7	138.2	57.4	-44.8	-62.2	20.8	392.9	392.8
Total change as percentage of total employment	1.8	-1.1	-1.2	2.7	2.8	1.1	-0.9	-1.2	0.4	7.9	7.3
Job creation	92.3	43.7	62.1	167.1	141.2	131.5	119.5	71.5	70.6	423.3	406.3
Job destruction	7.8	95.3	118.8	40.3	3.0	74.1	164.3	133.7	49.8	30.4	13.5
Job turnover as percentage of total employment	2.1	2.9	3.8	4.4	3.0	4.1	5.6	4.1	2.4	9.1	7.8

Source: Galiani and Nickell (1999).

Fig. 5.9. The Argentine economy in recent years

Sources: Panel a: CEPAL and INDEC press reports; b: household survey, all urban agglomerates; c: CEPAL; d: INDEC Press Reports.

manufacturing sector.[40] Thus, although it has been argued that the high levels of unemployment during the 1990s are the result of the reduction in the capital-labor price ratio, simple evidence shows this position to be false.[41]

The manufacturing sector shed labor between 1992 and 1995. However, in general, the remaining sectors show employment growth during most of the years except 1994. Indeed, at the industry level, job creation has been high in every year in which growth has been high. In this respect, 1994 is the exception, since the economy started to contract during the second half of the year. Second, although job creation was high, job destruction was also high, primarily as a result of the contraction in the manufacturing sector.

[40] There are reasons to expect that labor reallocation took place during the 1990s, as the privatized firms reduced their employment and, most importantly, the manufacturing sector faced a substantial decrease in its relative prices as it faced stronger foreign competition.

[41] It is sometimes argued that the rapid productivity growth of the early 1990s generated high unemployment because if output growth remains fixed, higher productivity growth must lead to lower employment growth. Of course, output growth does not remain fixed. Under sensible macroeconomic policies, output will expand with the supply potential of the economy.

5.5 Conclusion

The study of the Argentine labor market over the past century reveals some profound changes. Progress has been made in the rewards to labor in the forms of wages, benefits and increased leisure through shorter hours, vacation time, sick leave, and earlier retirement. Labor has also been granted greater security both on and off the job. But this study has also revealed that some aspects of the labor market have not progressed, while others have come full circle in the past century.

Labor market progress has interacted with social changes, alternately acting as cause and effect at given times. We identify three periods in the evolution of the Argentine labor market: (1) the "spot market" period from 1870 to 1929, (2) the institutional modern market period from 1943 to 1975, and (3) the period of a search for a modern, flexible labor market from 1976 to the present. Although these periods do not necessarily coincide with the phases of Argentine economic growth, they do match with phases of integration or isolation with regard to world goods and credit markets.

Appendix: Labor law in Argentina

Table 5.17 shows the development of the main Argentine labor laws. The Argentine labor relations system was mainly developed in the early 1940s, and although the collective laws system was then suppressed, just as the national constitution also has been suppressed in several periods, its structure has not been substantially modified (if at all) until the present (see Table 5.17).

During what we have called the spot era market, the general rule was freedom of contracting. Civil and commercial law constituted the basis of Argentine labor law until the early 1940s when, among many changes to the system, severance payment was generalized to the whole economy. We single out the generalization of the severance payment because that constitutes a clear property right conceded to workers in their jobs, which we have identified as a characteristic of the contract of employment in the modern era.

Notwithstanding, there were several attempts to legislate a labor code since the beginning of the nineteenth century. These labor codes contemplated several aspects of what has been legislated since the 1940s by both individual and collective labor laws. The first of these attempts was the code elaborated by J. V. González in 1904. This code was very ambitious and certainly could not be passed at that time. It tried to legislate the terms of a host of employment issues: the contract of employment, accidents and professional sickness, a legal rest regime including weekly and daily hours of work, work by minors and women, security and hygiene conditions, trade unions, and collective bargaining and arbitrage in collective conflicts (see, for example, Zimmermann 1995). The projects of Usain in 1921, Molinari in 1928, and Saavedra Lamas in 1933 all followed González's lead.

Obviously, the lack of a general code did not imply the lack of labor legislation apart from civil and commercial law. Labor law started to develop early in the twentieth century and had progressed somewhat during the 1930s, but only after 1940 did it take off. The system that developed was not based on a unique code, but on several laws

Table 5.17. *A summary of Argentine labor law*

Year	Law	Sum and substance of the legislation
1859/62	Civil and Commercial law	Individual labor law in the "spot market" era (there is not collective law during this period): The Commercial law constituted the basis of the Argentine labor law, especially after its reform in 1934. Nevertheless, this law only regulated the relations between workers and merchants in the trade sector. The labor relations in the remaining sectors of the economy were regulated by the Civil law.
1905/13	1st labor law (4.661 and 9.104)	This law established the prohibition against work during Sundays in the Federal District. This prohibition was then extended to the whole national territory in 1913. As it is commonly the case, these laws did not apply to domestic servant workers. The law 11.640 of 1932, which stretched the prohibition to Saturdays after 13 hours extended these laws.
1907	2nd labor law (5.291)	Prohibited the employment of individuals younger than 10 years old.
1915	Accidents and professional sickness (9.688)	This law regulated accidents and professional sickness. Although with modifications, it was the law in practice until 1995. It established objective employer responsibility with tariff compensations.
1929	Weekly and daily hours of work (11.544)	Legislated working time. It established the maximum duration of both daily and weekly working time. The law was only regulated in 1933 and it was in use through the Contract of Employment Law (1974 to 76) until 1991: 8 hours per day and 48 hours per week. The employment law (24.013) of 1991 relaxed these limits.
1933	Severance pay (11.729)	The law 11.729 reformed the severance payment system regulated in the Commercial law and also introduced paid vacations. Yet, until 1945, this law only applied to workers in the trade sector.
1934	Maternity leave (11.933)	Prohibited female employment since 30 days before childbirth to 45 days after it. It also created a maternity leave insurance system.
1940/47	Professional statutes	The statutory legislation begins in 1940 with the professional statute of the workers of the banking sector. Between 1944 and 1947 it expanded extensively, covering the workers of several industries. The professional statutes regulated the labor relations by profession. During the rest of the century, there have been legislated new statutes (and many have been modified).
1945	Severance pay (12.921)	This law extended the severance payment legislation to all wage earners.
1945	Paid vacation (DL 1.740)	Extended paid vacations to all wage earners.

Table 5.17. (Continued)

Year	Law	Sum and substance of the legislation
1945	DL 33.302	Legislated the minimum wage and established the creation of the National Institute of Remunerations for its determination. However, this Institute has never been created. It also increased the severance payment and instituted the thirteen wage.
1943	Professional associations (D 2.669)	Collective labor law in the rigid modern labor market era: Regulated the constitution, organization, and working conditions of the professional associations. It guaranteed freedom of association to all workers. However, the system was (and it still is) based on the existence of a unique union by craft or industry: The syndicate that holds trade union representation (Personeria Gremial) and not only civil representation. It also established that unions could constitute federations and confederations (second and third order associations).
1945	DL 23.852	It legislated the unions' rights and regulated the collective agreement procedures until they were fully regulated by law. It made firms the agents of retention of the contributions of affiliated workers to their unions.
1952	Professional associations law (14.295)	Regulated the constitution, organization and working conditions of the professional associations following D 2.669.
1953	Collective bargaining law (14.250)	Regulated the procedures and coverage of the collective agreements. It made collective agreements erga omnes.
1956	DL 9.270	It suppressed most of the dispositions of DL 23.852 and law 14.250. It established sindical freedom by eliminating the trade union representation. The principle of sindical freedom was also established in the Constitution of 1957.
1957	Equal payment (DL 2.739)	It established that the wages of workers performing the same task should not differ by gender.
1957	System of conciliation and arbitrage (DL 10.956)	It regulated the voluntary conciliation of conflicts. It also established the arbitrage role of the state in collective conflicts.
1958	Professional associations (14.455)	It undid DL 9.270. This (new) law of professional associations was similar to DL 23.852.
1964	Minimum wage (16.459)	It created the National Council of Minimum Wage. This institution was in charge of establishing the minimum wage in the country until 1990 when it was replaced by the Council of Productivity and Employment.

Table 5.17. (Continued)

Year	Law	Sum and substance of the legislation
1966	Individual contract of employment (16.881)	It is the first contract of employment law passed by congress. However, the project was only partially promulgated by the executive power. Indeed, only four articles were promulgated while the rest of the law was vetoed.
1966	Financial control of trade unions (D 969)	It regulates the auditing and control of the financial resources of the trade unions.
1970	Women and child work (18.624)	Regulated minimum ages and tasks at work for women and children complying with the ILO resolutions.
1972	New law of hygiene (19.587)	Improved the conditions of work satisfying ILO resolutions.
1969	Collective bargaining intervention (18.016 and successive modifications)	It established that collective agreements should not bargain wages since 1970.
1971	Collective bargaining (18.887)	New law of collective bargaining and workers and firms' commissions. It established that wage increases should not exceed the inflation rate plus productivity growth.
1974	Contract of employment law (20.744)	Contract of employment law: Unified diverse institutions of the labor law. It was preeminently prolabor: It improved workers' rights in many dimensions (longer annual leaves, higher severance payment, etc.). It may be said that almost every article in the law was based in the most favorable legal antecedent for workers. The general rule upheld by the contract of employment law is the principle of (relative) continuity of employment contracts. Employment contracts are settled for an indeterminate period of time.
1973	Professional associations (20.615)	It replaced law 14.455. However, the sindical model adopted was the same. It gave more power and homogeneity to the union movement. It also created the legal sindical jurisdiction.
1973	Collective bargaining: *Pacto Social*	Called to a social pact among firms, unions, and the government to establish wages and to reduce inflation. Industry level collective bargaining was fully reinstated in 1975 (just for a year).
1974	D 1.045	It allowed unions to charge sindical fees to all workers in the industry irrespective of whether or not they were union members.
1976	Reform of the Contract of employment law	Some rights granted to workers by law 20.744 were reduced or eliminated.

Table 5.17. (Continued)

Year	Law	Sum and substance of the legislation
1976	Law 21.261	It suspended both the right to strike and collective bargaining. The government established (reference) wages until the collective bargaining was reinstated during the late 80s.
1976	Professional associations (D 9)	It suspended all gremial activities.
1976	D 385	It derogated D 1.045.
1988	Professional associations law (23.555)	Regulated the constitution, organization, and working conditions of the professional associations. It follows law 14.455. The system is still based on the existence of a unique union by craft or industry: The syndicate that holds trade union representation (Personeria Gremial).
1988	Collective bargaining law (23.545 and 23.546)	Regulated the procedures and coverage of collective agreements. It made collective agreements erga omnes. These laws are essentially similar to law 14.250.
1991	Employment Law (24.013)	This law introduced several fix-term contracts and it constitutes the first attempt to flexibilize the Argentine labor market. Introduced fixed term contracts and special training contracts for young workers. It also created the unemployment benefit system.
1995	Flexibilization of the contract of employment law (24.465)	This law generalized the set of fix-term contracts regulated in 1991 by law 24.013. It also introduced a trial period up to six month.
1996	Accidents and professional sickness (24.557)	It modified the previous legislation severely. It establishes an insurance system.
1998	25.013	It eliminated the promoted contracts regulated by laws 24.013 and 24.465. However, it also decreased substantially the severance payment for the short-tenure employment relationships. It also increased the degree of centralization prevalent in the collective bargaining although law 25.250 undid this regulation.
2000	Decentralization of collective bargaining (25.250)	The main objective of this reform is the decentralization of collective bargaining. It is the first serious attempt to decentralize collective bargaining in Argentina. Although the law of professional associations is not modified, law 25.250 establishes the right to bargain at any level of representation, that is, bargaining can be conducted by any union that possesses enough representation even though there exist other unions with a higher degree of representation (e.g., a first grade union when there is a second grade union). Additionally, it establishes that whenever bargaining is at the firm level, the representation of workers must include members of the internal commission of workers of the firm.

Sources: Authors' elaboration based on Vázquez Vialard (1996, 1999).

that legislated diverse aspects of the individual contract of employment and a system of collective laws.

However, collective bargaining took place even before it was legislated (see Gaudio and Pilone 1983), and by its nature, it necessarily affected the individual contract of employment (as individual laws always shape and are shaped by collective bargaining).

A singular characteristic of the collective bargaining system in Argentina is that it was recurrently eliminated and reinstated by military and civil governments, respectively. While unique, this characteristic is hardly surprising given the country's institutional history. In spite of its constitutional guarantee since 1953, there were only a few windows of opportunity in which collective bargaining was unfettered.[42] Indeed, collective bargaining was banned from 1956 to 1958, 1967 to 1971, 1973 to 1975, and 1976 to 1988.

Clearly, the prolabor, Peronist party that possessed the support of all trade unions from 1946 (see Torre 1990) has passed the most favorable legislation for labor, both at the individual and collective level, first in the 1940s and early 1950s and again during the early 1970s. Although during the 1990s the party passed some flexible contractual forms that may not be considered prolabor, it favored trade unions when it left power in 1998.

The professional associations law only entitles one union to represent a group of workers by industry, profession, or enterprise in a determined geographical area in the bargaining process. Legal recognition was originally awarded to the most representative union. Given the union structure prevalent in Argentina, most collective agreements are national agreements that take place at the industry level. A collective agreement has to be endorsed by the ministry of labor and social security to be extended to all workers and employers of a determinate activity in a specific geographical location. Thus, collective agreements endorsed by government have *erga omnes* effects, and the system of collective bargaining is fairly centralized.[43]

The main regulatory framework of the employment relationship is the contract of employment law passed in 1974 and modified in 1976. The contract of employment law is the main institution in labor law. The general rule it upholds is the principle of continuity of employment contracts. Employment contracts are settled for an indeterminate period of time. However, this conceived stability of jobs by law is not absolute. Much to the contrary, any employer has the right to end an employment contract without explanation. To dismiss an employee, the employer only has to give the worker a legislated severance pay determined by the worker's wage and tenure. During the last decade, there have been three laws that changed the contract of employment law by introducing flexibility at the margin (introducing fixed-term contracts exempted of severance payment at termination). However, these reforms have already been undone by laws reflecting dissatisfaction with their results.

---

[42] Between 1945 and 1953 collective bargaining was also unfettered although it was regulated by decree and not by law.

[43] Although employer organizations are regulated by civil law, they deserve consideration here, given that employer organizations are parties to collective bargaining. In Argentina, these are pluralist organizations, which frequently are structured federatively (associations, chambers, or federations). Any of them may coexist with other important employer organizations in the same activity. Finally, the employer position in bargaining (indeed the position of each party) is decided by majority rule.

References

Abowd, John M., and Richard B. Freeman. 1991. *Immigration, Trade, and the Labor Market.* Chicago: University of Chicago Press.

Adelman, Jeremy. 1994. *Frontier Development: Land, Labour, and Capital on the Wheatlands of Argentina and Canada, 1890–1914.* Oxford: Clarendon Press.

Ashenfelter, Orley, and John Pencavel. 1969. American Trade Union Growth: 1900–1960. *Quarterly Journal of Economics* 83: 434–48.

Beccaria, Luis. 1991. Distribución del ingreso en la Argentina: Explorando lo sucedido desde mediados de los setenta. *Desarrollo Económico* 31: 319–38.

Booth, Alison. 1983. A Reconsideration of Trade Union Growth in the United Kingdom. *British Journal of Industrial Relations* 21: 377–91.

———. 1995. *The Economics of the Trade Unions.* Cambridge: Cambridge University Press.

Bunge, Alejandro E. 1928. *La economía argentina.* Buenos Aires: Agencia General de Librerás y Publicaciones.

Burgess, Simon, and Hedley Rees. 1996. Job Tenure in Britain 1975–92. *Economic Journal* 106 (March): 334–44.

Canitrot, Adolfo. 1975. La experiencia populista de redistribución de ingresos. *Desarrollo Económico* 15: 331–54.

———. 1980. La disciplina como objetivo de la política económica: Un ensayo sobre el programa económico del gobierno argentino desde 1976. *Desarrollo Económico* 19: 453–75.

———. 1981. Teoría y práctica del liberalismo: Política antiinflacionaria y apertura económica en la Argentina, 1976–1981. *Desarrollo Económico* 21: 131–89.

Comité Nacional de Geografía. 1941. *Anuario geográfico argentino.* Buenos Aires: Comité Nacional de Geografía.

CONADE-CEPAL (Consejo Nacional de Desarrollo (Argentina), and United Nations. Economic Commission for Latin America).1965. *Distribución del ingreso y cuentas nacionales en la Argentina.* 5 vols. Buenos Aires: CONADE.

Cortés Conde, Roberto. 1979. *El progreso argentino.* Buenos Aires: Editorial Sudamericana.

———. 1982. Income Differentials and Migrations. In *Economics in the Long View: Essays in Honour of W. W. Rostow,* edited by C. Kindleberger and G. Di Tella. London: Macmillan.

———. 1997. *La economía argentina en el largo plazo: Ensayos de historia económica de los siglos XIX y XX.* Buenos Aires: Editioral Sudamerica.

de Pablo, Juan Carlos. 1979. *Ensayos sobre economía argentina.* Buenos Aires: Ediciones Macchi.

Díaz Alejandro, Carlos F. 1970. *Essays on the Economic History of the Argentine Republic.* New Haven, Conn.: Yale University Press.

———. 1988. No Less Than One Hundred Years of Argentine Economic History Plus Some Comparisons. In *Trade, Development and the World Economy: Selected Essays of Carlos F. Díaz-Alejandro,* edited by A. Velasco. Oxford: Basil Blackwell.

Diebold, Francis X., David Neumark, and Daniel Polsky. 1997. Job Stability in the United States. *Journal of Labor Economics* 15 (2): 206–33.

Di Tella, Guido, and Manuel Zymelman. 1967. *Las etapas del desarrollo económico argentino.* Buenos Aires: Editorial Universitaria de Buenos Aires.

Doyon, Louise M. 1975. El crecimiento sindical bajo el peronismo. *Desarrollo Económico* 15: 151–61.

———. 1984. La organización del movimiento sindical Peronista 1946–1955. *Desarrollo Económico* 24: 203–34.

Doeringer, Peter B., and Michael J. Piore. 1971. *Internal Labor Markets and Manpower Analysis*. Lexington, Mass.,: Heath.

Ernesto Tornquist & Co., Limited. 1919. *The Economic Development of the Argentine Republic in the Last Fifty Years*. Buenos Aires: Ernesto Tornquist & Co., Limited.

Farber, Henry S. 1998. Are Lifetime Jobs Disappearing? Job Duration in the United States, 1973–1993. In *Labor Statistics Measurement Issues*, edited by J. Haltiwanger, M. E. Manser, and R. Topel. Chicago: University of Chicago Press.

Ferenczi, Imre, and Walter Francis Wilcox. 1929. *International Migrations*. 2 vols. New York: National Bureau of Economic Research.

Frenkel, Roberto. 1979. Decisiones de precios en alta inflación. *Desarrollo Económico* 19: 612–32.

————. 1984. Salarios industriales e inflación: El periodo 1976–82. *Desarrollo Económico* 24: 387–413.

Friedberg, Rachel M., and Jennifer Hunt. 1995. The Impact of Immigrants on Host Country Wages, Employment and Growth. *Journal of Economic Perspectives* 9 (2): 23–44.

Galiani, Sebastián. 2002. The Differential Evolution of Wages, Job Stability and Unemployment in Argentina. Universidad de San Andrés. Photocopy.

Galiani, Sebastián, and Hugo Hopenhayn. 2003. Duration and Risk of Unemployment in Argentina. *Journal of Development Economics*. Forthcoming.

Galiani, Sebastián, and S. J. Nickell. 1999. Unemployment in Argentina in the 1990s. Working Paper DTE 219, Instituto Torcuato Di Tella.

Gaudio, Ricardo, and Jorge Pilone. 1983. El desarrollo de la negociación colectiva durante la etapa de modernización industrial en la Argentina, 1935–1943. *Desarrollo Económico* 90: 255–86.

————. 1984. Estado y relaciones laborales en el período previo al surgimiento del peronismo, 1935–1943. *Desarrollo Económico* 94: 235–73.

Gerchunoff, Pablo, and Lucas Llach. 1998. *El ciclo de la ilusión y el desencanto: Un siglo de políticas económicas argentinas*. Buenos Aires: Ariel.

Goldin, Claudia D. 2000. Labor Markets in the Twentieth Century. In *The Cambridge Economic History of the United States, Volume III: The Twentieth Century*, edited by S. L. Engerman and R. E. Gallman. Cambridge: Cambridge University Press.

Gutiérrez, Leandro, and Juan Carlos Korol. 1988. Historia de empresas y crecimiento industrial en la Argentina: El caso de la fabrica Argentina de alpargatas. *Desarrollo Económico* 28: 401–24.

Hatton, T. J., and Jeffrey G. Williamson. 1998. *The Age of Mass Migration: Causes and Economic Impact*. New York: Oxford University Press.

Heymann, Daniel, and Axel Leijonhufvud. 1995. *High Inflation*. Oxford: Clarendon Press.

Hopenhayn, Hugo, and Pablo A. Neumeyer. 2001. Economic Growth in Latin America and the Caribbean: Country Study for Argentina. Universidad Torcuato Di Tella. Photocopy.

Horowitz, Joel. 1990. *Argentine Unions, The State and The Rise of Perón, 1930–1945*. Berkeley: Institute of International Studies, University of California Berkeley.

IEERAL (Instituto de Estudios Económicos sobre la Realidad Argentina y Latinoamericana). 1986. Estadísticas de la evolución económica de Argentina 1913–1984. *Estudios* 9 (39): 103–84.

Kydland, Finn E., and Carlos E. J. M. Zarazaga. 2002. Argentina's Lost Decade. *Review of Economic Dynamics* 5 (1): 152–65.

Layard, P. R. G., S. J. Nickell, and Richard Jackman. 1991. *Unemployment: Macroeconomic Performance and the Labour Market*. Oxford: Oxford University Press.

Lobato, Mirta Zaida. 1998. La vida en las fabricas: Trabajo, protesta y política en una comunidad obrera, Berisso 1907–70. Ph.D. dissertation, Facultad de Filosofía y Letras, Universidad de Buenos Aires.

Maddison, Angus. 1995. *Monitoring the World Economy*. Paris: OECD.

Mallon, Richard D., and Juan V. Sourrouille. 1975. *Economic Policymaking in a Conflict Society: The Argentine Case*. Cambridge, Mass.: Harvard University Press.

Marshall, Adriana, and Dora Orlansky. 1983. Inmigración de países limítrofes y demanda de mano de obra en la Argentina, 1940–1980. *Desarrollo Económico* 23: 35–57.

Matsushita, Hiroshi. 1983. *Movimiento obrero argentino, 1930–1945: Sus proyecciones en los orígenes del peronismo*. Buenos Aires: Ediciones Siglo Veinte.

Nickell, S. J., and P. R. G. Layard. 2000. Labor Market Institutions and Economic Performance. In *The Handbook of Labor Economics, Volume 3C*, edited by O. Ashenfelter and D. E. Card. Amsterdam: North-Holland.

OECD. 1994. *The OECD Job Study: Evidence and Explanations*. Paris: OECD.

OECD. 1996. *Employment Outlook*. Paris: OECD.

O'Rourke, Kevin H., Alan M. Taylor, and Jeffrey G. Williamson. 1996. Factor Price Convergence in the Late-Nineteenth Century. *International Economic Review* 37 (3): 499–530.

O'Rourke, Kevin H., and Jeffrey G. Williamson. 1997. Around the European Periphery 1870–1913: Globalization, Schooling and Growth. *European Review of Economic History* 1 (2): 153–90.

O'Rourke, Kevin H., and Jeffrey G. Williamson. 1999. *Globalization and History: The Evolution of a Nineteenth-Century Atlantic Economy*. Cambridge: MIT Press.

Parsons, Donald O. 1986. The Employment Relationship: Job Attachment, Work Effort, and the Nature of Contracts. In *The Handbook of Labor Economics*, vol. 2, edited by O. Ashenfelter and P. R. G. Layard. Amsterdam: North-Holland.

Portantiero, Juan Carlos, and Miguel Murmis. 1971. *Estudios sobre los orígenes del peronismo*. Buenos Aires: Siglo Vientiuno Argentina Editores.

Recchini de Lattes, Zulma L., and Alfredo E. Lattes. 1975. *La Población de Argentina*. Buenos Aires: República Argentina, Ministerio de Economía, Instituto Nacional de Estadística y Censos.

Sábato, Hilda. 1985. La formación del mercado de trabajo en Buenos Aires, 1850–1880. *Desarrollo Económico* 24: 561–92.

Taylor, Alan M. 1994. Mass Migration to Distant Southern Shores: Argentina and Australia, 1870–1939. In *Migration and the International Labor Market, 1850–1939*, edited by T. J. Hatton and J. G. Williamson. London: Routledge.

———. 1997. Peopling the Pampa: On the Impact of Mass Migration to the River Plate, 1870–1914. *Explorations in Economic History* 34 (1): 100–132.

Torre, Juan Carlos. 1990. *La vieja guardia sindical y Perón: Sobre los orígenes del peronismo*. Buenos Aires: Editorial Sudamericana.

Vázquez Vialard, Antonio L. R. 1996. *Tratado de derecho del trabajo*. Vol. 3. Buenos Aires: Editorial Astrea.

———. 1999. *Derecho del trabajo y de la seguridad social*. Vols. 1–2. Buenos Aires: Editorial Astrea.

Véganzonès, Marie-Ange, and Carlos Winograd. 1997. *Argentina in the 20th Century: An Account of Long-Awaited Growth*. Paris: OECD.

Villanueva, Javier. 1972. El origen de la industrialización Argentina. *Desarrollo Económico* 12: 451–76.

Western, Bruce. 1997. *Between Class and Market: Postwar Unionization in the Capitalist Democracies*. Princeton: Princeton University Press.

Williamson, Jeffrey G. 2002. Land, Labor, and Globalization in the Pre-Industrial Third World. *Journal of Economic History*. Forthcoming.

Zimmermann, Eduardo A. 1995. *Los liberales reformistas: La cuestión social en la Argentina, 1890–1916.* Buenos Aires: Editorial Sudamericana.

6

Capital accumulation

ALAN M. TAYLOR

University of California, Davis, NBER, and CEPR

The study of capital formation rightly remains one of the central concerns in the study of long-run growth and economic development. Ever since the seminal contributions of Abramovitz (1956) and Solow (1956), studies of economic growth have recognized the importance of accumulation of inputs as a source of output growth. The recent revival of economic growth as a field of inquiry has not diminished these issues, although we have now expanded our list of relevant inputs to include human capital, in addition to physical capital and labor (Barro and Sala-i-Martin 1995; Mankiw, Romer, and Weil 1992). Looking further back in history, and especially at a frontier economy like Argentina's, we are unlikely to forget the importance of the third "classical" factor, land. As we now know, explanations of nineteenth-century growth and convergence that omit an accounting for land endowments are missing a big part of the story (Taylor 1999). However, the focus on physical capital in the tried and tested Solovian model is a useful simplification, since even today's most refined growth econometrics have identified investment as the most important and robust explanatory variable in cross-country growth regression analysis (Levine and Renelt 1992).

These concerns motivate the study of investment and capital accumulation. Since the Argentine economy has always ranked as a small (and more or less open) economy, we must concern ourselves not just with the demand for investment, its uses, and its effects, but also with its sources of supply, domestic savings, and foreign capital inflows via the current account. Other chapters in this book deal with questions of human and natural resources in the Argentine growth experience and with the record of economic growth itself, so we will not dwell for too long on the relationships between these large topics. Still, it is useful to set the stage in this introduction to capital formation by reminding ourselves of the long-run patterns of growth and investment, and the role of for-

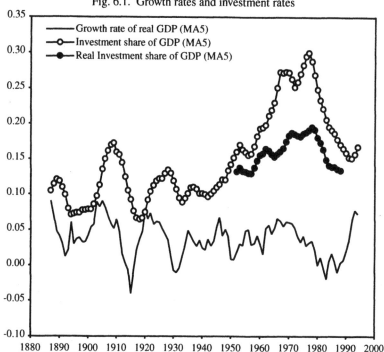

Fig. 6.1. Growth rates and investment rates

Sources: Obstfeld and Taylor (1998); Heston et al. (1994).

eign capital, to get a flavor for the historical record, overall trends, and major turning points.

Figure 6.1 shows the long-run evolution of the annual growth rate of real GDP

$$g = \frac{y_t}{y_{t-1}} - 1,$$

where y is real GDP, and the gross investment share of GDP in current prices, defined as the ratio of nominal investment I to nominal GDP Y,

$$\frac{I}{Y} = \frac{P_I i}{P_Y y},$$

where i is real investment, and P_I and P_Y are the nominal domestic prices of i and y, respectively. Data are shown for the period of just over a century for which we have data, and I employ five-year moving averages to smooth out short-run fluctuations.

Several features stand out from this chart. First, there is indeed a rough correlation, though this says nothing of causation, between investment and growth. The late 1880s emerge as Argentina's first major economic boom period, and both investment rates and growth rates were high. The downturn of the 1890s following the Baring Crisis saw a collapse in both measures, until 1900–14 when a long economic boom was sustained, a period commonly known as the *Belle Époque*. World War I was a massive downturn, on both measures, with a hesitant recovery in the 1920s, though to nothing like the previous peak. The Great Depression of the 1930s was mercifully brief for Argentina, at least as compared to other countries, and was followed by a stabilization of growth and investment rates at modest levels.

Tempting as it is, especially in a volume of this kind, to lump all data from different periods together, we know that the period after World War II is best regarded as a totally different kind of animal, and the empirical evidence must be handled accordingly. How else could one reconcile the very high and accelerating investment rates seen in the 1950s, 1960s, and 1970s with the dismal economic growth performance seen in the same period? The greatest of all Argentine economic historians, Carlos Díaz Alejandro (1970), suggested a reason for this apparent puzzle: investment rates were not really very high at all in real terms; rather, the ratio of investment expenditures to GDP was high in nominal terms because capital goods were rationed, via tariffs, quotas, and other barriers, at very high domestic prices relative to the rest of the world. Argentina spent a lot of output on investment, but got a very small quantity of real investment in return. This argument was formalized and tested econometrically (Taylor 1994) using the post-1950 data on cross-country comparisons of prices and quantities from the Penn World Table. The relevant measure of investment activity in that data set is real investment as a fraction of GDP measured at world prices,

$$\frac{I^W}{Y^W} = \frac{P_I^W i}{P_Y^W y}$$

where P_I^W and P_Y^W are the world prices of investment and output goods. This series is shown in Figure 6.1, and reveals a major source of the puzzle: measured at real international prices, Argentine investment was much lower than the raw national accounts data had indicated.

Since the 1980s, economic reforms have begun to nudge Argentina back toward a more open trading stance, and this has had measurable implications as seen here. Investment prices have converged back toward world levels, and, as a result, there is no longer such a large distortion driving a wedge between the measures I/Y and I^W/Y^W. In the 1990s, with this gap very small indeed, investment has started to boom, and growth too. Whilst this recent turnaround certainly has multiple causes, such as macroeconomic stabilization, one should not neglect here an important change in fundamentals – the boost to investment demand from the removal of capital goods price distortions. Capital accumulation is a key source of economic growth in the long run, so Argentine prospects for good economic performance are better now that the country no longer has to pay up to twice as much for each unit of capital accumulated as other countries.

Let us next turn to the role of foreign capital in this process over the last century. As we can see from Figure 6.2, which shows foreign capital stocks in the world at benchmark dates, this role has waned and waxed in importance, and in ways that accord with the conventional wisdom about international capital markets as a whole and about Argentina's engagement in those markets in particular. What is the larger context? From the perspective of the major foreign investing nations, such as the United States and Britain, the extent to which they sent capital overseas is measured by the ratio of their stock of outstanding foreign assets to their own GDP. Around 1900 this ratio was about 50 percent, but this fell by a factor of 2 to around 25 percent in the interwar period, a symptom of the implosion of global capital markets in the years after 1914. After World War II, the ratio was as low as 12 percent, smaller by yet another factor of 2. The postwar regime limited any recovery in these measures: the Bretton Woods system embraced the Keynesian notion that trade could be protected, and world economic stability enhanced, by limiting capital movements. Only in recent decades has the trend reversed: the ratio rose to 30 percent circa 1980, and 47 percent in 1990. It is higher still now.

What happened in some of the capital importing regions, such as Argentina and its Latin American neighbors? Figure 6.2 shows that relative to GDP, foreign investment was much more important in these developing countries than in the capital exporters of the core, for two reasons. First, they were poorer countries, so the denominator was smaller; second, relative to other parts of the world, Latin America, and especially Argentina, were heavily favored by foreign investors, at least in the early part of the twentieth century. But that favor did not persist, and as we see there was a dramatic decline in the importance of foreign capital after 1914, persisting even to the present.

To put it another way, Díaz Alejandro (1970) estimated that foreign capital in Argentina in 1913 comprised about 50 percent of the total Argentine domestic capital stock. This is a phenomenal ratio, never seen before or since in capital importing economies, and attests to the extreme exposure of Argentina to foreign investors in the *Belle Époque*. In contrast, by 1950, and throughout much

Fig. 6.2. Foreign capital stock as a fraction of GDP

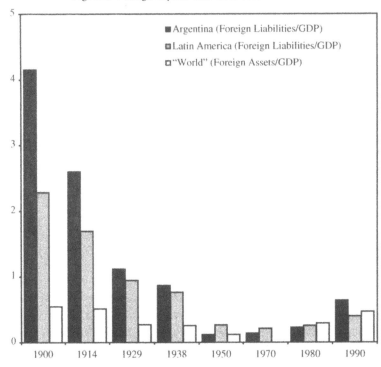

Sources: Taylor (1998); Obstfeld and Taylor (2001).

of the postwar period until the 1980s and 1990s, the use of foreign capital was trivial, and, for all intents and purposes, all capital was of domestic origin.

Of course, raising investment finance from domestic versus foreign sources poses very different sets of institutional, economic, and political problems. Thus, we will also need to keep in mind this remarkable pattern of shifts in the sources of Argentine finance over the years if we are to fully understand the causes and consequences of capital accumulation.

This introduction gives a flavor of some of the key questions in the history of Argentine capital accumulation. Why has investment (and thus growth) been so volatile? What policies have made a difference in these ups and downs? How does the pattern of investment relate to national savings? When, and under what circumstances, have foreign capital inflows made a difference? What underlying variables have affected the level of investment, saving, and the current account at different times? We have also seen a glimpse of a major conceptual and methodological issue that matters: one's interest in real versus nominal measures of investment activity will depend on the purposes at hand. Studies of growth will be best served by real measures, whereas a study, for example, of the national accounts or the external accounts will require nominal data for consistency with the standard accounting identities. In the rest of this chapter we will examine these issues, look at the relevant historical data that have been collected, and discuss the major hypotheses that research has addressed in the past, or has yet to confront in the future.

6.1 Quantities: Investment, saving, and the current account

In this section, I discuss the evolution of the three key variables in the current account identity, $CA = S - I$ where CA is the current account (surplus), S is gross national saving, and I is gross domestic investment. The nomenclature is not always so simple: equivalently, one may call CA capital outflow, or (outward) net foreign investment; for a receiving region we may also refer to $-CA$, the current account deficit, as (inward) net foreign investment. We also will need some kind of normalization to make comparisons feasible across time and space, and the usual procedure here is to normalize all variables as a fraction of GDP. Thus we shall study the three ratios S/Y, I/Y, and CA/Y, where Y is nominal GDP.

Finally, a word on the most serious of the measurement problems is necessary. Except for modern day national accounts, we rarely have comprehensive expenditure-side data that allows us directly to observe national saving, or to calculate it as the difference between the appropriate income and consumption measures. Instead, especially in historical settings, it is necessary to compute S as a residual, given by $S = CA + I$ from the above identity. It is often important to remember that S is constructed in this way, since any biases in CA or I will be built into S too; in particular, this can have important econometric consequences.

Given all these caveats, I will now present the time series evidence, dividing the last century or so into three major phases for this purpose. I first consider the period 1884–1913, when Argentina was well integrated into global capital markets, saving was low, and external inflows were large. Next, I examine the interwar period 1914–45, when external finance was scarce and saving slowly rose. Finally, I look at the post-1945 period when, until recently, inflows were also scarce, but domestic saving started to rise.

Table 6.1. *Saving, investment, and the current account, 1884–1913*

	Y	I	CA	S/Y	I/Y	CA/Y
1884	355	—	-54	—	—	—
1885	463	54	-42	.025	.116	-.091
1886	478	44	-73	-.061	.092	-.153
1887	513	44	-95	-.100	.085	-.185
1888	565	64	-115	-.090	.114	-.204
1889	795	93	-242	-.187	.117	-.304
1890	1,068	176	-262	-.081	.165	-.245
1891	1,482	181	16	.133	.122	.011
1892	1,285	95	-3	.071	.074	-.003
1893	1,265	90	-95	-.003	.071	-.075
1894	1,334	86	-102	-.012	.065	-.077
1895	1,602	109	-45	.040	.068	-.028
1896	1,473	116	-104	.008	.079	-.071
1897	1,428	112	-120	-.005	.079	-.084
1898	1,492	119	-62	.038	.080	-.042
1899	1,398	91	31	.087	.065	.022
1900	1,537	131	-41	.059	.085	-.026
1901	1,461	119	-29	.062	.082	-.020
1902	1,571	129	4	.085	.082	.002
1903	1,694	134	11	.086	.079	.007
1904	1,919	198	-43	.081	.103	-.022
1905	2,368	333	22	.150	.141	.009
1906	2,636	422	-227	.074	.160	-.086
1907	2,770	537	-290	.089	.194	-.105
1908	2,934	441	-143	.102	.150	-.049
1909	3,348	541	-186	.106	.162	-.056
1910	3,882	699	-406	.076	.180	-.105
1911	3,929	685	-608	.020	.174	-.155
1912	4,348	571	-362	.048	.131	-.083
1913	4,400	580	-422	.036	.132	-.096

Notes: Units of I, Y, and CA are millions of pesos (moneda nacional).
Source: Taylor (1998).

6.1.1 The period 1884–1913

Data for the period 1884 to 1913 are shown in Table 6.1 from Taylor (1998b). The construction of these series is quite fragile, and should be regarded as having a wide margin for error.

The basic investment data is from Di Tella and Zymelman (1967), which is based on the work of Alberto Fracchia and others. These estimates of aggregate investment activity are rough and somewhat incomplete. A major problem is that the raw data are real quantities and must be converted to nominal terms using a price deflator series. Here we use the deflator of della Paolera and Ortiz (1995). This is not ideal, since it is a general price level proxy, heavily biased toward tradable goods, and is unlikely to be a reliable measure of the price of the investment component of GDP, which quite probably had a different trend. Perhaps the major flaw in the raw data is the omission of estimates of investment in rural improvements on farms and ranches, principally fencing, drainage and other infrastructure.

Undoubtedly these were major components, but even the recent conjectural figures of Davis and Gallman (2001) cannot pin down these components precisely. However, even when that component is omitted the figures are quite high (by nineteenth century standards) and suggest, for example, an investment rate of between 11 and 16 percent of GDP during the peak of the late 1880s boom. After the 1890–91 Baring Crisis, the volatility of investment is revealed by a collapse in this ratio to around 6 or 7 percent for much of the decade of the 1890s. The investment rate did not recover to above 10 percent until 1904, and then averaged around 15 percent during the height of the *Belle Époque* from 1905 to 1913.

Our current account data for the period is in somewhat better shape. As do most macrohistorical data from this period, the external accounts provide rather good records. Gold values of exports and imports were compiled from customs documents by Cortés Conde et al., provided by Diéguez (1972); applying the paper-gold exchange rate (della Paolera 1988) allows us to figure the trade balance in nominal terms.

This leaves only the net factor payments abroad to be calculated, which, at first approximation, can be thought of as consisting of debt service. An absence of detailed accounts here requires a conjectural approach; before 1900 we can approximate based on the debit side of the "balance of borrowings" series of Williams (1920). After 1900 the data is more scarce and we can do no better than to use data from Phelps (1938) to build a trend approximation (12 percent per annum) from 1900 to 1912 to the growth of foreign debt service, a figure close to the rate of growth of debt itself (about 11 percent per annum over the same period). This kind of an approximation may overstate the debt in the years 1900–04, when Argentina was still establishing credibility in world capital markets after the 1899 gold standard resumption. By the same token, this procedure may understate debt in the peak of the *Belle Époque* of 1905–14, when the country was the darling of foreign investors and a surge of capital poured into this emerging market.

Given all these caveats, what do the data show? For comparison, we should note that it is very unusual for a country to experience a current account deficit in excess of 5 or 10 percent of GDP. It is clear then that the 1880s stand out as a period of totally unprecedented capital inflows into an emerging market at any time in history. Similarly, the years 1905–13 also emerge as years of heavy borrowing. It is probably no coincidence that at other times, when reputation in international capital markets had been lost due to macroeconomic policy mistakes, capital inflows were small, and even turned around into net payments to anxious creditors, the most striking episode of which were the events subsequent to 1890. The Baring Crisis prompted a huge, real structural shift in export, import, fiscal, and consumption allocations to free up resources for debt service (della Paolera 1988; della Paolera and Taylor 2001). Thus, though our immediate task here is to document the statistical evidence, we should remember that there were important institutional forces behind the numbers.

Do these estimates seem reliable? I would urge future research to delve deeper into this question, but I do not expect the claim that the two pre-1913 booms in Argentina witnessed some of the most spectacular capital inflows in the history of the world economy to be overturned. To see how much revision may be needed, let us consider perhaps the most mind-boggling estimate: can a current account deficit of 30 percent of GDP in 1889 be taken seriously? It is surely inaccurate, but by how much? Let us recall where this figure comes from in order to contemplate where the biases may lie. Exports were 90 million gold pesos and imports 164 million that year, for a trade deficit of 74 million gold pesos, or 134 million paper pesos. Output is estimated at 795 million paper pesos, so the trade deficit alone is about 17 percent of GDP. The debit in the balance of borrowings, which we assume is mostly interest paid, was 60 million gold pesos, or 108 million paper, or about 13 percent of GDP.

Where might problems lie in my calculation (Taylor 1998b)? Taxes fell on imports, not on exports, so it is unlikely that imports, and hence the trade deficit, are overstated, unless there are serious biases in the Diéguez series. Interest payments may be overstated, but even if biased by a factor of two, as seems very unlikely, this would yield a current account deficit of 24 percent of GDP, still huge. The only other alternative fix would be to assume that the denominator, 1889 output, is understated in nominal terms. Since all data for this period starts with a 1913 price and output index benchmark, such problems could arise for two reasons. First, because the rate of growth of output or of prices from 1889 to 1913 (the base year) has been set too high; or second, because the 1913 nominal level of output is set too low. Price and output series were taken from della Paolera and Ortiz (1995); but the output trend is not very different from that of Cortés Conde (1994), and the price trend closely matches the exchange rate trend, as expected under a hypothesis of purchasing power parity. The 1913 level of nominal output also closely matches the figures of IEERAL (1986) for 1913 nominal output, so these approximations survive reasonable cross checks against theory and the few independently constructed datasets that we have available.

But why would one worry about these potential upward biases in the current account ratio series? A glance at the residually constructed saving rate series shows why. Because the amplitude of the series CA/Y is so large relative to I/Y, we cannot avoid the conclusion that on average the saving rate S/Y in Argentina was very low, around 5 percent, and in many years was actually *negative* – in some years very negative. Depending on one's priors, this may or may not seem unreasonable. If the famous anecdotes about spendthrift *porteños* splurging their vast fortunes in the salons of Europe are to be believed, then a high propensity to consume might indeed drive saving rates this low! I think future research is needed to pin down estimates of saving rates more accurately before we embrace this popular stereotype as a reflection of macroeconomic conditions.

Still, as I have indicated, I do not expect radical corrections in the series to bring Argentine saving rates in this era up to the levels of European or other settler economies, say in the range of 15 to 20 percent. And this is for good reason, since we know that some important characteristics of the Argentine economy made a high savings rate less likely. Among these explanations we can count poor financial development and low income levels, though we still seek quantitative measures of these effects. One explanation that has been quantified relates to the life-cycle theory of saving. I have shown (Taylor 1992) that Argentina had a demographic structure with a comparatively high dependency rate: around 39 percent of the population was under 15 or over 65 in the years 1900–13, compared to 33 or 34 percent in Australia and Canada. With a higher fraction of children and elderly in the population, Argentina's propensity to consume was pushed higher. Nonetheless, this explanation is only partial and not exclusive. I expect future research to explore which other determinants of low savings rates mattered. At the same time, some of the puzzle of low saving rates might be a data problem, one that might be resolved, in part, by positive adjustments to the investment ratios (to add missing components and better deflators) and to the current account ratios (to better include interest remittances in the numerator and rescale nominal output in the denominator).

6.1.2 The period 1914–1945

Data for the period 1914–45 appear in Table 6.2. Several important historical developments are apparent relative to the picture presented in Table 6.1 for the preceding decades. Most important among these, capital inflows markedly diminished after 1913. During World War I this capital-scarce country was a net capital exporter of about 2 percent of GDP. In the 1920s, some inflows resumed in the range of 4 to 9 percent of GDP, but large flows tapered off after

Table 6.2. *Saving, investment, and the current account, 1914–45*

	Y	I	CA	S/Y	I/Y	CA/Y
1914	3,990	420	96	.129	.105	.024
1915	4,301	340	29	.086	.079	.007
1916	4,723	370	144	.109	.078	.030
1917	5,370	360	253	.114	.067	.047
1918	6,995	350	203	.079	.050	.029
1919	7,448	430	235	.089	.058	.032
1920	8,368	590	-340	.030	.071	-.041
1921	6,844	600	-538	.009	.088	-.079
1922	6,729	730	-616	.017	.108	-.092
1923	7,724	1,040	-394	.084	.135	-.051
1924	8,951	1,050	-312	.083	.117	-.035
1925	9,035	1,040	-312	.081	.115	-.034
1926	8,536	1,010	-268	.087	.118	-.031
1927	8,958	1,120	51	.131	.125	.006
1928	9,611	1,300	-113	.124	.135	-.012
1929	9,749	1,490	-379	.114	.153	-.039
1930	8,956	1,250	-851	.045	.140	-.095
1931	8,063	770	-260	.063	.096	-.032
1932	7,883	560	-57	.064	.071	-.007
1933	7,886	600	-247	.045	.076	-.031
1934	9,696	890	-27	.089	.092	-.003
1935	10,015	1,100	14	.111	.110	.001
1936	10,611	1,290	117	.133	.122	.011
1937	12,234	1,310	317	.133	.107	.026
1938	11,922	1,380	-557	.069	.116	-.047
1939	12,521	1,210	-69	.091	.097	-.006
1940	12,917	1,250	-182	.083	.097	-.014
1941	13,918	1,250	203	.104	.090	.015
1942	15,729	1,680	360	.130	.107	.023
1943	16,547	1,800	1,280	.186	.109	.077
1944	18,899	1,510	1,273	.147	.080	.067
1945	20,865	2,460	1,480	.189	.118	.071

Notes: Units of I, Y, and CA are millions of pesos (moneda nacional).
Source: Taylor (1998).

1930, and again during wartime from 1941 to 1945 the country was a net capital exporter.

This change in the pattern of capital flows comes as no surprise to the historian familiar with the dramatic disintegration of the global capital market in the interwar period (Obstfeld and Taylor 1998). From a comparative standpoint, the shrinkage of flows to Argentina was not unusual, since all countries experienced a reduction in capital movements, both export and import, after 1913. What is unique about the Argentine case is that such a change of regime should come sharp on the heels of a development path that had operated for many decades under the assumption of unrestricted and open access to capital on the world market. No other country, therefore, had so much to lose once this source of investment funds dried up.

I have explored in more quantitative detail some of the sources and implications of this regime change for Argentine development (Taylor 1992; 1994). An immediate challenge was for the Argentine economy to find domestic substitutes for foreign finance. This meant either enlarging the supply of domestic saving or enhancing the technologies of financial intermediation to more efficiently mobilize the savings. Neither came to full fruition in the short run. Despite fluctuations in the saving rate data, mostly driven by the residual construction methods noted above, we can see that, as expected, secular shifts in the saving rate tend to occur rather slowly. I would estimate that it took a span of almost two decades, from the 1910s to the 1930s, for Argentina to be able to claim with conviction a saving rate that had decisively moved into double digits.

These constraints on savings supply, which fed into a tight constraint on investment, have two proximate causes that we can identify so far. First, at the fundamental level of the determinants of saving supply, Argentina could not quickly escape the slowly evolving demographic dynamics that kept dependency rates persistently high during the interwar period (Taylor 1992). Not until the demographic transition to lower birth rates was under way did dependency rates converge to the levels of Europe or the other settler economies. Second, in terms of savings mobilization, domestic financial intermediation remained limited after 1913. Argentina was previously well served by solid international banks, which had ample diversification and insurance through their headquarters and global networks. When these banks left on the ebb tide of capital flows after 1913, they took that technology with them, and the domestic banks left in their wake were very different firms (della Paolera and Taylor 1998). Compared to the retreating foreign banks, the domestic banks were more cautious, meaning that they had lower leverage; and they were inherently more fragile – more prone to the risks of runs and capital crunches during downturns. As such, they were ill equipped to replace the financial void left by the withdrawal of foreign banks.

The effects of this new capital market regime were very adverse for Argentina's growth path (Taylor 1992; 1994). With investment rates I/Y constrained to be equal to relatively low saving rates S/Y, a major source of growth had been curtailed. Far from being able to reach investment rates of 15 to 20 percent as in the *Belle Époque* years, the Argentine economy of the 1910s and 1920s was held to an investment rate of about 10 percent. This ratio recovered only later as saving rates rose in the 1930s and 1940s to offset lost inflows.

Attributing a growth effect to a counterfactual "lost" capital flow of perhaps 5 to 10 percent of GDP is a speculative exercise, an approximation. But if we postulate a rate of return of 20 percent, the curtailed capital inflows would have had a growth rate effect of 1 or 2 percentage points of output growth per annum. This is a quantitatively significant effect, given the actual retardation of 1.6 percentage points from 1900–13 to 1913–29. Moreover, using the above-mentioned econometric methods to estimate demographic impacts on saving rates, one can show that this savings shortfall was due almost entirely to Argentina's comparatively high dependency ratios.

The interwar period of Argentina is interesting in the broader context of Argentine economic development because it represents an important turning point. Up to 1913, Argentine per capita incomes had been converging upward on the levels seen in the OECD. It was an emerging market, a developing country, to be sure, but one that seemed destined to join quickly the ranks of highly developed and wealthy economies. But after 1913 divergence set in at an accelerating pace: a slow relative decline from 1914 to 1929 was then followed much more serious retardation beginning in 1929 and especially in the postwar period. It is clearly important that we diagnose correctly the sources of this retardation, a development failure that has had such hard consequences for Argentines' economic and even psychological well-being.

As other chapters in this volume show, no one can dispute the importance of certain policy mistakes in the twentieth century that made matters much, much worse than they needed to be. At the same time, we should recognize some important external shocks to the Argentine economy that also mattered greatly, and helped set it on its divergent course in the first place. The dramatic change in the capital accumulation regime after 1913 seems like the most important example of such a change: here, by force of circumstance, not by choice, an autarkic response in the rest of the world left Argentina reliant on a very meager domestic savings supply.

6.1.3 The period 1945 to the present

Finally, the evidence on saving, investment, and the current account after 1945 can be found in Table 6.3. Note that the nominal figures in the table are subject to several recalibrations of units during this period of high inflation, and sometimes hyperinflation. The striking feature of this table is that, in nominal terms, most of the underlying constraints on saving seemed to have been lifted by the postwar period. Saving rates of 30 percent or more were not uncommon in the 1960s and 1970s, so that, even with the persistent closure of world capital markets, Argentina could mobilize a great deal of capital for investment in this period.

Table 6.3. *Saving, investment, and the current account, 1945–92*

	Y	I	CA	S/Y	I/Y	CA/Y
1945	20,865	2,460	1,480	.189	.118	.071
1946	28,252	3,100	1,999	.180	.110	.071
1947	38,825	5,150	852	.155	.133	.022
1948	47,305	6,090	214	.133	.129	.005
1949	56,792	6,510	-610	.104	.115	-.011
1950	67,275	7,740	561	.123	.115	.008
1951	96,390	16,900	-5,318	.120	.175	-.055
1952	111,540	19,600	-9,451	.091	.176	-.085
1953	128,761	22,700	7,761	.237	.176	.060
1954	142,652	22,400	2,100	.172	.157	.015
1955	168,598	27,600	-7,379	.120	.164	-.044
1956	220,731	31,600	-4,656	.122	.143	-.021
1957	283,051	44,100	-12,005	.113	.156	-.042
1958	399,515	62,800	-12,976	.125	.157	-.032
1959	762,791	126,500	878	.167	.166	.001
1960	1,006	218	-5	.211	.216	-.005
1961	1,214	261	-35	.186	.215	-.028
1962	1,455	306	-14	.201	.211	-.009
1963	1,922	317	48	.190	.165	.025
1964	2,710	500	25	.194	.184	.009
1965	3,834	1,081	38	.292	.282	.010
1966	4,840	1,235	54	.266	.255	.011
1967	6,427	1,698	43	.271	.264	.007
1968	7,498	2,007	-19	.265	.268	-.002
1969	8,938	2,625	-80	.285	.294	-.009

It may therefore seem surprising that this apparent success in generating a high saving rate did not lead to the same outcomes – high growth rates and a convergences in per capita incomes on the OECD – that was seen in other high saving and high investment rate countries, the East Asian "tiger" economies such as Korea and Taiwan. The answer, as may be surmised, can be traced back to our earlier Figure 6.1.

Although nominal spending on investment was as high as 30 percent as a fraction of output, in real terms this investment was much lower, around 15 to 20 percent, and was subject to serious misallocation problems. The low real value of investment stemmed from trade and fiscal policies that taxed capital goods heavily and drove a wedge between domestic and world prices. The misallocation came from a variegated structure of protection that distorted relative prices of different goods. These findings only beg the counterfactual question: how much did the misspent savings of Argentina cost the country in

Table 6.3. (Continued)

	Y	I	CA	S/Y	I/Y	CA/Y
1970	10,585	2,933	-62	.271	.277	-.006
1971	15,277	4,014	-176	.251	.263	-.012
1972	25,545	6,639	-113	.255	.260	-.004
1973	44,325	9,881	355	.231	.223	.008
1974	61,477	14,512	59	.237	.236	.001
1975	182,852	57,122	-4,708	.287	.312	-.026
1976	981,406	314,482	9,114	.330	.320	.009
1977	2,739,434	878,450	45,896	.337	.321	.017
1978	6,929,834	1,969,950	147,682	.306	.284	.021
1979	19,088,936	4,995,889	-67,562	.258	.262	-.004
1980	38,400	9,700	-877	.230	.253	-.023
1981	74,740	16,960	-2,075	.199	.227	-.028
1982	218,520	47,540	-6,099	.190	.218	-.028
1983	1,095,000	228,700	-25,651	.185	.209	-.023
1984	7,909,200	1,579,000	-168,787	.178	.200	-.021
1985	53,050	9,331	-573	.165	.176	-.011
1986	99,841	17,434	-2,696	.148	.175	-.027
1987	233,323	45,626	-9,080	.157	.196	-.039
1988	1,110,620	207,020	-13,760	.174	.186	-.012
1989	32,440,450	5,033,029	-552,406	.138	.155	-.017
1990	689,923	96,474	9,279	.153	.140	.013
1991	1,808,980	264,781	-26,739	.132	.146	-.015
1992	2,266,376	378,544	-82,913	.130	.167	-.037

Notes: Units of *I*, *Y*, and *CA* are millions of pesos moneda nacional until 1959, then billions to 1979, trillions to 1984, billion billions to 1989, then billion trillions to 1992.
Source: Taylor (1998).

terms of long run economic growth? It is a topic to which we shall return in a moment when we consider price distortions.

The story of the postwar period is therefore, at a deep level, in marked contrast to that of the interwar period. In brief, in the former period, distortions were few and accumulation was held back by scarce domestic savings and a trickle of foreign capital; Argentina knew then how to allocate capital, it just did not have enough in supply. In the postwar period, Argentina raised the saving rate, but capital goods prices were distorted so as to limit real capital accumulation, and misallocation was encouraged by an array of relative price distortions; in this latter era, Argentina had an ample supply of savings, but failed to use it wisely.

Only in the decade of the 1990s did investment prices in Argentina finally start to converge back to world levels, implying that investment goods were now more affordable and that savings would generate more and better capital accumulation. At the same time, world capital markets became much more open, and like many emerging markets, Argentina now has the chance to augment its own potentially high saving rate with flows of foreign capital that reappeared as a force in the global economy. In addition, favorable demographic trends promise even high rates of saving within Argentina (Taylor 1998b). As the accumulation bottlenecks of the last century are lifted – whether they were caused by external shocks, slow changes in fundamentals, or errant policies – Argentina should again find herself with great opportunities for growth by accumulation.

6.1.4 Sectoral allocation of investment

Macroeconomic statistics, of course, only tell one part of the history of Argentine investment. Where did this investment go and how was it used? Although space is limited, it is worth spending a moment to consider the sectoral allocation of investment among the three main categories of GDP, the primary, secondary, and tertiary sectors (corresponding to agriculture and extractive activity, manufacturing activity, and service activity). This decomposition for the years 1913 to 1984 is shown in Figure 6.3.

Certain major trends stand out. Investment in agriculture has been in decline for most of the century, falling from around 5 to less than 1 percent of GDP. This reflects both the decline in the relative size of the sector itself, but also the reallocation, on the margin, of funds to other uses. The main beneficiary here was the manufacturing (secondary) sector, although the service sector has also seen a sharp increase from a very low starting point. However, the overall impression is one of manufacturing as the main recipient of investment funds – over two-thirds in most years.

The chart also invites speculation over the very different trends in the volatility of each component. In part this may reflect the volatility of each sector within the business cycle. Manufacturing investment has been very volatile, with marked troughs during the crises of the world wars, the Great Depression, and the 1980s debt crisis. But service sector investment has been much steadier over time, and agricultural investment steadier still.

Other hypotheses may invite investigation here: for example, to what extent was agriculture shielded from volatility by its isolation from financial intermediation? We know that farmers were poorly served in general by banks, a phenomenon that dates back to the late-nineteenth century and one that put Argentine farmers at a relative disadvantage compared to their competitors in other settler countries such as Canada (Adelman 1994). If, absent external sources of finance, farmers relied more on retained earnings and saving from profits as sources of capital, then we might indeed expect to see a low correlation between their investment activity and the rest of the economy. This is

Fig. 6.3. Investment by sector as a fraction of GDP, 1913–84

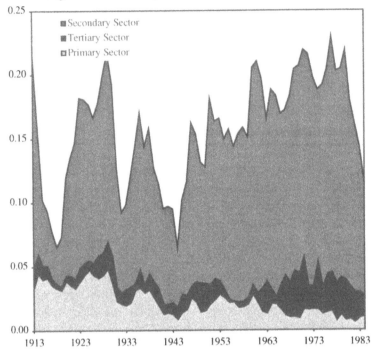

Sources: IEERAL (1986).

not to say such an outcome was efficient, of course: farmers probably would have benefited from access to a larger pool of capital, albeit with risk of higher volatility. Such sectoral cleavages in the national capital market remain little studied, and they merit attention in our future research. Another important question concerns the extent to which economic policies discriminated against agriculture, and therefore channeled excessive and inefficient investment in protected industries. There appears to be ample evidence of this force at work (Mundlak, Cavallo, and Domenech 1989).

6.2 Prices: Interest rates, risk premia, and the cost of capital

Although the preceding evidence gives an overview of the major quantity measures of capital market activity, an equally important statistical measure is the price of capital. Economic theory tells us that the key price is the user cost of capital, which can be further broken down into two components. First is the financial cost of borrowing, that is, the interest rate; second is the relative price of capital goods, a variable we have already discussed as a factor in translating nominal savings resources into real investment quantities.

Prices are important because we expect them to clear markets and drive allocation: in particular, prices should have an inverse relationship to investment demand. In this section of the chapter we examine the way in which price changes have related to investment outcomes in Argentine history and to what extent the capital market has effectively functioned. This narrative will stress the empirical evidence, but it ties in with important discussions of the institutional evolution of banks and financial markets, macroeconomic policies, and the relationship between business and government in other chapters.

6.2.1 Interest rates before 1940

We first examine the financial cost of capital, or the interest rate. For many countries, especially developing countries, this is not easy historical data to collect. In the case of a country such as Argentina, which experienced considerable controls on financial markets in the postwar period, even the existence of price data does not guarantee that transactions actually took place at those prices. The data may reveal very little about actual market conditions absent further institutional knowledge. Finally, we should note that there are often dozens of interest rates at any point in time, including for example bond rates, deposit rates, lending rates, and discount rates; for clarity we can only present a few series, and preferably only those that allow consistent comparisons across time. With these caveats in mind we can turn to the extant evidence. We will focus on the long-term government bond series since the mid-nineteenth century.

Before World War II we have long and continuous series for external bonds floated in hard currency (gold) in London. Gold bond yields are approximately equivalent to real interest rates given the stability of the London gold price for most of this period (excluding World War I, and at least until sterling left the gold standard in 1931). Such a bond yield gives a good representation of the marginal, external opportunity cost of capital imported from the rest of the world – at least for the sovereign borrower, the federal government, which probably obtained the most favorable (lowest) risk premium of any Argentine borrower. After World War II, little external capital flowed, and the best series we have are yields on domestic bonds in paper currency, which require somewhat different handling to convert nominal into real interest rates, especially in times of high inflation. The interest rates for the two epochs appear in Figure 6.4 and Table 6.4.

Fig. 6.4. *External government bond yields, 1870–1940*

External Bond Spread: Argentina v. 11 Core & Empire Bonds

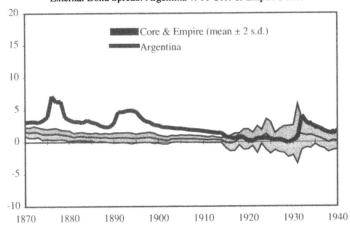

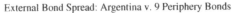

External Bond Spread: Argentina v. 9 Periphery Bonds

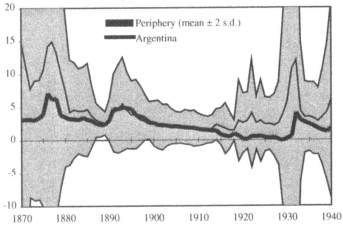

Notes and Sources: Underlying data from Global Financial Data and della Paolera (1988). Core and Empire = Australia, Canada, France, Germany, India, Netherlands, New Zealand, Norway, South Africa, Sweden, and the United States. Periphery = Chile, Greece, Hungary, Italy, Japan, Mexico, Portugal, Spain, and Uruguay.

Table 6.4. *Real and nominal government bond yields after 1950*

	Rate of Inflation	Interest Rate			Rate of Inflation	Interest Rate	
		Nominal	Real			Nominal	Real
1950	20	8	-12	1972	77	26	-51
1951	49	8	-41	1973	50	23	-27
1952	31	8	-23	1974	21	23	2
1953	12	8	-4	1975	196	41	-156
1954	3	7	4	1976	494	70	-424
1955	9	7	-2	1977	151	—	—
1956	26	10	-16	1978	145	172	27
1957	24	10	-14	1979	148	135	-13
1958	31	11	-20	1980	74	98	24
1959	133	11	-123	1981	110	—	—
1960	16	11	-5	1982	256	—	—
1961	8	11	3	1983	361	—	—
1962	30	14	-17	1984	575	—	—
1963	29	17	-12	1985	663	76	-586
1964	26	17	-9	1986	64	91	27
1965	24	17	-7	1987	123	126	3
1966	20	17	-3	1988	413	167	-246
1967	26	17	-9	1989	3433	443	-2989
1968	10	17	7	1990	1607	274	-1333
1969	6	16	10	1991	110	86	-25
1970	14	16	2	1992	6	32	26
1971	39	18	-21	1993	2	25	23

Source: della Paolera and Ortiz (1995).

Figure 6.4 shows the London bond yield for Argentine bonds in the years 1870 to 1940. What do these series have to say about how well Argentina was integrated into world capital markets? Argentina's cost of borrowing varied dramatically over the years, and the *risk premium*, or the excess yield demanded on Argentine bonds relative to safe bonds, such as the British consol, also proved very volatile. To explore how Argentina was treated relative to other bond issuers in the London market we can compare spreads with those of other borrowers. We show two comparsions: how Argentina's yield compared to the distribution (mean yield plus or minus two standard deviations) in a sample of core country bond yields, and also the same statistics for a sample of periphery country yields.

Before 1913, it is apparent that during times of Argentine macroeconomic stability, such as the 1900s, Argentine bonds could be floated at rates only slightly above those in core countries, and at a yield not atypical for periphery borrowers. In the 1870s and 1880s, Argentina was even a favored borrower compared to many peripheral countries, obtaining much lower bond spreads than most. In contrast, during crisis episodes in the 1870s and 1890s, bond spreads widened. More than a century ago, the international financial markets were swift to punish countries that flirted with macroeconomic policy mistakes. By the 1920s Argentina was doing even better: the risk premium had almost vanished relative to the core, and was much lower than in other periphery countries. Markets took the view that Argentina was something of a safe haven, especially as its macroeconomic reputation grew and core countries went to war. Of course, there are a couple of problems with taking this as a uniformly positive statement about interwar borrowing conditions. First, we are looking just at the secondary market's assessment of Argentine risk and, at times, especially for the decade after 1914, very little new capital actually flowed at these rates. Second, it is clear that all was lost in the Great Depression, as spreads widened and international lending came to a total standstill.

However, a most striking feature of these data is that they do correlate to some degree with major capital inflow episodes, and the investment booms that resulted from them. When lending was low cost in the 1880s and 1900s, and again in the 1920s, surges in investment and growth took place. In crises, when spreads widened, capital inflows dried up and investment was curtailed. We should like to know more about causality here. It probably ran both ways: poor news about fundamentals raised risk premia, but at the same time high interest rates also discouraged new investment. To the extent that these shocks were exogenous, they reflected world capital market conditions over which Argentina had no control. But an open area for research concerns the extent of "contagion" effects in world capital markets and, for our purpose, how they might have affected Argentine conditions. The crisis of 1890 was home-grown, but the downturns of the 1870s and 1890s were also global crises, as were World War I and the Great Depression. These shocks were international in origin and impact. In those crises it remains to be shown to what extent adverse price and quantity effects on investment were based on fundamentals, and how that compares with recent experience (Bordo, Eichengreen, and Irwin 1999).

6.2.2 Interest rates after 1950

After 1950 we can consider the internal government bond yields and annual averages shown in Table 6.4, converted into real rates using a CPI inflation rate. Again, we are using the government bond yield as a proxy for interest rates in the economy as a whole.

The contrast between the data in this table and the pre-1940 data in Figure 6.3 reveals, in another way, the dramatic change in the capital market from the 1940s until the reforms of the 1990s. In almost all years, with increasingly rampant inflation, real interest rates were negative. How could this be so? In a free market this price could not be sustained as a competitve equilibrium. Here the figures instead are revealing of the conditions of financial repression that existed in Argentina for four decades after 1950. As researchers in the financial markets of developing countries have shown, financial repression is a common market failure, and exists in economies in which interest rates are subject to caps or other controls, banks are heavily regulated, and inflation rates are high or accelerating (Fry 1995; McKinnon 1973). This phenomenon is well known in postwar Latin America, and its adverse impacts have been explored quantitatively (Roubini and Sala-i-Martin 1992).

Essentially, the problem is this: at negative real interest rates, everyone will want to borrow and nobody will want to save. The price mechanism is destroyed as a rationing device, so other allocation mechanisms have to be brought into play. On the investment demand side, this means even more burdensome project evaluation by financial intermediaries or the explicit direction of investment funds by bureaucrats or governments. On the savings supply side, absent any financial incentives to willingly hold bonds yielding negative real returns, legislation and regulation must be introduced to require savings in this form by individuals or institutions (e.g., banks). Implicit subsidies are then created to make sure such assets are unwillingly held, creating further dead-weight loss.

Such a scenario of financial repression played out in postwar Argentina. National saving rates were high, as we saw earlier, but the allocation of those funds was not governed at all by normal considerations of market pricing of financial capital. Instead, nonprice allocation of investment became the norm. This also must be reckoned as one of the pivotal changes between the early- and late-twentieth century, and another culprit, therefore, in the long-term economic decline arising from the misuse of investment.

6.2.3 *The relative price of capital*

Our discovery of peculiar, negative trends in the real interest rate after 1950 raise the question: if the real interest rate did not ration investment and clear the market, what did? Although financial repression and nonprice credit rationing devices are part of the answer, a complementary explanation might be found by examining the other important component of the user cost of capital, the relative price of the capital goods themselves.

We have already made reference to the pioneering work of Díaz Alejandro (1970) on this issue. He noted that the price of machinery and equipment, the most tradable of all capital goods, was perhaps twice as high in Argentina in some of these years as in, for example, the United States. Under the uncontroversial assumption that demand curves slope downward, this kind of inflated

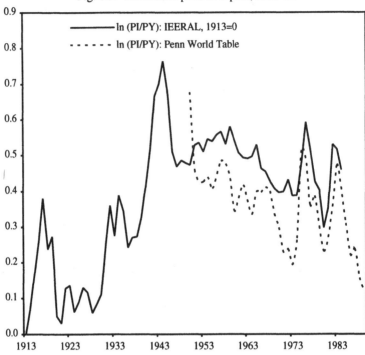

Fig. 6.5. The relative price of capital, 1913–89

Sources: IEERAL (1986); Heston et al. (1994).

price would tend to dampen investment and hence growth. With longer-run data series at our disposal, as in Figure 6.5, we can see the full extent of these distortions in the postwar period, and their swift emergence after 1929. The series of domestic prices (from IEERAL) does not compare Argentine prices to world prices, but assuming distortions are small in 1913, we can see that a price twist of up to 30 percent emerges during World War I and in the 1930s as imports are rationed in economic crises. The distortion ratchets higher still in World War II, but thereafter, as a result of the implementation of policies that kept it in place, it does not decline. After 1950 we have the Penn World Table data to give us an accurate picture of local versus world relative prices, and their match to the above IEERAL series is quite close, suggesting that our 1913 normalization was reasonable. The postwar data reveal a very persistent and high relative price twist of 40 to 80 percent from the 1940s to the 1980s, a feature of the Argentine economy that has only been altered decisively by the reforms of the 1990s.

How did these price twists emerge? These distortions took the form of trade restrictions. Initially they arose out of macroeconomic policies in the 1930s, and out of the adoption of successful heterodox policies in reaction to the collapse of the Gold Standard (della Paolera and Taylor 1999). These policies included competitive devaluations and the introduction of assorted exchange controls, but by the late 1930s the multiple exchange rate regime had been recognized as a powerful tool for protectionism of nascent industrial sectors (Salera 1941). The impacts were eventually codified and extended as a part of Argentine commercial policy in the form of tariffs and quotas. An emphasis on developing home-grown manufactures, including capital goods, was the hallmark of this Import Substituting Industrialization (ISI). Space is short, so I refer the reader to the chapters in this volume on macroeconomic policy, trade and commercial policy, and business and government to find more details on the interplay of all these forces.

What was the political economy of these developments? The traditional explanation is that the Peronist economic agenda deprioritized investment goods relative to other objectives in the allocation of foreign exchange (Díaz Alejandro 1970). Populism required bread and circuses for the working-class constituents, so imports of consumption goods could not be compressed too hard; equally, imported raw materials were essential to the short run task of keeping the factories operational. To maintain external balance, something had to be squeezed, and unfortunately this turned out to be the goods that form the basis of long-run growth, the capital goods. The cost was very high indeed, and had investment price distortions been removed, virtually all of Argentina's retardation relative to the OECD could have been abated (Taylor 1994). Although this explanation is persuasive, future research on the political economy of the Peronist years and the emergence of ISI could shed new light on exactly how this process both got underway and persisted for many decades.

In a comparative study (Taylor 1998a), I provide an even broader empirical basis for this conclusion, extending the idea to a broad sample of countries that includes a key comparison of East Asia and Latin America. In its postwar policy mix Argentina was not alone: many countries reacted to the global isolationism that developed in the 1920s to the 1940s in just the same way. But Argentina stands out as the poster child of ISI in the postwar period, with policy distortions that were similar to, but more pronounced than, those applied elsewhere in Latin America. In contrast, those countries in the 1960s and 1970s that did succeed in removing these distortions to investment price do appear to have spurred investment and economic growth – notable are the success cases in East Asia

6.3 Conclusion

The record of superior economic growth in the *Belle Époque* and relative economic retardation ever since has always divided Argentine economic history into two major phases, years of convergence and divergence. As this survey of capital accumulation shows, that record of economic growth is highly correlated with patterns of investment. We can learn a great deal from both the simple time-series measures of investment activity and the quality of that investment as revealed by quantitative price distortions and by qualitative institutional characteristics.

Overall, the investment record helps us understand some of the underlying causes of growth performance, highlighting the channels through which exogenous global economic shocks or domestic policy choices affected outcomes. Seen this way, history presents a more complex story than the simple two-period framework of success followed by failure. Perhaps we can better summarize Argentine experience in three phases.

The first phase was 1884–1913, when investment demand boomed and open world markets channeled other countries' savings into very productive use in the Argentine economy. In that era, despite some occasional and now infamous policy mistakes, the economy prospered. In the second phase, the interwar period, investment demand was held back by a reliance on purely domestic saving as global capital markets seized up; growth slowed and matters were made more difficult by a fragile financial system. In the third, postwar period, policy interventions were much more widespread, and, by poor design, extremely detrimental to capital accumulation. High relative prices for investment goods were stimulated by tax and tariff measures and financial repression created allocation mechanisms divorced from price incentives. The great tragedy of the postwar era is that most of the very generous supply of savings was misspent on investment activities that were either overpriced or unnecessary or both. In conclusion, to look forward, we can hope that Argentine investment is now entering a fourth phase, hopefully reminiscent of the first phase, when domestic and foreign savings are abundant and market allocation mechanisms once again operate effectively to channel precious resources for growth to their most efficient use.

References

Abramovitz, Moses. 1956. Resource and Output Trends in the United States Since 1870. *American Economic Review* 46 (2): 5–23.
Adelman, Jeremy. 1994. *Frontier Development: Land, Labour, and Capital on the Wheatlands of Argentina and Canada, 1890–1914.* Oxford: Clarendon Press.

Barro, Robert J., and Xavier Sala-i-Martin. 1995. *Economic Growth.* New York: McGraw-Hill.

Bordo, Michael D., Barry Eichengreen, and Douglas A. Irwin. 1999. Is Globalization Today Really Different Than Globalization a Hundred Years Ago? *Brookings Trade Forum.*

Cortés Conde, Roberto. 1994. Estimaciones del PBI en la Argentina 1875–1935. Ciclos de seminarios no. 3/94, Departamento de Economía, Universidad de San Andrés.

Davis, Lance E., and Robert E. Gallman. 2001. *Evolving Financial Markets and International Capital Flows: Britain, The Americas, and Australia, 1865–1914.* Japan–U.S. Center Sanwa Monographs on International Financial Markets. Cambridge: Cambridge University Press.

della Paolera, Gerardo. 1988. How the Argentine Economy Performed During the International Gold Standard: A Reexamination. Ph.D. dissertation, University of Chicago.

della Paolera, Gerardo, and Javier Ortiz. 1995. Dinero, intermediación financiera y nivel de actividad en 110 años de historia económica argentina. Documentos de Trabajo no. 36 (December), Universidad Torcuato Di Tella.

della Paolera, Gerardo, and Alan M. Taylor. 1998. Finance and Development in an Emerging Market: Argentina in the Interwar Period. In *Latin America and the World Economy Since 1800*, edited by J. H. Coatsworth and A. M. Taylor. Cambridge, Mass.: Harvard University Press.

———. 1999. Economic Recovery from the Argentine Great Depression: Institutions, Expectations, and the Change of Macroeconomic Regime. *Journal of Economic History* 59 (3): 567–99.

———. 2001. *Straining at the Anchor: The Argentine Currency Board and the Search for Macroeconomic Stability, 1880–1935.* NBER Series on Long-Term Factors in Economic Growth. Chicago: University of Chicago Press.

Díaz Alejandro, Carlos F. 1970. *Essays on the Economic History of the Argentine Republic.* New Haven, Conn.: Yale University Press.

Diéguez, Héctor L. 1972. Crecimiento e inestabilidad del valor y el volumen físico de las exportaciones en el período 1864–1963. *Desarrollo Económico* 12: 333–49.

Di Tella, Guido, and Manuel Zymelman. 1967. *Las etapas del desarrollo económico argentino.* Buenos Aires: Editorial Universitaria de Buenos Aires.

Fry, Maxwell J. 1995. *Money, Interest, and Banking in Economic Development.* 2d ed. Baltimore, Md.: Johns Hopkins University Press.

Heston, Alan, Robert Summers, Daniel A. Nuxoll, and Bettina Aten. 1994. The Penn World Table, Version 5.6. National Bureau of Economic Research, Cambridge, Mass. Internet <http://nber.harvard.edu>.

IEERAL (Instituto de Estudios Económicos sobre la Realidad Argentina y Latinoamericana). 1986. Estadísticas de la evolución económica de Argentina 1913–1984. *Estudios* 9 (39): 103–84.

Levine, Ross, and David Renelt. 1992. A Sensitivity Analysis of Cross-Country Growth Regressions. *American Economic Review* 82 (4): 942–63.

Mankiw, N. Gregory, David Romer, and David N. Weil. 1992. A Contribution to the Empirics of Economic Growth. *Quarterly Journal of Economics* 107 (2): 407–37.

McKinnon, Ronald I. 1973. *Money and Capital in Economic Development.* Washington, D.C.: The Brookings Institution.

Mundlak, Yair, Domingo Cavallo, and Roberto Domenech. 1989. Agriculture and Economic Growth in Argentina, 1913–1984. Research Report no. 76 (November), International Food Policy Research Institute.

Obstfeld, Maurice, and Alan M. Taylor. 1998. The Great Depression as a Watershed: International Capital Mobility in the Long Run. In *The Defining Moment: The Great Depression and the American Economy in the Twentieth Century*, edited by M. D. Bordo, C. D. Goldin, and E. N. White. Chicago: University of Chicago Press.

———. 2003. *Global Capital Markets: Integration, Crisis, and Growth, Japan-U.S. Center Sanwa Monographs on International Financial Markets*. Cambridge: Cambridge University Press. In press.

Phelps, Vernon Lovell. 1938. *The International Economic Position of Argentina*. Philadelphia: University of Pennsylvania Press.

Roubini, Nouriel, and Xavier Sala-i-Martin. 1992. Financial Repression and Economic Growth. *Journal of Development Economics* 39: 5–30.

Salera, Virgil. 1941. *Exchange Control and the Argentine Market*. New York: Columbia University Press.

Solow, Robert M. 1956. A Contribution to the Theory of Economic Growth. *Quarterly Journal of Economics* 70: 65–94.

Taylor, Alan M. 1992. External Dependence, Demographic Burdens and Argentine Economic Decline After the *Belle Époque*. *Journal of Economic History* 52 (4): 907–36.

———. 1994. Tres fases del crecimiento económico argentino. *Revista de Historia Económica* 12 (3): 649–83.

———. 1998a. Argentina and the World Capital Market: Saving, Investment, and International Capital Mobility in the Twentieth Century. *Journal of Development Economics* 57 (1): 147–84.

———. 1998b. On the Costs of Inward-Looking Development: Price Distortions, Growth, and Divergence in Latin America. *Journal of Economic History* 58 (1): 1–28.

———. 1999. Sources of Convergence in the Late-Nineteenth Century. *European Economic Review* 43 (5): 1621–45.

Williams, John H. 1920. *Argentine International Trade Under Inconvertible Paper Currency, 1880–1900*. Cambridge, Mass.: Harvard University Press.

7

International trade and commercial policy

JULIO BERLINSKI
Instituto Torcuato Di Tella and Universidad Torcuato Di Tella

This chapter provides a long view of Argentine international trade and commercial policies based on selected data for the twentieth century. Foreign shocks caused by wars and exogenous changes in commodity prices of exports and imports have affected international trade in Argentina, thus inducing domestic policy responses. Those responses were formulated within a framework of alternative development paths, resulting in a specific interdependence of devices used to control imports and promote exports, with both price and quantity instruments, by either fixing nominal exchange rates or regulating trade flows and the types of goods eligible for differential incentives.

It is tempting to assign certain sets of policy choices to different kinds of regimes, and attempt some sort of periodization, but this is no simple task. Of the various policy experiments, some bear similarities, but nevertheless are differentiated by intensity and foreign context. Trade policy in some periods was based on greater trade liberalization with a policy mix influenced by different ideas or fashions. After the adoption of foreign exchange control in 1931, policies based on closed-economy models were introduced with the purpose of maintaining prior levels of activity. Due to the importance of bilateral agreements, priority was placed on foreign exchange availability to satisfy the demand for imported inputs induced by import-substituting industrialization (ISI).[1]

The conventional historiography usually highlights 1931 as the major turning point in Argentine trade and commercial policy, and the subsequent decade has thus been seen as the start of a new, inward-looking regime in which industry was the leading sector of the economy – or at least, was intended as such.

The comments of the conference participants are gratefully acknowledged, especially those of Alan Taylor, Gerardo della Paolera, and George McCandless. The efficient assistance of Nicolás M. Depetris Chauvin is gratefully acknowledged. The points of view are my own.
[1] See the chapter on industry in this volume.

But this did not imply that the external sector was thereafter unimportant as a force in aggregate performance. Berlinski (1966) estimated a model of growth for the period 1935–53.[2] In these years ISI was promoted by protectionist devices (e.g., exchange rate controls and import tariffs) and other policies (e.g., subsidized credit lines, especially after 1943). These policies were intended to compensate for countervailing effects caused by a sharp fall in exports, mainly caused by external conditions.[3] Accordingly, in 1935–53, changes in trade variables accounted for 60 percent of total deviations (direct plus indirect) from trend, while only 16 percent corresponded to deviations in domestic absorption and 24 percent to technological change.[4]

Without recourse, then, to an over-simplified periodization, this chapter begins by discussing the trends in the terms of trade and the reaction of domestic policies over the course of the last century. This includes a detailed examination of several important periods, with a selective discussion of the different instruments used to control imports and promote exports. The next major section estimates some of the determinants of the real exchange rate. The final section discusses changes in factor prices and endowments.

7.1 Terms of trade and commercial policies

7.1.1 The trends of the century

We begin with a look at the long run trends of some key variables. Figure 7.1 shows the compensatory nature of the movement through time of the domestic terms of trade (DTT, the ratio of the wholesale prices of agriculture to industry) following shocks in the foreign terms of trade (FTT, the ratio of the unit values of exports to imports).

In Figure 7.2 the relationship of both indices (foreign and domestic terms of trade) provides a trade policy index in which the adjustment of relative nominal (trade-weighted) exchange rates diverges little from the trend. This is

[2] In order to explain the Argentine pattern of growth, the model applied followed that of Chenery et al. (1962), and estimated changes in output as caused by deviations in autonomous elements such as domestic absorption, exports, imports, and technological change.

[3] Comparing 1934–38 and 1950–54 the share of Argentine exports (in tons) in world markets was respectively maize (61 percent and 21 percent), wheat (19 percent and 9 percent), linseed (68 percent and 44 percent) and meat (40 percent and 19 percent). This meant a slowdown in exports as a leading element of growth; before the crisis, one-third of GDP was agricultural in origin, and 50 percent of its production was exported.

[4] The main target of the ISI program was traditional industries; the lags in those producing intermediate goods, vehicles, and machinery meant that during the fifties, there occurred a shift in the external vulnerability of the economy from the export to the import side. This shift in vulnerability brought, in its turn, a misallocation of resources that mainly was due to the preferences given to existing industries. On the growth-retarding effects of such policies see the chapter on investment in this volume.

Fig. 7.1. Domestic and foreign terms of trade, 1913–99

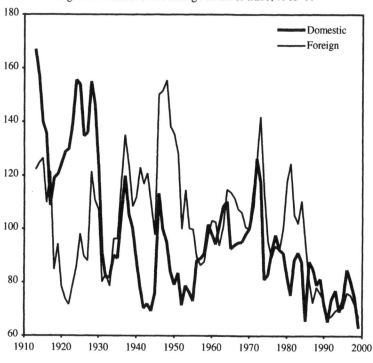

Notes and sources: Author's estimations based on national statistics.

a commercial policy (CP) index, measuring freer trade with lower values and greater protection with higher values.

Figure 7.2 also shows the ratio of trade to GDP (the trade share). The trend of the trade share shows a strong reduction after the 1930s, when the protection index increased sharply.[5] But after the 1940s and toward the end of the century fluctuations in the trade share around 20 percent reveal the restrictive effect of the slow growth in exports. This was partly the outcome of both foreign restrictions on the market access of Argentine exports and domestic supply shortcomings induced by changes in the system of incentives.

In Figure 7.3 we see that the real exchange rate (RER, the ratio of foreign to domestic common-currency prices) increased between 1913 and 1943, declined to 1955, increased again to 1960, and then declined with some variability to 1975. The index reached still lower values in 1980 and in several years of the 1990s, with high peaks in 1985 and 1989 – clearly demonstrating some

---

[5] Where we measure the trade share as the ratio of exports plus imports to GDP.

Fig. 7.2. Relative trade policy and trade shares, 1913–99

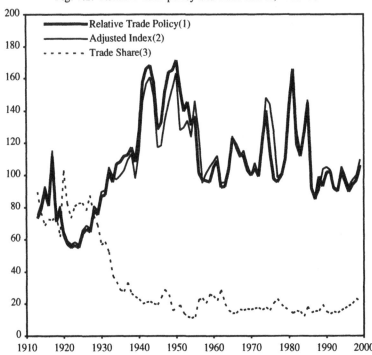

Notes and sources: Author's estimations based on national statistics and Díaz Alejandro (1981). (1) Ratio of foreign and domestic terms of trade. (2) Relative trade policy index adjusted by relative nominal exchange rates. (3) Share of exports and imports in GDP.

very volatile behavior. The picture is similar to that obtained from comparing (as does Salter) the import and domestic prices of manufacturing goods in Argentina, assuming that they represent, respectively, the behavior of tradable and nontradable types of goods.

Figure 7.4 depicts the trend in the overall trade tax burden, measured as the ratio of tax revenues to the values of imports and exports. The most impressive feature is that the import tax ratio increased steadily until the mid-1930s (to around 30 percent), declined sharply until the early 1960s, increased again (though to a lower level of about 25 percent) in the mid-1960s, and finally declined to the 10 percent level in the 1990's, which is – with several fluctuations in between – similar to the level at present.[6] Export taxation was important in the late-1960s, 1970s, mid-1980s, and early 1990s; it has since almost disappeared.

[6] Here, for the period 1958–62, there is a discrepancy, with the IEERAL (1986) statistics showing a lower decline.

Fig. 7.3. Real exchange rates (RER) and ratio of WPI for industrial imports and domestic production, 1913–99

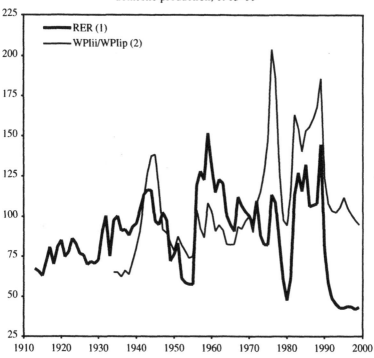

Notes and sources: Author's estimations based on national statistics and Díaz Alejandro (1981). (1) Average nominal exchange rate times US WPI and divided by CPI of Argentina. (2) WPI for industrial imports divided by WPI for industrial production.

The increases in the ratio of tariff revenues to import values until the 1930s, which appear again in the 1960s, are related to the payment of tariffs in a freer foreign exchange market, while the declines of the 1930s and mid-1960s are related to foreign exchange controls that gave priority to imports of intermediate inputs with low or zero tariffs.

Naturally, these trends had broader public finance implications. There was a sharp decline in the share of trade taxes in total tax revenue; the level was around 45 percent in the 1920s and just 5 percent in the 1950s. Since then the share has fluctuated around 18 percent with values as low as 8 percent in the 1990s. Another dimension can be seen from the comparison of the total tax revenue-to-GDP ratio to the trade tax revenue-to-GDP ratio, which shows an important increase in domestic taxation from the 1950s onwards as a substitute for falling trade taxes.

Fig. 7.4. Ratios of tariff revenue to value of imports and of export taxes to value of
exports, 1913–99

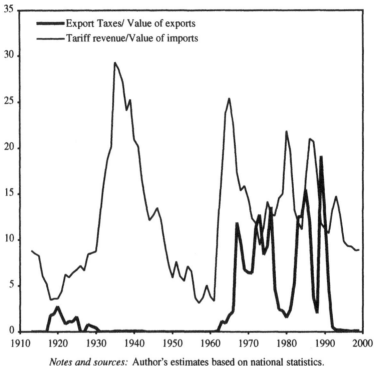

Notes and sources: Author's estimates based on national statistics.

Figure 7.5 shows that, in 1900, imports of consumer and intermediate goods
each represented 40 percent of total imports. A strong decline in the share
of consumer goods then set in, reaching very low values in the 1960s, but
with a peak in the early 1980s and a higher level for the 1990s. This trend
was complemented by an increase in the share of intermediate goods to 50–60
percent between the 1930s and 1960s, followed by a further increase to 70
percent from the mid-1960s to the mid-1970s, with spikes in some years of the
1980s. In the early 1980s and 1990s the share of intermediate goods declined
to just 50 percent. The highest share of capital goods imports (40 percent) was
reached in the early 1960s, with additional peaks near 30 percent in the 1950s,
early 1980s, and 1990s.

These descriptive figures provide us with something of an overview of the
effect of ISI on tariff revenue, import composition, and the transfer of the
tax revenue base to domestic activity. As mentioned, the particular form of
tariff escalation adopted implied lower tariff rates for intermediate goods than

Fig. 7.5. Shares in imports by type of goods, 1900–99

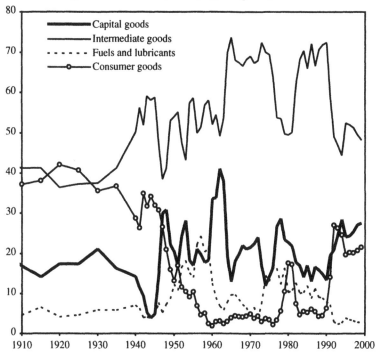

Notes and sources: Author's estimations based on national statistics.

for final goods; so, as the ISI process was reinforced, domestic production (consumption) bore the brunt of taxes. It is also worth remembering that, in terms of incentives, there were serious distortions acting through even higher rates of effective protection, since there were higher tariff rates on final goods produced and sold domestically than on intermediate inputs, whether produced or imported.[7]

With this overview complete, we move onto a more detailed look at history, in both data and narrative forms. The next section is chronologically organized around a database of three-year moving average time series of major indicators of trade policy between 1913 and 1999, using the most consistent and comparable data available for all years, as shown in Table 7.1. The discussion focuses on aggregates such as the merchandise and current accounts, the terms of trade, and

---

[7] The effective rate of protection (ERP) is a measure of the incidence of tariffs on a value-added basis. On ERP and trade policy in various developing countries see the survey by Edwards (1993).

Table 7.1. *The current account, terms of trade, and trade policy, 1913–99*

Years	1913	1916	1919	1922	1925	1928	1931	1934	1937	1940
	-15	-18	-21	-24	-27	-30	-33	-36	-39	-42
Trade balance (1)	103.0	225.7	183.3	-17.0	149.7	74.7	93.3	133.0	118.0	124.0
Exports	472.3	623.0	812.3	630.0	855.7	821.3	370.7	482.0	565.0	465.0
Imports	369.3	397.3	629.0	647.0	706.0	746.7	277.3	349.0	447.0	341.0
Current account	-27.0	63.7	2.3	-174.0	-70.7	-172.7	-55.3	2.7	-18.0	31.0
Trade shares (%) (2)	78.3	73.2	82.4	78.9	82.9	66.9	49.4	30.1	28.1	21.4
GDP growth rate (annual %)	-4.9	1.9	4.7	9.7	3.9	2.1	-1.9	4.5	3.9	2.7
Deficit/GDP (%)	-2.4	-2.1	-0.5	-1.3	-2.0	-2.8	-2.1	-1.8	-2.9	-3.4
Terms of trade (1970 = 100)										
Domestic (3)	154.8	121.1	124.8	141.6	141.6	141.6	84.9	94.8	108.5	79.1
Foreign (4)	124.8	102.1	83.3	78.7	92.3	113.6	80.6	103.4	122.7	117.2
Exports	72.1	111.6	101.9	67.6	80.2	77.3	33.7	30.2	35.8	38.7
Imports	57.8	109.3	122.3	85.9	86.9	68.1	41.8	29.2	29.1	33.0
Exchange rates (1970 = 100)										
Relative (5)	103.3	103.3	103.3	103.3	103.3	103.3	103.3	91.8	94.7	92.5
Real (CPI) (6)	65.2	73.8	80.1	82.2	74.1	71.5	88.4	96.2	91.1	104.4
WPlii/WPlip (7)								64.0	66.8	92.5
Relative trade policy (1970 = 100)										
Index (8)	80.6	84.4	66.8	55.6	65.2	80.2	94.9	109.0	113.1	148.3
Adjusted index (9) = (8) × (5)	83.3	87.1	68.9	57.4	67.3	82.9	98.0	100.1	107.1	137.2

Table 7.1. (Continued)

Years	1943 -45	1946 -48	1949 -51	1952 -54	1955 -57	1958 -60	1961 -63	1964 -66	1967 -69	1970 -72
Trade balance (1)	407.0	189.0	-109.0	-38.0	-255.0	-130.0	-84.0	365.0	202.0	-4.0
Exports	678.0	1472.0	1090.0	946.0	949.0	1025.0	1182.0	1497.0	1482.0	1818.0
Imports	271.0	1283.0	1199.0	984.0	1204.0	1155.0	1266.0	1132.0	1280.0	1822.0
Current account	339.7	229.3	-121.0	-127.7	-231.0	-259.3	-2.0	157.0	-20.0	-257.0
Trade shares (%) (2)	20.4	26.2	17.5	12.4	19.4	23.7	23.6	14.6	16.5	18.3
GDP growth rate (annual %)	2.3	9.2	1.0	1.4	5.2	2.4	2.0	8.3	6.6	4.9
Deficit/GDP (%)	-5.6	-3.7	-4.7	-3.6	-4.1	-5.3	-5.6	-4.5	-1.7	-3.1
Terms of trade (1970 = 100)										
Domestic (3)	72.4	102.7	82.1	75.5	83.4	96.8	101.2	98.9	95.9	111.6
Foreign (4)	108.2	166.2	133.5	104.7	91.9	95.9	98.9	113.3	104.6	113.1
Exports	54.1	104.3	117.0	106.7	92.5	87.1	87.1	98.6	93.1	114.9
Imports	50.0	62.8	87.6	101.9	100.6	90.8	88.2	87.0	89.0	101.6
Exchange rates (1970 = 100)										
Relative (5)	93.8	88.8	90.3	93.1	109.1	105.9	102.9	100.5	101.5	101.0
Real (CPI) (6)	109.9	98.1	77.0	59.0	101.5	134.9	119.3	95.1	107.1	101.2
WPIii/WPIip (7)	133.9	98.0	82.8	77.8	88.7	98.4	92.2	82.4	94.2	98.8
Relative trade policy (1970 = 100)										
Index (8)	149.5	161.8	162.7	138.7	110.2	99.1	97.7	114.6	109.1	101.3
Adjusted index (9) = (8) × (5)	140.1	143.7	146.9	129.2	120.3	104.9	100.5	115.1	110.7	102.3

Table 7.1. (Continued)

Years	1973 -75	1976 -78	1979 -81	1982 -84	1985 -87	1988 -90	1991 -93	1994 -96	1997 -99
Trade balance (1)	116.0	1647.0	-565.0	3047.0	2422.0	5815.0	-876.0	-1619.0	-3848.0
Exports	3386.0	5323.0	8325.0	7856.0	7201.0	10343.0	12435.0	20205.0	25328.0
Imports	3270.0	3676.0	8890.0	4809.0	4779.0	4528.0	13311.0	21824.0	29176.0
Current account	-146.0	1258.0	-3344.0	-2404.0	-2700.0	-321.0	-6649.7	-6884.3	-12873.0
Trade shares (%) (2)	16.6	20.4	15.8	14.3	16.1	16.8	14.4	17.3	21.7
GDP growth rate (annual %)	4.1	1.8	1.1	0.8	0.9	-2.6	8.6	2.7	2.8
Deficit/GDP (%)	-8.3	-5.9	-6.6	-9.2	-4.3	-4.3	-0.2	-1.4	-1.9
Terms of trade (1970 = 100)									
Domestic (3)	93.7	93.8	82.8	89.0	79.4	77.4	71.8	75.7	72.4
Foreign (4)	112.9	91.7	114.1	105.7	81.9	74.7	79.6	79.2	71.4
Exports	204.3	193.4	289.0	245.6	201.3	250.3	246.0	252.6	214.6
Imports	181.0	211.0	253.2	232.3	245.9	335.2	309.0	318.9	300.7
Exchange rates (1970 = 100)									
Relative (5)	109.4	110.1	100.6	103.3	101.0	101.4	101.0	103.3	103.3
Real (CPI) (6)	84.2	101.8	56.2	118.5	115.0	110.8	50.7	43.0	42.8
WPIii/WPIip (7)	128.4	166.0	101.3	152.2	156.4	154.4	104.5	107.2	97.5
Relative trade policy (1970 = 100)									
Index (8)	120.4	97.8	137.8	118.8	103.1	96.5	110.8	104.7	98.6
Adjusted index (9) = (8) × (5)	131.7	107.7	138.7	122.7	104.1	97.9	111.9	108.1	101.8

Notes and sources: Author's estimations based on national statistics and Díaz Alejandro (1981). Deficit/GDP figures are based on Véganzonès and Winograd (1997). (1) Millions of current US dollars. (2) Share of exports and imports to GDP. (3) WPI for agriculture divided by WPI for industry. (4) Index of unit prices of exports divided by unit prices of imports. (5) Relative nominal average exchange rate for exports and imports. (6) (RER) average nominal exchange rate times US WPI and divided by CPI of Argentina. (7) WPI for industrial imports divided by WPI for industrial production. (8) Trade policy index. (9) Trade Policy index adjusted by relative exchange rates.

a relative commercial policy index, and also provides more detailed evidence on specific commercial policies.

In the parallel narrative discussion we will see that the different instruments used in trade were the result of decisions taken in the past, either on a national level or through multilateral (and even bilateral) arrangements. After the 1930s the mix of instruments used to control imports and/or promote exports became increasingly complex, mainly because of exchange controls and quantitative restrictions. In the 1990s a transition from unilateral trade liberalization to participation in the regional trade agreement known as Mercosur, with its reciprocal concessions of preference margins, added even more complexity.

7.1.2 From World War I to the Great Depression (1913–1930)

7.1.2.1 The aggregates

This was a period in which freer trade allowed for the transmission of foreign terms of trade fluctuations to the domestic economy (Table 7.1); this was the case for both negative shocks (1913–15 to 1922–24) and positive shocks (1925–27 to 1928–30). In 1913–18 the positive merchandise balance implied a high trade share with a compensatory increase in the real exchange rate and little protection against imports. This was followed by the period 1919–30, with a negative current account balance, high trade shares, and a declining real exchange rate. Regarding protection against imports, the trend of low protection inherited from earlier periods was maintained.

7.1.2.2 Tariffs (1909 and 1927)

Table 7.2 shows tariffs in seven categories.[8] The overall weighted average of tariffs was 23 percent in 1909 compared with 19 percent in 1927.[9] As expected, the arithmetic means are higher, showing in both cases a dispersion of 66 percent and 68 percent. For 1927 the data show that the weighted average using real values was 16 percent, which is lower than the rates based on tariff values, but with a similar dispersion.

Even this early in the century, tariff rate escalation (from raw to finished goods) was an important aspect of the tariff structure. For cotton, wool, and silk, the tariff rates for spun fibers varied between 5 percent and 14 percent, the rates for cloth varied between 23 percent and 46 percent, and the rates for final products varied between 40 percent and 46 percent.[10]

---

[8] Based on Díaz Alejandro (1970, Table 5.4).

[9] As is well known, weighting by import values results in a downward bias of the protective effect.

[10] Based on Díaz Alejandro (1970, Table 5.5).

Table 7.2. *Import duties in 1909 and 1927*
Percent

	1909 Tariff values	1927 Tariff values	1927 Real values
Foods and beverages	43	24	15
Textiles and manufactures	27	22	17
Chemical products	34	18	20
Wood and paper	27	19	14
Leather and manufactures	39	36	27
Metals and manufactures	10	16	14
Stone, glass, and manufactures	23	15	14
Weighted Average	23	19	16
Mean	28	24	19
Standard deviation	18	16	12
Dispersion (%)	66	68	65

Notes and sources: Author's calculations based on Díaz Alejandro (1970) Table 5.4. Individual rates are weighted averages using real import values. Tariff values are based on official prices (aforos). No real value estimate is available for 1909.

This escalation led to effective rates of protection that were much higher than the nominal rates on domestic production. Looking at the rates for the 7 categories (Table 7.2) the highest weighted average using tariff values in 1909 was 43 percent corresponding to foods and beverages, compared with 24 percent in 1927. The decline between those years was significant for chemical products, wood and paper products, stone and glass; the only increase to be found was for metal products. Regarding the 1927 tariff rates based on real values, the aggregate weighted average is much more representative of the true rates for the different categories.

7.1.3 From exchange controls to the end of World War II (1931–1945)

7.1.3.1 The aggregates

In 1931 exchange controls were adopted, and in 1933 the *margen de cambios* were introduced for importers. Both changes made for a strong policy discontinuity. In 1931–39, even with growth in exports and imports, the trade share declined (Table 7.1), while the foreign terms of trade increased (especially the export index). At the same time a high RER persisted, and an increase in protectionism took place in 1934–39. In the wartime years of 1940–45 there were, as expected, increased exports and diminished imports, and these implied an increase in the merchandise balance and in the current account, most strongly in 1943–45. Trade shares declined slowly with declining FTT and another round of increased protectionism.

In an attempt to apply a Rostovian model, Zymelman (1958) defined the period 1933–52 as the take-off period, when industry became the leading sector of the economy. This process implied an increase in the manufacturing share of GDP and a reduction in the share of agriculture, developments that were accompanied by a reallocative shift in the labor force. Díaz Alejandro (1966) characterized government policies after 1930 as mainly concerned with greater protection, income distribution, maintenance of employment, and a lessening of the role of foreign capital. On the one hand there were the protective barriers (cum foreign exchange controls) that promoted manufacturing, as well as the increase in domestic demand that was due to higher salaries and subsidies. On the other hand, a key element in delaying technical change after 1943 was a new hostility towards foreign capital – a hostility that would not see a reversal until 1953.

7.1.3.2 On foreign exchange controls

Foreign exchange control implied that the authorization of the Comisión de Control de Cambios was needed to buy or sell foreign currency.[11] Thus, exporters could not deliver their shipments before relinquishing the currency generated from the proceeds of their sales. The underlying objective was to control evasion in the capital market. In 1932 a priority scheme was established for foreign exchange uses. In decreasing order of priority, the uses were: public sector needs, raw materials for domestic industries, fuels, indispensable consumption goods, small immigrant transfers, travelers' needs, and payment of debt services. The main problem of the period was the unexpected variability in exchange rate levels.

In 1933 the old foreign exchange control commission was transformed into an office within the treasury. Importers were required to have a permit to be entitled to buy at the official exchange rate. An exchange rate for importers, as well as for exporters, was later established. This provided revenue to finance the maintenance of the domestic prices of the three principal agricultural products (wheat, corn, and linseed), which were administered by the grain regulating board (Junta Reguladora de Granos).

At first this system restricted *all* imports, but later on it was eased for imports from those countries that bought Argentine goods. Also, importers could buy foreign exchange in the free market; this led the government to introduce an additional tariff of 20 percent on imports made without an official permit. To this was added the requirement of consular invoices to validate the origin of goods and regulations on the commission rates banks could charge on foreign

---

[11] This section draws on Prados Arrarte (1944) and Salera (1941).

exchange transactions. Soon several exceptions were established, such as free market sales of exchange in exchange for gold and silver, for public funds uses, for trade with neighboring countries, and for the transfers of railroad firms as a *quid pro quo* for reduced freight rates – all of these further distorting the price system.

By the end of 1940, a bilateral imbalance of payments with the USA was the main problem facing the authorities with respect to foreign exchange control. In earlier years the main objective had been to restrict imports; at this time, imports were welcomed given the scarcity of products in the international market related to the war. This disappearance of the principal sources of international import supply encouraged the authorities to become more liberal around 1941. In that year import permits, as well as the office of exchange control itself, were eliminated; but that did not mean the end of import restrictions as a system of multiple exchange rates was then introduced. For this purpose, countries were divided into three subsets, the most favored being a group that comprised the British Empire and several neighboring countries including Peru. The Corporación para la Promoción del Intercambio was created in response to the scarcity of foreign exchange. Its proceeds were to be used for imports of non-traditional intermediate and capital goods. At the same time strong restrictions were imposed on the movement of funds and transfers of capital.

7.1.3.3 Tariff-exempt imports (1920–1953)

Exemptions of tariffs are, in a sense, tax expenditures. In other words, they reduce fiscal revenues by reducing the costs to eligible users. For imports competing with domestic production, exemptions may push domestic prices downward if competition among eligible importers is strong. Exemptions on inputs might be reflected in lower prices of final goods or higher factor rewards for privileged activities related to the lower input protection.

The size of tariff-exempted imports between 1906 and 1940 varied between 26 percent and 30 percent; this implies, for instance, that the *ad valorem* rate for dutiable imports was 23 percent in 1927, compared with 16 percent if the calculation is based solely on tariff revenues.[12] In Table 7.3 additional estimates of this effect are presented up to 1953, and it can be seen that while those early proportions of tariff-exempted imports were maintained up to 1947, in 1949–50 the average was 54 percent, similar to the figure for the period 1951–53. The second column of this table shows tariff revenue as a proportion of dutiable imports. As expected, the increase in exempted imports brought the tariff rate paid from a high of 33 percent in 1931–35 to only 12 percent in 1951–53. The

[12] Díaz Alejandro (1970).

Table 7.3. *Tariff-exempted imports, 1920–53*

	Duty-free imports (percent)	Tariff revenue as percent of dutiable imports	Real import value as percent of official tariff base
1920	26	10	286
Average 1921–25	27	17	165
Average 1926–30	31	24	105
Average 1931–35	25	33	100
Average 1936–40	28	28	108
Average 1941–45	29	16	192
1946	32	15	199
1947	27	13	241
1948	34	11	255
1949	52	12	242
1950	55	12	223
Average 1946–50	40	12	236
1951	47	12	378
1952	57	12	371
1953	63	11	266
Average 1951–53	55	12	342

Source: CEPAL (1961).

last column shows that the decline in the tariff rate paid was also related to an official tariff base that was lower than the real values of imports and that declined through time.

7.1.4 Reinforcing ISI (1946–1975)

7.1.4.1 The aggregates

The immediate postwar period 1946–54 saw increases in exports and imports, leading to frequent negative merchandise and current account balances (Table 7.1). Trade shares declined very strongly after reaching the high value of 1946–48, as did FTT. There was a declining RER and increases in protectionism. In 1955–75 the continuation of ISI policies again implied frequent negative merchandise and current account balances. The trade share increased in 1955–63 with a strong decline afterwards, as RER first increased (in 1955–60), and then declined as protection was scaled back.

Some policy oscillations can also be detected. In the 1960s and 1970s similarities can be seen regarding trade policy experiments. The years 1964–66 had commercial policies quite similar to those of 1973–75; conversely, the period 1967–69 is more in line with the policies of 1976–81 (Cavallo and Cottani 1991). Of course, the latter were framed in a very different policy context, as they sprung from a decade under the influence of ideas quite unrelated to those that had influenced the trade liberalization experiment of 1967–69.

The 1960s saw perhaps the most determined attempt at trade liberalization, albeit with a great deal of manipulation along the way. In the period 1964–66 the foreign terms of trade were higher than in 1967–69, with smaller exposure to world trade. In 1964–66 the economy started off highly protected on the import side with strong foreign exchange regulations, but new legislation concerning the financial promotion of nontraditional exports was introduced. In 1967–69 a rationalization of the system of incentives was enacted with the intention of introducing greater transparency in trade policy. Foreign terms of trade declined, as did taxation of traditional exports, while implicit protection for import-competing goods was also reduced. This was done through a compensated devaluation whereby tariffs were reduced to a level that did not change domestic prices, given the nominal increase in the exchange rate. The compensation, however, was imperfect since it did not apply to certain goods and there were products where the tariff reduction could not fully compensate for the cost increases arising from a 40 percent devaluation (for details, see Cavallo and Cottani 1991; de Pablo 1972).

Liberalization did not endure. In 1973–75 strong quantitative restrictions were again introduced, together with foreign exchange controls and generous promotion devices for nontraditional exports. The 1973–75 policies, along with an economic model closed to imports, required additional foreign exchange to fund the complementary imports induced by ISI. This was achieved through subsidies to nontraditional exports, and taxation of traditional exports such as foods and grains.[13]

7.1.4.2 The incentive system (1943–1958)

Credit and protection policies were very influential in the course of industrialization during the postwar period.[14] The exchange rate applied to industrial raw materials and much machinery represented a partially subsidized rate, which increased through time particularly because of the slow devaluation of the official exchange rate. The import duties paid were quite low, and increased protection in 1944 included concessions for industries designated as being of national interest. Later the government's five-year plan called for the protection of several existing industries and the promotion of new ISI and exports.

By the end of 1948 the Central Bank was issuing foreign exchange permits for all commodities, most extant import quotas were maintained, and new im-

[13] Di Tella (1983).
[14] This section draws on Schwartz (1968).

port prohibitions were introduced. By 1950 imports of certain consumer goods were banned if domestic substitutes were available. During the crisis of 1952 the import prohibition was extended to capital goods and persisted until 1958. It is difficult to estimate the level of protection prevailing after the war, but the evidence of Loser (1971) shows that the average effective rate of protection for the period 1947–50 was substantially higher (310 percent) than that corresponding to 1943–46 (181 percent). The average effective rate was higher still when foods were excluded from consideration, demonstrating the sharp incentives provided to the rest of the domestic manufacturing sector.[15]

In the immediate postwar period the expansion of credit was perhaps more significant even than the increase in protection, though the pattern was later reversed. From 1945 to 1947 several industries experiencing rapid growth also received large increases in bank loans, such as the rubber, metallurgy, chemical, and petroleum refining industries. The increase in import restrictions also acted to promote industrialization, but the impact was limited by the difficulty of importing intermediate and capital goods. The Central Bank was more willing to provide permits for intermediate than capital goods, implying a high effective protection for existing industries and causing delays in introducing the innovations embodied in the imports of new vintages of capital goods.

If an industry was deemed by the government to be in the national interest, it saw the imposition of quotas on competitive imports, a reduction of duties on imported raw materials and capital goods, and favorable treatment in getting bank credit and foreign exchange at the official rate. But this kind of protection was also extended to other industries lacking such a designation. The industries officially selected for differential protection after 1945 included, apart from agricultural inputs, those producing intermediate goods, such as metals, newsprint, plywood, glass, vehicles, and machinery. Finally, after 1955 when supplementary tariffs and prior deposits increased differential protection, there was no longer any reference made to efficiency standards in the selection of industries for protection.

7.1.4.3 Tariffs (1959 and 1969)

With the change of government in 1955, the components of a new economic program included a unified official exchange rate, a free market exchange rate, free mobility of capital, and official prices for some exports. These rules were maintained up to 1958, and by the end of 1958 quotas and import permits were eliminated, and temporary tariffs were introduced based on three classifications

---

[15] In a report to the Ministry of the Economy (Macario 1961), an effective rate of 300 percent was considered feasible for activities using agricultural inputs and having nominal rates of 150 percent.

of goods. For products not included in the classification lists, a 300 percent tariff was applied. Pre-import deposits were introduced (but eliminated by 1959) following the same pattern as tariffs – lower levels for goods on the lists, and higher for those not included. The list also included a tax on exports. As to the level of legal tariffs, in 1959 Argentine average nominal duties were 151 percent, much higher than those in the rest of Latin American and in Europe.[16]

In Table 7.4 a comparison is made between legal rates of protection for selected activities in 1959 and 1969.[17] The weighted average rate for 1959 was 141 percent – higher than the average for consumer and capital goods and lower than that for intermediate products. In 1969 the weighted average of 107 percent was similar to that of 1976, with the lowest rates for intermediate and capital goods, and with similar arithmetic and weighted averages, and dispersions around 40 percent. The pattern of rate escalation is now seen to have been an important and persistent characteristic of the protection system for most of the century, with a long-run policy of discrimination against consumers and capital users intended to provide higher incentives for industrialization in final-goods sectors.[18] In a more detailed study for this period covering all protected activities, Berlinski and Schydlowsky (1982) found that in 1969 the economy was highly protected on many fronts. The average effective rate on manufactures was 97 percent compared with –13 percent in agriculture. The former basically reflected the tariff escalation of the 1967 reform and the latter the bias against exports.[19]

7.1.5 From trade liberalization to quantitative trade restrictions (1976–1987)

7.1.5.1 The aggregates

At the start of this period, in 1976–81, an unsuccessful trade liberalization episode led to an increase in imports and exports with a high negative current

---

[16] See Macario (1964).

[17] Berlinski (1977). For this selection a three-sector framework was used to describe the economy: agriculture (at international prices); agroindustries, users of internationally competitive agricultural inputs; and all other industrial activities (at domestic prices) of which forty ISIC (five-digit) industries were chosen.

[18] In *Consejo Nacional de Desarrollo* (1970) estimates of legal tariff rates for six sectors (based on the 40 industries mentioned above) showed a weighted average in 1965 of 205 percent and in 1967 of 98 percent, with both subject to a similar escalation pattern.

[19] This study also highlighted redundant tariffs, which became an important characteristic of the protective system. Redundant tariffs occur when domestic price increases are smaller than those resulting from legal tariffs. The rationale for this would be to use high legal tariffs to restrict foreign competition so that domestic prices would be determined either by demand elasticities or by price controls introduced by the authorities.

Table 7.4. *Legal tariff rates, 1959–97*

	1959	1969	1976	1988	1991	1993	1997
Non durable consumer goods	197	142	200	53	25	30	23
Durable consumer goods	198	142	149	63	21	20	19
Intermediate goods	118	102	86	44	17	20	14
Machinery	147	93	87	57	22	8	14
Transport equipment	188	124	132	57	27	9	21
Weighted average	141	107	99	48	19	17	16
Mean	145	103	97	52	19	17	15
Standard deviation	56	42	41	16	5	8	5
Dispersion (%)	38	41	42	30	27	44	30

Notes and sources: Author's calculations; 1959 based on Macario (1964); 1969 and 1976 based on Berlinski and Schydlowsky (1982), and Berlinski (1977); 1988, 1991, 1993 and 1997 taken from Berlinski (1994 and 1998). Detailed rates are weighted averages using data of production.

account balance in 1979–81 (Table 7.1). Trade shares increased and later declined with a similar pattern for RER and the level of protection against imports. In 1982–87 there was a decline in exports and, especially, in imports, as well as a decline in the FTT; the RER increased and there was a decline in protection against imports.

As noted above, the period 1976–81 was an unsuccessful case of southern cone liberalization-stabilization policies, mainly due to an exchange rate overvaluation which depressed exports and raised imports to hitherto unknown levels (Nogués 1986). This experiment ended with a massive increase in foreign debt, as the size of net interest remittances increased steadily from an average of $400 million (in 1976–78) to $1.5 billion (in 1979–81). A large current account deficit of $3.3 billion opened up, setting the standard for the rest of the 1980s.

Real exchange rates for exports were at their highest in the 1970s, but reached their lowest values in 1979–81 as a result of an overvaluation policy later called an "active crawling peg" (Martirena-Mantel 1981). Berlinski's (1982) simulation of the effect of reducing the levels of effective protection on relative prices showed that such a change in relative prices did not take place in the official tariff-dismantling exercise mainly because of the size of the offsetting real appreciation of the exchange rate.

In July 1982, because of the Malvinas (Falklands) War, a priority list of trade and exchange restrictions was reintroduced. By the end of 1983 quantitative restrictions were firmly in place and based on several lists. Among other things, the rules required the approval of a committee formed by public officials and private sector representatives for the import of goods competing with domestic production.

During 1985–87 a deficit in the current account of $2.7 billion current was the outcome of a positive balance of merchandise trade of $2.4 billion and the payment for financial services of $5.1 billion, of which foreign debt servicing accounted for more than 80 percent. This picture is similar to the one for 1982–84: both periods were affected by shocks in the foreign terms of trade, especially export prices, which declined sharply. Thus it is not surprising that positive balances of merchandise trade ($3 and $2.4 billion in 1982–84 and 1985–87) were made possible by strong quantitative restrictions on imports, with a predictable side effect being a boost in the sales of domestic firms.

7.1.5.2 Legal tariffs (1976)

There are strong similarities between the 1967 and 1976 general tariff reforms, as noted by Berlinski (1977). In both cases a similar framework was used to classify tariff items according to three characteristics: the degree of fabrication (10 groups), the type of goods (consumer, intermediate, capital), and the importance of domestic supply. Rates on consumer goods, which in 1967 were in the range 110 percent–140 percent, were reduced by 1976 to 80 percent–100 percent (and for imports the range was 25 percent–95 percent). Intermediate goods fell from 40 percent–130 percent and fell to 30 percent–95 percent in the same period (imports varied from 5 percent–30 percent). Capital goods in 1967 ranged from 40 percent–100 percent, and were reduced in 1976 to 30 percent–70 percent (import rates fell to 25 percent–35 percent).[20]

Tariffs paid as a proportion of CIF value were lower than the legal *ad valorem* rates, a difference that can be easily explained by tariff exemptions. In 1979–80 the average tariff paid on imports was 10 percent (20 percent in 1987) and the proportion of tariff-exempted imports was 44 percent, a fact that suggests the need to examine more closely the effect of tariff exemptions on domestic prices and incentives.[21]

The aggregate averages and dispersions of legal tariff levels were similar in 1976 and 1969 (Table 7.4). At a more detailed level, however, the averages declined (especially for intermediate goods and machinery). The reduction in realized rates between 1969 and 1977 was not enough to eliminate the relative bias against exports; rebates in 1969 were large (12 percent) but were made in few sectors. In 1977 the average reimbursement of 14 percent compared to

---

[20] The estimate of realized protection rates showed that effective rates were higher for firms exporting more than 3 percent of their total sales. It is an open question whether this was a deliberate action to protect the domestic market and allow firms to export at marginal cost, or just inertia related to the ignorance of bureaucrats. Also, as mentioned above, the existence of redundant tariffs was still important, and the margins as measured in 1969 and in 1977 showed higher proportions in the latter year (Berlinski 1979).

[21] See Berlinski et al. (1984).

a realized nominal import protection level of 37 percent, showing that a bias persisted. The high dispersion of effective rates in the 1970s still discriminated against exports but was partially compensated by other devices.

7.1.6 Dismantling restrictions, liberalization, and privatization (1988–1999)

7.1.6.1 The aggregates

In 1988–90 the dismantling of quantitative restrictions (QRs) and other major restrictions began, leading to an increase in exports and in the merchandise trade balance (Table 7.1). The FTT declined, reinforced by a declining RER, so that protection against imports declined as well. In 1991–99 trade liberalization continued along with the privatization of state enterprises. A strong increase in exports and imports took place, but with it emerged a strong negative current account. The FTT initially increased then declined later in the period, along with the RER, while protection against imports followed the same pattern.

7.1.6.2 The 1980s

The 1988 tariff reforms were part of a trade policy package that included a change in tariff rates, a reduction in the number of items under QRs, the introduction of specific rates, and the temporary application of a dual exchange rate. The 1988 levels in Table 7.4 describe the initial conditions of tariffs before the reform (circa June 1988). Tariff rates were then highly concentrated in the 46 percent–60 percent range. For the most part tariffs on intermediate and capital goods were also located in this same range. Unweighted protection rates show an overall average of 52 percent, but with lower levels for intermediate than for consumer and capital goods.[22] Dispersion of these rates, while not high, was still lower than the average for machinery only. Weighted rates show a similar pattern, as the average of 48 percent is only undercut by intermediate goods. At the same time, export tax rebates, with average rates of 12 percent, were also lower in the intermediate goods category.

In the new tariff schedule the most common bracket for rates was 31 percent–45 percent, where a high concentration of intermediate and capital goods were found. The similarity between unweighted and weighted rates was high, and the pattern described above remained – the average tariff rate was now 36 percent but with the lowest rates for intermediate goods. On the other hand, the scope of QRs was reduced, from a list of around 3,000 items introduced by the end of 1983 to just 1,000. The remaining items in the QR list were highly concentrated in textiles, metal products, and machinery, with a lower incidence in chemicals

---

[22] Tariff surcharges were not included here.

and nonmetallic minerals. Textile protection was also reinforced by the effect of new specific tariff rates and the survival of some official prices.[23]

7.1.6.3 The 1990s

In Table 7.4 a final comparison is made between tariffs in 1991 and 1993. In 1991 weighted tariffs averaged 19 percent (once again with a lower rate for intermediate goods), while in 1993 the average weighted tariff was 17 percent (with a higher rate for consumer goods and a lower one for capital goods). The dispersion of average tariffs was quite low in 1991, but increased in 1993 with the reduction of tariffs on capital goods and an increase in the statistics tax (with several exceptions). Nontariff restrictions were concentrated in textiles (with minimum specific tariffs), basic metals (with antidumping measures), transport equipment (with quotas on automobiles), and paper (more use of quotas). Export reimbursements increased from 1991, and the average tariff rate for the same activities was reduced, implying a decline in the bias against exports.

The completion of the Mercosur regional trade agreement had important effects on Argentine trade policy. Under the Ouro Preto protocol of December 17, 1994, a Common External Tariff (CET) was negotiated. Exceptions included capital goods, where the tariff increased to 14 percent in 2001, and information technology and telecommunications, where the tariff is to reach 16 percent in 2006. A transition regime was to be completed in 1998–99. Other aspects of discussion concerned the treatment of sugar, textiles, automobiles, the institutional structure of Mercosur, policies regarding safeguards, nontariff restrictions, dumping, customs issues, and guidelines related to policies that distorted competition.

The average of the eleven different levels of the CET was 11 percent with a high dispersion of 56 percent. The exceptions to the CET (and the transition regime) implied that country-specific tariff rates still existed, modifying the CET system of incentives. Thus, the CET also required rules of origin to ensure that the benefits of regional free trade were distributed according to plan. Also, tariff escalation was still an important characteristic of the tariff structure, and estimates for 1996 showed that the tariff paid on dutiable imports was 13 percent, resulting in an average rate on tariff-exempted imports of 11 percent. The main exemptions were related to industrial promotion, turnkey plants, industrial specialization, and temporary admissions.

---

[23] The exchange rates prevailing by the end of 1988 were characterized by two markets. First, the rate for imports was the highest (the black market rate was similar); second, the official rate (20 percent lower than the black market) was applied to traditional exports while nontraditional exports were assigned an average of both rates.

Reimbursements to extraregional exports in 1997 had an average rate for manufacturing of 6 percent and lower rates for agriculture and mining. Exports made through Patagonian ports received an additional reimbursement for goods originating south of the Rio Colorado. The remaining export taxes in 1998 were oilseeds at 3.5 percent and raw hides at 10 percent for exports to the rest of the world, and 5 percent to the regional market. Finally, average nominal tariff protection for the group of manufacturing activities mentioned earlier fell from 17 percent in 1993 to 15 percent in 1997, with a reduction in dispersion and lower export reimbursements (Table 7.4). This was a result of reducing the higher tariffs and increasing the lower ones, relative to 1993, and especially of the changes for capital goods. Comparing the general averages between 1993 and 1997, the lower level of protection for import-competing activities and the reduction of export reimbursements clearly increased export incentives to the Mercosur area.

Unilateral liberalization implied lower levels of protection than those known in the past, and came about through the dismantling nontariff restrictions, with some exceptions related to industrial promotion and other special regimes. As QRs fell the extent of tariff redundancy was diminished. Thus tariffs have become once again the relevant instrument (though still with a high dispersion) that should be considered as part of the cost of protection. The transition to Mercosur implied that intraregional trade increased strongly (comparing, say, the averages of 1988–90 and 1995–97). The shares of Mercosur in world trade for those periods showed a slight reduction in exports and a strong increase in imports. The regionalization of trade raised questions about the danger of trade diversion, but the evidence presented by the World Bank (2000, Chapter 3), isolating trade diversion in the context of a gravity model in the 1980s and 1990s, would seem to indicate the absence of any large effects.

7.1.7 Final comments

The most intense periods of protective policy corresponded to the years 1940–54 and 1973–75. Less protective periods were 1934–39, 1955–72, 1976–78, 1982–84 and 1991–99. In all of the latter periods (except in 1991–99) high fiscal deficits existed, as did a negative current account balance in several cases. In most cases an improvement in the FTT brought an increase in the growth rate, except in 1961–63 (owing to a change in the nominal exchange rate) and in 1979–81 (owing to a real appreciation).

Regarding trade policies, the agricultural sector was more heavily taxed during the 1980s as compared with the 1970s and 1960s, while the highest levels of import protection came in 1964–66 and 1973–75, and then declined in 1979–

81 and to a smaller extent in 1985–87. Yet the two declines were associated with different policies: the former was an import liberalization policy realized through an overvalued exchange rate; the latter was the effect of a stabilization policy in which a subsequent price freeze was the basis for restraints in manufacturing profitability within a framework of large quantitative restrictions.

Looking at the aggregates, the deterioration of the FTT reinforced the effect of trade policies on foreign exchange availability and growth. All policy experiments set ceilings on the induced shifts in domestic terms of trade; this was done either by price controls (for several years between the mid-1940s and the mid-1950s, in 1964–66 and 1973–75, and to a different extent in 1967–69, 1976–78 and 1985–87) or by removing restrictions on imports competing with domestic activities (notably in 1967–69 and 1979–81). In all cases the trade policy package was completed by a decision to tax traditional exports.

Finally, in 2000 and 2001 several policy reversals overturned the trends of the 1990s. Exports were around $26 billion in both years, similar to the 1997–99 average, while recessions and uncertainty sent imports into sharp decline from an average of $29 billion on 1997–99 to $20 billion in 2001. The increase in the trade balance reduced the deficit on the current account to an estimated –$5 billion in 2001, compared with an average of –$13 billion in 1997–99. Fiscal deficits increased in both years, reaching 3.5 percent of GDP in 2001. At this time tariff protection increased, reversing the trend toward trade liberalization of the past decade.

7.2 The real exchange rate (1913–1975)

7.2.1 The background

The price of foreign exchange, together with the foreign terms of trade (FTT), is one of the fundamental prices in an open economy. Interest in the long-run real exchange rate (RER) has revived for the industrial countries, but the empirical literature on RER for developing countries has remained less prolific (see Edwards and Savastano 2000). In what follows, RER was estimated as a function of standard fundamentals, but it must be kept in mind that the equilibrium RER is not observable.[24] This calculation of RER was related to fluctuations in FTT, to commercial policies (CP), and also to some additional variables intended to control for the effect of the cycle, namely fiscal deficits as a percentage of GDP, GDP, or the ratio of GDP to employment (as a substitute for changes in productivity). The results provide some explanations of patterns of RER evolution

---

[24] Measured as the average of the nominal exchange rates for exports and imports times US WPI, all divided by the local CPI.

in the periods identified earlier, despite the existence of different exchange rate regimes.[25]

Before World War II the influence of the United Kingdom and United States in Argentine foreign trade was important. In the 1920s a real depreciation took place as compared with the period 1913–15. After 1933 multiple exchange rates were a normal feature of the regime. In the 1930s real depreciation was more intense as compared with the 1920s, and this may have enabled the government to overcome the effects of the Great Depression. During World War II depreciation continued, but in 1946–54 a real appreciation took place with an RER level similar to the one of the 1920s. From 1955 real depreciations have dominated but have been mixed with real appreciations in some periods. Real depreciations can be detected especially in the abrupt changes of 1955–57, 1958–60, 1967–69, and 1982–84, whereas the outstanding periods of real appreciation are 1964–66, 1973–75, 1979–81, and the years after 1991.

It is well known that RER appreciates with improvements in FTT, more protective commercial policies, increases in productivity, foreign capital inflows, and peak phases of the cycle. But for the period under analysis, the nominal exchange rate was exceptionally free in its fluctuations, and it is doubtful that domestic prices would adjust immediately to the yearly gyrations of the exchange rate. It was further assumed that all the explanatory variables used are exogenous. Finally, it turns out that there is a positive correlation between CP and FTT. Under the small country assumption this might just be a spurious result; or on the other hand, a large-country assumption would allow trade policy, via the optimal tariff, to affect a real appreciation and, thus, an improvement in FTT (at least in the early part of the century where the correlation is higher).[26]

An overview of the period suggests at least three major subperiods. The period 1913–29 is the tail end of a period of rapid growth from 1900 to the 1929 crisis that ended outward-oriented growth with agriculture as the engine of the economy. During that period, land under cultivation continued to grow, employing a large share of the labor force.[27] The next period, 1930–43, began with the Great Depression and ended in a world war, with high volatility in international goods and financial markets and with industrial developments partially offsetting the slowdown of agriculture. Finally, the 1944–75 period mainly revolved around ISI, implying the emergence of a welfare state and

---

[25] See Figure 7.3, which is based on annual figures of observed RER, and Table 7.1, which presents three-year averages.

[26] The share of Argentine exports in world markets was then very important for maize, wheat, linseed, and meat.

[27] For that period the average share of the labor force in agriculture was 39.3 percent (with a standard deviation of 4.6 percent).

extensive intervention in the economy through the detailed control of imports as well as fixed prices for agricultural products. This last period is far from uniform as, both in 1955–57 and 1967–69, there were attempts to change the incentive system of the regime itself (albeit with short-lived results).

7.2.2 The estimates

The simple model developed here uses estimates that bear some similarity to the efforts of Díaz Alejandro (1981). Table 7.5, panel (a) shows a breakdown for 1913–29, 1930–43 and 1944–75. In the first period of freer trade the RER showed a mean value of 252.9 (with a standard deviation of 23.2). The ongoing increase in restrictions raised means and dispersions with a mean of 322.0 and standard deviation of 41.5 in 1930–43, and a mean for the ISI period of 333.3 and a standard deviation of 77.8.

The estimated equations were of the form:

$$\log RER_t = a + b_1 \log(FTT_t) + b_2 \log(CP_t) + b_3 \log(DEF_t) + u_t,$$

$$\log RER_t = a + b_1 \log(FTT_t) + b_2 \log(CP_t) + b_3 \log(GDP_t) + u_t,$$

$$\log RER_t = a + b_1 \log(FTT_t) + b_2 \log(CP_t) + b_3 \log(GDPLAB_t) + u_t,$$

where the different indices are, as before: FTT, foreign terms of trade; CP, commercial policies; DEF, fiscal deficit as a share of GDP; GDP, gross domestic product; GDPLAB, ratio of GDP to employment. AR(1) denotes the first-order autoregression parameter.

Table 7.5 shows for the period 1913–29 a negative relationship of the RER to FTT when either GDP or GDPLAB are included, but for 1930–43 a positive relationship between RER and CP in every equation is shown. On the other hand, in 1944–75 the coefficient on the CP variable is negative. In sum, a real appreciation was taking place before the 1930s because of the improvement in FTT and in 1944–75 because of a change in commercial policy. Real depreciation took place in 1930–43 together with an expansion of commercial policy intervention.

In panel (b) of Table 7.5 the idea is to capture the effects of change in the international payments regimes; thus, the samples are the interwar period (1918–39) and the Bretton Woods era (1945–73). We see here a positive relationship between RER and CP in the first period and a negative one in the second. The large overlap with the period of ISI did not affect the sign for the period 1944–75. But it did affect it for the interwar period, which overlapped between 1913–29 (with no significance for CP) and 1930–43 (with a positive and significant co-

Table 7.5. *Some determinants of the real exchange rate, 1913–75*

(a) Domestic trade regimes

	Constant	FTT	CP	DEF	GDP	GDPLAB	AR(1)	$\bar{R}^2$	DW	F
1913–29	6.425* (11.83)	-0.296 (-1.39)	0.107 (0.51)	-0.012 (-1.39)	—	—	0.030 (0.09)	0.25	2.02	2.30
1913–29	6.223* (4.56)	-0.452* (-2.06)	0.196 (0.78)	—	0.052 (0.50)	—	-0.119 (-0.38)	0.15	2.07	1.67
1913–29	6.227* (2.57)	-0.441* (-1.80)	0.171 (0.60)	—	—	0.064 (0.27)	-0.130 (-0.41)	0.13	2.08	1.60
1930–43	3.156* (4.12)	-0.073 (-0.45)	0.641* (4.29)	-0.071 (-0.94)	—	—	-0.248 (-0.70)	0.47	2.32	3.85*
1930–43	1.284 (0.32)	-0.239 (-0.83)	0.492* (2.14)	—	0.304 (0.56)	—	-0.158 (-0.49)	0.43	2.16	3.44*
1930–43	6.956 (0.69)	-0.027 (-0.09)	0.595* (3.93)	—	—	-0.422 (-0.34)	-0.186 (-0.56)	0.41	2.10	3.31*
1944–75	8.864* (5.62)	0.053 (0.21)	-0.689* (-2.38)	-0.040 (-0.56)	—	—	0.631* (4.41)	0.57	1.86	11.33*
1944–75	7.546* (2.55)	0.078 (0.30)	-0.720* (-2.50)	—	0.111 (0.53)	—	0.624* (4.31)	0.57	1.89	11.33*
1944–75	7.346* (2.24)	0.070 (0.27)	-0.731* (-2.52)	—	—	0.164 (0.53)	0.625* (4.33)	0.57	1.89	11.32*

Table 7.5. (Continued)
(b) International payments regimes

	Constant	FTT	CP	DEF	GDP	GDPLAB	AR(1)	$\bar{R}^2$	DW	F
1918–39	4.509*	-0.142	0.404*	-0.013	—	—	0.324	0.32	2.00	3.43*
	(6.44)	(-0.77)	(2.49)	(-1.22)			(1.42)			
1918–39	4.371*	-0.187	0.357*	—	0.051	—	0.263	0.26	1.96	2.84*
	(2.54)	(-0.91)	(1.96)		(0.23)		(1.09)			
1918–39	6.545	-0.098	0.368*	—	—	-0.228	0.323	0.26	2.06	2.88*
	(1.41)	(-0.42)	(2.20)			(-0.41)	(1.47)			
1945–73	9.220*	0.155	-0.864*	-0.053	—	—	0.567*	0.56	1.68	10.03*
	(5.54)	(0.52)	(-2.42)	(-0.65)			(3.38)			
1945–73	7.895*	0.129	-0.836*	—	0.107	—	0.561*	0.56	1.70	9.93*
	(2.39)	(0.42)	(-2.26)		(0.48)		(3.24)			
1945–73	7.923*	0.121	-0.848*	—	—	0.137	0.560*	0.56	1.69	9.87*
	(2.12)	(0.39)	(-2.31)			(0.40)	(3.21)			

Notes and sources: Author's estimations based on national statistics and Diaz Alejandro (1981). OLS of log transformations, *t*-values in parentheses, * denotes statistically significant at 10% or less. FTT, foreign terms of trade; CP, commercial policy; DEF, deficit as GDP share; GDPLAB, ratio of GDP to employment. Interwar period (1918–39), Bretton Woods (1945–73).

efficient for CP), suggesting the importance of exchange rates and commercial policy manipulations under the exchange control regime.

A comparison with Díaz Alejandro (1981) shows similarities in the signs and significance of the variables related to FTT and CP, even though a different proxy was used for the latter. Finally, in a recent paper, Taylor (2002) investigates the purchasing-power-parity (PPP) hypothesis for the twentieth century in twenty countries, including Argentina. His conclusion is that short-run deviations from PPP are largely related to monetary shocks; the agreement of the estimates used herein with his hypothesis should be the subject of further inquiry into the exogeneity of the explanatory variables used.

7.3 Factor and product prices, endowments, and trade

7.3.1 The background

How has trade in Argentina been related to income distribution? One answer follows from studying rewards by factor type. Williamson (2002) and O'Rourke and Williamson (2002) have discussed the effect of the strong reduction in transport costs in the last quarter of the nineteenth century and in 1940. Their aim was to consider the convergence in goods prices and factor rewards, and as expected, price convergence increased the returns to the abundant factors and reduced the returns to scarce ones, consistent with the Heckscher-Ohlin theory. In Asian countries the price of abundant unskilled labor increased substantially with increases in the ratio of wages to land prices (W/R) while in Argentina, Australia, and the United States, the same ratio declined.

O'Rourke, Taylor, and Williamson (1996) undertook a systematic test using a specific factor trade model in which they divided their sample into the new world (Argentina, Australia, Canada, and the United States), and the relatively open old world (the United Kingdom, Denmark, Ireland, and Sweden) plus the more protectionist old world (France, Germany, and Spain). The evolution of the ratio of wages and land prices between 1870 and 1910 is summarized by a strong increase in the wage-rental ratio in the old world and a substantial reduction in the new world. By way of an explanation they note the importance of three elements: the role of factor endowments as determinants of trade and factor rewards; the importance of relative price convergence, specifically that of agriculture versus nonagriculture; and the relationship between relative goods prices and relative factor prices.

7.3.2 *The estimates*

A test similar to the specific factor model can be applied to the available Argentine historical data (all transformed into logs).[28] On the left hand side of the equation below is the ratio of average wages to the value of land (a substitute for the land rental value); of course, as markets are imperfect, this ratio between prices of flows and stocks may not be perfect. The right hand side contains relative factor endowments and relative goods prices. Relative endowments included are the ratio of the stocks of productive land to agricultural labor and nonagricultural capital to nonagricultural labor.

In the context of the specific factor model, the expected sign on factor endowments is positive since foreign demand should induce changes in the frontier of natural resources used. The situation is not so clear regarding the capital-labor ratio for nonagricultural (and mostly nontraded) importables. The relative price variable would have a negative sign depending on how close the relationship is between the value of stocks in agriculture and its implicit price.

The dependent variable, W/R, shows high variability. Thus, estimation on several aggregates and on several subperiods was undertaken, with the latter mainly related to changes in policy instruments in 1913–29, 1930–43 and 1944–75. The first period of freer trade gave a mean value of 0.624 (with a standard deviation of 0.141); in the next period from the 1930s and early 1940s the ratio became 0.662 (with a standard deviation of 0.072); and the mean for the ISI period was 0.773 (with a standard deviation of 0.202).

The estimated equation was:

$$\log(W/R_t) = a + b_1 \log(LAND/TEMP_t) + b_2 \log(CANA/TEMP_t)$$

$$+ b_3 \log(APRI/NPRI_t) + u_t,$$

where the different indices are: W, average salaries; R, prices of land; LAND, land weighted by value of production; TEMP, total employment; CANA, capital in nonagriculture; APRI, implicit prices in GDP of agriculture; and NPRI, implicit prices in GDP of nonagriculture. AR(1) denotes the first-order autoregression parameter. The results are shown in Table 7.6.

This application of the specific factor model tells us that increases in endowments would be related positively to wages and negatively to rents, and that the opposite would be the case for increases in labor. In the period of freer trade, 1913–29, a significant positive elasticity resulted from the downward trend in W/R (continuing the trend observed in the last years of the nineteenth century and early years of the twentieth) and a decreasing movement of LAND/TEMP.

---

[28] The data was based in IEERAL (1986).

Table 7.6. *Factor and product prices, endowments, and trade*
Dependent variable: W/R

Period	Constant	LAND/TEMP	CANA/TEMP	APRI/NPRI	AR(1)	$\bar{R}^2$	DW	F
1913–29	-12.892*	1.481*	-0.058	0.021	0.551*	0.77	2.11	13.36*
	(-2.56)	(2.16)	(-0.07)	(0.08)	(2.59)			
1930–43	4.373	0.878	-2.382*	0.055	0.015	0.21	1.58	1.86
	(1.23)	(1.34)	(-2.38)	(0.27)	(0.04)			
1944–75	9.818	-0.566	-1.028*	-0.558*	0.570*	0.65	1.96	15.00*
	(1.15)	(-0.65)	(-2.63)	(-2.02)	(3.63)			

Notes and sources: AR(1) first order autoregression to correct for autocorrelation, *t*-values in parentheses, * denotes statistically significant at 10% or less. Data from IEERAL (1986). W: average salaries. R: prices of land. LAND: land weighted by value of production. TEMP: total employment. CANA: capital in non agriculture. APRI: agriculture implicit prices in GDP. NPRI: nonagriculture implicit prices in GDP.

For the period 1930–43 (after the world crisis and during the exchange control period) the elasticity for the CANA/TEMP variable was negative and statistically significant, this being the outcome of a negative trend in nonagricultural capital-labor ratios and a positive trend in W/R.

In the period 1944–75 the wage-rental ratio was driven by changes in relative prices (higher increases in nonagricultural prices) and by a negative and significant elasticity in CANA/TEMP. In these relationships the positive trend in W/R was reversed after the mid-1950s, with oscillations since then related, among other things, to short-lived attempts to change incentives (e.g., 1955–57 and 1967–69). This was combined in the whole period with a negative trend in LAND/TEMP and a positive one in CANA/TEMP. Also, in the mid-1950s a strong change in regime took place regarding capital accumulation and growth in the manufacturing industry. This was the outcome of industrial promotion policies that, by lowering the cost of capital, induced foreign firms to undertake new investments, leading to a change in factor proportions towards labor savings. So, up to the mid-1950s, support of ISI policies resulted in the increase of nonagricultural prices and wages, which can be seen as a reversion to the W/R behavior of the 1913–29 period, while the high volatility of relative prices since the mid-1950s can be considered the main driving force of W/R.

A comparison with O'Rourke, Taylor, and Williamson (1996) shows similarities regarding the positive sign and significance of the land-labor ratio in the early part of the century and a negative relationship with relative prices for the period 1944–75. These data tell us a story about the effect of changes in agricultural prices on land prices in the first part of century brought about by the increased profitability of agriculture, and about the effect of nonagricultural price increases on wages in the ISI period. The latter effect was mainly related to the well-known change in the incentive system – a strong promotion of manufacturing industry at the expense of agriculture.

7.4 Conclusions

This chapter has surveyed the evolution of trade and trade policies in Argentina in the twentieth century, highlighted certain major trends and stylized facts, and identified topics for future research. The important historical developments can be summarized as follows.

Before the 1930s the economy was driven by a more open trade policy with growing agricultural rents on the export side and intermediate inputs and capital goods on the import side. After the 1930s the trade regime was characterized by the interaction of several instruments: tariffs, quantitative restrictions, export promotion (via rebates, drawbacks, and financing instruments), and several special tools – all of which were frequently reinforced by strong foreign exchange regulations as well as by multiple exchange rates. But those instruments were applied with varying strength through time. Tariff revenue was especially important up to the mid-1930s.[29] Afterwards, the rationalization of the system of protection was difficult not only on technical grounds but also because of the political economy of adjustment.

In terms of policy distortions, tariff escalation is seen always to have been an important characteristic of the incentive system, providing higher rates for consumer goods than for intermediate and capital goods. This resulted in high effective rates of protection, with a dispersion higher than that of nominal rates. This dispersion went beyond what could be justified on normative grounds and should be added to the cost of protection. Protected markets, by increasing their private rates of return, provided attractive points of departure for several projects. The outcome was inhibited levels of exports and increased resistance from domestic users to further ISI, where the latter was due to the higher protection provided to new import-competing activities.

The more protective commercial policy periods corresponded to the periods 1940–1954 and 1973–75. Lower levels of protection were found in the periods 1934–39, 1955–72, 1976–78, 1982–87 and 1991–99. In most of these episodes high fiscal deficits prevailed, as did negative current accounts in several cases. However, an improvement in FTT brought an increase in the growth rate in most cases.

Real depreciation took place in the 1920s, and became more intense in the 1930s, a trend that might have enabled Argentina to overcome the Great Depression. During Word War II depreciation continued, but during 1946–54 RER appreciated. After 1955 real depreciation returned, mixed with phases of real appreciation in 1964–66, 1973–75, 1979–81, and post-1991. The outcome of estimating a single-equation model of the real exchange rate for the period 1913–75 showed interesting results. Real appreciation taking place before the 1930s was due to the improvement in the FTT and during 1944–75, which in turn was due to a change in commercial policy. Real depreciation took place during 1930–43 together with a change in commercial policy and management of the foreign exchange market.

Regarding the relative price of factors and products, the estimated equation showed that the ratio of the average wage to the price of land had, in the period 1944–75, a negative relationship to relative prices (agriculture/nonagriculture) because of policies that favored ISI and so allowed greater increases in wages. For the periods 1913–29 and 1930–43 the coefficients for changes in the land-

---

[29] It was less important in the mid-1960s, late 1970s, and mid-1980s.

to-labor ratio are positive, and thus, are related to the increase in available land as the profitability of agriculture's expansion was still high. Later on the effect of nonagricultural price increases on wages was due to a system of incentives biased towards the protection of manufacturing for sales in the domestic market.

References

Berlinski, Julio. 1966. The Pattern of Growth of Argentina, 1935–1953. Harvard University. Photocopy.

———. 1977. La protección arancelaria de actividades seleccionadas de la industria manufacturera argentina. Ministerio de economía. Photocopy.

———. 1979. La relación empírica entre tasas de protección y algunos de sus determinantes: Argentina, 1977 y 1969. Working Paper no. 87, Instituto Torcuato Di Tella.

———. 1982. Dismantling Foreign Trade Restrictions: Some Evidence and Issues on the Argentine Case. In *Trade, Stability, Technology, and Equity in Latin America*, edited by M. Syrquin and S. Teitel. New York: Academic Press.

———. 1987. Choice of Growth Strategy: Trade Regimes and Export Promotion. In *External Debt, Savings, and Growth in Latin America*, edited by A. M. Martirena-Mantel. Washington, D.C.: International Monetary Fund.

———. 1992a. Trade Policy and Industrialization. In *Towards a New Development Strategy for Latin America: Pathways from Hirschman's Thought*. Washington, D.C.: Inter-American Development Bank.

———. 1992b. Trade Policies in Argentina. In *National Trade Policies*, Handbook of Comparative Economic Policies, vol. 2., edited by D. Salvatore. New York: Greenwood Press.

———. 1994. Post-Trade Liberalization: Institutional Issues in Argentina. Working Paper no. 182, Instituto Torcuato Di Tella.

———. 1998. El sistema de incentivos en Argentina: De la liberalización unilateral al Mercosur. Working Paper no. 217, Instituto Torcuato Di Tella.

———. 2000. The WTO Trade Policy Review of Argentina, 1999. *World Economy* 23 (9): 1195–1213.

Berlinski, Julio, Heber Camelo, and María Pazmiño. 1984. Importaciones exentas de aranceles en algunos países de la ALADI. *Integración Económica* 89: 3–15.

Berlinski, Julio, and D. Schydlowsky. 1982. Argentina. In *Development Strategies in Semi-Industrial Economies*, edited by B. A. Balassa. Baltimore, Md.: Johns Hopkins University Press.

Cavallo, Domingo, and Joaquín Cottani. 1991. Argentina. In *Liberalizing Foreign Trade in Developing Countries: The Lessons of Experience*, edited by A. M. Choksi, M. Michaely, and D. Papageorgiou. Oxford: Basil Blackwell.

Cavallo, Domingo, Roberto Domenech, and Yair Mundlak. 1989. *La Argentina que pudo ser: Los costos de la represión económica*. Buenos Aires: Manantial.

CEPAL (United Nations, Economic Commission for Latin America). 1961. Derechos aduaneros y otros gravámenes y restricciones a la importación en países latinoamericanos y sus niveles promedio de incidencia. E/CN.12.554.

Consejo Nacional de Desarrollo (CONADE). 1970. La protección aduanera efectiva en la República Argentina. Photocopy.

Chenery, Hollis B., Shuntaro Shishido, and Tsunehiko Watanabe. 1962. The Pattern of Japanese Growth, 1914–1954. *Econometrica* 30 (1): 98–139.

de Pablo, Juan Carlos. 1972. *Política antiinflacionaria en la Argentina, 1967–1970.* Buenos Aires: Amorrortu Editores.

Di Tella, Guido. 1983. *Perón-Perón, 1973–1976.* 2d ed. Buenos Aires: Editorial Sudamericana.

Díaz Alejandro, Carlos F. 1966. *Stages in the Industrialization of Argentina.* Buenos Aires: Instituto Torcuato di Tella, Centro de Investigaciones Económicas.

———. 1970. *Essays on the Economic History of the Argentine Republic.* New Haven, Conn.: Yale University Press.

———. 1981. Tipo de cambio y terminos de intercambio en la República Argentina 1913–1976. Documentos de Trabajo no. 22, Centro de Estudios Macroeconomicos Argentinos (Marzo).

Dornbusch, Rudiger, and Juan Carlos de Pablo. 1988. *Deuda externa e inestabilidad macroeconómica en la Argentina.* Buenos Aires: Editorial Sudamericana.

Edwards, Sebastian. 1993. Openness, Trade Liberalization and Growth in Developing Countries. *Journal of Economic Literature* 31 (3): 1358–93.

Edwards, Sebastian, and Miguel Savastano. 2000. Exchange Rates in Emerging Economies: What Do We Know? What Do We Need to Know? In *Economic Policy Reform: The Second Stage,* edited by A. O. Krueger. Chicago: University of Chicago Press.

Fundación de Investigaciones Económicas Latinoamericanas (Buenos Aires Argentina). 1989. *El control de cambios en la Argentina: Liberación cambiaria y crecimiento.* Buenos Aires: Manantial.

Garcia Heras, Raúl. 1996. La Argentina y el Club de Paris: Comercio y pagos multilaterales con la Europa occidental, 1955–1958. *El Trimestre Económico* 63 (4): 1277–1308.

IEERAL (Instituto de Estudios Económicos sobre la Realidad Argentina y Latinoamericana). 1986. Estadísticas de la evolución económica de Argentina 1913–1984. *Estudios* 9 (39): 103–84.

Loser, Claudio. 1971. The intensity of trade restrictions in Argentina, 1939–68. Ph.D. dissertation, University of Chicago.

Macario, Santiago. 1961. La protección industrial. Report to the Ministry of the Economy, *Panorama de la economía argentina,* vol. 3, no. 17.

———. 1964. Proteccionismo e industrialización en America Latina. *Boletín Económico de America Latina* 9 (1): 61–101.

Mangiante, Eduardo L., and Aníbal E. Marquesto. 1952. *Tecnica del control de cambios en la Argentina.* Buenos Aires: Editorial Alejandro Bunge.

Martirena-Mantel, Ana María. 1981. Crawling Peg Systems and Macroeconomic Stability: The Case of Argentina. In *Exchange Rates Rule: The Theory, Performance, and Prospects of the Crawling Peg,* edited by J. Williamson. London: Macmillan.

Nogués, Julio J. 1986. The Nature of Argentina's Policy Reforms During 1976–81. *World Bank Staff Papers* no. 765. Washington, D.C.: World Bank.

O'Rourke, Kevin H., and Jeffrey G. Williamson. 2002. The Heckscher-Ohlin Model Between 1400 and 2000: When It Explained Factor Price Convergence, When It Didn't, And Why. In *Bertil Ohlin: A Centennial Celebration, 1899–1999,* edited by R. Findlay, L. Jonung, and M. Lundahl. Cambridge, Mass.: MIT Press.

O'Rourke, Kevin H., Alan M. Taylor, and Jeffrey G. Williamson. 1996. Factor Price Convergence in the Late-Nineteenth Century. *International Economic Review* 37 (3): 499–530.

Prados Arrarte, Jesús. 1944. *El control de cambios.* Buenos Aires: Editorial Sudamericana.

Taylor, Alan M. 2002. A Century of Purchasing Power Parity. *Review of Economics and Statistics* 84 (1): 139–50.

Salera, Virgil. 1941. *Exchange Control and the Argentine Market.* New York: Columbia University Press.

Schwartz, Hugh H. 1968. The Argentine Experience with Industrial Credit and Protection Incentives, 1943–1958. Ph.D. dissertation, Yale University.

Vázquez-Presedo, Vicente. 1986. *Estadísticas históricas argentinas (Compendio 1873–1973).* Buenos Aires: Academia Nacional de Ciencias Económicas, Instituto de Economía Aplicada.

———. 1994. *Estadísticas históricas argentinas.* Buenos Aires: Academia Nacional de Ciencias Económicas, Instituto de Economía Aplicada.

Véganzonès, Marie-Ange, and Carlos Winograd. 1997. *Argentina in the 20th Century: An Account of Long-Awaited Growth.* Paris: OECD.

Williamson, Jeffrey G. 2002. Land, Labor, and Globalization in the Third World, 1870-1940. *The Journal of Economic History* 62 (1): 55–85.

World Bank. 2000. *Trade Blocs.* Oxford: Oxford University Press.

Zymelman, Manuel. 1958. The Economic History of Argentina, 1933–52. Ph.D. dissertation, Massachusetts Institute of Technology.

8

Agriculture

YAIR MUNDLAK
Hebrew University of Jerusalem

MARCELO REGÚNAGA
Universidad de Buenos Aires

The field of economics is organized around thematic subdisciplines; this volume is about economic history. In many ways, economic history addresses the domain of economic growth, but nevertheless these subdisciplines tend to remain isolated, and there is little resemblance between the questions asked by economic historians and those asked by growth theorists. That growth has become an important subject of macroeconomics is an interesting development because such analysis is not naturally connected to the economic fluctuations that have been the traditional subjects of macroeconomics. Because this difference in subjects and approaches is very relevant to this paper, we will begin by elaborating on it briefly.

Much growth theory has been concerned with finding the conditions under which steady state growth would prevail. Presumably, if such conditions were maintained, the future development of an economy could be charted in a smooth and linear fashion as if it were on "automatic pilot." The engine for the journey consists of parameters of social preferences, and is easier to navigate if those parameters are kept simple. Although insightful, this approach is antithetical to the theatre of the economic historian, which stages flights more akin to the path of roller coasters.

The interplay between models and data, or more bluntly between models and reality, requires explanation. Of course, all economic fluctuations can be dismissed as random variations and ignored, but doing this amounts to a refusal to face the challenge of data. To be sure, growth theory is inspired by actual data in that it tries to explain recorded growth rates. Too often, however, the explanation of the variability of growth rates ignores the economic environment within which the data are generated, and the exercise becomes indistinguishable from the assumption that the fortunes of the economy are written in the stars. If that were the case, the growth rates would eventually be realized, if not this year then in the future. One can think of many countries that would be happy to believe that this were true. In the policy arena, this approach can be used to justify no action, or perhaps excessive action, because the stars are silent.

The problem with this line of thinking is twofold. First, it implicitly assumes that economic theory can predict the starred rates. This is a false assumption because innovations (or whatever term we use to describe the changes in the available technology) is the trigger of growth. The pace of innovation is not a subject that economics can predict with reasonable accuracy because there is no production function for innovation (Mundlak 1993, 2000). The best we can do is to assume that the past monotonic relationships between expenditures on education, research, and development, on the one hand and related innovations on the other hand, will also prevail in the future. But even under this assumption, we cannot quantify the future input-output relationships of the process or determine its convexity. History provides fascinating anecdotes, but unfortunately they lack predictive power. The second problem is that innovations are not immediately put into action at the time of their appearance. Rather, the implementation is gradual and delayed, meaning that implemented technology is not identical to the available technology. The data we use are generated by implemented technology, and therefore cannot be used to describe accurately all available technology. The gap between available and implemented technology is a function of the economic environment, a term we will specify below.

The impact of the economic environment on growth is a subject for productive economic analysis. This is the theme taken by Cavallo and Mundlak (1982) and Mundlak, Cavallo, and Domenech (1989) in investigating the performance of the Argentine economy. The latter study (hereinafter referred to as MCD) covers the period 1913–1984. Over this period, exogenous shocks and wide fluctuations in the political environment and economic policies generated a considerable variability in economic performance. This was bad for Argentina, but ironically has provided useful data for economic analysis and makes Argentina a good case study for examining the possible impact of the economic environment. This impact is manifested through several outlets, and those are discussed here with reference to the analysis in MCD. The time coverage of that study is extended here on both ends. We go back almost forty years further to review the development of the economy from the beginning of the federal government, and we bring the discussion up to the end of the millennium. This extension reinforces the picture drawn by MCD on the role of the economic environment in growth.

The economy is specified to consist of two private sectors, agriculture and nonagriculture, and the public sector. The sectoral model is an aggregate, but it consists of several blocks. As such it is sufficiently detailed to complicate the empirical analysis. There is, however, more to the model that is relevant to understanding the process of growth than the mere mechanical exercise per se. To support this claim, we review the rationale of that study and some of its more important conceptual elements.[1] This is followed by a discussion of the qualitative nature of the results and their evaluation in light of the developments in Argentina in the poststudy period.

The plan of the paper is as follows. The next section provides background information. It is followed by an overview of the model and its main components, or blocks: production, growth of inputs and sectoral allocation, and the price block that covers the internal terms of trade and incentives. The main results are summarized and their policy relevance is discussed. The final section reviews developments, mainly in agriculture, in the poststudy period, and evaluates them with reference to the model.

8.1 Background

In its early days Argentina had a startling growth performance, surpassing that of many similarly endowed reference countries. During the period 1880–1930, GDP per capita grew more rapidly than in the United States, Canada, Australia, and other countries (Table 8.1). In that period, agriculture and related industries were the backbone of the Argentine economy; thus, the story of agriculture was pretty much the story of the economy and vice versa. In evaluating the performance at the time and, to a degree, in subsequent periods, it is important to emphasize that the impressive performance of agriculture is not solely a story about land. The utilization of agricultural potential benefited from a combination of prominent factors such as relative macro stability, free markets, resource flows, and the buildup of infrastructure.

The availability of land increased substantially with the consolidation of the federal government in 1880. At the end of the war with Paraguay, the Argentine army turned to the expansion of the agricultural frontier (The Expedition to the Desert) by taking over territories that had been partially controlled by indigenous people. This resulted in an impressive growth of territory in the span of just a few decades. The territories expanded from 400,000 km^2 in 1867 to 858,000 in 1890. The Expedition also improved the security of people and of property rights in the main areas of the Pampas (the most productive area of Argentina), and thereby made the areas more attractive to new settlers. Arable land (for pastures and crops) expanded by around 30 million hectares. Cultivated (crop) land and pastures increased by almost 50 percent (Cortes Conde 1997).

---

[1] The exposition also benefits from MCD (1990) and Mundlak and Domenech (1995), which are based on MCD (1989).

Table 8.1. *Comparative growth rates of income and population*
Argentina and selected countries, annual average in percent

	Argentina	Australia	Brazil	Canada	U.S.A.
1900–1904 to 1925–1929					
Population	2.8	1.8	2.1	2.2	1.1
Income	4.6	2.6	3.3	3.4	2.9
Per capita income	1.8	0.8	1.2	1.2	1.3
1925–1929 to 1980–1984					
Population	1.8	1.7	2.5	1.5	1.3
Income	2.8	3.9	5.5	3.9	3.1
Per capita income	1	2.2	3	2.4	1.8
1981 to 1990					
Population	1.4	1.5	1.8	1.4	0.9
Income	-1.1	3.4	2.2	2.9	3.2
Per capita income	-2.5	1.9	0.5	1.5	2.3
1991 to 1998					
Population	1.3	1.2	1.4	1.1	1
Income	5.8	3.5	2.7	2.2	3
Per capita income	4.5	2.3	1.3	1.1	2

Source: Cavallo, Domenech, and Mundlak (1989) plus IMF data for the period 1981–98.

The country was on the gold standard; the economy was open, had little intervention in the markets, and enjoyed relative price stability. The growing world markets for food products and a vast availability of resources created a very favorable environment for agricultural growth that resulted in significant increases in GDP and foreign trade. Between 1884 and 1913 cultivated land grew at an annual rate of 9 percent, while production grew at an annual rate of 10.5 percent, prima facie evidence for productivity growth. Exports rose from 15 percent of GDP in 1884 to 21 percent in 1913 (Cortés Conde 1997).

The development of agriculture benefited from the development of the railways that connected the main production areas with the ports. Transportation costs declined, which improved the competitiveness of Argentine agriculture. The availability of land and a favorable economic environment attracted European immigration, which expanded considerably the labor supply. This expansion was essential for the expansion of cultivated land. The land was initially rented from the landowners. The inflows of capital constituted an important source for financing the investment in crops, improved livestock, pastures, and other farm infrastructure, particularly wire fences. Processing and distribution apparatuses for agricultural products such as slaughterhouses, mills, constructions, ports, and other transportation facilities also required huge investments. The absence of government distortions helped the efficient allocation of resources and the development of private markets for land and commodities. For instance, in the 1920s the Rosario grain market was of a similar size as the Chicago market.

The growth of agricultural investment exceeded that of manufacturing, which in itself consisted mainly of food industries. Between 1895 and 1914 agricultural investment (in constant terms) grew at an annual rate of 12.1 percent, as compared to 5.5 percent in manufacturing (Cortés Conde 1997).

The agricultural practice at the time was based on a rotation scheme in which three years of crops were followed by pasturing. This scheme improved the soil's fertility. The improved breeds and pastures allowed for a move away from the traditional production of hides to more sophisticated beef production for the European market. Crop production was the main driving force during the period 1875–1913, as shown clearly in Figure 8.1 (based on Cortés Conde's data). While total GDP increased elevenfold between 1876–80 and 1911–15, the crop subsector grew thirty-twofold, and the livestock subsector grew only threefold. Consequently, the share of crops in GDP increased from only 4.4 percent in 1876–80 to 15.7 percent in 1911–15. At the same time livestock production declined from 56.5 percent of GDP in 1876–80 to 16.2 percent in 1911–15. To sum up, the development of agriculture and the economy was largely the result of factor accumulation under favorable economic conditions.[2]

In the 1930s Argentina's economic vitality began to deteriorate, particularly in agriculture, and the good times came to an end. The deterioration of economic performance came about, initially, as a result of the Great Depression. The worsening of economic conditions at that time, however, was common to other countries – even to those that performed better during the crisis. This resulted in a deterioration of the performance of Argentina relative to the reference countries, as shown in Figure 8.2. The deterioration continued into the later periods. Postwar policies, even when well intentioned, were notorious for their time inconsistency as well as internal inconsistency. Perhaps more importantly, they not only damaged the natural comparative advantage of the country, but also ruined the competitive structure of the economy by generating monopolies in key industries. Striking evidence from the agricultural sector of the consequences of these policies is shown in Figure 8.3, which compares the yield of the leading crops grown in Argentina with those of the same crops in the United States. Until the mid-1930s the two countries had the same level

---

[2] Some authors consider land abundance and low population density to be retarding factors in agricultural growth (e.g., Hayami and Platteau 1997, in the context of Africa). Binswanger and Townsend (2000, 1076) accept this view but give more weight to the importance of incentives and policies. This view of resource endowment is inconsistent with the experience of Argentina, where the development had its golden period when land was most abundant and population density was low. In fact, land abundance did not prevent agricultural growth in the United States, Australia, or Canada.

Fig. 8.1. Aggregate and sectoral indices, 1875–1930

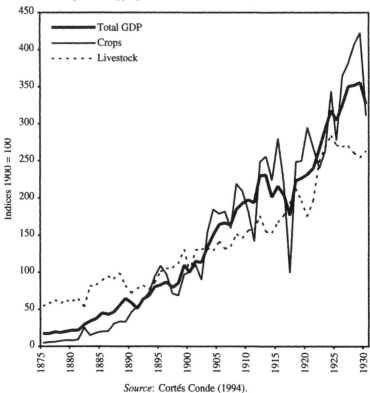

Source: Cortés Conde (1994).

of yields, with a slight edge to Argentina. Thereafter, Argentina started to lag behind the United States, and the gap increased with time. Comparing averages for the periods 1913–1930 and 1975–1984, U.S. agricultural yields tripled whereas Argentine yields did not even double. That is, Argentina did not benefit from the changes in available technology that, in the case of agriculture, were freely available.

If growth depends only on human capital, then perhaps the effect of the external shocks and the internal policies should not have been as strong as they were. After all, the level of education certainly did not decline in Argentina. Moreover, if growth is induced solely by knowledge that accumulates with time or experience, then weaker growth performance in Argentina should have been observed in the earlier years rather than later. Thus, it appears that human capital is not the only factor determining growth and that Argentina, like many other countries, could make further progress given its prevailing level of human

Fig. 8.2. Growth trends in Argentina, Australia, and Canada, 1929–84

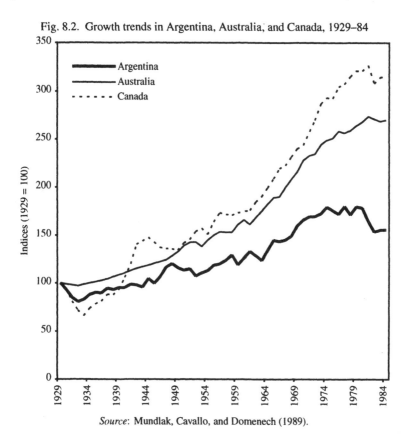

Source: Mundlak, Cavallo, and Domenech (1989).

capital. For this reason it is necessary to broaden the framework of analysis and to examine the effect of the economic environment on the growth process.

8.2 Framework

To examine the effect of the economic environment on growth we summarize the main features of the MCD model to describe the sectoral evolution of the economy in Argentina. The model, empirical in nature, intends to trace the path of the economy over time and to show how the economic environment influences that path. Even though our ultimate interest is agriculture, the model deals with the economy as a whole. Agriculture does not operate in isolation, and its fortunes are related to what happens in the rest of the economy (and vice versa). The analysis takes an explicit account of the dependence of agriculture on the economic environment, namely the available technology, world prices,

Fig. 8.3. Average yields, Argentina and United States, 1913–98
Tons per hectare

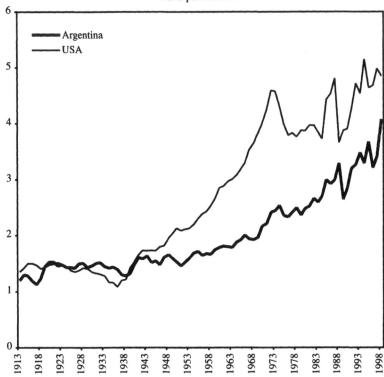

Sources: 1913–80 from Mundlak, Cavallo, and Domenech (1989); 1981–98 from S.A.G.P. y A.
and U.S.D.A. data.

domestic policies, political instability, and the like. It does this by analyzing the competition between sectors in the factor market, tracing the impact of shocks that affect factor accumulation in the economy and the real exchange rate, and examining the impact of political instability on the main sectors of the economy. The discussion describes the empirical equations, the logic of the specification, and provides a general summary of the empirical results. This is followed by a summary discussion of the implications. The reader who is not interested in the structure of the model can move to the summary and the policy implications.

In the model, the economy consists of three sectors: agriculture, nonagriculture (private), and government. Most of the analysis is concerned with the two private sectors. However, the government sector plays an important role through its market and trade policies. The model consists of several blocks. We begin with the production block.

8.3 Production

Changes in output are the outcome of changes in inputs and in technology. Whatever is not accounted for by inputs is attributed to changes in total factor productivity. To calculate the contribution of the inputs to the changes in outputs, they are aggregated to yield a change in the aggregate or total factor. This requires data on inputs and a calculation of the inputs' productivity to serve as weights in the aggregation. There are no serious conceptual or practical problems with input data beyond availability. The productivity measure, however, is a different story.

Two basic approaches have been employed in the literature in the calculation of factor productivity: market data and empirical production functions. The first approach assumes that real factor prices are always equal to the marginal productivity of the factors or, equivalently, that factor shares are equal to the production elasticities. Thus, the input aggregation is achieved through the use of the observed factor shares. The second approach, which has been used more frequently, derives the production elasticities from empirical production functions. Still, in a competitive environment, the elasticities should equal the factor shares, so both approaches should come up with estimates that are consistent with the data.

Factor shares, in Argentina as elsewhere, have fluctuated considerably. For instance, the capital (nonlabor) share in Argentine agriculture, which reached a low value of 0.31 in 1951, fluctuated in the range of 0.6 to 0.8 in several periods: 1913–1920, the 1930s, and the late 1970s and early 1980s. Such wide fluctuations could not have been generated by a Cobb-Douglas production function where factor shares are constant. The alternative is to attribute the variability in the factor shares to changes in the economic environment (Mundlak 1987). This, of course, requires an explanation.

One does not have to be an engineer to realize that production in any sector of the economy actually consists of several techniques of production. In other words, technology is heterogeneous. A production function estimated from aggregate data, where the output is an aggregate of production via more than one technique, is affected by the composition of the implemented techniques. Thus, the composition affects the calculated productivity of inputs. To make this point tangible, we can ask, for example, what the marginal productivity of water is. To answer this question we have to know the irrigated crops, their season, and the amount of other inputs. But the composition of crops depends on prices and on many other constraints, such as the cultivated area. The productivity of water is therefore a function of prices as well as the supply of other inputs. But the level of inputs is determined simultaneously with the techniques of production. It is in this sense that the implemented technology is endogenous. This is also true for the measure of total factor productivity (TFP).

The foregoing discussion serves as a background to the procedure followed in MCD. That study presents estimates of sectoral production functions for agriculture and for private nonagriculture for the period 1913–84. The functions have the Cobb-Douglas form but the elasticities and the overall productivity level are allowed to be functions of the variables representing the economic environment. This is the mechanism through which the economic environment affects factor productivity and thereby TFP and growth. The state variables that describe the economic environment are grouped as follows: technology, incentives, constraints, and institutional environment.

The analysis indicates that the following variables are capital using (labor saving): capital deepening, technical change, real sectoral prices, and the real exchange rate. This result is consistent with the hypothesis that capital accumulation, technological change, and favorable prices are all conducive to a shift in the direction of capital intensive techniques. The impact of government expenditures is ambiguous because it represents two contradictory effects. The expansion effect is likely to be capital intensive, like the other expansionary variables; on the other hand, government demand is biased toward labor-intensive techniques.

8.4 Resource growth

8.4.1 Labor supply

Population growth is taken as exogenous, but employment and investment are determined endogenously. Considerable effort was required to patch together the various sources of labor data to come up with a series for the whole period (see IEERAL 1986). The empirical analysis explains variations in the labor force. It shows that employment was positively related to the population and to the real wage in the private sector. Real wages fluctuated widely around an upward trend, reflecting the short-run cycles of the economy. The labor force was negatively related to the government wage that acted as a floor on wages in the rest of the economy.

8.4.2 Cultivated land

Land is basically a resource specific to agriculture. The area of cultivation responded positively to sectoral profitability and negatively to credit restrictions on agriculture; it also grew at a rate of 1.3 percent annually during the period

1913–30, considerably less than the strong growth observed in the earlier period reviewed above. Thereafter, profitability in agriculture started to deteriorate, and this affected the size of the area of cultivation, which reached approximately 26.7 million hectares in 1930 and remained unchanged until the late 1950s. Then it increased again, reaching nearly 30 million hectares during the 1960s, but by the end of the 1980s this figure had declined again to the 27 million hectares level. These figures do not include pasture, which serves as a substitute to crops. As such, the annual variations are also affected by the relative price of crops to livestock.

Alternatively, we can look at the changes in cultivated land adjusted for quality. An index that weights the cultivated areas by the crop's value of production grew at an average annual rate of about 1 percent during the period 1913–89. This growth was faster during 1913–39 (1.6 percent) and 1970–89 (1.8 percent) compared to the period 1940–69 (0.8 percent) during which nonagriculture, and particularly industry, had a rapid expansion.

8.4.3 Capital accumulation

Capital accumulation in the private sector is determined by net private investment. Argentina has at times been an open economy and historically drew a considerable amount of foreign capital. The inflow of capital is taken to be a function of the profitability of capital in domestic production relative to returns abroad.

The empirical results show that private investment responded positively to the expected rate of return to capital and to the acceleration in output growth. In an open economy, domestic and (net) foreign savings finance investment. Thus, domestic investment is competing for resources with the rest of the world, and it is gaining ground as domestic profitability is improving. The results also show that private investment responded positively to public investment. This is consistent with the view that public investment has provided the infrastructure necessary to host private investment. However, the results also show that increasing fiscal deficits had a negative effect on private investment. When public investment is financed through borrowing, the crowding-out effect causes a rise in interest rates and a decline in investment. As indicated below, it also has an indirect effect on the real exchange rate and, therefore, on the profitability of production, which affects the rate of return. Thus, the net effect of public investment depends on the relative strengths of these two opposing effects.

Moderate levels of borrowing to finance fiscal deficits and well-planned government investment in infrastructure during the period 1958–72 encouraged private investment, which grew at a cumulative rate of 5.6 percent. This was a period of rapid industrialization that also affected incentives. However, the financial foundation for this expansion was not sustainable; fiscal deficits and corresponding government debts were increasing significantly in the early 1970s, and private investment started to slow down. To conclude, the empirical investment function shows that a favorable economic environment has a positive effect on investment.

8.5 Factor allocation

The production function determines the factor productivity in each sector. The factor productivity and prices determine the returns to factors in each sector. In line with the Economic Law of Gravity, sectoral differences in factor returns determine the intersectoral allocation of labor and capital.

The rate of labor migration out of agriculture depends on income in agriculture relative to that in nonagriculture. After 1947, wage differentials turned in favor of urban activities because of the expansion of industries and services. The steady process of migration that took place throughout the postwar period satisfied this upward shift in urban labor demand. As a result, the agricultural labor force declined from a historical peak of 1.63 million persons in 1948 to around 1.24 million persons during the 1980s. Although it was found that urban unemployment had a negative effect on migration, the incentive provided by relative sectoral incomes was stronger until the end of the 1980s. Since then, higher unemployment in urban activities reduced the migration rate and has stabilized the agricultural labor force in the last decade. The labor series used by MCD has not been updated, and it is impossible to give a definitive answer on the direction and pace of migration in the more recent years. However, information from other sources provides the following estimates of agricultural and total (in parentheses) employment in millions: 1993, 0.783 (12.54); 1995, 0.853 (12.52); 1997, 0.942 (13.34). This amounts to a share of agriculture in total employment of 6.2, 6.8, and 7.0 percent respectively. At the same time, the share of the rural population in the total population showed a downward trend. The numbers here are: 21, 17, 13, and 11 percent in 1970, 1980, 1991 and 1999 respectively.

The sectoral allocation of net investment was also affected by the differential rate of return to capital between agriculture and nonagriculture. During the period 1930–89, the incentives to invest turned in favor of nonagriculture. In the period 1913–1930, the agricultural share of investment averaged 31 percent, which was lower than the levels reviewed above for the earlier period. The share continued to decline, reaching approximately 14 percent during the 1940s and 1950s and less than 4 percent during the 1980s. The share of private nonagriculture increased until the end of the 1960s, but the trend was reversed in favor of public investment during the 1970s and 1980s. This reversal was the combined result of a sharp decline in private investment and a moderate increase in public investment.

The trends in the sectoral allocation of investment resulted in much more pronounced capital deepening in nonagriculture, particularly in manufactures. During the period 1913–40, agriculture and nonagriculture had approximately equal shares in the total capital stock, whereas by the 1980s the shares were around 20 and 80 percent respectively.

8.6 Sectoral prices and the real exchange rate

In an open economy, world prices, nominal exchange rates, and taxes determine the prices of tradable products. However, some products are not tradable and, therefore, their prices are determined by domestic supply and demand. Economic decisions depend on relative prices and that includes the price ratio of tradables to that of nontradables, or in other words, the real exchange rate. Clearly, the real exchange rate is determined domestically within a framework that has the important features of a closed economy. As such it depends on domestic determinants of supply and demand, including actions by the public sector. In reality, there are no sectors of the economy that can be classified as purely tradable or nontradable. Thus, in the evaluation of price differentials over time or across sectors or countries, we have to consider the influence of the degree of tradability.

The degree of tradability measures the share of the tradable component in the price of a product. Hence, policies or shocks that affect the prices of tradables affect product prices according to their degree of tradability. Similarly, policies or shocks, which affect the prices of domestic resources, affect the product prices according to their degree of nontradability. This conceptual framework is useful in evaluating the response of sectoral prices to policies that are not sector specific. It is applied empirically by first analyzing the determinants of the real exchange rate and second by relating the real exchange rate to sectoral prices.

The equation for the real exchange rate includes the effects of macro variables that are often ignored in such analysis. The structural relationships depend on the degree of openness of the economy. Two measures of openness are relevant to this discussion: commercial (DOC) and financial (DOF). The DOC is determined empirically jointly with the other variables in the system, whereas DOF is treated as exogenous. Thus, the empirical analysis of the price block consists of simultaneous estimation of four equations: the real exchange rate, two sectoral prices, and the degree of commercial openness of the economy.

The dependent variable in the equation for the real exchange rate is the ratio of the price of exportables to that of nontradables or home goods. The latter is measured by the price of the government services, taking into account the dependence of this price on the macro policies. The effect on the real exchange rate of export and import taxes is unambiguously negative. The strength of this effect depends on the economy's openness. Before 1930 when the economy was very open, the price of the home good was more closely related to the price of imported goods than to that of exported goods. This reflects a relatively high degree of substitution in production and demand between domestic and imported goods. As the economy was closing in on itself through import restrictions to protect industry, the price of home goods became more closely related to the domestic price of exports, reflecting a high degree of substitution in production and demand between exported and home goods. This has often been mentioned as a structural characteristic of the postwar Argentine economy: the domestic prices of exports affect the cost of living because exports are mainly wage goods. As such, they strongly influence wages and domestic prices.

When the economy is closed to imports, the very low degree of substitution in production and demand between imported and home goods found in the data bears important consequences regarding the effect of commercial policy. In this case, a reduction in the taxes on exports resulted in an increase of the real exchange rate for exports of only 25 percent of value of the tax cut, i.e., not by the full amount of the cut. This is because the incentive to increase the production of exportables generates a trade surplus and thereby a rise in the money supply. This liquidity is channeled to domestic goods; their prices increase, and the real exchange rate decreases. Clearly, the outcome would be different if imports were not restricted, and the rise in liquidity was spent on imported goods as well.

The empirical analysis shows clearly the sensitivity of the real exchange rate to government expenditures and related macro variables. This reflects several effects. First, government expenditures contain a larger component of nontraded goods than the private expenditures taxed to finance them. Consequently, the increase in such expenditures inflates the price of nontradables and thereby depresses the real exchange rate. This effect is stronger when the economy is closed to imports. It was found that in this case, a 10 percent increase in the share of government consumption decreased the real exchange rate by 7.5 percent. Second, the increase in government borrowing to finance the fiscal deficit also depresses the real exchange rate. The strength of this effect is related to the financial openness of the economy. In periods of unrestricted capital movements, increased borrowing raises the interest rate and produces capital inflows. This, in turn, produces a decline in the nominal exchange rate, an increase in domestic prices, or both. When capital movements are restricted, the effect is milder because government borrowing crowds out private expenditures. Third, monetary expansion in excess of nominal devaluation, foreign inflation, and money demand growth affect the real exchange rate negatively. In this case, the effect is stronger when the economy is more closed to financial transactions with the rest of the world.

The impact of changes in the real exchange rate on the prices of agriculture and nonagriculture relative to the price of home good depends on the sectoral degree of tradability. In Argentina, the average degree of tradability for the period 1916–1984 was 0.68 and 0.48 for agriculture and nonagriculture respectively. Consequently, changes in the real exchange rate had a stronger effect on the agricultural price. Similarly, the differential effect of economy-wide policies on sectoral prices also depended on the sectoral degree of tradability. The same effect exists for price ratios of different products within each sector. This is important, considering that some industrial activities, particularly during the last two decades, have increased their traded component of final output.

8.7 Discussion

The empirical results were assembled to build a sectoral growth model of the Argentine economy. When we sum it up we obtain the following picture. The foreign terms of trade, domestic taxes on trade, degree of commercial openness, and excess demand for goods as affected by macro policies all affect the real exchange rate. The real exchange rate, in turn, affects sectoral prices differently, depending on the sectoral degree of tradability. Because agriculture is more tradable than nonagriculture, its price is more sensitive to variations in the real exchange rate, and indeed, to all variables that affect the real exchange rate, especially policy.

Total investment and, hence, the capital stock are favorably affected by profitability, and as such respond positively to all variables that increase the rate of return, especially real product prices and productivity. Similarly, agricultural profitability has a positive effect on the size of the cultivated area.

The choice of techniques is affected by changes in available technology and by other state variables. Incentives affect output through their effect on the level of inputs and through their effect on the choice of techniques. To the extent that new techniques are more capital intensive, the pace of capital accumulation favorably affects the degree of their implementation. Production functions and product prices determine the returns to factors at the sectoral level, and thereby the allocations of investment and labor across sectors, and the growth of sectoral output.

Each of the blocks describes important economic processes that are a subject of research in their own right. Here, we are interested in the larger picture that comes out of this formulation that shows us how to view the growth of the economy and how to evaluate the impact of policies on the growth path.

8.8 Policy implications

The model presented here in outline was put to work by MCD to evaluate the cost in terms of long-term growth of the economic policies that were applied to cope with external shocks or short-term economic goals for three important periods in Argentine economic history. To do this, we compare the trajectories that the economy could have attained under alternative economic policies.

The first episode begins in 1929 and continues through the end of the 1930s. Here, the analysis examines how economic policy reacted in the face of the drastic disruption in world trade that was caused by the Great Depression. The second episode occurred from 1946 to the mid-1950s. Here, attention is paid to the income distribution program implemented by President Perón during his first and second administrations. Finally, the third episode extends from 1970 to the mid-1980s, covering a period of very contradictory policies. Initially, the aim was a deepening of the import substitution process and redistribution of income in favor of labor. Later, the policies were changed in the opposite direction in a time of extreme macroeconomic instability and excess liquidity in world financial markets.

As indicated above, the single most striking characteristic of Argentine economic history is the long-lasting reversal of its formerly large share in world trade and finance. For several decades prior to the Great Depression, Argentina's growth had been tightly linked to that of the world economy. However, from 1929 and in reaction to a combination of external shocks and internal decisions the economy turned inward and became less and less integrated with world goods and capital markets.

To evaluate the costs in terms of long-term growth of the inward-looking strategy, the model was used to simulate the trajectory of the economy under a set of policies designed to preserve the outward-looking strategy that prevailed before 1930. The results are then compared to the actual trends. In this simulation, public expenditures were adjusted so as to avoid the sharp increases that were not sustainable in the longer run. Reducing public expenditures reduced the need for borrowing, so the fiscal deficit financed by borrowing was adjusted accordingly. The monetary-exchange policy was designed to stabilize the ratio of money to income, evaluated in terms of foreign prices, at the average level actually observed for the period 1930–84. Commercial policy was set as a uniform and constant tariff on imports of 10 percent with an elimination of taxes on exports, quantitative restrictions on trade, and controls on the exchange rate.

The results of this exercise show that relative prices strongly responded to the policy changes. On average, during the 55-year simulation period, real agricultural prices would have been 45 percent higher and real prices of private nonagriculture 20 percent higher. By the end of the period, agricultural output would have more than doubled its historical level as a consequence of both input expansion and productivity growth. Employment in agriculture would have increased by 64 percent, physical capital by 59 percent, and cultivated land by 37 percent. In private nonagriculture, output would have increased by 65 percent with a small decline in employment and a 50 percent increase in the stock of capital.

To allow for such factor growth and reallocation in the private sectors of the economy, employment in the government sector would have been 35 percent lower. This decline in government employment is consistent with the same level of government services, assuming that labor productivity in this sector increases at the same rate as in the rest of the economy. The figures for the overall economy are quite impressive. Total output would have been 63 percent higher; investment would have doubled and exports almost tripled.

These results have all the limitations that econometricians are well aware of when working with simulations involving large policy changes. With this caveat, the results can be put in perspective, allowing the readers to judge their relevance for themselves. MCD (1989, 119) compare the output simulated by the model for Argentina under free trade and macroeconomic discipline with the actual trajectories of output in Argentina, Australia, and Canada as shown in Figure 8.2 above. The outcome of the proposed policies is that Argentina's performance could have been very similar to that of the reference countries, which were similarly endowed but managed to take advantage of the opportunities offered by world markets.

All this is, of course, a retrospective evaluation. We now turn to evaluate (in terms of the model) developments since 1984 and, specifically, since the introduction of the convertibility plan and associated economic reforms.

8.9 The 1980s

The economic policies of the 1980s can be seen as a continuation of those prevailing in previous decades, with relatively high levels of government ex-

Fig. 8.4. Public expenditure and fiscal deficit, 1913–98
Percent of GDP

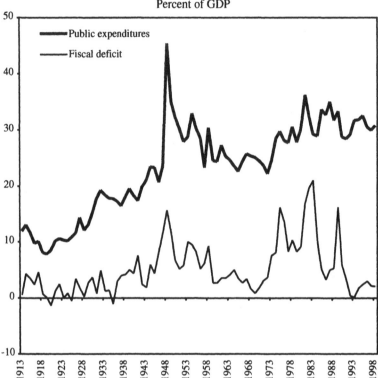

Sources: IEERAL (1986) and Secretary of Economic and Regional Programming data.

penditure and large budget deficits financed by borrowing and printing money
(see Figure 8.4). Public expenditures averaged 32.5 percent of GDP in 1980–88
and reached a level of 33.4 percent in 1989. The share of the fiscal deficit in GDP
increased from an average level of 7.3 percent for the period 1980–88 to 16.2
percent in 1989. Consequently, inflation skyrocketed; consumer prices grew
at an average annual rate of 876 percent for the period 1981–1990, reaching a
peak of 4,924 percent in 1989. In this environment the annual budget stated in
current pesos was totally meaningless and the difference between actual public
revenues and expenditures was closed by inflationary tax (Llach 1997).

The main message that comes out of this period is that such policies are
unsustainable and will eventually explode. It is true that the country reached
this situation out of the storm of political events in the 1970s, and that in the
early 1980s Argentina faced external shocks that placed it in the company of

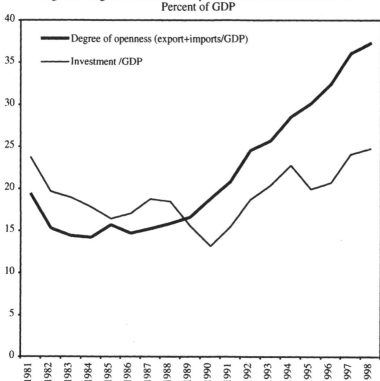

Fig. 8.5. Degree of commercial openness and investment, 1981–98
Percent of GDP

Sources: IEERAL (1986) and Secretary of Economic and Regional Programming data.

other Latin American countries. But at the end of the day, internal developments were a direct outcome of internal policies.

Although the crisis was an outcome of expansionary fiscal policies, the attempted stabilization policies also missed the target. They involved heavy overseas borrowing and the application of price and other controls such as export taxes; very high import taxes; quantitative restrictions on trade, particularly on capital and consumer durable goods; and controls on domestic prices and foreign transactions.

Overall, the impact of these policies was to cause the effective closure of the economy. The degree of commercial openness (the ratio of trade to GDP) remained at very low levels, around 15 percent of GDP, during most of the period (Figure 8.5), and the ratio of the black market to the nominal rate of exchange averaged 1.38 and was subject to high variability. Gross fixed investment declined steadily, from an average of 19.3 percent of GDP in the period 1981–85

Table 8.2. *Total factor productivity, 1900–90*

Periods	Average annual growth rate (percent)
1900–1929	0.9
1929–1947	1.9
1947–1973	0.8
1973–1990	-1.5

Sources: Elias (1995).

to 16.6 percent in the period 1986–90, reaching a minimum of 13.2 percent in 1990 (Figure 8.5).

As shown in Table 8.2, total factor productivity, which prior to the 1970s had shown a positive trend, declined during the period 1973–1990 by an average annual rate of 1.5 percent (Elías 1995). Real GDP declined during the period 1981–90 at an average annual rate of 1.06 percent. During the same period, Australia, Canada, and the United States grew at annual rates of 3.4 percent, 2.9 percent and 3.2 percent, respectively; and thus, the gap in the growth observed in previous decades between Argentina and these reference countries continued to grow (Table 8.1).

In addition to this unfavorable economic environment, agriculture was suffering from a decline in world agricultural prices in the second half of the decade. Land cultivated with annual crops declined by 9.9 percent from 1981–83 to 1988–90. Agricultural production continued to be relatively extensive, but still, some of the main Argentine crops registered small productivity gains, based mainly on improved seeds. This, however, was not sufficient to offset the drop in harvested area, and total production of annual crops declined from an annual average of 56 million tons in 1981–83 to 49 million tons in 1988–90. Exports of agricultural primary goods also declined from an annual average of 3.7 billion dollars in 1981–83 to 2.6 billion dollars in 1988–90.

8.10 The 1990s

8.10.1 The reform

The broad economic reforms first introduced in April of 1991 changed dramatically the economic environment of Argentina. A major goal of the reforms was to stop inflation and, at the same time, to better utilize the potential of the economy. This was done through the restoration of fiscal and monetary discipline. The reforms, however, were far broader in scope, and they involved institutional changes and affected drastically the supply side of the economy and the integration of the economy within the world economy. Before turning

Table 8.3. *Export taxes for agricultural products, 1989–93*

Taxes as of	Wheat	Corn	Soybean
05/89	20	20	31
08/89	30	30	41
11/90	15	17	26
03/91	0	0	6
09/93	0	0	3.5

Sources: Secretary of Industry, Commerce, and Mining data.
Note: Not included are the statistics tax (3%), which was eliminated in November 1991, and the tax for INTA (1.5%), which was eliminated in September 1993.

to agriculture, we list briefly some of the more important elements of the reform and their general consequences.

The imposition of fiscal discipline required a reduction in public expenditures and the elimination of various subsidies and redundant or low-priority programs. After decades of steady growth in the share of public expenditures in GDP, the ratio dropped to 28.4 percent in 1991 from an annual average of 32.5 percent in the 1980s (Figure 8.4). The privatization of public companies alleviated the burden they had imposed on the budget and provided revenue for other uses. The public debt was rescheduled, thus reducing the ongoing interest payments.

The Convertibility Law established a free convertibility of the domestic currency to the dollar. Under the plan, the Central Bank operates as an independent currency board, and the local currency is fully backed by foreign reserves and gold. This eliminated the possibility of monetizing government deficits and the scope for foreign exchange controls.

The market reforms included:

(a) establishing complete freedom of prices in domestic and foreign trade and freedom of action in foreign exchange transactions as well as other transactions in the financial and capital markets;

(b) eliminating restrictions and regulations on most economic activities, including domestic and external trade, professional services, insurance, financial services, medium and long distance transport, ports, and other services;

(c) eliminating differential exchange rates used for foreign transactions;

(d) eliminating most of the export taxes for agricultural products, as seen in Table 8.3;[3]

(e) and substantial reductions in the levels and spreads of import taxes, the statistics tax which provided funds to promote exports and local maritime fleets,

---

[3] In 1993 export rebates were introduced for most agricultural and nonagricultural products (major oil seeds were excepted). In 1996 the export rebates were reduced for fiscal reasons.

Table 8.4. *Evolution of the import tax structure, 1987–91*

Taxes on	1987	1989	1990	April 1991
Capital Goods	37	34	22	12
Intermediate Goods	41	27	20	6.4
Consumer Durable	48	34	24	11.5
Consumer Non Durable	34	27	18	5.4

Source: Conci and Bozzalla (1992).

Table 8.5. *Import taxes in selected years*
Percent

	1987	1991	1992	1995	1995[1]
Average	39.4	14	11	11	11
Standard Deviation	21.6	6.9	6	6.2	6
Maximum Tariff	102.5	39.5	35	35	20[2]
Minimum Tariff	0	0	0	0	0
Statistics Tax	3	3	3	3	0

[1] Mercosur common external tariff.
[2] Mercosur countries were allowed to maintain exceptions (300 tariff lines for Argentina) at a maximum of 35 percent.
Sources: IEERAL and Secretary of Industry, Commerce, and Mining data.

and the currency transfer tax; Table 8.4 shows the evolution of the import tax structure in the time around the reform.[4]

With some oversimplification, it can be said that three tariff levels were established in 1991: 0 percent for raw materials, 11 percent for intermediate goods, and 22 percent for manufactured goods; a three percent statistics tax was also maintained. Some changes were introduced later on without a substantial change in the overall picture. Other minor changes were introduced in 1995 when the MERCOSUR set its common external tariff (Table 8.5).

On the whole, the tax system was simplified and made more transparent, and distorting taxes were reduced dramatically; representing 3.2 percent of GDP in 1989–90, they declined to 0.5 percent in 1995 (Llach 1997). Emphasis was placed on V.A.T., income tax, luxury goods, gasoline, and labor taxes to finance the social programs. Taxes on foreign trade were reduced significantly. However, despite the good results of this policy, some of the distorting taxes (such as fuel and import taxes) were applied again in the second half of the 1990s.

A deliberate effort was made to reduce the cost of production and thereby to improve the competitive position of the country. In addition to the afore-

---

[4] The statistics tax is just another tax, so named for historical reasons.

mentioned tax reforms, this effort involved the deregulation of most economic activities and the privatization of services, including energy, transportation, ports, telecommunications, grain elevators, and agricultural markets. Consequently, the prices of services declined considerably – 26 percent in industrial electricity, 67 percent in port costs for containers, 48 percent in port service charges, 43 percent in maritime freights, and 33 percent in truck freights to Brazil (Obschatko, Sguiglia and Delgado 1994; Union Industrial Argentina, Machinea, and Gerchunoff, 1996). In the case of grain exports, the elimination of the various taxes and the reduction in the costs of export quality controls, loading, unloading, and storage resulted in reductions of around 15 percent in free-on-board (FOB) prices.

8.10.2 Results

The impact of the reforms was swift and strong. Inflation converged to international rates, and foreign trade, investment, rural employment, and cultivated land all increased. Output (at constant prices) in the period 1991–98 grew at an average annual rate of 5.8 percent (Table 8.1). The higher growth rates in GDP and GDP per capita registered in Argentina during the 1990s exceeded the rates achieved in the reference countries.

Foreign trade expanded considerably from the beginning of the Convertibility Law. Initially there was an import boom, particularly of capital goods and other inputs, which accounted for 80 percent of the import growth. Annual imports of capital goods, which averaged 2 billion dollars during the 1980's, grew to an annual average of 8.7 billion dollars during the period 1991–1998. Up until 1996 most of the capital goods were imported with reduced or zero import duties, which contributed to the modernization of the private production sector.

The response of exports, however, did not begin until 1993. On the demand side, there was initially a strong positive response of domestic consumption to the program, which competed with exports. On the supply side, agricultural world prices were very low in 1991 and 1992, and that discouraged a sizable output expansion. Total exports of goods in current dollars, nevertheless, more than doubled in the period 1991–98, as compared to a growth of about 35 percent in the previous decade. During the 1990s the degree of commercial openness of the economy grew steadily until 1998, reaching 37 percent of GDP in the last year as compared to 19 percent in 1990 (Figure 8.5).

The supply of credit increased with local savings and with foreign capital inflows. Perceived country risk, which had reached very high levels by the end of the previous decade, registered a dramatic reduction from the second half of 1991, and interest rates declined gradually. Interest rates for loans denominated in U.S. dollars, provided by Banco Nacion Argentina (the main source for the agricultural sector), declined from 18 percent by the end of 1991 to 17 percent by the end of 1992; they remained at around 16 percent in 1993, 1994, and 1995, and declined to 13 percent by the end of 1996 and to 12 in 1997.

The improved climate for investment attracted domestic and foreign investors. Increased foreign direct investment helped to incorporate modern technologies in different sectors. Gross fixed investment grew from an annual average of 16.6 percent of GDP during the period 1986–90, to 19.5 percent in the period 1991–95, and 23.2 percent in the period 1996–98 (Figure 8.5). This was associated with a sharp increase in total factor productivity, particularly during the first half of the 1990s. A study conducted by Cavallo and Mondino (1995) shows that total factor productivity grew at an annual rate of 6.5 percent in the period 1990–1994.

The supply of credit to agriculture increased more than threefold in a short period of time, from an annual average of $1.9 billion in 1988–1990 to $6.3 billion in 1996–1998. This change resulted in an increase of the share of agriculture in total credit supply.

8.10.3 Agriculture

Agriculture benefited from the various measures taken under the reform, specifically: the elimination of quantitative restrictions on imports; the reductions in import taxes for agricultural inputs (fertilizers, herbicides, pesticides, machinery, and irrigation equipment); the elimination of distorting taxes on fuels, commercial and financial transactions; the elimination of export taxes; the deregulation of economic activities; and the removal of inefficiencies and monopoly profits in the trade channels (elevators, transportation, and ports). These changes reduced the factor costs and thereby the spread between the cost-insurance-freight (CIF) and farm prices. This is clearly reflected in the output-input price ratio at the farm level, as seen in Table 8.6.

The improvement in the price ratio resulted in the increased use of chemicals and improved conservation practices. During the period 1990–1998 there were impressive rises in the use of fertilizers (fivefold), herbicides and pesticides (threefold), and tractors (around 50 percent).[5] New techniques were introduced that have resulted in a better use of water and soils, reduced costs, and improved

---

[5] As to the slower growth in the number of tractors, the number reflects two developments. First, the average size of tractors (in terms of horsepower) grew around 10 percent during the last decade. Second, changes to no-tillage or low-tillage practices replaced machinery with chemicals.

Table 8.6. *Relative prices for selected inputs and crops*
Tons of grain needed to purchase 1 ton, 1,000 liters, or 1 unit

	Herbicide		Fertilizer		Fule oil		Tractor	
Period	Wheat	Soya	Wheat	Soya	Wheat	Soya	Wheat	Soya
1985–87	66	37	3.6	2.0	2.6	1.4	231	125
1988–90	55	35	3.4	2.1	2.5	1.6	211	127
1991–93	43	25	3.2	1.8	2.8	1.6	252	144
1994–96	32	22	2.6	1.7	1.9	1.2	174	120

Notes: The herbicide is Treflan; the fertilizer Diamon.
Sources: S.A.G.P. y A. and Margenes Agropecuarios data.

Table 8.7. *Growth in yields, 1986–98*
Tons per hectare

Period	Wheat	Corn	Soybean	Sunflower
1986–90	1.80	3.42	2.02	1.39
1991–95	2.12	4.34	2.16	1.67
1996–98	2.27	4.89	2.17	1.74

Sources: S.A.G.P. y A. data.

yields. They have also contributed to the sustained productivity of soils in the Pampas, a subject of major public concern during the 1980s.

Another major technological change has been the use of high-yield seeds, mainly transgenic, which are resistant to selected herbicides and pesticides. Such seeds reduce costs significantly and facilitate double cropping. The efficient use of no-tillage practices and resistant seeds allow for a better selection of the planting period. As a consequence, a high percentage of Argentine soybeans are now grown as a second crop after wheat. Currently, the transgenic seeds account for around 80 percent of area planted with soybeans, a crop that accounts for more than 40 percent of value of production of total annual crops. Between the periods 1986–90 and 1996–98 the major Argentine crops registered significant growth in yields (see Table 8.7).

This amounts to a growth of 26 percent in wheat, 43 percent in corn, 7 percent in soybeans, and 25 percent in sunflower seed. The growth in the yield of soybeans was tame because during the last decade there was a shift from growing soybeans as a single crop to double crop. Thus, the productivity growth was manifested in terms of having a second crop in the same year. Most of the soybean currently planted in the Argentine corn belt is double crop, in contrast to the United States where it is still grown as a single crop. On the whole, the gain in yields exceeded those registered in the United States in the same period, thus reversing a long-term trend of a growing gap (Figure 8.3).

The improved domestic economic environment for agriculture, supplemented by better world prices from 1994, had a positive impact on the size of the planted area. Land area sown to the 31 main annual crops expanded by 24.6 percent between the period 1988–90 and the period 1996–98. Production capacity was also increased with the use of supplementary irrigation for extensive crops (particularly corn) in the Pampean region. Investment in irrigation was significant during the period 1994–97, when profits rose.

New techniques introduced during the 1990s emphasized cost reduction. Deteriorating international agricultural prices discouraged the use of more productive, but also more expensive, practices being used elsewhere in countries that subsidized their agriculture. According to recent OECD estimates for 1998, these subsidies amounted to 22 percent, 16 percent, and 45 percent of the farmers' income in the United States, Canada, and the European Union respectively.

The increase in the planted area of main crops and in their yields resulted in a 7 percent annual growth in production during the period 1988–90 to 1996–98. This impressive growth allowed for a substantial expansion of exports during the 1990s; the value of exports of primary agricultural goods doubled in the period 1990–1998. The output growth of agricultural products destined primarily for domestic consumption was somewhat weaker because, unlike exported products, it was constrained by the growth of domestic demand. Thus the annual growth rate in the same period was 4.4 percent for fruits and 5 percent for milk.

In sum, the economic environment for agriculture is best reflected in land prices. As shown in Table 8.8, land prices in dollars that were fairly stable in the 1980s started to take off in the 1990s and reached high levels in 1996–98.

8.11 Conclusion

The higher the position from which an overview is made, the flatter the observed landscape. Still, the contours of high mountains and wide valleys can be observed even from high above. Our chapter-length attempt to evaluate the development of the Argentine economy in a period exceeding a century (and no one can claim that is has been a dull one) has required a very high position. The result is a view with which one can dare to assess the broad forces that have affected the development of the economy and their impact.

Building on the MCD framework and empirical analysis of the period 1913–1984, our attention was very directed. The observed picture is that without having the necessary economic environment the economy does not utilize its potential. Economic growth at the pace observed in other countries is not an in-

Table 8.8. *Land prices*

U.S. dollars per hectare or product units per hectare

	Corn Belt ($/ha)	Wheat Area ($/ha)	Livestock Area ($/ha)	Corn Belt (t/ha)	Wheat Area (t/ha)	Livestock Area (kg/ha)
1977–78	1,734	825	733	22.8	10.1	1,828
1979–81	2,432	1,011	1,080	21.0	8.1	1,304
1982–84	1,813	727	701	27.9	9.8	1,538
1985–87	1,562	582	575	26.6	8.4	1,374
1988–90	1,768	657	644	24.8	7.0	1,249
1991–93	2,338	867	916	23.8	7.9	1,111
1994–96	2,599	1,048	1,087	20.8	6.5	1,303
1997–99	4,300	1,557	1,667	44.1	13.0	1,753

Notes: Prices in U.S. dollars, and in units of corn, wheat, or meat, respectively, per hectare.
Source: Margenes Agropecuarios.

herent human right, and it is not written in the stars. What is true for individuals is also the case for society: one has to work for it. The importance of this study is that it covers a very long period that shows that society can shortchange itself even for long periods of time. The fact that the country is blessed with natural resources provides it with greater potential, but it does not make the job easier. This very general statement is illustrated in the counterfactual simulation in MCD for the period 1930–1984 and is reinforced here by the straightforward comparison of the events in the 1980s and the 1990s. It is also consistent with the developments in the early period, which was a period of expansion.

References

Binswanger, Hans P., and Robert F. Townsend. 2000. The Growth Performance of Agriculture in Subsaharan Africa. *American Journal of Agricultural Economics* 82 (5): 1075–86.

Cavallo, Domingo, Roberto Domenech, and Yair Mundlak. 1989. *La Argentina que pudo ser: Los costos de la represión económica*. Buenos Aires: Manantial.

Cavallo, Domingo, and Guillermo Mondino. 1995. Argentina's Miracle? From Hyperinflation to Sustained Growth. Paper presented at The World Bank, Annual Bank Conference on Development Economics.

Cavallo, Domingo, and Yair Mundlak. 1982. *Agricultural and Economic Growth in an Open Economy: The Case of Argentina*. Washington, D.C.: International Food Policy Research Institute, Research Report 36.

Conci, L., and C. Bozalla. 1992. *Estimaciones de la serie de tipo de cambio efectivo real de las importaciones*. Buenos Aires: Photocopy. Area Estadísticas Económicas, Banco Central de la República Argentina.

Cortés Conde, Roberto. 1994. Estimaciones del PBI en la Argentina 1875–1935. Ciclos de seminarios no. 3/94, Departamento de Economía, Universidad de San Andrés.

———. 1997. *La economía argentina en el largo plazo: Ensayos de historia económica de los siglos XIX y XX*. Buenos Aires: Editorial Sudamerica.

de Obschatko, Edith S., Eduardo Sguiglia, and Ricardo Delgado. 1994. *Efectos de la desregulación sobre la competitividad de la producción argentina.* Buenos Aires: Grupo Editor Latinoamericano.

Elias, Victor. 1995. *Infrastructure and Growth: The Latin American Case.* Washington, D.C.: The World Bank.

Hayami, Yujiro, and Jean-Philippe Platteau. 1997. Resource Endowments and Agricultural Development: Africa vs. Asia. In *The Institutional Foundation of Economic Development in East Asia,* edited by M. Aoki and Y. Hayami. London: Macmillan.

IEERAL (Instituto de Estudios Económicos sobre la Realidad Argentina y Latinoamericana). 1986. Estadísticas de la evolución económica de Argentina 1913–1984. *Estudios* 9 (39): 103–84.

Llach, Juan José. 1997. *Otro Siglo, Otra Argentina.* Buenos Aires: Ariel.

Mundlak, Yair. 2000. *Agriculture and Economic Growth: Theory and Measurement.* Cambridge, Mass.: Harvard University Press.

Mundlak, Yair, Domingo Cavallo, and Roberto Domenech. 1989. *Agriculture and Economic Growth, Argentina 1913–1984.* Washington, D.C.: International Food Policy Research Institute, Research Report 76.

———. 1990. Effects of Macroeconomic Policies on Sectoral Prices. *World Bank Economic Review* 4 (1): 55–79.

Mundlak, Yair, and Roberto Domenech. 1995. Agricultural Growth in Argentina. In *Agriculture on the Road to Industrialization,* edited by J. W. Mellor. Baltimore, Md.: Johns Hopkins University Press.

OECD. 1999. *Agricultural Policies in OECD Countries: Monitoring and Evaluation.* Paris: OECD.

Sturzenegger, Adolfo, Wylian Otrera, and Beatriz Mosquera. 1990. *Trade, Exchange Rate, and Agricultural Pricing Policies in Argentina.* Washington, D.C.: World Bank.

Union Industrial Argentina, José L. Machinea, and Pablo Gerchunoff. 1996. *Evolución reciente y situación actual de la industria argentina.* Buenos Aires: Boletín Informativo Techint (Julio–Septiembre).

9

Industry

MARÍA INÉS BARBERO
Universidad de Buenos Aires and Universidad Nacional de General Sarmiento

FERNANDO ROCCHI
Universidad Torcuato Di Tella

This chapter analyzes the evolution and performance of the Argentine industrial sector in a long-run perspective, aiming to unveil some phenomena that historical studies restricted to shorter spans of time cannot grasp. It begins in the 1870s with the establishment of the first factories and ends a century later when the industrialization model, the core of which was the satisfaction of domestic demand through an increasing process of import substitution, suffered a crisis from which there emerged a new industrial profile.

To focus our view of the terrain, we look to studies of industry for details of the quantitative and qualitative transformations that have occurred. Throughout, the market and government appear as characters in a story whose plot is complex, but which may be clarified with a long-run viewpoint. This perspective also offers the possibility of a new periodization, one that is quite different from those seen in the traditional studies of industrial history. As an inescapable shortcoming, this kind of summary discussion affords only a high degree of generalization.

The general question permeating this chapter is to what extent the analysis of Argentine industrial evolution provides a means to explain the poor comparative performance that the Argentine economy has had in the last fifty years. Even as a sectoral study, then, it shares some major questions with other essays in this volume that also target the causes of Argentine decline. At the same time, it does not ignore the fact that the debate over the causes of decline has not ended; rather, the Argentine case, as stated by Carlos Díaz Alejandro, remains "one of the most puzzling and misunderstood national stories in the development literature."[1]

We thank Pablo Gerchunoff, Stephen Haber, and Andrés Regalsky for their comments.

[1] Díaz Alejandro (1988, 230). For a long-run study of the Argentine economy see Gerchunoff and Llach (1998). For the debate on the causes of the Argentine decline see della Paolera and Taylor (2001).

The absence of successful industrialization is seen – by quite a number of scholars – as one of the roots of Argentina's stagnation. From theoretical and methodological standpoints, studies on Argentine (and, in general, Latin American) industry can be classified into two analytical schools: the structuralist and the neoclassical.[2] The former prevailed from the 1950s to the 1970s and was strongly legitimized and propagated by the United Nations Economic Commission for Latin America (CEPAL). Structuralists argued that industrialization was the avenue toward development and that markets by themselves would not necessarily foster it, especially in underdeveloped countries. As a consequence, it was the task of government to enforce active policies to achieve this goal and to work against market deficiencies. For them, industrialization meant not only an increase in industrial output but also structural changes that were equated with modernization. Their main historical observation was that industrial growth during the export-led period, from the late nineteenth century to 1930, was negligible. They embraced the idea that Latin American states were allegedly captive to land-owning elites and operating as impediments to industrial development. In this view, it was only a shock with the magnitude of the Great Depression that forced elites to change economic policies and foster industrial growth.[3]

However, structuralist ideas soon faced a challenge. The neoclassical perspective began to emerge in the academic field in the 1970s with the research of Díaz Alejandro (1970) and a group of scholars working at the Instituto Torcuato Di Tella in Buenos Aires. Neoclassicists did not identify development with industrialization, but instead strongly criticized the intervention of the state in the market's allocation of resources. The costs that such policy had in terms of efficiency was, from their point of view, great. Such policy resulted mainly in the distortion of relative prices and the diversion of resources from more competitive sectors to manufacturing. In their revision of the structuralist interpretation, neoclassicists assigned to the export-led period, with its open economy and non-interventionist state, a much more positive role in terms of industrial growth. Industry, then, not only existed and expanded before 1930 but it did so in a much more efficient way than occurred later.

Both paradigms coexist at present and, thus, represent alternative readings of the past. The neoclassical approach gained strength with the crisis surrounding

---

[2] This classification, only offered as a tool for a general view, assumes some simplification and does not include other perspectives such as dependency theory or the Marxist approach. Two influential collections following the general neoclassical approach but emphasizing instititutionalism, in one case, and cliometrics, in the other, are Haber (1997) and Coatsworth and Taylor (1998). For other perspectives see Korol and Sábato (1990), and C. Lewis and Suzigan (2000).

[3] See Ferrer (1963) and Peralta Ramos (1972). An exception was the pioneer work of Dorfman (1942).

Keynesianism, and proposed a still more detailed vision with the rise of the new institutionalism. Structuralists, on the other hand, still have an important presence in the academic world through neostructuralism, which supports a more nuanced perspective; as such, they have a more critical stance on the import-substitution model, especially in its domestic market orientation and restrictive policies regarding primary goods exports.[4]

Since this article represents a summation of recent research on Argentine industry, it depends on the respective strengths and limitations of those research agendas. We must note that, in the case of Argentina, new scholarly perspectives – such as institutionalism and cliometrics – have not had the same degree of success as in other Latin American case studies, such as Brazil and Mexico.[5] In addition, neoclassicism has been used as a framework for analyzing the general performance of the economy, as well as individual sectors, but not of manufacturing in particular.[6]

This chapter also incorporates our own research into business history and the study of consumption. In doing so, it benefits from new insights that highlight the micro aspects of industry; at the same time, it allows for departures from the traditional macro approach that both structuralism and neoclassicism embody.[7] Finally, it considers the most recent studies on topics – such as the capital market, investment, and saving – that shed indirect light on some aspects of historical industrial performance.[8]

Despite such a broad approach, our chapter, like the extant literature, still leaves much ground uncovered, revealing the perspectives and methodological issues that have yet to be tackled by future researchers. Our approach, then, has necessarily been eclectic. This means that we have not taken any single theoretical or methodological perspective as the solely valid (or even predominant) model. Our goal has been to summarize debates, to elucidate the process, and to consider different variables in explaining the evolution of industrial performance. We conclude that this evolution has been the outcome of economic and noneconomic forces (including social, political, and cultural ones), of macro and micro aspects, and of national and international contexts. Thus, we propose to analyze manufacturing as the byproduct of market and government activity, observing how both combined in the different stages into which we divide Argentine industrial history.

---

[4] See, for example, Ffrench-Davis, Muñoz, and Palma (1994), and Katz and Kosacoff (1989).

[5] See C. Lewis (1986, 1998), Topik (1987), Haber (1989), and Bulmer-Thomas (1994).

[6] See Cortés Conde (1997).

[7] See Barbero (1990, 2000), Barbero and Ceva (1997), and Rocchi (1994, 1997, 1998).

[8] See della Paolera and Taylor (1998), Nakamura and Zarazaga (1998), Regalsky (1992, 1999), and Rougier (2001).

The chapter is arranged chronologically, defining periods of expansion and stagnation according to two main considerations. One can be derived easily from the numbers, namely, the trend in the annual growth rates of the manufacturing industry. The other comes out of the microeconomic aspects we have studied in our own research. The periodization we propose does not follow the usual pattern used in the literature and probably will come as a surprise to some readers. In such periods, however, we have found continuities that we will help us set the stage for each section.

To that end, we have constructed a time series of industrial product that incorporates various extant estimates and combines them into a common series, shown in Tables 9.1 and 9.2 and Figure 9.1.[9] Table 9.1 provides a global picture of industry's ups and downs and offers a quick comparison with the performance of the economy as a whole. The periods of expansion are relatively protracted through time – they range from twenty to thirty-eight years – while the periods of stagnation never exceed one decade.[10] Expansions include the periods 1875–1913, 1920–1948, and 1954–1974, and show high annual growth rates of around 8 percent, 5 percent, and 6 percent per annum, respectively. Downturns include the periods 1913–1920 and 1948–1954 and exhibit growth rates close to zero.[11] However, it is striking that from 1975 onward Argentina's manufacturing history changed dramatically, and industrial growth began to show negative rates of growth – a "de-industrialization" trend that would be reversed (though only briefly) in the early to late 1990s (Table 9.3). More importantly, the profile of the industrial sector in this last period of decline is significantly different from the one that had persisted until the mid-1970s.

9.1 The birth of industry, 1875–1913

From the closing of the nineteenth century to the Great Depression, the boom of the Argentine economy was linked to its integration into the world market. The amount of research conducted on industry during this period has been meager. Again, scholars long assumed that manufacturing essentially did not exist at that time. The idea that Argentina may have had some industrial development during the export boom was first suggested only in the 1960s. It obtained its

---

[9] Data on Gross Domestic and Industrial Products have been drawn from different series. For the period before 1935, we have taken into account the research of Cortés Conde (1994). For the period from 1935 to 1990, we have consider the series of United Nations, CEPAL (1978), and Martínez (1999). We chose Cortés Conde's estimates rather than the CEPAL for the period 1900–1935 as a result of the more careful methodology of his estimation. Had we chosen the CEPAL numbers, industrial growth in the 1920s would have been significantly higher than presented in this article.

[10] See Heyman (1980) and his idea of "intuitive periodizations."

[11] The annual growth rates were calculated for the beginning and the final years of each period.

Table 9.1. *Annual rate of growth of industry and GDP, 1875–1990*

Percent

Period	Industry	GDP
1875–1913	7.97	6.85
1913–1920	0.28	0.04
1920–1948	5.36	3.64
1948–1954	0.42	0.68
1954–1974	5.89	4.07
1974–1990	-2.02	-0.18
1875–1990	4.66	3.93

Source: Authors' calculation based on Cortés Conde (1994) for the period 1875–1935; CEPAL (1978) for the period 1936–76; and Martínez (1999) for the period 1977–90.

Table 9.2. *Evolution of industrial output, 1875–1990*

Index 1900 = 100

1875	14.46	1904	149.97	1933	461.31	1962	1,955.07
1876	13.13	1905	169.56	1934	513.70	1963	1,659.76
1877	15.96	1906	185.40	1935	621.51	1964	1,972.67
1878	14.83	1907	179.12	1936	659.81	1965	2,244.99
1879	15.95	1908	182.08	1937	700.44	1966	2,259.79
1880	14.57	1909	207.93	1938	742.22	1967	2,294.03
1881	15.84	1910	217.85	1939	770.65	1968	2,443.10
1882	18.38	1911	231.79	1940	755.56	1969	2,707.79
1883	20.67	1912	247.18	1941	785.74	1970	2,878.67
1884	19.85	1913	266.19	1942	871.05	1971	3,156.60
1885	22.40	1914	226.41	1943	909.35	1972	3,344.78
1886	25.50	1915	235.14	1944	998.72	1973	3,557.41
1887	31.76	1916	248.13	1945	951.71	1974	3,773.92
1888	31.75	1917	246.28	1946	1,037.02	1975	3,668.11
1889	30.00	1918	258.97	1947	1,206.47	1976	3,494.03
1890	31.62	1919	284.52	1948	1,172.23	1977	3,767.15
1891	35.62	1920	271.50	1949	1,090.40	1978	3,370.68
1892	40.61	1921	297.89	1950	1,112.46	1979	3,706.37
1893	39.85	1922	322.98	1951	1,141.60	1980	3,572.58
1894	58.10	1923	349.94	1952	1,120.03	1981	3,012.59
1895	60.37	1924	348.97	1953	1,113.78	1982	2,859.95
1896	73.39	1925	389.66	1954	1,202.04	1983	3,146.89
1897	70.27	1926	390.05	1955	1,349.10	1984	3,272.30
1898	81.42	1927	419.51	1956	1,442.61	1985	2,934.41
1899	104.83	1928	431.70	1957	1,556.53	1986	3,317.14
1900	100.00	1929	427.23	1958	1,513.10	1987	3,298.80
1901	108.92	1930	417.35	1959	1,512.24	1988	3,078.96
1902	109.05	1931	405.58	1960	1,664.33	1989	2,859.30
1903	130.12	1932	411.45	1961	1,831.04	1990	2,723.26

Sources: As in Table 9.1.

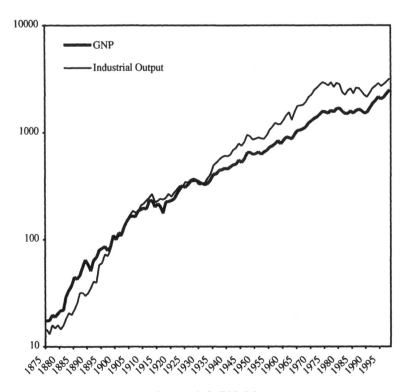

Fig. 9.1. Comparative growth of GDP and industrial output, 1875–1998
Logarithmic scale, index 1900 = 100

Sources: As in Table 9.1.

Table 9.3. *Share of industrial output in GNP, 1900–90*

Percent

1900–09	15.35
1910–19	16.54
1920–29	18.65
1930–39	21.06
1940–49	24.22
1950–59	24.80
1960–69	28.18
1970–79	27.23
1980–90	23.60

Source: Kosacoff (1992).

final form with the followers of the "staple theory" who pointed to the absence of conflict between the growth of exports and industry, since the former could actually help increase the demand for domestic manufactured products.[12] The neoclassical school asserted that it was precisely in this period that industry showed its strongest growth and ascribed it to the laissez-faire policies that allowed for an optimum allocation of resources.[13]

Industry's growth in the period 1875–1913 was around 8 percent per annum, the highest of all rates considered in the periodization of our study (Table 9.1). The high growth rates attained are only partly explained by the large proportional changes that may be expected starting from a base of virtually zero industrial activity. A division of this period into two stages – before and after 1900 – shows that the pace of growth was firmly sustained throughout the whole period. From 1875 to 1900, industry grew at 8.04 percent per annum (but with stagnant performance in the late 1870s) and at 7.82 percent per annum from 1901 to 1912.

The relationship between industrial growth and the time of greatest economic expansion is enlightening, and shows the importance of the linkages associated with the agricultural boom – linkages that generated the momentum for manufacturing at its initial stages. Industry at this time, mainly based on the manufacturing of consumer goods, was the result of a three forces: domestic consumption, external demand, and import substitution.

The growth in domestic demand (the result of an increase in total population fueled by high immigration and the rise in GDP per capita) generated a market for consumer goods of relatively simple manufacture whose costs of production domestically allowed for a decline in imports. Within this period, GDP increased thirteen times and allowed for the possibility not only of substituting products formerly imported but also the creation of demands for new products, which began to be manufactured in the country. In addition, the foreign demand for some manufactures of agricultural origin (in particular those at cold storage plants) partly explains the sustained industrial growth, especially during the period 1900–1913 (Rocchi 2000).

Tariff protection was applied on the basis of two criteria. On the one hand, tariffs imposed in response to crises, such as that of 1876, led the government to a commercial policy that could produce a surplus in the balance of trade through the reduction of imports and generate needed income for the treasury. The result was the domestic production of goods, such as biscuits and matches, that were easily manufactured and that might have emerged as industries in

---

[12] See Gallo (1970), Cortés Conde (1979), Geller (1975), and Warwick (1985).

[13] See Díaz Alejandro (1970, 208–214). For a similar approach see P. Lewis (1990, 30–32).

later years without the need for protection. On the other hand, the protection of particular products, such as sugar, was the result of the activity of regional lobbyists, who manufactured at costs significantly above world levels.

The substitution of imports deepened in the 1890s – one of the periods with the most impressive industrial growth in Argentina – as a result of new tariffs generated by another economic crisis and the protection implied by the domestic currency devaluation. The index of industrial product that had doubled from a nearly null base between 1875 and 1890 tripled during the 1890s. The industries leading the growth were strongly protected: textile products were now manufactured by companies that formerly imported them from their head offices, while wine production in the western provinces was carried out under a shielding (and lobbying) scheme similar to that of sugar production. The textile sector grew faster than the food sector in the 1890s, though the latter easily remained in prime position. In 1895, a national census was made, the results of which provide a picture of this new industry. The food sector accounted for 44 percent of the capital invested, the clothing and toiletry industries 11 percent, and construction, which had linkage effects on the woodworking and the metal industries, nearly 11 percent.

At times it is better to think in terms of goods than in terms of branches when analyzing Argentine industrial development. The textile industry of the 1890s was mainly devoted to final manufacturing of garments while weaving (particularly cotton weaving) was insignificant and spinning nonexistent. The metal industry, on the other hand, included a number of goods of mass consumption and simple manufacture, such as nails and nuts, as well as a number of craft activities mainly produced on order.

The substitution effects, however, were limited; the fact that such goods started to be manufactured domestically did not necessarily imply the elimination of imports. Moreover, this process shows a characteristic that reappears in the later development of Argentine industry as well as similar processes in other countries. Namely, the production of goods starts from the stage of final manufacturing and implies a strong dependence on imported raw materials and inputs. The case of the textile industry provides an example. While imported garments were in short supply by the 1900s, the import of cotton fabrics had increased from 11,390,169 kg in 1893 to 20,688,000 kg in 1904, and the import of yarns from 298,392 kg to 4,759,000 kg in the same period.[14]

In this period, selective tariff protection was very far from being part of a grand plan for industrial promotion. Nevertheless, it prompted a few isolated

---

[14] See Rocchi (1997). This process took place in different industrializing countries as analyzed by Hirschman (1958).

complaints from agricultural producers who feared the threat of retaliation by countries that were agricultural export destinations (Hora 2000). It was at that point that the idea was born that opposite to the "natural industry" of agriculture, which generated resources in an efficient manner, there appeared an "artificial industry," namely manufacturing, which could survive only because of the protection it received. All the same, such protection lived on, as was clearly shown by the Customs Law of 1905 that established import reference prices (the so-called *aforos*, or fixed market values) and the import duties applicable thereon.

The export boom of the twentieth century gave rise to a market that allowed for the growth of industry as described above, but it emerged that this process had only a fragile basis. The importance of the growth of domestic demand, and not the substitution effect, for the promotion of industries may be clearly seen in the period 1900–13, when industry grew at a 7 percent annual rate, but was countered by an almost equivalent increase in imports, including manufactured goods. By that time, a few large companies that had standardized manufacturing came to the fore, and faced with stiff competition in their attempts to gain market share, they merged, giving rise to manufacturing trusts.

Within that market, the state appeared as an early and eager customer. In 1895 the first National Buying act was passed, which ordered the army quartermaster services to opt for domestic instead of foreign products of equal prices and qualities. As a result, Argentine manufacturers began to sell blankets, uniforms, and footwear to a buyer that increased its purchasing power with the establishment of compulsory military service in 1902. Such purchasing laws were later extended to public hospitals, schools, and the administration itself (Rocchi 1997).

Still, the impact of import substitution and National Buying was as selective as it was limited. It set a tone for further developments rather than a true basis for industrialization. The strengths of manufacturing growth, on the contrary, were based during this period on the working of quite free markets for factors. Inputs and machinery could enter without difficulty due to a generally open economy. The labor market, fuelled by immigration that lowered real wages, worked in a deregulated atmosphere.[15] The provision of capital, finally, was easier than is usually assumed and deserves further discussion.

Most studies on Argentine industry correspond with the well-established belief in the alleged anti-industrial bias of financing institutions prior to the 1940s. Not surprisingly, researchers only touched briefly on the issue in their work, treating it as an unquestionable truth needing no further research. This lack of attention was reinforced in the 1960s and 1970s when an overemphasis

---

[15] See the chapter by Gerchunoff and Galiani in this volume.

on the real sector in economic analysis promoted an even wider acceptance of the canonical version.[16] Providing some relief from this version's homogenous perspective, some works offered important nuances that could have provided the basis for further debate. With its variants, the traditional version held that beyond food processing and personal ties industry was bereft of access to credit, while the market mechanisms that could have provided loans to the industrialists did not work.[17]

Recent research has shown the importance of economic groups in the financing of industrial firms (Barbero 2000). In addition, the role of private banks now seems to have been crucial in the origins of the industrial sector (Regalsky 1999). Moreover, drawing upon the methods provided by neo-institutionalism and cliometrics, other studies demonstrate that firms had access to capital in a simpler and more fluid manner than has ever been supposed through the issue of self-financed shares on the stock exchange and the help of state banks. This is surprising, since the latter were supposed to be the very institutions that embodied the alleged anti-industrial bias of the capital market (Rocchi 1997). Foreign direct investment, on the other hand, was crucial in some branches, such as meatpacking, and for some specific firms (Villanueva 1972). In sum, industry in this period found a wider variety of methods to increase its working capital and obtain money for its investments than traditionally has been thought.

Thus, the first period of Argentine industrialization was characterized by industries that were protected on a selective basis, dependent on imported inputs, and working in a quite favorable economic and institutional atmosphere. Although the big manufacturing plants in operation were still few in number, a trend toward modernization had begun. This was true even by the time of the first period of stagnation since the inception of industry in the 1870s.

---

[16] Dorfman (1942, 189) and Ortiz (1964, 550 and 657–58). For the 1960s and 1970s see Ferrer (1963, 190), Jorge (1971), and Cornblit (1967, 641–91). For neoclassicism see Díaz Alejandro (1970). There is no equivalent of agrarian credit analysis for the case of manufacturing. See Tulchin (1978) and Adelman (1994, chap. 6).

[17] Cortés Conde (1967, 66–67) suggested that part of the industrial sector, for example food processing, did not suffer from capital constraints. Geller (1975, 180) stated that industry was profitable, though his staple theory framework limited his conclusions to agroindustry. Guy (1982, 351–74) moved the discussion to a fresh area and delved into the legal constraints restricting access to loans, but put too much emphasis on the importance of personal networks in overcoming this challenge. Finally, P. Lewis (1990, 67, 65, and 72) highlighted the existence of aggressive entrepreneurs in contrast to the passively suffering stereotype, but continued to support the idea of a primitive capital market with personal savings as the main source of financing in an environment of government credit hostility.

9.2 The war problems, 1913–1920

The first period of stagnation resulted from an external shock caused by an economic crisis (which had begun in 1913) and by the First World War (Cortés Conde 1994; Taylor 1992). Assessments as to impact of the war have been many and contradictory. The estimates used in this chapter show the negative impact that the crisis and war had (Table 9.1). This data cannot be consistent with a strand in the literature that perceived the wartime closed economy and its "forced protection" as a favorable environment for the development of domestic industry. While theoretically these circumstances could have generated a substitution process, the degree of dependence of most Argentine manufactures on imported raw materials and inputs strangled industrial activity at this time. Only those industries that had enough capacity, and used domestic raw materials, could benefit from the war, such as the wool industry (and particularly the wool scouring mills).[18]

Some of the forces that had a positive influence in the previous period for the promotion of industrial growth, such as immigration and capital flow, ebbed after 1913, and this partly explains the stagnation of the period. In turn, sectors that had multiplier effects on industrial production, in particular construction, lost momentum.

The problems generated by the war may be seen in examples taken from the industrial companies themselves. A viable strategy to cope with the scarcity of inputs was the substitution of intermediate goods, a strategy used by some firms. However, the overall balance, in light of the empirical evidence, is definitely negative; by 1920, industrial output was almost at the same level as in 1913. At the same time, the obvious inefficiencies generated by a lack of inputs, and the rise of small firms attempting to cope with the war, were long at work, and it took some years (and sacrifice) for a more optimal arrangement to appear. Perhaps the main legacy of this period was an exposure to the possible ill effects for Argentina of extreme dependence on the international economic order. As a result of this new scenario, a long-standing interpretation has been that the state could have started a deep import-substitution process in order to industrialize the country. But since it did not see this opportunity, a long delay began that lasted into the 1930s (Di Tella and Zymelman 1967).

---

[18] A later position has claimed that it hurt manufacturing growth because of the halt in imports of vital capital equipment and raw materials. See Miller (1981) and Gravil (1976). A more recent perspective associates the slow development of manufacture during the war with structural weaknesses and limitations. See Albert and Henderson (1988, 181).

9.3 Substitution changes the pace, 1920–1948

In this period, industry grew at an average annual rate of 5 percent. A look at the subperiods defined by the Great Depression and World War II shows that from 1920 to 1930, the annual industrial growth rate reached 4.4 percent, from 1930 to 1939 it was 7.1 percent, during the war years it decreased to 3.6 percent, and in the postwar recovery of 1946–48 it was 6.3 percent (see Table 9.1).[19] Within this context of shifting fortunes, the similarities stand out more clearly than the differences when we consider qualitative transformations.

In the 1920s industry grew as a result of the same forces that had operated at its inception: an increase in aggregate demand, new tariffs, and a favorable exchange rate. Rates of economic growth are a subject of debate for this decade. An optimistic view highlights the strong performance of the period while other studies consider it as one marked by a strong deceleration in growth. Since the pace of industrial growth was so dependent on the pace of economic evolution at that time, the impact that this disputed *Belle Époque* might have had on the demand for industrial goods in the domestic market is crucial. Thus, the optimistic view would affirm that manufacturing regained its strength of the 1900s, while the pessimists would support a certain but less dramatic increase in output.[20]

Regarding the impact of exchange rates and tariffs, both contributed to support industrial production in different periods. Domestic inflation had the effect of reducing the strength of the tariffs established in 1905, since import duties were calculated on the basis of the above mentioned *aforos,* which remained unchanged in nominal terms. This decline in protection was countered by the depreciation of the peso until 1922. When the peso began to appreciate, pressure for the determination of a new set of tariff rates mounted. The result was new legislation in 1923 that inflated the values of *aforos* (Jorge 1971; Solberg 1973). Thus, industry was neither excessively protected nor unprotected in the 1920s, since the two currents that confronted it with foreign competition did not conjoin in any given period. Overall, the impact of substitution appears to have been much less than that of domestic demand, and, in fact, the percentage of imports needed to satisfy consumption increased slightly from 49.2 percent to 51.1 percent (CEPAL 1959).

Early in the 1920s, industry resumed its growth, although at a slower pace than in the previous period of expansion (Table 9.1). By this time, qualitative changes had initiated a new industrializing phase that would have its consolidation halted

---

[19] The CEPAL estimates show a higher increase for industry in the 1920s, 5 percent.

[20] For the optimistic view see Díaz Alejandro (1970) and Nakamura and Zarazaga (1998). For the less optimistic see Taylor (1992) and Cortés Conde (1997).

Table 9.4. *Shares of industrial output, by branch, 1914–94*

Percent

	1914	1935	1947	1954	1964	1974	1984	1994
Food, beverages, tobacco	53	41	34	30	30	28	24	29
Textiles, leather	11	21	26	23	16	13	13	9
Wood items	5	3	5	4	2	2	2	3
Printing	2	6	5	4	4	4	5	6
Chemicals, oil products	3	10	11	12	19	20	29	26
Metals, machinery	5	14	14	21	27	33	27	24
Others	21	5	5	6	2	0	0	3

Source: Industrial censuses.

only at the end of the 1940s. In parallel, production began to change its profile, led by light industry, the progression of food production (representing a relative step backwards), and a simultaneous growth of the textile and metal industries. The latter two sectors demonstrated the greatest expansion in the industrial development of the entire period 1920–48 (Table 9.4).

The share of industry in GDP slowly increased from 18.7 percent in the 1920s to 24.2 percent in the 1940s (Table 9.3). Changes in industrial structure, which became noticeable in the 1920s, led to the assertion in a pioneer study that it was in that very decade that modern industry first appeared in Argentina (Villanueva 1972, 1987). Such an assertion may now look exaggerated when we take into account our discussion of the pre-1913 period, which showed that some factories already possessed standardized methods. The 1920s, however, witnessed a change in terms of both scale and quality.

Modern industrial plants increased in number and expanded into the manufacture of new products. The organization of corporations, which was interrupted in 1913, resumed, and there was a renewed trend towards capital concentration through the organization of trusts and mergers. At the same time, a new phenomenon appeared – the arrival of foreign capital, mostly American and in substantial amounts. From 1921 to 1930, forty-three foreign companies established operations in Argentina as compared with the thirteen that had done so between 1900 and 1920. In particular, they invested in new expanding industries, such as cement, oil, pharmaceuticals, chemicals, metals, home appliances, rubber, and automobile assembly.[21]

Sectors that were formerly expanding – food, beverages, and textiles – grew at a slower pace than the overall average for industry (Table 9.4). However, there were some changes that favored the subsequent development of the still unsettled textile industry with the launching of domestic production of raw

[21] See Villanueva (1972), Schvarzer (1996), and Barbero and Ceva (1997).

Table 9.5. *Intercensus variation in output, employment, and labor productivity, 1895–1974*

	Output index	Workers	Output per worker
1895	60.37	145,641	0.41
1914	226.41	410,201	0.55
1935	621.51	463,424	1.34
1947	1,206.47	1,023,032	1.18
1954	1,202.04	1,167,928	1.03
1964	1,972.67	1,320,120	1.49
1974	3,773.92	1,525,221	2.47

Source: Table 9.2 for industrial output (1900 = 100) and industrial censuses for workers. The output per worker index is multiplied by 1,000.

materials such as cotton (which grew from 2,460 tons in 1917 to 92,644 in 1929) and silk.[22] The rapid growth of metallurgical production, in turn, was notable: production quadrupled in the years from 1920 to 1929 in response to an increase in demand generated by construction and an improvement in manufacturing techniques.[23]

At the microeconomic level, it should be noted that there was a trend on the part of companies towards vertical integration that might be attributed to the experience gained during the war and to the costs of imported products in an externally dependent economy. There was also a remarkable technological and administrative change in companies that was partly introduced by newly established international firms (Rapoport 1988). Taylor's theories, which had only been implemented at American cold storage plants, began to spread, while an increase in real wages led a number of companies to implement strategies to substitute for labor through the purchase of machinery (Lobato 1988). The acquisition of equipment resulted in high volumes of imported industrial machinery (Di Tella y Zymelman 1967). The census of 1935, not surprisingly, showed an increase in labor productivity as compared to the figures for 1914 (Table 9.5).

In addition to cement, oil extraction and distillation were among the new industrial activities: oil production increased from 262,000 m³ in 1920 to 1,500,000 m³ in 1929, while cement production rose from 79,000 m³ to 343,000 m³ in the same years (García-Mata and Llorens 1939, 265–66). In the case of oil, the role of the government was crucial and did not leave much room for private capital. The newly created state company YPF (Yacimientos Petrolíferos Fiscales), which set up its first distilling plant in 1925, dominated this sector.

[22] See Petrecolla (1968) and García-Mata and Llorens (1939, 260).
[23] See CEPAL (1959) and Di Tella and Zymelman (1967, 366).

Table 9.6. *Substitution rates, 1900–54*

Percent

Period	Demand for industrial goods	Total Imports	Con-sumer goods	Capital goods	Industrial inputs	Industrial output
1900–04	100.0	58.6	22.2	8.7	27.7	41.4
1905–09	100.0	59.8	21.1	12.3	26.4	40.2
1910–14	100.0	58.0	21.0	11.1	25.9	42.0
1915–19	100.0	46.3	22.6	6.1	17.6	53.7
1920–24	100.0	49.2	20.2	8.4	20.6	50.8
1925–29	100.0	51.1	18.9	11.1	21.0	48.9
1930–34	100.0	37.3	14.6	5.2	17.5	62.7
1935–39	100.0	36.7	12.3	7.0	17.4	63.3
1940–44	100.0	19.5	5.9	1.9	11.6	80.5
1945–49	100.0	25.9	6.2	6.3	13.4	74.1
1950–54	100.0	21.2	2.7	4.4	14.1	78.8

Source: CEPAL (1959, 159–60). The rate of substitution is defined as the fraction of consumption goods produced domestically.

Moreover, by then the military had become involved in a project for industrialization that heavily featured this industry and the manufacturing of army equipment. Ever since the armed forces have unfailingly supported the development of industry.

The years following the 1930 depression witnessed a modification of the patterns of industrial evolution, with a strengthening of import substitution, via the official control of foreign exchange and tariff increases. By this time, the countercyclical policies adopted also affected the industrial sector without being part of any industrializing plan (Prebisch 1986). The growth of industry in the 1930s was not linear. Industrial product declined as a consequence of the great crash but bounced back in 1933; it grew at a 16 percent annual rate from 1933 to 1935 and at a rate of 5.5 percent between 1935 and 1939. The rate of substitution (defined as the fraction of consumption goods produced domestically), which had been around 50 percent between 1925 and 1929, increased to 63 percent between 1930 and 1939 (Table 9.6; CEPAL 1959).

This expansion was led by cotton textiles, which grew during the 1930–35 period at an annual rate of 10.5 percent, versus a 4.3 percent rate in the food and beverages sectors (Cortés Conde 1997). The evolution of textiles was especially pronounced in the production of fabrics and yarns. In 1930 there were 6 cotton-spinning mills with 60,000 spindles; in 1937 the companies numbered almost 20 with 340,000 spindles (García-Mata and Llorens 1939, 123). Other industries expanding at a rate greater than the average were oil byproducts, motor vehicles, and, with less momentum, the metal industry. Rubber products, machinery, and electric appliances showed the most impressive growth – close to 40 percent annually, although much of that performance is explained by the fact that they were virtually nonexistent in the previous period.

The program of public works, such as road construction, generated an incentive for the production of certain kinds of goods. In 1930 the consumption of cement was approximately 755,000 tons with imports of 409,000 tons; in 1938 those figures were 1,254,000 and 83,000 respectively (Rapoport 2000, 319). By that time the purchasing role of the state had grown considerably: in 1930 a decree passed by the military administration established a 5 percent premium applicable to public biddings in favor of domestic industry (Llamazares 1943). The changes that had occurred in the structure of industrial sectors, as much as the continuities, are reflected in the census carried out in 1935 compared with that of 1914 (Table 9.4).

Starting in the 1930s, manufacturing became the sector of greatest expansion in the economy, a process that lasted until the late 1970s. This would cause the 1930 depression to appear to many as a key breakpoint in Argentine industrial development. The relationship between the industrial development of the 1933–48 period and that of the 1920s, however, is much closer than it appears. On the one hand, a micro perspective shows that the 1930s witnessed an expansion of the sectors that had already appeared dynamic prior to the crisis. On the other hand, the spread of foreign companies (mainly American) continued with already established branches substituting local production for imports, as well as with other firms that started their activities in Argentina as a result of the foreign exchange controls and tariff increase. From 1931 to 1943, the number of foreign companies established in the industrial sector reached 45, a number similar to that of the 1920s (Jorge 1971, 99–100, Table 9).

The relative price of industrial goods fell as a result of the stability of real wages and the availability of labor offered by domestic migration to the cities where manufacturing activities were expanding. In fact, following the large investments of the 1920s, industry was able to grow on the basis of increased stock of labor; this was true particularly for large companies (Table 9.5; Llach 1984). Moreover, although regulations on the labor market had begun to be enacted, they were not yet enforced.[24] The institutional financing network did not change much in the 1930s, in spite of a more regulated economy and the creation of the Central Bank in 1935. The provision of raw materials and machinery was a more difficult problem to resolve, and proposed solutions were not always the most efficient ones.

---

[24] See the chapter by Galiani and Gerchunoff in this volume.

Parallel to an increase in labor productivity that had grown out of the 1920s, the rise of new plants generated inefficiencies within the context of a more closed economy. The Second World War led this situation to a climax. Technological designs were antiquated, equipment consisted of used or obsolete machinery, and subcontractors and suppliers of inputs and spare parts were lacking.[25] In contrast to the previous decade, the 1930s saw a process of industrial deconcentration that was heightened by the war and continued into the mid-1950s.[26] The consequences in terms of labor productivity were negative, as can be seen when comparing the 1935 and 1947 census data (Table 9.5).[27]

Consumer products led the expansion in the so-called easy substitution period. Since machines and inputs were, to a significant degree, imported, there was not only a potential problem for the current account but also a potential crisis in supply. The war exposed this problem. Given the development attained by Argentine industry in the late 1930s, the war offered an opportunity for industrial expansion through two routes. The first was through a deepening in the level of substitution: the rate of substitution, the fraction of consumption goods produced domestically, rose from 60 percent to 80 percent. The second was by an increase in industrial exports to countries formerly served by the belligerent nations (CEPAL 1959). The impact of war varied according to the particular part of industry, but, as in the First World War, it benefited those branches that used domestic raw materials and inputs.

The expansion of industrial exports – geared to the Latin American market – was a new phenomenon with volumes scarcely surpassed thereafter and, in some branches, never attained again. During those years, the markets for the economy as a whole diversified: from 1937–39 to 1943–45 the percentage of exports to the whole of the Americas increased from 21 percent to 47 percent, with the figures for the United States growing from 12 percent to 23 percent (Llach 1984).

In the midst of the war, the government considered a plan prepared by the Minister of Finance, Federico Pinedo, with the idea of promoting modifications to the structure of production in order to cope with actual or potential cyclical unemployment. The plan proposed an industrial development strategy based on exports and specialized in those branches that used domestic raw materials, thus promoting trade with neighboring countries (particularly Brazil) and with

[25] Katz and Kosacoff (1989). For an approach based on the retarding effects of Argentina's late industrialization see Vitelli (1999).

[26] Goetz (1976). See also Jorge (1971) and Llach (1972). Dorfman (1942), however, points out an opposite trend in the concentration of capital.

[27] Between 1914 and 1935 it was around 20 percent, while between 1935 and 1947 it fell to 13 percent. The analogous figure for the period 1914–47 is 4 percent.

the United States. The aim was to favor industrial exports in those activities through foreign exchange incentives. The Pinedo Plan was never implemented, but stands out as the first state document in which the possibility of modifying the country's economic development path was considered (Weil 1944).

Towards the end of the war, part of the debate over industry considered whether exports or the domestic market should be privileged. The export strategy did not imply an increase in wage costs and was favored by large companies. A number of smaller manufacturers, on the other hand, began to favor domestic market orientation. The debates on the industrialization model that should be adopted were discussed in the Consejo Nacional de Posguerra (National Postwar Council) that was founded in 1944, inspired by the U.S. New Deal and Soviet planning agencies, and presided over by Juan Perón. Opinions were diverse, but the issues that were gaining favor among those leading the debate (and who would later govern the country) were full employment and the need to reduce the social costs of either policy. In the end, the domestic market option prevailed and was implemented during the Peronist era that began in 1946.

By then, the military's goal of industrialization had gained more strength because of its role in administration after the coup of 1943. The creation of Fabricaciones Militares, as a compound of strategic industries, including the manufacture of weapons, is the best example of this strength. During the military administration, the Bank of Industrial Credit was created in 1944 with the aim of offering industrialists long-term credit at cheap rates (Rougier 2001).

The market's dimensions limited industrial expansion, rapidly making apparent the shortcomings of closed economic policies in a small country. Those dimensions revolved around the size and distribution of income, which were crucial since they affected – via the composition of demand – the profile of industry and the development of technology. The increase in manufacturing volumes during the war arose for three reasons: improvements in the daily wages of some industries, certain technical aspects, and longer working hours on the part of industrial workers. But even given this, the purchasing power of Argentine employees appeared unchanged (Llach 1984; Gerchunoff and Llach 1998). Dr. John Hopkins, part of a mission of the Armour Research Foundation, arrived in Argentina to make a report for the Corporación Argentina para la Promoción del Intercambio, which was published in 1944. An entrepreneur warned him: "Don't forget that the Argentine market is made up of three and a half million people and not of 13 million [the actual population of the country]" (Hopkins 1944, 29). According to the report, which provides some crucial insights into the trade-off inherent in the domestic market approach, the Argentine unskilled worker received a salary equivalent to two thirds that of a German worker, half that of a British worker, or one third that of a U.S. worker.[28] The Peronists wished to change that story.

In the first two years of the Peronist administration, the growth model based on the domestic market appeared to be successful. Between 1946 and 1948, industry grew at an annual rate of 6.3 percent with some variation among the various branches (Table 9.4). A comparative analysis of the 1935 and 1945 censuses, on the other hand, shows insignificant changes in industrial structure.[29] However, it was the year 1948 that would demonstrate the serious limitations posed by this model.

The domestic market orientation chosen by the Peronist administration was unsuitable for industrial growth. From 1946 to 1955, manufacturing industry grew at an annual rate of just 3.0 percent, a figure that, taking into account the growth rate of population, appears desultory. However, this result, as well as the closure to foreign trade, were more related to external conditions – Argentine foreign policy and the social and income distribution policy of Peronism – than to the industrial debate per se (Gerchunoff and Llach 1998). Still, after such a quick rise, manufacturing suffered only its second period of relative decline since its inception. Such weak growth is paradoxical in light of the administration's aims, but reinforces the contemporary view of policy as being mainly geared to distribution and – subject to unintended consequences – having very little to do with accumulation and growth.

9.4 1948–1954: A second "long-delay"?

After 1948, industrial sector growth slowed to a crawl. The annual average growth rate was just 0.42 percent until 1954. In 1948 the expansion of the immediate postwar era ceased, and 1947 levels of output were recovered only in 1954.[30] The share of the industrial sector in GDP remained almost unchanged throughout the 1940s and 1950s (Tables 9.1 and 9.2).

This deficient performance partly reflects the critical situation faced by the Argentine economy in this period, a time of recurring crises in the external sector and growing macroeconomic instability. The imbalances of the foreign sector and the shortage of foreign currency were due, to a large degree, to the sector's import requirements and its reduced exporting capacity. Manufacturing was partly a victim of and partly responsible for, its own situation. The

[28] See Hopkins (1944, 57) and Llamazares (1943, 80). A discussion on the controversy over the *Informe Armour* can be found in Di Tella (1979) and O'Connell (1979).

[29] Díaz Alejandro (1970). The higher growth rates (based on the period 1937–39 to 1948–50) were those of the textile industry (9.1 percent), electric appliances and machinery (8.7 percent), motor vehicles and machinery (8.3 percent), and chemicals (7.7 percent).

[30] Not all authors agree on this point. See Gerchunoff and Llach (1998) and Gerchunoff (1989).

industrial standstill of this period, rather than highlighting problems related to demand, revealed the limitations of substitution based mainly on consumer goods and the difficulties in shifting to new dynamic activities such as intermediate and capital goods (Table 9.4). The development of the lagging sectors was hindered not only by official policy, but also by the problems faced by some industrial branches such as technological complexity, high capital intensity, or the unavailability of domestic raw materials.

Toward the end of the 1940s, the possibility of substitution in light industries had been exhausted. At the same time, inasmuch as industrial production was almost exclusively destined for the domestic market, it did not generate the foreign currency needed to match its import requirements (unlike agriculture). During the war, restrictions on imports and the growth in industrial exports made this less obvious. But at the end of the war, imports grew sharply, offsetting the previous restrictions and meeting the unsatisfied demand. The high level of purchases could be sustained while there was foreign currency available, but the fall in primary exports and the depletion of reserves after 1948 precluded industry from growing by the same process as previously.

The policies adopted by the Peronist administration had also reinforced characteristics of the manufacturing sector that had developed in previous decades. As soon as currency restrictions began, the government favored the import of raw materials, intermediate goods, and some spare parts and machinery, while the import of consumer goods was simultaneously closed off. The subsidies to imported inputs were considerable, and implemented through an overvaluation of the exchange rate and the granting of import licenses and foreign exchange permits, assigning absolute priority to those goods required for normal operation of plants (Díaz Alejandro 1970).

An analysis of these policies leads us to ask why there were no measures adopted for the promotion of manufacturing exports that would have permitted the maintenance of war-time levels and why substitution was not further deepened. The answer lies in the objectives of social policy, which lacked any strictly industrial context. The promotion of industrial exports could only be attained at the cost of reducing the level of wages and domestic consumption, which the administration was seeking to increase. Real wages, which had remained stable during the war and had permitted relatively low manufacturing costs, grew after 1945 as an official objective of policy, generating a rise in production costs that made exporting more difficult. The unexploited exporting possibilities thus present a potential exercise in counterfactual history, since the international environment had changed and, with it, extraordinary new market possibilities that had not existed during the world conflict.

The failure to further substitution was also the result of an indiscriminate

Table 9.7. *Inflation, nominal interest rate issued by the Industrial Bank, and implicit subsidies*

Percent

	1944	1945	1946	1947	1948	1949
Interest rate	5.5	5.5	5.5	6.5	6.5	7.0
Inflation rate	8.2	9.0	15.8	3.5	15.5	23.0
Implicit subsidy	2.7	3.5	10.3	-3.0	9.0	16.0
	1950	1951	1952	1953	1954	1955
Interest rate	7.0	7.5	7.5	7.5	7.5	7.5
Inflation rate	20.2	49.1	31.2	11.6	3.2	8.9
Implicit subsidy	13.2	41.6	23.7	4.1	-4.3	1.4

Source: Rougier (2001).

protection to existing industry that, in turn, resulted from the desire to sustain employment levels and the supply of mass consumer goods. Another aim was to avoid the closing of companies conceived or enlarged because of the protection offered during the war. From 1935 to 1947, the number of establishments had more than doubled, and so had the labor employed, which exceeded one million persons in 1947 (Llach 1984). It is no surprise that during the period from 1947 to 1954, the trend toward deconcentration continued (Goetz 1976, 511).

In the meantime, however, the financial environment could not have been better for industry. We have already seen that the manufacturing sector did not find major constraints in the capital market in the first decades of its evolution. Since the creation of the Industrial Bank, the story took a new direction with the provision of subsidized credit. The implicit subsidies or negative real interest rates, reckoned as the difference between the nominal interest rate on industrial loans and inflation, reached impressive levels, especially between 1948 and 1952 when they ranged from 9 percent to 42 percent (Table 9.7; Rougier 2001).

It was not until 1953 that the Peronist administration tried to modify the course of policy, promoting the substitution of intermediate goods and machinery and the attraction of foreign capital. Large ventures in this type of activity – particularly the manufacturing of trucks and automobiles – would start appearing from the time of the Law on Foreign Investments in 1953 (Sourrouille 1980). Between 1953 and 1955, 73 percent of foreign investment originated in the United States; of this, 67 percent was in motor vehicles and 16 percent in chemicals (Villanueva 1987, 102–103). In 1954, Perón convened the Congress on Productivity with the purpose of reducing costs in domestic industry. His overthrow in 1955 prevented the administration from capitalizing on the results of these measures, which had been poorly implemented for bureaucratic and political reasons.

Despite its weak growth rates, industry experienced significant changes in sectoral structure, which may be seen in a comparison of the 1954 and 1947 censuses (Table 9.4). The most outstanding feature is the relative decline of textiles and the advance of the metal working industries. This growth mainly was due to the opening of a significant number of small workshops engaged in the repair or manufacture of spare parts in response to import restrictions and the obsolescence of equipment.[31] The 1954 census also reflects the trend of industry toward light activities. Throughout the 1950s, the substitution of consumer durables was completed with significant progress in machinery, equipment, and electric appliances. Upon completion of this process, domestic production leveled out or even declined. This was the case, for example, with washing machines, stoves, sewing machines, bicycles, motorcycles, and railroad and agricultural machinery and equipment (Mallon and Sourrouills 1973).

9.5 The climax before the fall: Deepening of substitution and promotion of exports, 1954–1974

After 1954, industrial activity surpassed its 1948 levels, commencing a new period of expansion with an average annual growth rate of 5.7 percent (Table 9.1). This period consists of two distinct decades. From 1954 to 1964, growth was slower (5.1 percent) and less regular, since production fell in 1958 and 1963 as a result of economic slowdowns. A time of faster expansion followed from 1964 to 1974 with a 6.7 percent average annual rate of uninterrupted growth. Productivity, wages, employment, and exports grew simultaneously, and the expansion took place in all branches of industry.

Irrespective of the difference in ideologies, circumstances, and interests represented, industrialization was an objective of economic policy from the end of the 1940s until the mid-1970s (Canitrot 1981). A coalition formed by industrialists, trade unions, and the armed forces became so strong that political instability and the accompanying succession of civil and military administrations did not bring about major changes in the goals of industrial policy.

The distinguishing element between the 1954–1974 period and the preceding one was the intention to rise above the limits of simple substitution through two mechanisms: a greater level of import substitution (in input supplying sectors and, to a lesser degree, in capital goods) and the promotion of industrial exports. The expansion of the manufacturing industry is shown by its growing share in GDP, which rose from less than 25 percent in the 1950s to more than 28 percent

---

[31] The number of metal working and machinery plants rose from 23,020 to 48,215; employment from 258,196 to 420,207; and the sector's share of production from 14 percent to 21 percent. See Sourrouille (1980).

in the 1960s (Table 9.2). In those twenty years, the international economy presented favorable conditions, while new laws on foreign investment, starting in the late 1950s, attracted foreign capital and gave multinational corporations a growing presence. In parallel, the trend toward deconcentration that had prevailed since the Great Depression was reversed.

The initial indications of the limitations of substitution based on light industry became apparent in the last years of the Perón administration and exploded after its fall in 1955. Criticism of simple industrialization increased in a debate in which the rhetoric directed against the fallen administration overlapped with that concerning the role of the state in the economy. Both the Preliminary Report on the Argentine Economic Situation by Raúl Prebisch (1955) and the volumes published by CEPAL (1959) proposed as one of the basic objectives of economic policy an effort to fight against foreign currency constraints (the foreign exchange "gap") by developing further the basic domestic industries. They also both recommended the promotion of industrial exports (with other Latin American countries as the primary target).

Deeper transformations began with the economic program of the so-called *desarrollismo* (developmentalism) in 1958–62, which revived the idea of accelerating growth through a boost to investment concentrated in a few capital intensive and import substituting sectors. Its proposals consisted of furthering substitution to the fullest extent and the attaining the highest level of autarky, a strategy that implied, in no uncertain terms, an "absolute and plain rejection of the theory of comparative advantages" (Gerchunoff and Llach 1998). It also contemplated an increase in productivity through a rapid incorporation of technology as the basis of industry's structural transformations. The fundamental objective was the development of an integrated industrial complex, with emphasis on basic goods and the intensive exploitation of natural resources, fixing as priorities oil and gas, steel, electric power, cement, paper, equipment and machinery, as well as infrastructure works. In addition, the plan worked toward national economic integration and the geographic decentralization of activities.

The program included an explicit invitation to foreign capital, which it was thought would provide the resources necessary to drive investment. In 1958, the government passed a new law on foreign investment that guaranteed them equal treatment with domestic companies, placed no restriction on the scope of their activities, and authorized the transfer of earnings abroad. Concurrently, it deregulated the import of capital goods with the purpose of promoting the re-equipment of domestic industry and offered tax allowances to spur new investments. Some of these measures achieved the desired results within a few years, particularly in the inflow of multinational corporations. The contracts with oil companies boosted production, which between 1958 and 1962 grew at an annual rate of 30 percent, allowing the country to attain oil self-sufficiency by the end of 1962. This implied a significant saving of foreign currency since oil imports in 1957 represented almost 25 percent of imports (Gadano 1998).

From 1959, capital began to flow and investment grew; between 1959 and 1962 foreign investment reached $500 million, twice the aggregate of all permits granted between 1954 and 1958 and between 1963 and 1970. Ninety per cent of the newly established companies (60 percent of them American) focused on the chemical, petrochemical and oil byproduct, transport, metallurgy and electrical, and mechanical machinery industries (Sourrouille, Kosacoff, and Lucángeli 1985). At the same time, domestic companies were re-equipping with effects that would be seen in the increase of productivity throughout the following decade (Petrecolla 1989).

However, the measures adopted by the *desarrollismo* did not render the expected results in terms of the balance of payments. Paradoxically, imports increased instead of falling; between 1960 and 1962 they were 30 percent above those of 1959. The reasons for such an increase are found in the fact that the mix of production was geared toward import-intensive, dynamic industries (Felix 1970). Unblocking the import of inputs and capital goods also implied an expansion of imports (Petrecolla 1989). In the mid-1960s, and especially after the recession in 1962–63, the limits of *desarrollismo* became obvious with respect to its capacity to initiate sustained development and to solve the imbalances of the external sector, as deficits in the current account continued.

A strong tendency to import was also the result of a regressive redistribution of income (the wage earners' share of income dropped from 47 percent to 42 percent between 1955 and 1957), with a consequent increase in the demand for consumer durables (Díaz Alejandro 1966). The case of the automobile industry is illustrative. Demand had been strongly constrained in the previous decades by import restrictions (Table 9.8). Unable to obtain domestic input supply in sufficient amounts, this industry required imported inputs. The Promotion Regime under which it operated authorized the import of spare parts, which would be restricted from initially high levels over time with the growth of domestic production (Sourrouille 1980). In the end, net substitution was only achieved for oil, and the results of the growth in manufacturing capacity, and per-capita productivity, did not become apparent until 1963.

By 1964, the industrial scene began to show positive signs that had few parallels in Argentine history. For the expansion of 1964–74, several explanations have been attempted in relation to supply and demand. The structure of domestic consumption changed because of an income distribution that favored the middle class and an increase in real wages (Gerchunoff and Llach 1975). The increasingly capital-intensive nature of industry and technological devel-

Table 9.8. *Number of cars and trucks, 1926–75*

	Imports	Local production
1926–30	250,000	—
1931–35	52,000	—
1936–40	130,000	—
1941–45	23,305	—
1946–50	136,365	—
1951–55	50,561	13,901
1956–60	96,990	171,252
1961–65	15,058	731,986
1966–70	6,221	973,936
1971–75	4,719	1,416,994

Source: Sourrouille (1980).

opments, related both to the presence of affiliates of multinational corporations and the evolution of domestic companies, explain the transformation in supply (Katz and Kosacoff 1989). According to our estimates, labor productivity increased as well (Table 9.5). As a consequence of these changes, industry experienced a bout of modernization with a parallel rise in employment, which in 1974 exceeded 1.5 million persons.

As in other Latin American countries, the results of policies that had penalized production and the export of primary goods, and that demonstrated an excessive confidence import substitution, began to be perceptible. This fact, of course, seems more obvious *ex post* than it was at the time that decisions were being made (Ffrench-Davis, Muñoz, and Palma 1994). By the early 1960s, the industrial structure had reached a level and a complexity comparable to countries with high per-capita incomes, such as Australia, Canada, and Italy. However, Argentina had only a slight exporting capacity. In 1963, it exported just 2 percent of its industrial production while in Italy that figure reached 28 percent, and in Canada, 24 percent. Production for the highly protected domestic market generated a distorted structure of costs and relative prices, with low productivity and oligopolistic tendencies. At the same time, substitution was unable to further reduce the share of imports, despite the sustained efforts made in the 1960s. The import-to-GDP ratio fell from 23 percent in 1935–39 to 12 percent in 1950–54, but no further improvements occurred (e.g., it stood at 11 percent in 1962–66) (Brodersohn 1970).

Within this context, new strategies for industrialization began to be debated. The promotion of industrial exports appeared to be the way to balance the foreign accounts and allow for sustained development by expanding on the size of a relatively small domestic market that barely exceeded 20 million potential consumers in 1960. A scholarly debate paralleled the policy measures (as revealed in the 1964 National Development Plan) with a discussion as to the kinds of goods in which industry should specialize. The discussion included those who proposed an indiscriminate promotion of exports, as well as those who only wished to support goods with comparative advantage.[32] Incentive mechanisms were made up of a diversified and cumulative structure of fiscal, tax, exchange, and financial arrangements, which operated differently for each sector. In parallel, the creation in 1960 of the Latin American Free Trade Association (ALALC) renewed the old idea of a regional common market. This idea had already been put forward by Alejandro Bunge in the 1920s, revisited by Prebisch in the 1950s, and actively promoted by CEPAL in the 1960s. The results, however, were disappointing.[33]

The effect of these laws was an increase in the export of industrial manufactures: between 1969 and 1974 they grew from $166 to $794 million, representing 10 percent and 20 percent, respectively, of total exports (Ablin 1985). These figures merit our attention in at least two respects. First, the proportion of products of industrial origin in relation to total exports still remained low. Second, the Argentine economy was so closed that the impact of the increase was less dramatic than expected. In addition, the increase in manufactured exports flowed from newly established industries, technologically advanced and of a larger scale, but whose relative prices were high compared to those of other economies. This was the result of financial incentives that permitted these industries to export at prices lower than total cost and of certain advantages bestowed upon branches of multinational corporations in terms of distribution networks, inter-company trade, and lower vulnerability to the fluctuations in the relative value of currencies.[34]

Despite the efforts to promote industrial exports, between 1973 and 1975 the export of primary goods still represented almost 40 percent of total exports. In turn, manufactured goods explained the other 60 percent, out of which two-thirds corresponded to processed agricultural products, and only one-third to industrial products (i.e., they constituted only 20 percent of total exports). At the same time, the ratio of total exports to GDP was very small, hardly reaching 4 percent (Bisang and Kosacoff 1995). Overall, external demand was still low compared to domestic consumption (Table 9.9).

Except for the food sector, industry was still intensively oriented toward the domestic market. In the first half of the 1970s, Argentine industry began exporting a few nontraditional goods, among which were automobiles and an array

---

[32] See Brodersohn (1970), Felix (1970), Berlinski (1986), and Gerchunoff and Llach (1998).

[33] See Berlinski (1986, 1989) and Katz and Kosacoff (1989).

[34] See Mallon and Sourrouille (1973), Berlinski and Schydhowsky (1977), and Berlinski (1985).

Table 9.9. *Share of exports in industrial production*
Total and in selected branches, percent

	1951	1958	1964	1972
Total	2.1	4.3	3.5	5.7
Total excluding food	0.2	0.3	3.5	5.7
Food	8.3	15.5	12.8	18.2
Tobacco	0.0	0.4	2.6	7.0
Textiles	0.3	0.5	0.3	2.7
Shoes and ready-to-wear	0.1	0.2	0.2	2.6
Printing	0.1	0.2	4.0	4.8
Chemicals	0.1	1.4	1.3	7.1
Basic metals	0.0	0.1	1.6	2.7
Machinery	0.1	0.4	1.3	4.7
Transport equipment	0.0	0.0	0.1	2.0

Source: Gerchunoff and Llach (1998).

of heavy engineering goods that included agricultural machinery, calculating machines, and industrial machinery (Bisang and Kosacoff 1995). Although some of these exports became important for particular companies, they had little impact on the overall picture given the anemic export volumes involved (Gerchunoff and Llach 1998).

Attempts to deepen substitution through the domestic production of basic inputs continued in the meantime. One of the big pushes took place in the early 1970s through financial facilities and tax reductions. In the first case the main instruments were long-term facilities granted by Banco Nacional de Desarrollo (Banade) and the loans of international financial institutions (such as the Banco Interamericano de Desarrollo) guaranteed by the state through Banade. The most favored areas were those of paper and pulp, petrochemical, and steel production, which significantly increased their capacities later in the decade (Schvarzer 1978). One effect of these policies, which mainly favored companies of domestic origin, was the growth of national economic groups that began to contest the leadership of multinational corporations. It was at that point that industry collapsed.

9.6 Conclusions

One of the most salient features of manufacturing evolution in Argentina is its record of growth at high rates even in periods with very different political-economic environments. At its beginning, it expanded during an era of export orientation, when policies mainly followed open-economy principles. But it also grew rapidly after the Depression, when the economy became more closed to international commerce and more regulated by unstructured state intervention. Manufacturing also regained high rates of growth in the period 1963–74, at a time when closed-economy principles and regulation continued, but when industrialization had become a state policy.

In comparison to other Latin American countries, the Argentine story presents more nuances. Until 1930 Argentine industry grew at a rate similar to those seen in the region's largest nations, namely, Brazil and Mexico. In the 1930s and 1940s, industry in these other countries grew at higher rates. The gap in growth rates widened further after the 1950s and continued in the following decades. This outcome invites a number of explanations. The poor industrial performance of Argentina in the second half of the twentieth century cannot be solely attributed to the implementation of import substitution, as this policy prevailed in all three countries, though to differing degrees. Other reasons should also be explored.

One of the possible explanations relates to the shortcomings of a small domestic market for import-substitution policies. Argentina reached these limits earlier than Brazil and Mexico for two reasons: its relatively smaller population from the 1930s onward, and the rapid integration of the national market. Argentina, following this argument, finds a closer comparison case in Chile, a country that had a similar timing to its industrial evolution.

As we have seen, the financial atmosphere was not hostile to industrial growth. On the contrary, from 1944 it even provided the sector with highly subsidized loans. As a consequence, one might ask to what extent problems usually related to the lack of capital were not in actuality shortcomings resulting from the difficulty in accessing the most modern technology. A closed economy made this goal harder, and our historical account supports this conclusion: only in the 1920s (under relatively free trade) and in the 1960s (led by multinational corporations) did Argentine industry have good access to techniques at the cutting edge.

Another possible reason for Argentina's relative backwardness can be found in the political sphere. Discontinuities in public policies were recurrent in the Argentine case, partially as a result of conflicts in the social and political arenas. The coalition behind industrialization (industrialists, organized labor, and the armed forces) became increasingly unstable due to struggles over income distribution. Distributional struggles fostered an atmosphere of instability that affected not just absolute, but relative prices. On the one hand, instability promoted inflation; on the other hand, it increased industrial labor costs. By the mid-1970s this process had reached its climax.

Labor costs alone, however, do not explain the lack of competitiveness in Argentine industry. In global terms, its relative prices were higher than those of the industrialized countries with high production costs (mainly in branches that used imported inputs), with an underutilization of capacity and a failure to exploit economies of scale. The last two problems were related to the small size of the domestic market. The high level of protection generated high profit margins and a lack of incentives to improve efficiency. The industries with relatively higher returns were more concentrated and operated in oligopolistic markets and with strong lobbying power.

Looking at this situation as it prevailed in the 1970s, one question that arises is why industrial output fell so sharply from that point on. The answer might be found in the extreme dependence of protected industries on state support. There was a marked change in the rules of the game following the rise of the military administration in 1976, when new policies aimed at opening the economy strongly affected the manufacturing sector. That opening exposed the fact that a substantial number of domestic firms were unable to compete successfully with foreign imports, in part because of the overvaluation of the local currency, but also because of newly revealed structural problems that had been masked for a long period.

The major limitations of the import-substitution model were, undoubtedly, the excessive protection of the state, the lack of competitiveness, and the limited capacity to generate foreign currency to cover import requirements. Early in the 1970s, industry still operated under high import duties and took loans at negative real interest rates. This implied that the possibilities for growth, or even survival, were tied to the continuity of the state's protectionist devices. In addition, the internal shock was accompanied by the troubles arising in the international scene following the oil crisis of 1973, and by the changes in the global context of technological change. Successes and failures of Argentina's industry, then, might be explained as a result of a complex combination of economic and noneconomic forces.

Import substitution schemes had been put into operation from the beginnings of industry in the 1870s through a selective protection of certain goods. Following the 1890 and 1930 crises, an ever-wider array of goods ended up being protected, but it was only in the 1940s, under the economic plan of Perón, that protectionism took a form so radical as to seem unprecedented. These essential features remained unchanged following 1955, except for the adoption of import restrictions and the stronger promotion of input substitution and of manufactured product exports. The role of the state as a regulator of industrial and economic activity was not discussed, while the protection of industry was associated with the maintenance of employment. As regards import requirements and the power to generate foreign exchange, the main issue was still the domestic-market bias of Argentine industry.

An explanation of industry's performance cannot avoid considering both the macroeconomic as well as the political contexts in which substitution took place. We have noted the slow growth of the economy in general, its volatile cyclical behavior, inflation, and fluctuations in exchange rates, coupled with political instability, disputes over distribution, and a lack of continuity in economic policy – this does not constitute the most promising environment for any economic activity. To what extent the industrial sector was also responsible for its own fate is a question yet to be answered. But the fact that the collapse occurred in conjunction with the depths of the political conflicts in the years 1974–75 does not seem to be a coincidence.

References

Ablin, Eduardo R. 1985. *Internacionalización de empresas y tecnología de origen argentino.* Buenos Aires: CEPAL/Eudeba.

Adelman, Jeremy. 1994. *Frontier Development: Land, Labour, and Capital on the Wheatlands of Argentina and Canada, 1890–1914.* Oxford: Clarendon Press.

Albert, Bill, and Paul Henderson. 1988. *South America and the First World War: The Impact of the War on Brazil, Argentina, Peru, and Chile.* Cambridge: Cambridge University Press.

Barbero, María Inés. 1990. *Grupos empresarios, intercambio comercial e inversiones italianas en la Argentina: El caso de Pirelli (1910–1920).* Estudios Migratorios Latinoamericanos 15–16. Buenos Aires: Centro de Estudios Migratorios Latinoamericanos (CEMLA).

———. 2000. *Mercados, redes sociales y estrategias empresariales en los orígenes de los grupos económicos: De la Compañía General de Fósforos al Grupo Fabril (1889–1929).* Estudios Migratorios Latinoamericanos 44. Buenos Aires: Centro de Estudios Migratorios Latinoamericanos (CEMLA).

Barbero, María Inés, and Mariela Ceva. 1997. El catolicismo social como estrategia empresarial: El caso de Algodonera Flandria (1924–1955). *Anuario IEHS* (Tandil, Argentina: Universidad Nacional del Centro de la Provincia de Buenos Aires, Facultad de Ciencias Humanas, Instituto de Estudios Histórico-Sociales) 12: 269–89.

Berlinski, Julio. 1985. *La protección efectiva de actividades seleccionadas de la industria manufacturera argentina.* Buenos Aires: Instituto Torcuato Di Tella, Centro de Investigaciones Económicas.

———. 1986. *La elección de una estrategia de crecimiento: Los regimenes de comercio exterior y la promoción de las exportaciones en América Latina.* Buenos Aires: Instituto Torcuato Di Tella, Centro de Investigaciones Económicas.

———. 1989. *Trade Policies in Argentina.* Buenos Aires: Instituto Torcuato Di Tella, Centro de Investigaciones Económicas.

Berlinski, Julio, and Daniel Schydhowsky. 1977. Incentives for Industrialization in Argentina. Buenos Aires: Centro de Estudios Monetarios y Bancarios.

Bisang, Roberto, and Bernardo Kosacoff. 1995. Tres etapas en la búsqueda de una especializaciòn sustentable: Exportaciones industriales argentines, 1974–1993. In *Hacia una nueva estrategia exportadora: La experiencia argentina, el marco regional y las reglas multilaterales,* edited by B. Kosacoff and E. R. Ablin. Buenos Aires: Universidad Nacional de Quilmes.

Brodersohn, Mario S., ed. 1970. *Estrategias de industrialización para la Argentina*. Buenos Aires: Editorial del Instituto.
Bulmer-Thomas, Victor. 1994. *The Economic History of Latin America Since Independence*. Cambridge: Cambridge University Press.
Canitrot, Adolfo. 1981. Teoría y práctica del liberalismo: Política antiinflacionaria y apertura económica en la Argentina, 1976–1981. *Desarrollo Económico* 82: 131–89.
CEPAL (United Nations, Economic Commission for Latin America). 1959. *Análisis y proyecciones del desarrollo económico, vol. 5: El desarrollo económico de la Argentina*. Mexico City: CEPAL.
———. 1978. *Series históricas del crecimiento de América Latina*. Santiago de Chile: CEPAL.
Coatsworth, John H., and Alan M. Taylor, eds. 1998. *Latin America and the World Economy Since 1800*. Cambridge, Mass.: Harvard University Press.
Cornblit, Oscar. 1967. Inmigrantes y empresarios en la política argentina. *Desarrollo Economico* 24: 641–91.
Cortés Conde, Roberto. 1967. Problemas del crecimiento industrial argentino. 1880–1914. In *Argentina: Sociedad de masas*, edited by Torcuato S. Di Tella, Gino Germani, et al. Buenos Aires: Eudeba.
———. 1979. *El progreso argentino*. Buenos Aires: Editorial Sudamericana.
———. 1994. Estimaciones del PBI en la Argentina 1875–1935. Ciclos de seminarios no. 3/94, Departamento de Economía, Universidad de San Andrés.
———. 1997. *La economía argentina en el largo plazo: Ensayos de historia económica de los siglos XIX y XX*. Buenos Aires: Editioral Sudamerica.
della Paolera, Gerardo, and Alan M. Taylor. 1998. Finance and Development in an Emerging Market: Argentina in the Interwar Period. In *Latin America and the World Economy Since 1800*, edited by J. H. Coatsworth and A. M. Taylor. Cambridge, Mass.: Harvard University Press.
———. 2001. *Straining at the Anchor: The Argentine Currency Board and the Search for Macroeconomic Stability, 1880–1935*. Chicago: University of Chicago Press.
Di Tella, Guido. 1979. Controversias económicas en la Argentina. In *Argentina y Australia*, edited by J. Fogarty, E. Gallo, and H. L. Diéguez. Buenos Aires: Instituto Torcuato Di Tella.
Di Tella, Guido, and Manuel Zymelman. 1967. *Las etapas del desarrollo económico argentino*. Buenos Aires: Editorial Universitaria de Buenos Aires.
Díaz Alejandro, Carlos F. 1966. *Devaluación de la tasa de cambio en un país semi-industrializado: La experiencia de la Argentina, 1955–1961*. Buenos Aires: Editorial del Instituto.
———. 1970. *Essays on the Economic History of the Argentine Republic*. New Haven, Conn.: Yale University Press.
———. 1988. No Less Than One Hundred Years of Argentine Economic History Plus Some Comparisons. In *Trade, Development and the World Economy: Selected Essays of Carlos F. Díaz Alejandro*, edited by A. Velasco. Oxford: Basil Blackwell.
Dorfman, Adolfo. 1942. *Evolución industrial argentina*. Buenos Aires: Editorial Losada.
Felix, David. 1970. Más allá de la sustitución de importaciones: Un dilema latinoamericano. In *Estrategias de industrialización para la Argentina*, edited by M. S. Brodersohn. Buenos Aires: Editorial del Instituto.
Ferrer, Aldo. 1963. *La economía argentina: Las etapas de su desarrollo y problemas actuales*. Mexico City: Fondo de Cultura Económica.
Ffrench-Davis, Ricardo, Oscar Muñoz, and José G. Palma. 1994. Latin American

Economies, 1950–1990. In *The Cambridge History of Latin America*, vol. 4, edited by L. Bethell. Cambridge: Cambridge University Press.

Gadano, Nicolás. 1998. *Determinantes de la inversión en el sector petróleo y gas de la Argentina*. Santiago de Chile: CEPAL (United Nations, Economic Commission for Latin America).

Gallo, Ezequiel. 1970. Agrarian Expansion and Industrial Development in Argentina, 1880–1930. In *Latin American Affairs*, St. Antony's papers, no. 22, edited by R. Carr. Oxford: Oxford University Press.

García-Mata, Rafael, and Emilio Llorens. 1939. *Argentina económica*. Buenos Aires: Compañía Impresora Argentina.

Geller, Lucio. 1975. El crecimiento industrial argentino hasta 1914 y la teoría del bien primario exportable. In *El Régimen oligáriquico*, edited by M. Giménez Zapiola. Buenos Aires: Amorrortu Editores.

Gerchunoff, Pablo. 1989. Peronist Economic Policies, 1946–55. In *The Political Economy of Argentina, 1946–83*, edited by G. Di Tella and R. Dornbusch. Basingstoke: Macmillan.

Gerchunoff, Pablo, and Lucas Llach. 1998. *El ciclo de la ilusión y el desencanto: Un siglo de políticas económicas argentinas*. Buenos Aires: Ariel.

Goetz, Arturo. 1976. Concentración y desconcentración en la industria argentina desde la década de 1930 a la de 1960. *Desarrollo Económico* 60: 507–48.

Gravil, Roger. 1976. Argentina and the First World War. *Revista de Historia* 54 (108): 385–417.

Guy, Donna. 1982. La industria argentina, 1870–1940: Legislación comercial, mercado de acciones y capitalización extranjera. *Desarrollo Económico* 87: 351–74.

Haber, Stephen. 1989. *Industry and Underdevelopment: The Industrialization of Mexico, 1890–1940*. Stanford, Calif.: Stanford University Press.

Haber, Stephen, ed. 1997. *How Latin America Fell Behind: Essays on the Economic Histories of Brazil and Mexico, 1800–1914*. Stanford, Calif.: Stanford University Press.

Heyman, Daniel. 1980. *Las fluctuaciones de la industria manufacturera argetnina, 1950–1978*. Cuadernos de la CEPAL 34. Santiago de Chile: CEPAL.

Hirschman, Albert O. 1958. *The Strategy of Economic Development*. New Haven, Conn.: Yale University Press.

Hopkins, John. 1944. *Informe presentado por el Dr. John Hopkins, integrante de la Misión de Investigadores de la Armour Research Foundation*. Buenos Aires: Corporación Para la Promoción del Intercambio.

Hora, Roy. 2000. Terratenientes, empresarios industriales y crecimiento industrial en la Argentina: Los estancieros y el debate sobre el proteccionismo (1890–1914). *Desarrollo Económico* 40 (159): 465–92.

Jorge, Eduardo F. 1971. *Industria y concentración económica*. Buenos Aires: Siglo Veintiuno Argentina Editores.

Katz, Jorge M., and Bernardo P. Kosacoff. 1989. *El proceso de industrialización en la Argentina: Evolución, retroceso y prospectiva*. Buenos Aires: Centro Editor de América Latina, CEPAL (United Nations, Economic Commission for Latin America).

Korol, Juan Carlos, and Hilda Sábato. 1990. Incomplete Industrialization: An Argentine Obsession. *Latin American Research Review* 25 (1): 7–30.

Kosacoff, Bernardo P. 1992. *El sector industrial argentino*. Buenos Aires: CEPAL.

Lewis, Colin. 1986. Industry in Latin America before 1930. In *The Cambridge History of Latin America*, vol. 4, edited by L. Bethell. Cambridge: Cambridge University Press.

————. 1998. Industry in Latin America. In *Industrialisation: Critical Perspectives on the World Economy*, edited by P. K. O'Brien. London: Routledge.

Lewis, Colin, and Wilson Suzigan. 2000. Industry and Industrialization in Latin America: In Pursuit of Development. London School of Economics. Photocopy.

Lewis, Paul H. 1990. *The Crisis of Argentine Capitalism*. Chapel Hill, N. C.: University of North Carolina Press.

Llach, Juan. 1972. Dependencia, procesos sociales y control del estado en la década del treinta. *Desarrollo Económico* 12 (45): 173–83.

————. 1984. El Plan Pinedo de 1940: Su significado histórico y los orígenes de la economía política del peronismo. *Desarrollo Económico* 92: 515–58.

Llamazares, Juan. 1943. *Examen del problema industrial argentino: Aspectos de política económica y social*. Buenos Aires: Facultad de Ciencias Económicas, Universidad de Buenos Aires.

Lobato, Mirta Zaida. 1988. *El "taylorismo" en la gran industria exportadora argentina: 1907–1945*. Buenos Aires: Centro Editor de América Latina.

Mallon, Richard, and Juan Sourrouille. 1973. *La política económica en una sociedad conflictiva: El caso argentino*. Buenos Aires: Amorrortu Editores.

Martínez, Ricardo. 1999. Recopilación de series históricas del Producto y del Ingreso. N.p.: CEPAL.

Miller, Rory. 1981. Latin American Manufacturing and the First World War: An Explanatory Essay. *World Development* 9 (8): 707–16.

Nakamura, Leonard I., and Carlos E. J. M. Zarazaga. 1998. Economic Growth in Argentina in the Period 1905–1930: Some Evidence from Stock Returns. In *Latin America and the World Economy Since 1800*, edited by J. H. Coatsworth and A. M. Taylor. Cambridge, Mass.: Harvard University Press.

O'Connell, Arturo. 1979. "Comentario a." In *Argentina y Australia*, edited by J. Fogarty, E. Gallo and H. L. Diéguez. Buenos Aires: Instituto Torcuato Di Tella.

Ortiz, Ricardo M. 1964. *Historia económica de la Argentina, 1850–1930*. Buenos Aires: Ediciones Pampa y Cielo: Plus Ultra distributor.

Peralta-Ramos, Mónica. 1972. *Etapas de acumulación y alianzas de clases en la Argentina (1930–1970)*. Buenos Aires: Siglo Veintiuno Argentina Editores.

Petrecolla, Alberto. 1968. Prices, Import Substitution and Investment in the Argentine textile industry (1920–1939). Ph.D. dissertation, Columbia University.

————. 1989. Unbalanced Development, 1958–62. In *The Political Economy of Argentina, 1946–83*, edited by G. Di Tella and R. Dornbusch. Basingstoke: Macmillan.

Prebisch, Raúl. 1955. *Informe preliminar acerca de la situación económica*. Buenos Aires: Secretaría de Prensa y Actividades Culturales de la Presidencia de la Nación.

————. 1986. Argentine Economic Policies Since the 1930s: Recollections. In *The Political Economy of Argentina 1880–1946*, edited by G. Di Tella and D. C. M. Platt. New York: St. Martin's Press.

Rapoport, Mario. 1988. El triángulo argentino: las relaciones económicas con Estados Unidos y Gran Bretaña, 1914–1943. In *Economía e historia: Contribuciones a la historia económica argentina*, edited by M. Rapoport, E. Azcuy Ameghino, R. Prebisch, C. Taylor, and F. J. Weil. Buenos Aires: Editorial Tesis.

————. 2000. *Historia económica, política y social de la Argentina: (1880–2000)*. Buenos Aries: Ediciones Macchi.

Regalsky, Andrés M. 1992. El Banco Francés del Rio de la Plata y la emergencia de nuevas formas de crédito, 1886–1914. Photocopy.

————. 1999. Banca y capitalismo en la Argentina, 1850–1930: Un ensayo crítico. *Ciclos* 9 (18): 33–54.

Rocchi, Fernando. 1994. La Bagley di Buenos Aires: Una fabbrica di biscotti alla conquista del mercato interno (1887–1930). *Ventesimo Secolo* 4.

———. 1997. Building a Nation, Building a Market: Industrial Growth and the Domestic Economy in Turn-of-the-Century Argentina. Ph.D. dissertation, University of California, Santa Barbara.

———. 1998. Consumir es un placer: La industria y la expansión de la demanda en Buenos Aires a la vuelta del siglo pasado. *Desarrollo Económico* 148: 533–58.

———. 2000. El péndulo de la riqueza: La economía argentina en el período 1880–1916. In *Nueva historia Argentina*, edited by M. Z. Lobato and J. Suriano. Buenos Aires: Editorial Sudamericana.

Rougier, Marcelo. 2001. La política crediticia del Banco Industrial y la política económica del peronismo, 1944–1955. Documento de trabajo no. 5, Universidad de Buenos Aires, Facultad de Ciencias Ecónomicas, CEED.

Schvarzer, Jorge. 1978. Estrategia industrial y grandes empresas: El caso argentino. *Desarrollo Económico* 71: 307–51.

———. 1996. *La industria que supimos conseguir*. Buenos Aires: Planeta.

Solberg, Carl. 1973. The Tariff and Politics in Argentina 1916–1930. *Hispanic American Historical Review* 53 (2): 260–84.

Sourrouille, Juan V. 1980. Apuntes sobre la historia reciente de la industria argentina. *Boletín informativo Techint* 217.

———. 1980. *El complejo automotor en Argentina: Transnacionales en América Latina*. México City: Editorial Nueva Imagen.

Sourrouille, Juan V., Bernardo P. Kosacoff, and Jorge Lucángeli. 1985. *Transnacionalización y política económica en la Argentina*. Buenos Aires: Bibliotecas Universitarias Centro Editor de América Latina.

Taylor, Alan M. 1992. External Dependence, Demographic Burdens and Argentine Economic Decline After the *Belle Époque*. *Journal of Economic History* 52 (4): 907–36.

Topik, Steven. 1987. *The political economy of the Brazilian State, 1889–1930*. Austin, Tx.: University of Texas Press.

Tulchin, Joseph. 1978. El crédito agrario en la Argentina, 1910–1926. *Desarrollo Económico* 71: 381–408.

Villanueva, Javier. 1972. El origen de la industrialización argentina. *Desarrollo Económico* 12 (47): 451–76.

———. 1987. Industrial Development in Argentina: The Process up to the 1960s. Buenos Aires: Instituto Torcuato Di Tella and Universidad Católica Argentina. Photocopy.

Vitelli, Guillermo. 1999. *Los dos siglos de la Argentina: Historia económica comparada*. Buenos Aires Argentina: Prendergast Editores.

Warwick, Armstrong. 1985. The Social Origins of Industrial Growth: Canada, Argentina and Australia, 1870–1930. In *Argentina, Australia and Canada: Studies in Comparative Development, 1870–1965*, edited by G. Di Tella and D. C. M. Platt. London: Macmillan.

Weil, Felix José. 1944. *Argentine Riddle*. New York: John Day.

10

Banking and finance, 1900–1935

LEONARD I. NAKAMURA
Federal Reserve Bank of Philadelphia

CARLOS E. J. M. ZARAZAGA
Federal Reserve Bank of Dallas

Globalization and financial openness were defining themes of the world economy in the last decade of the twentieth century, much as they were during the first decade of the century. Indeed, in the years 1900 to 1913, international financial flows in relation to the size of the world economy were larger than they are today.

In the wake of the East Asian financial crisis of 1997–98, however, economists and policymakers have been questioning the value of the unhindered flow of international finance. In particular, some have argued that such financial flows can destabilize domestic economies, as overseas investors rush into emerging markets and rush out as quickly, exacerbating both booms and downturns.

This article focuses on a crucial stage in Argentine financial development, the period from 1900 to 1935, during which Argentina evolved from an economy highly dependent on external (primarily British) finance to one more nearly self-sufficient. This period permits a detailed case study of the consequences, for one country that was highly dependent on foreign finance, of the breakdown in the international financial system. Moreover, at least since Taylor's seminal paper (1992) this has been an important area of research for Argentina, so that data and analyses are, while still incomplete, comparatively well developed. Thus we are able to build on the work of Taylor (1992), della Paolera and Taylor (1998; 2001; 2002), and Nakamura and Zarazaga (1998) to examine the failure of domestic finance to adequately fill the void left by the decline of London and the breakdown of the gold standard and the world financial system in the interwar period. In addition, we extend the statistical series for the Bolsa de Comercio de Buenos Aires (stock exchange) in Nakamura and Zarazaga (1998) with data from 1931 to 1935.

The views expressed here are those of the authors and do not necessarily reflect those of the Federal Reserve Bank of Philadelphia, the Federal Reserve Bank of Dallas, or the Federal Reserve System. Victoria Geyfman and Olga Zograf provided excellent research assistance.

The story that we tell is one in which neither the Buenos Aires Bolsa nor the private domestic banks developed rapidly enough to replace fully the British investors as efficient channels for financing private investment. One consequence is that Argentine investable funds were increasingly concentrated in a single institution, the Banco de la Nación Argentina (BNA), creating a lopsided financial structure that was vulnerable to rent seeking and to authoritarian capture. Despite this weakness, we should remain aware of the very impressive level of development that Argentina did achieve during this period. Several measures, including gold reserves, interest rates, money supply, bank credit, and the market capitalization of domestic corporations attest to the vibrancy of Argentine financial development.

In his pathbreaking article, Taylor (1992) used the example of Argentine economic divergence to argue that Argentina's financial dependence on Great Britain in the early years of the century was a counterexample to the notion that foreign investment can jumpstart prosperity. He showed that Argentina's financial dependence and demographic profile made it vulnerable to the decline of British financial leadership. Recent work by della Paolera and Taylor (1998; 2002) pointedly analyzes the decline of private banking relative to the quasi-public Banco de la Nación Argentina as a crucial element in the failure of Argentina's response to the challenge of British financial decline.

In the international arena, financial leadership after the *Belle Époque* passed from London to New York. This decline not only tended to raise world interest rates, favoring savers over borrowers, but also deprived Argentina of the benefit of British knowledge of Argentine economic investment opportunities. Nakamura and Zarazaga (1998) and Taylor (this volume) document the improved *relative* reception of large Argentine issues in the 1920s, so that Argentina was not, in aggregate, deprived of access to international finance.

But in a period of creative destruction such as occurred in the early decades of the century, the ability of financial intermediaries to make fine-grained determinations about capital allocation can be crucial to the long-run success of economic enterprise. While the United States was willing to take over the British role of investing in the official bonds of Argentina and of Buenos Aires, and indeed did so at rates below those that would have been on offer in London, it did not step into a similar role for direct private investment.

A second theme in this paper is thus the development of domestic alternatives to international financial investors. The Buenos Aires Bolsa, domestic private banks, and the BNA were all channels for directing domestic savings into private investment. Of the three, as we shall see, only the BNA was able to rise in importance over the entire course of the period we investigate. As a quasi-public entity, the BNA was in a strong position to provide inside money to the

Argentine economy, but it was probably not nearly as appropriate a provider of private investment finance.

Indeed, a recurrent question in economics has been the relative economic importance of the two sides of the banking ledger – loans on the asset side and deposits on the liability side. A long tradition of monetarism has focused on the importance of the stability of the growth of the money stock as a key determinant of the efficiency of economic regimes (for example, Friedman and Schwartz 1963). From this perspective, the liability side of the banking ledger is of key macroeconomic significance. On the other hand, at least since Bagehot (1873) and Schumpeter (1934), economists have argued that the allocation of business finance has been a key contribution of the development of the banking system, thereby emphasizing the asset side of the banking ledger.

The policy relevance of this issue has risen rather than diminished over the years, as economic theory has come to play an ever more decisive role in debates over public policy. For example, if monetary and price stability are crucial prerequisites of development, and problems of credibility and intertemporal consistency of behavior are paramount, then the development of a regime such as adherence to a gold standard, a currency board, or dollarization may cut through knotty problems of institutional development. But if the efficient allocation of private finance is seen to be crucial to economic growth, then the development of legal and financial institutions that encourage the growth of private monitoring intermediaries like commercial banks and liquidity-enhancing markets like stock exchanges cannot be discounted.

In this paper, we seek to discuss Argentine financial development as seen through the lens of its stock market by examining in some detail the monthly stock returns of the banking and nonbanking sectors of Argentina, as well as examining some basic banking balance sheet data.

One motivation for following stock returns is that they are less subject to the serious measurement and methodological issues that arise in the reconstruction of the national accounts of the time, which seem to have blurred the debate with potentially conflicting stories.[1] Perhaps more important, a look at the relative valuation of stocks in different sectors of the economy may provide some useful insights into the microeconomic details of the Argentine development process that might escape the scrutiny of the usual macroeconomic aggregates.

---

[1] For instance, according to Maddison (1995), the hopes that Argentina would resume the 3 percent annual growth rate in per capita terms that the country had experienced in the period 1900–13 did materialize, since the equivalent growth rate for the period 1918–29 was, on average, around 4 percent – even higher than before the Great War. By contrast, a recent revision of the National Accounts of the time by Cortés Conde (1994) suggests that growth did slow down after 1914–18. Examining longer run trends (not just trough-to-peak rates) the same conclusion had been reached by Taylor (1992), both for absolute and relative growth performance.

Our data show, for example, that the domestic private banking sector of Argentina seems to have been struggling even before the Great War, while the industrial sector initiated a steady expansion right after it. We argue, in detail, that the banking crisis of 1912–14 played a large role in weakening the private banks in Argentina, and that this weakness contributed to the excessive development of the quasi-public Banco de la Nación. In turn, the lopsided development of Argentine finance made it vulnerable to the political economic chicanery described in della Paolera and Taylor (2001).

Judging by the behavior of banks' stock prices and returns, the markets do not seem to have been particularly optimistic about the prospects of domestic banks after the Great War, perhaps an early warning of the massive bailout that would have to be engineered in 1935 under the auspices of the newly founded central bank, with characteristics that, in the view of della Paolera and Taylor (2001), are reminiscent of the bailout implemented more recently in East Asia after the 1997–98 crisis.

It is unclear, however, why financial resources in Argentina were not channeled through institutional mechanisms other than banks. Why did the stock market remain relatively small during a period of rapid economic expansion? Were the regulatory bodies regarding corporate finance or its legal framework important impediments to a more solid development of Argentinean domestic capital markets? Did the fact that the London Stock Exchange listed the most important Argentine issues inhibit the development of the Buenos Aires Bolsa? These are urgent questions whose answers remain relevant to today's economic and financial debates.

10.1 Analytical framework

At least since Schumpeter (1934), economic growth has been associated with financial development. One theoretical strand in the literature has placed the efficient working of delegated monitors at the center of our understanding of financial intermediation (Diamond 1984; Diamond and Dybvig 1983). In a more nuanced view, private banks are privileged as delegated monitors because their crucial role in the transactions mechanism gives them a heightened ability to perform credit monitoring functions also (Black 1975; Fama 1985). As such, public provision of deposit insurance that protects private banks from destabilizing runs may be preferable, despite the moral hazard problems it may engender, to narrow banks that are barred from making risky commercial advances. As Mester, Nakamura, and Renault (2001) show, commercial banks do have access to information from checking accounts that is valuable in monitoring borrower activity.

This "credit" view of banking's role in development has been emphasized for Argentina by della Paolera and Taylor (1998) where they point out that private banking was sharply curtailed during the crucial decade of the 1920s in the wake of the 1913–14 crisis. Below, we take a modest further step toward the important task of analyzing that crucial crisis. In particular, we point out that the Banco de la Nación's quasi-official status may have aided it vis-à-vis private banks that lacked deposit protection.

King and Levine (1993) identify bank credit (loans by banks and other deposit-taking institutions) and stock turnover rate as key financial variables that measure the ability of a financial system to abet the economic development of a country. Levine and Zervos (1998) use bank credit and stock capitalization as indicators. We use these variables to frame a more detailed narrative of Argentine financial and economic development in the early twentieth century.

In this paper, we have generally used the United States as our basis for comparison with Argentine financial development. Arguably, the basis for comparison could be other small settler countries such as Canada and Australia, rather than the outsized United States. But Taylor (1992) points out that Canada and Australia, also closely tied financially to the London capital markets, were likewise poor performers in the interwar period. Because the United States, given its large size, was naturally more autarchic than other settler countries, it is a potentially more telling comparison.

10.2 The world capital market and Argentine finance

During the period of the *Belle Époque*, Argentina successfully joined the world on the gold standard (Ford 1962; della Paolera 1988). Argentina provided for gold redemption and currency stability in the wake of the Baring Crisis by setting up two institutions, the Caja de Conversión (currency board) and the Banco de la Nación. As described in della Paolera and Taylor (2002), the former was responsible for external convertibility and the maintenance of the gold standard while the latter dealt with inside money and engaged in normal commercial banking operations, yet also was the state's bank. For a substantial period of time, these two institutions operated admirably. Unfortunately, a weakness in the system eventually emerged. The BNA – in two steps, first in the banking crisis of 1913–14 and then in the banking crisis of 1929 – bailed out bankrupt private domestic banks, and in the process itself succumbed and was folded into the newly created central bank in 1935.

Despite this shortcoming, this institutional setup enabled Argentina to attract and hold a large proportion of the world's total stock of gold, given its size. At the end of 1913, this total world stock, according to the *Economist* (cited in

Keynes 1930), was 1.579 billion pounds sterling, of which 965 million pounds was in central banks and treasuries. Also, according to the *Economist*, the gold stock of Argentina, including gold in circulation, was 59 million pounds sterling of which 55 million pounds was held in the Caja de Conversión and the BNA. Thus Argentina had some 3.7 percent of the world's monetary gold and 5.7 percent of the gold held in the world's central banks and treasuries. Since, according to Maddison, Argentina's economy represented about 1.2 percent of the world's output and 2.8 percent of the world's exports, these are impressive figures. The figures in the *Economist* are notable because they represented the facts as known to the business community of the time: it was evident to market participants that Argentina, at the end of the *Belle Époque*, was a considerable actor in world markets. Moreover, as World War I began, even more gold, held by foreign delegations to Argentina, entered the country. At the war's end, foreign legations held 117 million gold pesos (23 million pounds sterling) in reserves.

According to Baiocco, in December 1913, the gold reserves in the country (*oro visible*) were 287.39 million gold pesos with 233.45 in the Caja de Conversión, 32.27 in the Banco de la Nación (the Caja and BNA held the equivalent of 53 million pounds, some 4 percent less than the Economist's figure), 18.73 in foreign banks, and a total of 53.94 in banks, implying 2.94 in other private banks. The numbers are close enough: in the first six months of 1913, 43 million gold pesos flowed into the Caja, and then 33 million fled back out in the next six. Given this instability, a 4 percent margin of error may be attributable to small differences in accounting.

But as column 4 of Table 10.1 shows, throughout the period from 1913 to 1928, Argentina held an enviable fraction of the world's gold, one that was more than ample given the size of its economy and trade – almost always between 4 and 6 percent.[2] Argentina's ability to maintain a substantial horde of gold no doubt bolstered its reputation on world financial markets.

Column 1 of Table 10.1 shows rates of return from long-term Argentine debt instruments, primarily the 5 percent custom loan of 1886–87 which was regularly quoted on the London stock exchange market.[3] This loan was secured by Argentine custom receipts, and was the largest loan ever floated abroad by the Argentine government. Columns 2 and 3 show rates of return on British

---

[2] These data come from a third source, the U.S. Federal Reserve's statistics from 1943. They generally agree with Baiocco within a range of about 10 percent.

[3] From 1900 to 1913, della Paolera (1988); from 1914 to 1919, the *Boletín de la Bolsa de Comercio*; and from June 1920 to June 1935 (the *Economist*, last issue in June of each year). For 1931 to 1935, the rate quoted is for the Argentine 4 percent rescission loan, maturing in 1952. The rates for the rescission loan and the custom loan are almost identical in 1929 and 1930 when they are quoted side by side.

Table 10.1. *Interest rates and gold*

	Yield on external bond (Argentina customs loan)	Yield on British consols	Yield on U.S. corporate bonds	Argentina's share of world monetary gold stocks (percent)[1]
1900	5.4	2.8	3.30	—
1901	5.2	2.9	3.25	—
1902	5.2	2.9	3.30	—
1903	5.0	2.8	3.45	—
1904	4.9	2.8	3.60	—
1905	4.9	2.8	3.50	—
1906	4.9	2.8	3.55	—
1907	4.9	3.0	3.80	—
1908	4.8	2.9	3.95	—
1909	4.8	3.0	3.82	—
1910	4.8	3.1	3.87	—
1911	4.8	3.2	3.94	—
1912	4.8	3.3	3.91	—
1913	4.9	3.4	4.02	5.27
1914	4.9	3.3	4.16	4.52
1915	5.1	3.8	4.20	3.83
1916	5.3	4.3	4.05	4.00
1917	5.3	4.6	4.05	4.03
1918	5.1	4.4	4.82	4.47
1919	5.3	4.6	4.81	4.95
1920	5.6	5.3	5.17	6.53
1921	5.4	5.2	5.31	5.87
1922	5.0	4.4	4.85	5.61
1923	5.0	4.3	4.68	5.39
1924	5.0	4.4	4.69	4.94
1925	5.0	4.4	4.50	5.01
1926	5.0	4.6	4.40	4.88
1927	4.9	4.6	4.30	5.52
1928	4.9	4.5	4.05	6.04
1929	5.3	4.6	4.45	4.20
1930	5.7	4.5	4.40	3.76
1931	7.0	4.4	4.10	2.23
1932	9.1	3.7	4.70	2.08
1933	4.9	3.4	4.11	1.99
1934	4.3	3.1	3.91	—
1935	4.0	2.9	3.37	—

[1] Gold at Caja and BNA as a percent of total gold at world central banks and treasuries.
Sources: Column 1: see text; Column 2: Mitchell (1962); Column 3: United States Bureau of the Census (1975); Column 4: Board of Governors of the Federal Reserve System (1943).

consols and on twenty-year U.S. corporate bonds. Broadly speaking, world and Argentine interest rates were somewhat higher in the period after 1922 than before 1914. From 1901 to 1913, the custom loan yielded just under 5 percent, and from 1922 to 1928 it yielded an identical amount (similarly, in the earlier period the prime rate averaged 6.3 percent, and in the later averaged 6.9 percent). Over the two periods, the spread between the custom loan and the British consol narrowed.

Thus, while it is evident that there was some upward drift in the real interest rate in Argentina, its magnitude appears small and in keeping with changes in the world marketplace, and not suggestive of an abrupt change in Buenos Aires's role therein. For example, in New York, 20-year corporate bonds yielded between 3.25 and 4 percent from 1901 to 1913, while they yielded between 4 and 5 percent from 1922 to 1929. If anything, we see that the British consol rate was drifting higher with respect to long-term rates for U.S. issues, while the Argentine custom loan and prime rate were holding their own. The transition from British to U.S. dominance of the capital markets appears to have been a relatively smooth one for Argentine borrowing, in so far as sovereign, well-secured borrowing is concerned.

Moreover, as documented in Taylor (this volume), although the risk premium on Argentine debt expanded considerably in 1931 and 1932, it narrowed again in 1934 and 1935, with Argentine spreads vis-à-vis United States corporate debt being quite low. This is remarkable given that the gold standard had been abandoned all around. Incredibly, in 1934, the spread between Argentine and U.S. debt was less than in 1912.

On the other hand, it remained the case that international financial flows in the 1920s and 1930s were much smaller than they had been, as Taylor (this volume) also documents. The question that arises is how well domestic financial markets were able to replace these financial flows. The aggregate figures argue strongly that Argentine average saving rates were low in the first decades of the twentieth century. But domestic saving is calculated as a residual and thus is subject to considerable error. So while it appears likely that domestic saving was inadequate for Argentine economic development, there is value in examining the extent to which quantitative characteristics of financial institutions in Argentina resemble those in relatively well-developed countries. It is to this task that we now turn, first to the stock market and then to the banking system.

10.3 Equity trading on the Buenos Aires Bolsa, 1900–1935

This paper documents one step in a long-term project to construct a complete series of prices and dividends for all the firms that quoted on the Bolsa de Comercio de Buenos Aires in the twentieth century. Currently, our data stretches from 1900 to 1935.

We document the fact that new listings and the overall capitalization of the Bolsa were relatively high for an emerging market when compared to GDP. However, the overall rate of transactions was rather low. In part, this may be due to the fact that the largest Argentine companies, the railroads, were listed on the London Stock Exchange rather than the Bolsa; these shares would naturally have had the highest rate of trading. A slow rate of turnover means that the stock market was less liquid and that the ability of the stock market to attract fresh capital for entrepreneurs was weakened. In addition, a low quantity of transactions means that brokerage commissions were also low, with the implication that the Bolsa was not an important source of income for equity brokers. As a result, news and analysis of Argentine equities would not have the monetary value that they would have had on a more active exchange.

On the other hand, by listing on the London Stock Exchange, the railroads had access to large quantities of capital at low rates and were thus able to efficiently finance growth. As the development of the Pampas and the port city of Buenos Aires, as well as most industry in Argentina, were direct beneficiaries of railroad development, the tradeoff was no doubt to the country's overall advantage, as Lewis (1983) has emphasized. Moreover, the active attention paid to Argentine affairs inspired by the railroads also aided other Argentine issues on the London market, such as the custom loan. Thus, while the fact that the most important Argentine securities traded there has implications for the development of the Buenos Aires Bolsa, it by no means suggests that Argentina would have been better off floating them domestically.

10.3.1 Data

Certainly, the collection of the necessary data for this project has proved to be extremely painstaking, suggesting that investors at the time may have had concerns regarding the transparency of corporate governance and the protection of shareholders' rights. This impression is reinforced by the Banco Español scandal uncovered in 1924 (discussed below), an indication of a potentially serious failure in the supervision and regulation of the banking sector that contributes to the comparison between East Asian economies and the early stages of Argentina's development.

Several challenges had to be confronted in the task of data retrieval. The first and most serious one was the lack of a single reliable source of data on prices, volumes, and dividends until the year 1921. The data for the period

1900–21 had to be collected, therefore, from a variety of sources as discussed in the following section.

10.3.2 Period 1900–1905

The only source that summarizes monthly data on prices for this period is the *Boletín Estadístico de la Bolsa de Comercio de Buenos Aires,* issued back then on about the fifteenth of each month. Only a handful of companies were actively traded each month during this period. Additionally, data on dividends and volumes are not systematically reported by any source, and it was necessary to reconstruct that information piecemeal from the daily summaries of the newspaper *La Prensa.*

Even then, information on dividends would have been incomplete without further investigation. For example, it is not rare to find *La Prensa* announcing the date of payment of a dividend without mentioning the amount. That information had to be supplemented by drawing on other sources that occasionally reported annual dividends, such as the *Anuario Pillado* and its successor, the Argentine Yearbook. Combining these different sources, we are able to reconstruct all the dividends paid by the banks in our stock market index in that period, Banco Español del Río de la Plata and Nuevo Banco Italiano.

10.3.3 Period 1906–1913

For this period, the *Review of the River Plate* provided weekly summaries of the prices of most companies quoted in the stock market. We adopted the last price of the last week of each month as representative of the monthly prices.

This source also reports information on annual dividends, although the assigned date is that of the end of the fiscal year, rather than the actual date of payment; and it misses, most of the time, the payment of provisional dividends. To correct these problems, it was necessary again to rely on alternative sources, such as the newspaper *La Prensa* until 1907 and *El Monitor de Sociedades Anónimas* from that year on. This latter publication also provided systematic information on annual dividends for the period 1907–35, and typically contained some references to provisional ones, which, in combination with the other sources already mentioned – the newspaper *La Prensa* and the *Review of the River Plate* – made it possible to determine, at least to a good approximation, both the amount and date of payment of provisional dividends.

Unfortunately, volumes traded for this period were reported only in *La Prensa,* and it was not possible to retrieve them at this stage of the project because of difficulties with the only two public libraries in Argentina that have the necessary issues in their collections.

10.3.4 Period 1913–1921

Monthly prices were taken from the weekly reports of the Bolsa de Comercio because starting in 1913 this source, unlike the *Review of the River Plate*, reports the exact amount of provisional dividends, although not their exact dates, which had to be extracted or inferred from the information reported in *El Monitor de Sociedades Anónimas*. Monthly prices were taken to be the first price quoted in the report of the first week of the subsequent month or, if that was missing, the price on the closest date to the last day of the month in which the stock was traded within a fifteen-day interval. Volumes traded for this period were also extracted from the *Boletín Oficial*.

10.3.5 Period 1921–1935

In 1921, the *Boletín Oficial de la Bolsa de Comercio de Buenos Aires* started to report the exact dates and amounts of all dividends paid. Therefore, this single source could be used to compile the information on prices, volume traded, and dividends. Occasional typos or inconsistencies between partial dividends and annual dividends had to be cleared by consulting other sources, such as the *Review of the River Plate* or *El Monitor de Sociedades Anónimas*. Monthly prices were assigned as in the previous period.

For all periods, the evolution of prices had to be monitored closely in order to filter spurious changes originating in cosmetic institutional features, such as stock splits or changes in share denomination. We have limited the indices constructed for this volume to the stocks with relatively continuous trading throughout the period. For these stocks we constructed quarterly price indices, annual average dividend-price ratios, and annual total investment returns. All these indices are constructed on the principle utilized in constructing the Dow Jones index, which is share-price weighting.[4]

---

[4] Our data on market capitalization is not complete for all the years we cover, so consistent market capitalization weights are not possible for this entire period. One natural alternative would be to average rates of return across all stocks, therefore giving each stock a weight of one in each period. However, a chained ratio of growth rates series introduces a systematic upward bias into the index. To give a simple example, consider an index with only two stocks, A and B, valued in year zero and year two at 100 each; in year 1 stock A rises to 150 while stock B falls to 50. A share-weighted index would give a price of 100 in each year while a chained growth rate series would show 100 in years zero and one and 133 1/3 in year 2 because it would average a 100 percent increase with a 33 1/3 percent decline.

10.3.6 The market capitalization of the Bolsa

The Buenos Aires Bolsa had a market capitalization of roughly 900 million paper pesos (p.p.) in 1929 when GDP was 9.7 billion p.p., so that the market capitalization was 9 percent of GDP. In that same year, the market capitalization of the New York Stock Exchange (NYSE) was $65 billion when U.S. GNP was $103 billion, so that U.S. market capitalization represented over 60 percent of GDP. But the U.S. stock market bubble in 1929 exaggerated the size of the market capitalization with respect to the economy. For the NYSE, 1924 would be perhaps more representative, and in that year, market capitalization was 32 percent of GDP. To offer another comparison, the Italian stock market in 1992 had a capitalization of less than 15 percent of Italian GDP.

Two further points should be noted. First, the Argentine stock market did not list the major railway issues – the Southern, the Western, the Pacific, and the Central. Together, the Argentine railway issues had a market capitalization in 1929 of 92 million British pounds, or 1.1 billion p.p. at the average exchange rate of that year. If we were to add those issues to the Argentine stock market, its capitalization would rise to above 20 percent of GDP. Second, we have included only ordinary stock, whereas the NYSE figures include preferred stock as well.

Demirgüç-Kunt and Levine (1996) show that for 18 non-OECD countries with formal stock exchanges, using data from 1986–93, the median ratio of market capitalization to GDP was 21 percent, which is similar to the capitalization of Argentina's equity issues if the railway shares in 1929 are included. For OECD countries, the ratio was 24 percent. Thus the market value of publicly traded Argentine companies, including those listed on the London exchange, was quite high for a modern economy, and substantial for an emerging market. Although it did not represent Argentina's foremost industrial concerns, the railroads, it represented a high proportion of the remaining ones and a substantial share of asset value.

10.3.7 Turnover on the Bolsa

Turnover – the extent to which outstanding shares are actively traded – varies considerably across stock markets and within stock markets over time. Trading on the Argentine Bolsa represented some 5 percent of market capitalization during the 1920s, that is, on average only one share in 20 turned over in a given year. Again, this figure does not include the most heavily traded issues, the railroads. In the hectic New York market of the 1920s, trading volume sometimes more than equaled the market capitalization. However, in the 1950s and 1960s, trading volume on the NYSE was more like 15 to 20 percent of

Table 10.2. *Stock market transactions relative to GDP*
Percent

Year	Ratio	Year	Ratio
1901	0.47	1918	0.89
1902	0.49	1919	0.71
1903	0.94	1920	0.37
1904	3.14	1921	0.59
1905	2.08	1922	0.66
1906	2.09	1923	0.53
1907	0.96	1924	0.29
1908	—	1925	0.21
1909	—	1926	0.31
1910	—	1927	0.48
1911	—	1928	0.38
1912	0.66	1929	0.41
1913	0.88	1930	0.27
1914	0.2	1931	—
1915	0.19	1932	—
1916	0.23	1933	—
1917	0.47	1934	—
1918	0.89	1935	—
1919	0.71		

Sources: Stock market data from *El monitor de sociedades anonimas y patentes de invención*; GDP from della Paolera and Taylor (2001).

market capitalization, and today it is roughly 50 percent. In 1992, trading on the Italian stock market was 20 percent of market capitalization. Demirgüç-Kunt and Levine (1996) present data that showed that the trading turnover on modern emerging markets (1986–93) is about 20 to 25 percent.

Thus the Bolsa's trading rate in the 1920s was relatively slow by either contemporary or past standards, but was by no means trivial. While the Bolsa cannot be considered highly liquid, it would be a mistake not to take seriously this market as a channel of finance.

Table 10.2 shows estimates of the volume of transactions in paper pesos on the Argentine Bolsa from 1901 to 1907 and 1912 to 1930 for trades in stocks denominated both in paper pesos and in gold pesos.[5] In nominal terms, volume peaked in 1918, but just barely. As a fraction of GDP, transaction volume may have peaked as early as 1904. It should be noted that the shares of the largest firms on the exchange traded regularly, to the extent that a trade is recorded in virtually every week for which we have records. This rate of trade is certainly sufficient to provide a reasonable record of valuations.

[5] The comparable data in Nakamura and Zarazaga (1998) consider only shares denominated in paper pesos.

The railroads were the companies with the highest capitalization in the country and would likely have been traded very actively on the Bolsa had they been listed there. The fact that they were traded on the London Stock Exchange meant that the Buenos Aires Bolsa was deprived of trading income and stature, and this may have substantially reduced the likelihood that stock trading in general would thrive on the Bolsa. On the other hand, the greater liquidity and legal stature of the London Stock Exchange bolstered the railroads' ability to raise capital, and by raising the value of information about Argentina in London, information spillovers no doubt helped other capital issues there as well.

10.3.8 Rates of return on equity

10.3.8.1 Dividend-price ratio

One measure of the expected return to stocks is the dividend-price ratio. If price movements are difficult to forecast, as one expects on an equity market, movements in the dividend-price ratio may reflect changing *ex ante* returns to the market. In this respect, there do not appear to have been enormous changes in the *ex ante* returns on the Argentine Bolsa. Table 10.3 reports dividend-price ratios for a group of common stocks with nominal capitalizations in excess of 10 million paper pesos. Generally speaking, these represent the bulk of the Bolsa's market capitalization.

In the period from 1900 to 1905, dividend-price ratios were low, and stock prices rose rapidly. It appears that in this period the exchange was dominated by stocks whose prices were expected to appreciate and did so. This seems generally appropriate for an era that *ex post* was one of spectacular growth. For much of the rest of the period, dividend-price ratios were relatively higher (around 6 percent) until the bear market of the 1930s, and dividends rather than capital gains dominated the *ex post* returns to the stocks. Returns were strong in the 1920s, and then weakened in the early 1930s with a bear market extending from 1928 to 1934. Low dividend-price ratios in the early 1930s suggest that during this period investors remained hopeful of a return to higher prices.

10.3.8.2 Price indices

Table 10.4 and Figure 10.1 show Argentine stock prices based on continuously traded stocks. This index is constructed like the Dow Jones stock index, with the shares included weighted by their share value. From 1906 to 1912, in the *Belle Époque*, the real value of shares on the Argentine stock market was roughly stable. After 1912, however, the stock market dropped for two years and continued to sink until 1920. Then, beginning in 1920, the stock market

Table 10.3. *Argentine equities: frequently traded stocks*
Percent

	Average dividend-price ratio	Average total returns	
		Nominal	Real
1900	4.2	22.4	8.6
1901	4.1	-0.2	13.4
1902	4.6	4.7	-4.1
1903	6.2	38.1	45.7
1904	4.4	14.4	12.0
1905	6.5	24.2	14.3
1906	5.9	-1.1	-6.7
1907	8.2	5.6	2.8
1908	7.3	12.3	16.6
1909	6.8	25.3	14.5
1910	6.6	29.9	20.5
1911	6.9	18.6	19.6
1912	5.8	10.9	8.2
1913	8.3	-16.0	-16.0
1914	6.2	-12.5	-13.1
1915	7.2	1.8	-4.9
1916	5.3	11.7	-1.9
1917	2.5	19.6	-3.8
1918	11.0	44.6	32.3
1919	6.3	18.9	15.1
1920	9.6	7.2	2.5
1921	7.3	-5.0	19.5
1922	7.4	10.6	22.0
1923	6.4	9.0	4.5
1924	6.7	5.0	-1.9
1925	7.0	5.2	3.5
1926	6.8	15.0	28.1
1927	6.6	14.1	16.2
1928	5.5	12.5	11.8
1929	5.7	1.2	4.4
1930	5.3	-8.3	-4.1
1931	6.3	-11.0	-8.3
1932	5.7	-10.7	-11.8
1933	4.9	10.6	15.7
1934	4.4	-1.9	-13.9
1935	5.5	1.6	2.8
1900–09	5.8	13.9	10.9
1910–19	6.6	11.4	4.5
1920–29	6.9	7.3	10.7
1930–35	5.4	-4.0	-3.7

Sources: See text. Real returns deflated using wholesale price indices from della Paolera (1988) and IEERAL (1986).

Fig. 10.1. Stock price indices: bank and nonbank firms
1899Q4 = 100

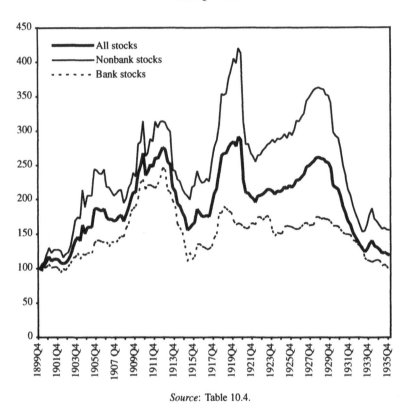

Source: Table 10.4.

stabilized and rallied spiritedly from 1925 to 1928; in 1930, the stock market was still well above its level in the first half of the decade.

Figure 10.1 shows that bank and nonbank stock prices showed broadly similar secular and cyclical movements, but that after the 1920s bank stock prices were less volatile, and there seems to have been relatively little secular movement. This quieter behavior of bank stocks reflected a period in which the private banks were not particularly robust.

In sum, from a high plateau around 1910, bank and nonbank stocks alike fell during the great liquidity crunch and recession of 1912 to 1914. Both series rose but while nonbank stocks rose above their 1910 level, bank stock prices on average managed only to recover to about four-fifths of their peak. The divergent path of bank stocks will be discussed further below.

Table 10.4. *Stock price indices: bank and nonbank firms*
1899Q4 = 100

	All	Bank	Nonbank		All	Bank	Nonbank
1899Q4	100.0	100.0	100.0	1911Q1	240.5	268.3	220.7
1900Q1	101.3	106.4	97.0	1911Q2	251.0	288.8	221.2
1900Q2	105.1	109.8	101.3	1911Q3	248.2	285.0	219.2
1900Q3	110.5	120.1	102.6	1911Q4	261.3	313.7	216.7
1900Q4	117.5	130.3	106.8	1912Q1	259.5	304.9	222.2
1901Q1	111.5	123.2	101.7	1912Q2	268.6	313.6	232.0
1901Q2	113.9	127.5	102.6	1912Q3	275.9	314.2	246.5
1901Q3	114.2	127.8	103.0	1912Q4	273.7	312.4	243.9
1901Q4	112.6	127.8	100.0	1913Q1	255.0	303.8	213.9
1902Q1	108.8	125.7	94.7	1913Q2	251.2	299.2	210.8
1902Q2	107.6	116.7	100.0	1913Q3	217.7	243.7	198.8
1902Q3	108.3	121.2	97.6	1913Q4	212.4	241.5	190.2
1902Q4	112.7	123.9	103.4	1914Q1	194.3	229.6	165.0
1903Q1	120.0	134.2	108.1	1914Q2	190.3	226.7	159.7
1903Q2	132.2	152.4	115.4	1914Q3	181.2	215.5	152.4
1903Q3	140.9	169.8	116.9	1914Q4	174.8	209.3	133.7
1903Q4	146.6	174.8	123.1	1915Q1	156.3	205.5	111.0
1904Q1	141.0	173.3	114.1	1915Q2	159.7	200.2	123.6
1904Q2	163.8	214.4	121.8	1915Q3	163.8	217.9	113.7
1904Q3	151.2	189.2	119.7	1915Q4	167.0	220.5	117.6
1904Q4	160.7	205.9	123.1	1916Q1	186.3	241.8	135.5
1905Q1	160.7	205.9	123.1	1916Q2	180.9	230.7	136.0
1905Q2	160.7	205.9	123.1	1916Q3	176.1	224.6	132.2
1905Q3	186.1	244.5	137.6	1916Q4	176.1	226.0	130.9
1905Q4	187.4	242.7	141.5	1917Q1	177.3	230.8	128.2
1906Q1	185.4	238.3	141.5	1917Q2	175.4	226.4	128.9
1906Q2	183.6	237.4	138.9	1917Q3	191.7	255.4	132.6
1906Q3	186.6	244.1	138.9	1918Q1	215.7	286.3	150.4
1906Q4	175.0	218.5	138.9	1918Q2	241.5	308.8	180.6
1907Q1	171.3	218.0	132.5	1918Q3	264.3	354.0	180.9
1907Q2	172.1	212.1	138.9	1918Q4	267.6	352.1	189.9
1907Q3	169.3	206.0	138.9	1919Q1	267.5	354.7	186.9
1907Q4	170.8	209.0	139.1	1919Q2	276.2	375.7	183.2
1908Q1	175.5	213.3	144.0	1919Q3	282.1	389.1	181.6
1908Q2	177.8	214.2	147.5	1919Q4	284.3	404.9	169.5
1908Q3	168.8	195.0	147.0	1920Q1	277.8	397.9	163.5
1908Q4	178.8	202.2	159.4	1920Q2	291.3	420.0	166.1
1909Q1	188.9	217.2	165.4	1920Q3	286.7	412.8	164.4
1909Q2	201.6	223.5	183.3	1920Q4	228.8	313.5	160.8
1909Q3	210.6	239.0	187.0	1921Q1	209.4	280.7	158.7
1909Q4	209.9	233.3	190.4	1921Q2	209.6	281.0	158.7
1910Q1	238.0	281.2	202.1	1921Q3	203.8	267.5	165.1
1910Q2	250.1	284.0	224.3	1921Q4	201.6	263.1	166.0
1910Q3	267.7	314.4	229.3	1922Q1	196.2	254.9	163.8
1910Q4	235.5	263.3	215.4	1922Q2	205.1	264.8	174.3

Table 10.4. (Continued)

	All	Bank	Nonbank		All	Bank	Nonbank
1922Q3	205.6	265.0	175.6	1929Q2	254.3	352.1	171.8
1922Q4	207.9	271.6	170.7	1929Q3	254.1	352.0	171.6
1923Q1	211.1	275.5	173.8	1929Q4	246.5	340.4	168.3
1923Q2	214.8	280.1	177.3	1930Q1	220.4	298.0	162.4
1923Q3	214.5	282.3	172.2	1930Q2	217.4	292.8	162.4
1923Q4	212.2	287.5	155.1	1930Q3	215.3	289.5	161.6
1924Q1	207.6	283.3	147.9	1930Q4	205.8	275.2	157.3
1924Q2	212.4	289.3	152.5	1931Q1	190.0	250.2	152.5
1924Q3	211.3	288.0	151.1	1931Q2	180.5	234.7	150.1
1924Q4	212.8	290.5	151.5	1931Q3	169.2	214.8	150.3
1925Q1	218.6	295.6	160.9	1931Q4	163.8	206.2	149.1
1925Q2	215.5	289.4	162.3	1932Q1	152.7	190.8	141.3
1925Q3	220.4	298.5	161.5	1932Q2	146.7	180.8	140.4
1925Q4	217.5	293.7	161.1	1932Q3	140.8	173.2	135.5
1926Q1	221.9	302.5	158.7	1932Q4	134.1	163.0	132.7
1926Q2	228.9	315.5	157.7	1933Q1	128.5	153.6	131.8
1926Q3	228.1	313.7	158.3	1933Q2	124.4	155.4	115.3
1926Q4	232.9	320.4	161.3	1933Q3	128.9	164.9	112.4
1927Q1	237.2	325.7	165.4	1933Q4	136.1	178.0	111.3
1927Q2	247.9	343.8	166.9	1934Q1	140.8	187.1	109.6
1927Q3	249.4	348.4	162.9	1934Q2	132.8	172.4	111.2
1927Q4	252.4	353.6	163.2	1934Q3	131.0	168.3	112.8
1928Q1	255.9	359.3	163.8	1934Q4	127.5	162.8	111.8
1928Q2	260.8	362.0	174.9	1935Q1	122.2	157.5	104.2
1928Q3	261.3	362.8	174.8	1935Q2	124.0	159.7	106.1
1928Q4	259.4	360.9	172.3	1935Q3	121.6	156.8	103.6
1929Q1	259.2	360.1	173.2	1935Q4	119.3	156.4	97.0

Sources: See text.

10.3.8.3 Real rates of return

Prior to the 1930s, real rates of return on Argentina's Bolsa were generally quite strong. The periodization here has been chosen to match that in a careful study of international equity returns by Dimson, Marsh, and Staunton (2000). Table 10.5 shows that for our Argentine stocks real returns were above those in the United States from 1900 to 1920 and then faltered relatively in the 1920s. At least until 1929, then, stock market real returns do not appear to have been the reason for the weak turnover and declining initial offerings.

In summary, where the New York Stock Exchange continued to strengthen and provide substantial finance as the 1920s developed, the Buenos Aires Bolsa faltered as a source of capital during this period. Nevertheless, for much of the period under consideration, the Bolsa was a surprisingly strong source of capital funding and of good dividends.

Table 10.5. *Real equity rates of return, selected countries*
Percent per annum

	Argentina	U.S.	U.K.	Australia	Canada
1900–10	10.9	7.1	1.8	11.8	6.3
1910–20	4.5	-2.5	-1.4	3.9	0.1
1920–30	10.7	14.9	9.3	16.3	15.5

	France	Germany	Italy	Netherlands	Sweden
1900–10	5.3	3.6	4.4	4.8	19.1
1910–20	-3.1	-12.7	-2.8	1.3	0.7
1920–30	7.9	13.6	2.4	1.5	8.4

Notes: The returns are calculated January 1 to January 1.
Sources: Table 10.5 and Dimson et al. (2000).

10.4 Banking development and banking crises

Measuring Argentine banking development during the period 1900 to 1935 depends in large part on how one conceives of banking development. We shall show that Argentine banking development in the aggregate from 1900 to 1935 was quite substantial, but took place with a highly significant drawback – the steadily increasing importance of the BNA.

10.4.1 Bank loans

As shown in Table 10.6 and Figure 10.2, the ratio of bank loans to GDP in Argentina rose steadily for most of the period, beginning around 20 percent in the early 1900s, rising to over 40 percent in 1922, and thereafter remaining above 35 percent until 1935. On average, over the period from 1901 to 1935, bank loans averaged 32.8 percent of Argentine GDP. Over the same period, U.S. bank loans averaged 39 percent of GDP. For a somewhat shorter period, from 1921 to 1935, loans at London clearing banks averaged 33.1 percent of U.K. GDP.[6] Focusing on the period after World War I and before the Depression, from 1921 to 1929 Argentine banks lent an average of 37 percent of GDP, U.S. banks 39 percent, and London clearing banks 34 percent. Thus, overall, banks in Argentina mobilized a large proportion of domestic funds compared to two of the best-developed banking systems in the world.

However, as documented in della Paolera and Taylor (1998; 2002), the Argentine banking system during this period had an increasingly lopsided development as the huge BNA grew much more rapidly than either private domestic or foreign banks. The relatively slow growth of private domestic banking during this period can in part be ascribed to the boom of 1910 to 1912 and the crash

---

[6] In this period, London clearing banks accounted for 77 percent of U.K. gross bank deposits.

Table 10.6. *Credit supply and money supply*

Ratio to GDP

	Bank loans						Broad money		
	All banks	Private banks	Foreign banks	Banco de la Nación	U.S. all banks	U.K. London clearing banks	Arg.	U.S.	U.K.
1901	0.27	0.08	0.08	0.11	0.33	—	0.38	0.46	0.55
1902	0.19	0.08	0.06	0.05	0.35	—	0.37	0.48	0.55
1903	0.2	0.09	0.07	0.04	0.36	—	0.42	0.48	0.56
1904	0.24	0.1	0.08	0.05	0.36	—	0.44	0.48	0.55
1905	0.26	0.11	0.08	0.07	0.37	—	0.44	0.49	0.54
1906	0.27	0.11	0.09	0.07	0.37	—	0.41	0.49	0.52
1907	0.26	0.11	0.08	0.07	0.39	—	0.4	0.49	0.51
1908	0.27	0.12	0.07	0.08	0.4	—	0.39	0.56	0.54
1909	0.28	0.13	0.07	0.08	0.39	—	0.42	0.54	0.55
1910	0.3	0.15	0.07	0.08	0.41	—	0.42	0.54	0.55
1911	0.35	0.18	0.07	0.1	0.41	—	0.44	0.56	0.53
1912	0.34	0.18	0.07	0.1	0.41	—	0.42	0.55	0.52
1913	0.36	0.18	0.07	0.11	0.41	—	0.44	0.54	0.52
1914	0.35	0.15	0.07	0.13	0.45	—	0.43	0.59	0.56
1915	0.29	0.12	0.06	0.12	0.44	—	0.41	0.63	0.55
1916	0.28	0.12	0.06	0.1	0.4	—	0.41	0.58	0.51
1917	0.27	0.12	0.05	0.1	0.38	—	0.41	0.55	0.46
1918	0.28	0.11	0.06	0.12	0.33	—	0.41	0.48	0.46
1919	0.32	0.12	0.07	0.13	0.33	—	0.44	0.5	0.53
1920	0.32	0.12	0.07	0.13	0.36	—	0.45	0.46	0.55
1921	0.39	0.16	0.09	0.15	0.4	0.29	0.54	0.51	0.65
1922	0.4	0.16	0.08	0.17	0.38	0.28	0.55	0.57	0.69
1923	0.38	0.14	0.08	0.16	0.36	0.31	0.5	0.51	0.68
1924	0.35	0.12	0.07	0.16	0.36	0.33	0.44	0.53	0.65
1925	0.35	0.12	0.07	0.16	0.38	0.35	0.45	0.55	0.61
1926	0.38	0.13	0.07	0.18	0.38	0.37	0.48	0.52	0.64
1927	0.36	0.13	0.07	0.17	0.39	0.38	0.48	0.55	0.61
1928	0.34	0.12	0.06	0.16	0.41	0.38	0.49	0.57	0.62
1929	0.37	0.13	0.07	0.17	0.4	0.39	0.5	0.53	0.61
1930	0.42	0.14	0.08	0.2	0.45	0.38	0.53	0.59	0.62
1931	0.48	0.16	0.09	0.23	0.46	0.36	0.56	0.63	0.67
1932	0.45	0.15	0.07	0.23	0.48	0.33	0.54	0.76	0.69
1933	0.44	0.15	0.06	0.23	0.4	0.27	0.53	0.74	0.74
1934	0.36	0.12	0.05	0.19	0.32	0.28	0.43	0.7	0.68
1935	0.29	0.11	0.05	0.13	0.28	0.27	0.42	0.7	0.69
Average									
1901–35	0.33	0.13	0.07	0.13	0.39	—	0.45	0.55	0.58
1921–29	0.37	0.13	0.07	0.16	0.39	0.34	0.49	0.54	0.64

Sources: Argentina: loans from Baiocco (1937); money from della Paolera (1988) and Baiocco (1937); GDP from della Paolera and Taylor (2001). U.S.: loans from Board of Governors of the Federal Reserve System (1959); money from Friedman and Schwartz (1970); GDP from Balke and Gordon (1989) to 1929 and from United States Department of Commerce (1998) afterwards. U.K.: loans from Mitchell (1962); money from Capie and Webber (1985); GDP from Feinstein (1972).

Fig. 10.2. Credit supply
Ratio of loans to GDP, percent

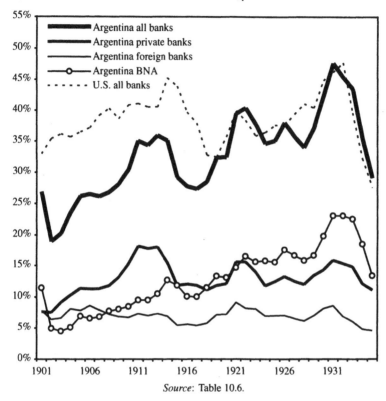

Source: Table 10.6.

that succeeded it, as we shall show below. In turn, the lopsided development of the Argentine banking system made the political capture of the financial system increasingly inviting, and the bailout of the Argentine private banks in 1935 documented in della Paolera and Taylor (2002) was one of the outcomes.

10.4.2 Monetary development

Another measure of financial development is money. A measure that is often used for international comparisons is M3, currency in circulation plus deposits at all financial intermediaries. This measure has two virtues: it is readily available for many countries, and by broadly defining depositories, it makes minor institutional differences between countries less important.

During the period under consideration, from 1901 to 1935, the ratio of M3 to GDP for Argentina was 45 percent (Table 10.6 and Figure 10.3). Over the

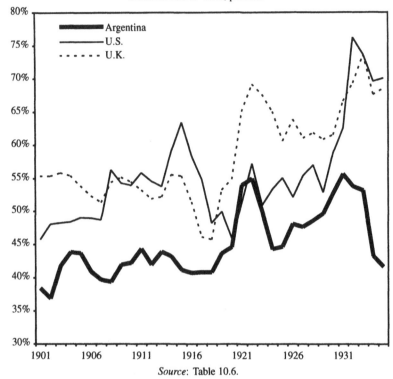

Fig. 10.3. Broad money supply
Ratio of M3 to GDP, percent

Source: Table 10.6.

same time period, the ratio for the United States was 55.5 percent and for the United Kingdom, 58.5 percent. Thus, on average, broad money in proportion to GDP was lower for Argentina than for the United States at a ratio of 0.82 and the United Kingdom at a ratio of 0.77.

All three countries saw their ratios of M3 to GDP grow over the period, and broadly speaking at about the same rate of nearly 1 percent per year. In the decade from 1901 to 1910 Argentina had an M3-GDP ratio of 41 percent, while in the decade ending in 1935 it had a ratio of 49 percent. For the United States, the comparable figures are 50.2 percent and 62.8 percent. For the United Kingdom, they are 54.4 percent and 65.5 percent.

10.4.3 Argentine private national banks

The Argentine private banks (*bancos privados nacionales*) proved their mettle as early as the Baring Crisis. In that crisis, when both the Banco Nacional (the forerunner of the Banco de la Nación) and the Banco de la Provincia de Buenos Aires failed, a number of private banks weathered the storm. But almost all of them were forced to suspend operations, at least briefly, during that period. Alone among domestic private banks,[7] Banco Español del Río de la Plata had managed to keep its doors open throughout the crisis, relying on a high reserve-to-deposit ratio that exceeded 50 percent. Although founded just four years before the Baring Crisis, the Banco Español was soon able to replace Banco de Italia y Río de la Plata as the top private bank as the result of the reputation it had won with its conservative investment strategy.

The period from 1900 to 1912 was a heady one for Argentina's financial community as the economy flowered and deposits rose rapidly. Deposits and loans of the private banks grew faster than GDP; indeed, their ratios to GDP roughly doubled. They also grew relative to deposits and loans of the BNA. But they may have grown too fast. Private banks used both security issues and deposits to grow, and while they generally used conservative banking principles, reserves did shrink somewhat relative to deposits.

From 1900 to 1914 during the *Belle Époque*, Argentina had generally benefited from rising world prices, and because Argentine export prices rose faster than import prices, there was a favorable terms of trade effect. This boom time for Argentina was perhaps comparable to the boom in Southeast Asia in the 1990s. As we shall see, weakness within the Argentine financial structure appeared well before the London Stock Exchange holiday.

In London, the bank rate was raised in late 1912, and monetary pressure was only relaxed by early 1914. The 1912–13 crop in Argentina was excellent. Yet bank stocks and dividends appeared to be already under pressure.

In the first quarter of 1913, gold continued to be imported into Argentina at a phenomenal rate (35 million gold pesos); and in the second quarter (10 million), gold was still being imported at the rate of the previous year. But in the second half of the year 42 million gold pesos were exported.

The 1913–14 crop did very poorly. Cereal exports for October 1913 to September 1914 fell to 182 million gold pesos, from 322 in 1912–13. By June 1914, a generalized depression had developed. Agricultural production had only one good year in the next three, 1914–15, and did not fully recover until 1917–18. The nonagricultural sector's production fell 15 percent from 1913 to 1914, and another 10 percent from 1914 to 1915. In all, from 1912 to 1917, Argentina's real GDP slid 19 percent while population rose nearly 14 percent. Output per capita thus fell nearly 29 percent with consequences that have reverberated throughout the century.

---

[7] The British Bank of London and the River Plate was the other private bank that did not.

Beginning in 1912, the disturbances of the domestic economy began to lead to widespread withdrawals of cash from the private banks, some of it in favor of the Banco de la Nación which was clearly perceived as a safe haven.

In retrospect it is clear that the closure of the London Stock Exchange on Friday, July 31, 1914 signaled the end of the *Belle Époque*, marking as it did the transfer of international financial leadership from London to New York. June 27, 1914 was the date of the assassination of Archduke Franz Ferdinand in Sarajevo, the spark that set off the war. The outbreak of war during the following month was accompanied by a desperate flight to liquidity, as foreign investors sold securities at exchanges around the world. In particular, many investors were afraid that they would not be able to liquidate and repatriate overseas assets as the war widened. They thus dumped assets on markets and withdrew liquidity, causing prices to tumble. This in turn threatened many institutions, particularly financial ones, with failure. In addition, the warring nations themselves had a sudden, pressing need to finance purchases of war materiel and the raising of armies. These rising pressures, over the course of July 1914, forced one exchange after another to close – most for extended periods. The world's major bond exchanges remained closed until the end of the year.

These liquidity needs naturally transmitted themselves to the Argentine markets, and in particular to the private banks. The most important private banks – Banco Español, Banco Italia, Banco Frances, and Nuevo Banco Italiano – were each identified with and dependent upon immigrant communities that maintained strong ties with their homelands. As their depositors were naturally responsive to European calls for liquidity, these banks were subject to extraordinary demands on liquidity.

In Diamond and Dybvig's model of a bank run, depositors hold liquid deposits because they expect to receive new information about the marginal utility of consumption. The events during 1914 appear closely to match this description of the demand for liquidity. Total deposits at Argentine banks fell by nearly 20 percent. The brunt of the hardship fell on the private banks, which lost over 45 percent of their deposits. It is useful to compare these losses with those in the United States during the banking panics of the Great Depression, where between the end of 1928 and the middle of 1933 commercial bank deposits fell by 39.5 percent. Thus the Argentine private banks experienced a worse deposit loss in two years than U.S. commercial banks did in the four and one-half years of the Great Depression.

As Table 10.7 shows, deposits at the five largest private banks fell by two-fifths. (Only the Banco Popular, the smallest of the five, had a deposit loss less than 20 percent.) It is remarkable that these banks could survive such

Table 10.7. *Deposits in the 1912–14 crisis*
Millions of paper pesos, end-of-year

	1912	1914	Percent change
Total	1,480.9	1,189.3	-19.7
Private domestic banks	674.3	365.4	-45.8
Banco Español	229.9	126.9	-44.8
Banco Italia	101.5	62.4	-38.5
Banco Francés	84.7	55.0	-35.1
Nuevo Banco Italiano	41.0	27.2	-33.7
Banco Popular Argentina	20.4	17.4	-14.7
Other private banks	196.8	76.5	-61.1
Banco de la Nación	478.3	552.7	15.6
Foreign banks	328.3	271.2	-17.4

Sources: Baiocco (1937) and Regalsky (1994).

intense drains. However, it was not just a demand for liquidity that propelled the deposit losses. For, as della Paolera and Taylor (2002) point out, the BNA actually gained deposits. On the one hand, then, a question arises as to whether the boom years from 1900 to 1912 had not themselves led the private banks to overextend. On the other hand, it could well be that some of the drain on deposits was due to contagious fears and a flight to safety that could have been stemmed by deposit insurance. Although the BNA, by rediscounting to the private banks, helped them weather the crisis, the BNA may also have by representing a safe haven encouraged flight.

One interpretation is that the banking crisis in this period was due to the end of London's role as financier to the world in general and Argentina in particular. An alternative interpretation argues that the extended boom from 1900 to 1912 had generated speculative conditions in Argentina that were in any case liable to cause the domestic financial structure to fall. This latter interpretation is close to that put forward in Ford's (1962) study of the crisis. We turn to detailed banking price data to shed additional light on this issue.

10.4.4 The stock market as a window on private banks

Detailed analysis of stock price movements offers a window on the public's view of the business prospects of some of the major Argentine private banks. We review some of the evidence below that shows significant stock price declines at the banks before the deep liquidity squeeze that began in June 1914.

Nuevo Banco Italiano, the fourth-largest private bank, had a stock price of 106 (pesos moneda nacional) in December 1899. The stock price hit a high of 420 in October 1912, but it fell to 325 in January 1913, stabilized at 305 in

November, and fell in February 1914 to 250. It then steadied during 1914 to 270 in September before falling to 165 in January 1915. NBI's stock had a pattern of falling around year end during this period. For this bank there appears to have been an important impact on its stock market value by the spring of 1914.

For Banco de Galicia, a medium-sized, private bank, our data begin with the stock trading at 138 in 1910. The price briefly shot up to 160 in January 1911, was still 160 in March 1911, fell back to 135 in April 1911, and was still 128 in January 1913. Over the course of the year it fell steadily to 85 in December 1913 and then to 40 in September 1914 before recovering to 60 in December 1914. When the generalized depression struck in July 1914, the Banco de Galicia's stock price had already fallen to 48.

Banco Frances del Río de la Plata was a large, forward-thinking bank that invested in industry – electricity, rails, and food manufacture – and came a cropper. Its shares peaked in 1911 at 175. The price fell steadily to 134 in December 1913 by which time it had lost nearly one-quarter of its nominal value. In February 1914, the stock traded at 112.5 and on the eve of war in June 1914 it had fallen to 92. But its true financial condition was revealed in the August through September hiatus, and when the Bolsa reopened in October 1914, the price was 37. Its group was ruined as a financial force.

Banco Español's stock price, which we first record at 128 in 1899, continued to do well throughout the 1912–13 crisis and did not begin to fall until 1914 opened. From 180 in February 1914, the stock price fell to 150 in July and was next traded at 100 in October. Thus Banco Español's stock price fall followed the agriculture failure and the generalized depression; the gold export in the second half of 1913 did not appear to be so important.

However, a decade later it was learned that Banco Español had beginning in 1914 entered into a policy of deception to avoid closing. *The Economist* of March 24, 1924 reported:

It is now public property that the Banco Español del Río de la Plata has, at an extraordinary general meeting, held on February 2, written down its capital by 75 percent – from $100 million Arg. paper to $25 million – and admitted losses which at the lowest reckoning total $103 million Arg. paper, and are generally believed to be in effect nearly thirty million more than this sum....As far back as 1914 the bank, taking the view that to suspend the dividend would have led to closing down, decided to pay dividends out of "funds other than profits," i.e., presumably out of capital.

The capital loss of about 100 million paper pesos represented roughly one-third of that paid in as capital of the private national banks as a group. Thus it would appear that even before the end of *Belle Époque*, the boom of that period had resulted in excesses that had severely harmed the major private banks in the domestic banking system. The picture that emerges is one not dissimilar to events in Southeast Asia where lack of financial controls during an economic boom inspired, in large part, by financial openness created banking sector weaknesses with dire economic consequences.

One consequence may have been that whereas the United States was able to ship industrial and military supplies to Europe and take advantage of the war boom, a similar growth in the industrial sector in Argentina was difficult to finance. Moreover, it is not clear how soundly banks were operating. In its report on the revelations at the Banco Español, *The Economist* notes that, "in 1918, the bank indulged in the purchase of ships (trying by hook or by crook to obtain the necessary profits). But the Armistice came along, and the only result of the shipping speculation was a further loss of $3 million m/n."

Banco Español shares had gone from 100 in October 1914 and 120 in January 1915 to 153 in December 1918. Some of the loss on the ships may have been reflected in its shares, which declined from 141 in August 1919 to 107 in January 1920. In the period surrounding the shareholders' meeting at which its losses were announced in February 1924, Banco Español's shares fell from 93 in September 1923 to 26.5 in January 1924 as the news leaked out, and then further to 16 in July 1924. It drifted up to 20.5 in January 1925 and then jumped abruptly to 72 in February 1925; it then stayed at that level until 1930.

Certainly the fact that both Banco Español and Banco Frances were ruined (one publicly, the other limping along by chicanery) at the end of the *Belle Époque* had important long-term consequences for the Argentine economy. The melancholy demise of the BNA in 1935 detailed in della Paolera and Taylor (2002) was due to bad loans that arose predominantly in the private banking system. They calculate that one-third of all private banking loans had gone bad by then. By the end, with the Caja rediscounting to the BNA and the latter rediscounting on the collateral of bad loans, there was simply no control in Argentina's system of credit allocation.

Inadequate development of the institutions for providing private credit must have been an important limitation to Argentina's economic development during this period. The creation of two durable institutions for maintaining the currency system was inadequate for the full development of a sound financial regime.

10.5 Conclusion

The failure of most developing countries to attain high levels of per capita output during the twentieth century is one of the most important questions for economics. One important cause of development failure is, no doubt, a failure of openness – countries that cut themselves off from world trade are unlikely to capture the benefits of technological progress abroad.

But an open financial regime is not a guarantee of domestic financial development as the progress of domestic financial institutions is by no means automatic. The traumatic events in Argentina associated with the close of the *Belle Époque* certainly warped its financial development. Despite a large stock market capitalization, good international credit, large gold reserves, a strong money supply, and apparently abundant bank credit, a careful study of the financial structure of Argentina reveals crucial weaknesses.

References

Bagehot, Walter. 1873. *Lombard Street: A Description of the Money Market.* London: H. S. King & Co.

Baiocco, Pedro J. 1937. *La economía bancaria argentina.* Buenos Aires: Universidad de Buenos Aires.

Balke, Nathan S., and Robert J. Gordon. 1989. The Estimation of Prewar Gross National Product: Methodology and New Evidence. *Journal of Political Economy* 97 (1): 38–92.

Black, Fischer. 1975. Bank Funds Management in an Efficient Market. *Journal of Financial Economics* 2: 323–39.

Board of Governors of the Federal Reserve System (U.S.). 1943. *Banking and Monetary Statistics.* Washington, D.C.: Board of Governors of the Federal Reserve System.

Board of Governors of the Federal Reserve System (U.S.). 1959. *All-Bank Statistics, United States, 1896–1955.* Washington, D.C.: Board of Governors of the Federal Reserve System.

Capie, Forrest, and Alan Webber. 1985. *A Monetary History of the United Kingdom, 1870–1982.* London: Allen & Unwin.

Cortés Conde, Roberto. 1994. Estimaciones del PBI en la Argentina 1875–1935. Ciclos de seminarios no. 3/94, Departamento de Economía, Universidad de San Andrés.

della Paolera, Gerardo. 1988. How the Argentine Economy Performed During the International Gold Standard: A Reexamination. Ph.D. dissertation, University of Chicago.

della Paolera, Gerardo, and Alan M. Taylor. 1998. Finance and Development in an Emerging Market: Argentina in the Interwar Period. In *Latin America and the World Economy Since 1800*, edited by J. H. Coatsworth and A. M. Taylor. Cambridge, Mass.: Harvard University Press.

———. 2001. *Straining at the Anchor: The Argentine Currency Board and the Search for Macroeconomic Stability, 1880–1935*, NBER Series on Long-Term Factors in Economic Growth. Chicago: University of Chicago Press.

———. 2002. Internal Versus External Convertibility and Emerging-Market Crises: Lessons from Argentine History. *Explorations in Economic History.* Forthcoming.

Demirgüç-Kunt, Asli, and Ross Levine. 1996. Stock Market Development and Financial Intermediaries. *World Bank Economic Review* 10 (2): 291–321.

Diamond, Douglas B. 1984. Financial Intermediation and Delegated Monitoring. *Review of Economic Studies* 51: 393–414.

Diamond, Douglas B., and Phillip H. Dybvig. 1983. Bank Runs, Deposit Insurance, and Liquidity. *Journal of Political Economy* 91 (3): 401–19.

Dimson, Elroy, Paul Marsh, and Mike Staunton. 2000. *The Millennium Book: A Century of Investment Returns.* London: London Business School.

Díaz Alejandro, Carlos F. 1970. *Essays on the Economic History of the Argentine Republic.* New Haven, Conn.: Yale University Press.

Fama, Eugene F. 1985. What's Different about Banks? *Journal of Monetary Economics* 15 (1): 29–39.

Feinstein, Charles H. 1972. *National Income, Expenditure and Output of the United Kingdom, 1855–1965.* Cambridge: Cambridge University Press.

Ford, Alec G. 1962. *The Gold Standard, 1880–1914: Britain and Argentina.* Oxford: Clarendon Press.

Friedman, Milton, and Anna Jacobson Schwartz. 1963. *A Monetary History of the United States, 1867–1960.* Princeton: Princeton University Press.

———. 1970. *Monetary Statistics of the United States: Estimates, Sources, Methods.* New York: National Bureau of Economic Research.

IEERAL (Instituto de Estudios Económicos sobre la Realidad Argentina y Latinoamericana). 1986. Estadísticas de la evolución económica de Argentina 1913–1984. *Estudios* 9 (39):103–84.

Keynes, John Maynard. 1930. *A Treatise on Money.* 2 vols. New York: Harcourt Brace and Company.

King, Robert G., and Ross Levine. 1993. Finance and Growth: Schumpeter Might Be Right. *Quarterly Journal of Economics* 108: 717–38.

Levine, Ross, and Sara Zervos. 1998. Stock Markets, Banks and Economic Growth. *American Economic Review* 88: 537–58.

Lewis, Colin M. 1983. *British Railways in Argentina, 1857–1914: A Case Study of Foreign Investment.* London: Athlone.

Maddison, Angus. 1995. *Monitoring the World Economy.* Paris: OECD.

Mester, Loretta J., Leonard I. Nakamura, and Micheline Renault. 2001. Checking Accounts and Bank Monitoring. Federal Reserve Bank of Philadelphia Working Paper no. 01-3 (March).

Mitchell, B. R. 1962. *Abstract of British Historical Statistics.* Cambridge: Cambridge University Press.

Nakamura, Leonard I., and Carlos E. J. M. Zarazaga. 1998. Economic Growth in Argentina in the Period 1905–1930: Some Evidence from Stock Returns. In *Latin America and the World Economy Since 1800*, edited by J. H. Coatsworth and A. M. Taylor. Cambridge, Mass.: Harvard University Press.

Regalsky, Andrés. 1994. La evolución de la Banca Privada Nacional en Argentina (1880–1914): Una introducción a su estudio. In *La formación de los bancos centrales en España y América Latina (siglos XIX y XX)*, edited by P. Tedde and C. Marichal. Madrid: Banco de España.

Schumpeter, Joseph Alois. 1934. *The Theory of Economic Development: An Inquiry Into Profits, Capital, Credit, Interest, and the Business Cycle.* Translated by Redvers Opie. Cambridge, Mass.: Harvard University Press.

Taylor, Alan M. 1992. External Dependence, Demographic Burdens and Argentine Economic Decline After the *Belle Époque. Journal of Economic History* 52 (4): 907–36.

———. 1998. Argentina and the World Capital Market: Saving, Investment, and International Capital Mobility in the Twentieth Century. *Journal of Development Economics* 57 (1): 147–84.

United States Bureau of the Census. 1975. *Historical Statistics of the United States, Colonial Times to 1970, Bicentennial Edition.* 2 vols. Washington, D.C.: Government Printing Office.

United States Department of Commerce. 1998. *National Income and Product Accounts of the United States, 1929–94.* Washington, D.C.: Government Printing Office.

11

Business, government, and law

SERGIO BERENSZTEIN
Universidad Torcuato Di Tella

HORACIO SPECTOR
Universidad Torcuato Di Tella

One of the most distinctive features of Argentine history is the growing presence of the state apparatus. Indeed, as soon as the country was able to resolve
internal disputes related to the crisis of the colonial system and the ensuing wars
of independence, a process of institution building helped to create political order as well as bolster economic growth and development. Thus, the foundation
of the modern state was instrumental in consolidating both the political system
and civil society. We argue that the relationship between business, government,
and law has grown increasingly significant since the so-called process of *Organización Nacional*, and that its complexity is linked historically to specific
changes in the state apparatus.

Not only did the state grow in size but also, and more importantly, liberal
principles faded and were replaced by interventionist, hyperregulatory, and usually authoritarian ideas and policies. This does not mean that during the liberal
era (roughly between the 1860s and late 1920s), there were no protectionist
policies or successful rent-seeking strategies. Nor do we claim that the prevailing political system was fully democratic. On the contrary, some sectors and
regions enjoyed policy shields against competition that can only be explained
by the result of political pressures and negotiations. Also, as already stated,
the very establishment of a modern state was crucial in encouraging capitalist
development in Argentina. Moreover, until the implementation of the electoral reform of 1912, the political system was far from democratic and was
thoroughly unrepresentative. However, liberal principles largely prevailed as
te premise for institution building, including both the development of the state
apparatus and the understanding and creation of laws and regulations.

Since the 1920s and 1930s, Argentina has experienced, as have many other
developing and developed countries, a critical change in both doctrine and po-

The authors thank Laura Ivanier for invaluable support in the preparation of this chapter. They
also thank Emily Stern for editing it.

litical dynamic. An inward-oriented, protectionist, and state-centered model emerged that, while not totally rejecting republican and liberal principles, certainly promoted corporatist, authoritarian schemes and policies. The interaction between international and domestic factors explains this outcome. Among the former we include the unstable international environment following World War I, the crisis of democracy caused by fascism and communism, and The Great Depression that quickly and substantially reduced international trade and finance. The main domestic factors were political and ideological. First, the radical party (Unión Cívica Radical, UCR) dominated the new political arena. The displaced and divided traditional elites found it difficult to return to power because, given the UCR's electoral power and hegemonic behavior, their incentives to support the current political system vanished. Second, there was a growing perception of threat caused by social and political conflicts related to the organized working classes. Finally, nationalist, antiliberal ideas gained broad acceptance and were disseminated particularly by powerful state institutions and agencies (for example, primary and secondary education and military service).

In this regard, we argue that while the populist experience and its aftermath brought about significant transformations in many areas, it can also be understood in the context of a long-term expansion of the state apparatus that limited, and sometimes even eliminated, the autonomy and vitality of civil society. We claim that Argentina experienced a critical turning point during the 1920s and 1930s as a series of institutional changes established the foundations of a state-centered economic and political system. Those mainfold changes encompassed legal principles, economic policy, and the expansion of the state apparatus. They created strong incentives for a narrowed relationship between state and society. Indeed, populism quickened this relationship even further as new social and political actors were incorporated through state supported, and usually state financed, mechanisms.

The fragility and instability of the few democratic experiences that took place before 1983 should be understood in light of this framework. The weighty presence of the state apparatus induced an ingrained leverage of state actors, such as military and bureaucratic cadres. Hence, firms, groups, and individuals developed strategies to take advantage of these opportunities, which perpetuated the cycle of state interventionism and political and economic decay. The pervasive consequences (i.e., violence, hyperinflation, stagnation, and the corrosion of the law) are still perceptible, although Argentina has been able to sustain a democratic political system since 1983. It is not fortuitous that this overall successful experience coincides with a collapse of the state that was wracked by fiscal and political crises.

This article aims to analyze the relationship between business, government, and law in contemporary Argentina. Our working hypothesis is that business interests take advantage of any possible set of institutional mechanisms to pursue their goals as economic agents. This entails the development of specific strategies to maximize their lobbying capacity vis-à-vis the executive, judiciary, and legislative branches. We believe the history of judicial review in Argentina shows that litigation cannot be taken as an exogenous variable in the strategic game between interest groups and government (Elhauge 1991; G. Miller 1994). Although lifetime tenure makes federal judges less susceptible to interest group pressure, in the medium and long run, interest groups can also influence the general trend of judicial review directly and indirectly. They do so directly by manipulating the economic information that nurtures judicial decision-making, and indirectly by influencing the political process related to judicial appointments and promotions.

According to Mancur Olson, small or oligopoly-type groups have the organizational capacity to provide themselves with a collective good since each member's contribution to the group effort is noticeable. Thus business lobbying is easily explained by the fact that the firms in the relevant industries constitute a small or medium-sized group. These industries are small enough to organize voluntarily to provide themselves with a lobby to purchase favorable legislation (Olson 1971, 45, 143). By contrast, large ("latent") groups are unable to organize themselves to provide a collective good (i.e., generous legislation), unless the collective good is a byproduct of the provision of non-collective goods ("selective incentives"). Latent groups, like agricultural producers, can be mobilized with the aid of selective incentives such as recreational and social benefits, technical information, business or political contacts, or public offices (Olson 1971, 158–9). Once a latent group is organized through selective incentives, it can grow further by means of governmental promotion.

The chapter is organized as follows. The next section reviews the state of the art in the research on government and business in Argentina. We find that the literature is quite limited both theoretically and in scope. Many studies are narrowly focused on particular sectors and/or have been informed by ideological views regarding the role of the state and the market. Other studies do examine the interaction between business, institutions, and policies, but still lack a thorough understanding both of the main patterns of interaction and of the actual mechanisms through which that interaction operated.

Section two examines the role of legal institutions in shaping government and business relationships from Organización Nacional to the legal and institutional changes introduced in response to group pressures that arose during the economic turmoil of the 1930s. We focus on property rights, rural law, liberty of contract, and police power. We will depict those changes against the background of a theoretical framework drawn from the law and economics literature and the interest-group literature. In particular, we show how the first provincial attempts to regulate industry were struck down by the Supreme Court, which consistently relied at that time on laissez-faire economic doctrines. However, since *Ercolano c/ Lanteri de Renshawn* in 1922, constitutional doctrine regarding commercial activity and property (in line with a trend followed by the U.S. Supreme Court) began to legitimize a vastly expanded state role in the economy. *Ercolano* had enormous implications for the politics of regulatory policies as a leading case for establishing precedence. We evaluate these implications and identify the main actors and political influences involved in this case in order to characterize the way in which private interests took advantage of existing institutional settings to pursue their strategic goals.

The third section examines the development and expansion of the state apparatus. We claim that this was the result not only of private interests' demands for rents, but also of the state elite's capacity to capture public resources for certain strategic areas (i.e., infrastructure and defense capabilities) – strategic according to their views and perceptions of real or potential external threats. In any case, the constant enlargement of the state apparatus eventually became autonomous as a result of institutional inertia and the state's relative capacity to regulate, and even control, social conflict. Also, by expanding the demand for goods and services, the state helped create new economic actors who were therefore *incorporated* into the system.

11.1 The state of the art

In this section, we discuss the main existing contributions to the relationships between government, business, and law in Argentina. Again, the literature is quite limited both theoretically and in scope. Few studies pay attention to the interaction between business and political actors, the institutional framework they created, and the resulting policies. Nor do we have a clear understanding of the distributional and developmental consequences of the particular coalitions forged in the context of conflict, crisis, and even ordinary periods. Most studies focus narrowly on particular sectors and/or political and economic actors, and we lack a clear understanding of the main mechanisms of interaction. These limitations notwithstanding, we offer this chapter as an initial contribution toward filling the existing gap in the literature. To that end, we will now examine some of the main works on this issue. Even though we certainly do not exhaust all the available resources, we include a wide range of them to illustrate their scope and trends.

There are some fairly solid pieces of academic scholarship aimed at explaining the divisiveness, high degree of domestic confrontation (political and social), instability, and eventual economic failure of Argentina in the twentieth century. They all share, either tacitly or explicitly, the purpose of explaining the sharp contrasts between the nation's amazing record between the 1860s and the late 1920s, and the – by all standards – puzzling and disappointing performance from the 1930s to the present. It can then be argued – to (ab)use the jargon – that these studies somehow have the same dependent variable; however, given the different theoretical and methodological conceptions, they focus on varied independent variables.

Two main approaches can be noted: theorists demonstrate a preference for either structural or for political/ideological explanations. Some contributions combine both in a sort of path-dependent fashion. In general, though, it is not difficult to perceive the biases of the period in which they were made. In the structural domain we include the work by Corradi (1985), de Sagastizábal (1990), P. Lewis (1990), Mallon and Sourrouille (1975), Peralta-Ramos (1992), and Randall (1978). We primarily examine the books by Waisman (1987) and Wynia (1978) as examples of political/ideological explanations.[1]

Particularly in regards to the relationship between business and government, some contributions argue that both economic and political factors explain the Argentine decline: the strength (and rent-seeking strategies) of the landlords (*terratenientes*);[2] the relative fragility (and, later, dependence upon the domestic market) of the industrial bourgeoisie; the transformation of the urban working class (originally well organized and articulated, although always quite divided both politically and ideologically) into a state-related, homogeneously Peronist-corporatist movement;[3] the growing power of the armed forces, unquestionably the most influential state actor in contemporary Argentine history;[4] the divisiveness and weakness of both political parties and civil society groups; and the increasingly recurrent violation of the Constitution and the rule

---

[1] While the Argentine experience is by many accounts quite unique, some of the processes and issues that we are addressing in this chapter can be compared to other countries in the region. Space does not permit us to embrace such a comparative-minded approach, for which the reader may consult, among others, Díaz Fuentes (1994); Hirschman (1987); Remmer (1976, 1984); and Rueshemeyer, Stephens, and Stephens (1993).

[2] Center-periphery relationships (by which we mean, in this context, federalism) are crucial to understanding the Argentine political system as well as the creation of rents, subsidies, tariffs, and other protectionist policies. We comment more on this issue below, but the origins and coalitions supporting protectionism emerged early in the 1860s (Chiaramonte 1962–63). Tucumán was the most effective province in bargaining for and securing tailor-made policies. See Bravo (1963), Girbal de Blacha (1988), Guy (1976), and Rosenzvaig (1987).

[3] See Munck (1987) and Cheresky (1981).

[4] See Rouquié (1978) and Buchrucker (1994).

of law. Thus, it is apparent that these factors combine to help explain the Argentine political-economic conundrum. However, many important questions remain unanswered, such as: Why were virtually all economic and political actors, including the armed forces, so prone to internal confrontations? Why was it so difficult to establish relatively stable economic and political compromises, democratic or not, which in turn could have contributed to more predictable business and political environments? Given the inefficacy of formal political arrangements, which institutional and political mechanisms contributed to prevent and/or buffer social and political conflicts? How exactly did those mechanisms affect the development of state agencies and public policies?

These questions lead us to consider another array of literature that focuses on the development of the state and its eventual impact on economic, political, social, and cultural issues. Drawing from the debate that dominated much of the social and political science community in the late 1970s and early 1980s, we can label this strand of scholarship "state centered". For example, authors such as Cavarozzi (1992), Most (1980, 1991), O'Donnell (1976), Oszlak (1997), Pomer (1988), and Sikkink (1993) claim, and to a certain extent also show, that state actors and agencies did indeed have enormous autonomy to set policy and political goals as well as to pursue them.[5] Interestingly, this pattern remained basically unchanged during both authoritarian and democratic periods, as there was an overall consensus about the importance of state interventionism among the main social and political actors. Moreover, many programs and policies have long-term implications as they create entitlements or demands for financing that are very hard to remove. In short, due to rigidities, inertia, and legal restraints, the enlargement of the state apparatus had multiple effects in the economic, political, social, and cultural realms.

We know that the infrastructural power of the state (Mann 1993) is fundamental in penetrating society and creating the actual capacity to control conflicts and secure territorial integrity. Oszlak studied the golden years of growth and development in Argentina. Even then, although the state had a limited role in the economy (reflecting the liberal economic principles that were popular in that era and that shaped the 1853–60 Constitution), the expansion of the state apparatus was critical to every aspect of society. From the railroad system that joined the country to urban infrastructure, the building of military capabilities, and the creation of the education system, the state's enlargement encouraged economic and social development, and vice versa.[6] Yet the actual state-centered

[5] The fiscal consequences of the state expansion were not trivial as demonstrated by Oszlak (1997) and Diaz Alejandro (1970). See also Alhadeff (1985) and Jones (1985).

[6] Indeed, the development of the railroad system was the key variable in the development of Argentine capitalism. See, in particular, C. Lewis (1985); see also López del Amo (1990).

economic and political model was set up in the 1930s and grew steadily until the early 1980s (Berensztein 1998; Cavarozzi 1992). What we lack is a clear understanding of this dynamic. Which areas grew the most? What sectors benefited from it? Who decided which spheres ought to be developed, and how? While we do not answer all of these questions, in the present chapter we do provide some data that helps us understand the scope, complexity, and intensity of this process.

Defining the winners and losers of state expansion is not a simple task, for proper sectoral and time considerations should be made. There is a general agreement that between the 1860s and 1930 a dynamic Argentine economy had trickled down to virtually all those formally included in the workforce (i.e., indigenous groups notwithstanding). Yet land owners, financiers, and others related to export services were particularly better off. Also, the increasing number of public employees (e.g., bureaucrats, teachers, military personnel) and other service sectors nourished the growth of the middle class. Deciding who has won or lost the most since the 1930s is, however, more controversial. Traditionally it has been argued that, to foster an import substitution industrialization scheme, there was a redistribution of wealth that was biased against the rural economy. Hence, the industrial bourgeoisie and the urban working class improved their standards, and increasingly so during the Peronist era.

In addition to considerations of wealth, incentives, and mechanisms for redistribution, it is apparent that since the 1930s, but principally since 1945, the so-called industrial bourgeoisie gained organizational resources and momentum as it became an important political and social actor (Acuña et al. 1998). It never was a homogeneous actor, though, for it was often divided by sector, size, and source (national and multinational).[7] But there was a common set of demands that united its different and even conflicting groups and sectors, including protectionism, an expansion of aggregate demand, low/subsidized credit, relatively low taxes, and control over organized labor. Therefore, it is not surprising that there was a close, but certainly not easy, relationship between the industrial bourgeoisie and Peronism (Lucchini 1990). That this relationship was established not only with a political movement, but also with the state itself (Mainwaring 1986), obviously implied the need to negotiate with both authoritarian leaders (O'Donnell 1976; Schvarzer 1991) and democratic ones (Villarreal, Palomino, and Itzcovitz 1986).

The fact that business actors had dealt directly with, and been related to, the state indicates that other means of interest representation, such as political parties, were not important. The literature on this issue corroborates such a

[7] See Katz and Kosacoff (1989) and Schvarzer (1991).

statement. Indeed, political parties did build relatively strong identities and networks (Cavarozzi 1995), but they failed to create a workable party system (de Riz 1986; Viguera 1995). In fact, firm identities can be considered a liability in so far as they impede the development of a working relationship with peers as symbolic factors prevailed over material ones (Berensztein 1990). As Smith (1974) suggests, the failure of democracy in Argentina can basically be understood as the result of sharp conflicts among political elites who were unable and/or unwilling to comply with the Constitution and the rule of law. The political system did not provide incentives, or effective constraints, to moderate political and social actors' behavior and strategies.[8] The failure of democracy in 1930 only made the situation more conflictual (Ciria 1968). The sweeping mutation of the Argentine political system since 1945 was only possible given the profound degree of erosion of the existing political-institutional framework and its leadership. Thus, the incorporation of the working class into the political arena (Collier and Collier 1991) was compensated both by the aforementioned new role for the industrial bourgeoisie, and by strategic changes on the part of rural interests (Lattuada 1988).[9]

In the legal literature there are scant references to the relationship between law and business groups. The general insulation of legal studies from political and economic research in all likelihood has hindered our understanding of how Argentine legal institutions, particularly in private law, shaped economic activities since 1860. The field of law and economics is in its infancy in Argentina, and hence we lack systematic applications of the growing literature in that discipline to Argentine private law. Legal research has also failed to apply interest group theory to legislative and judicial lawmaking in Argentina. However, Juan Bautista Alberdi, the founding father of the Argentine Constitution, left a thorough study of its economic foundations (Alberdi 1977). Judicial review has also been well studied. It is generally accepted that *Lochner* style judicial review prevailed in Argentina from the 1880s to the 1930s, particularly during Antonio Bermejo's tenure (J. Miller 1997).

11.2 From laissez-faire to interventionist legal institutions

The system of property rights that developed during the second half of the nineteenth century was well suited to economic growth chiefly based on exports of

---

[8] It is worth noting that during the recent democratic experience that began in 1983, the political elite finally created a successful, workable (but by no means transparent) pattern of interaction and negotiation (McGuire 1995), but that its relationship with the business community is still far from fluid or cooperative.

[9] The latter had been represented in the main political forces before 1945, but the emergence of Peronism forced a reassessment of their modus operandi.

land-intensive commodities. Pampean land, which had a very low opportunity cost, became advantageous as a result of growing European needs for primary goods, the rapid expansion of the railroad network, and massive immigration of labor and capital (Díaz Alejandro 1970, 9). The economic policy applied in those years can be seen as the application of the law of comparative advantages. Because of its template climate and fertile land, Argentina was very appropriate for cattle raising and grain cultivation.

The land ownership regime was founded on the national Constitution, the Civil Code, various land laws, and the provincial rural codes. Alberdi explicitly held that the Argentine Constitution embraced the liberal economic school of Adam Smith, as exposited by Jean Baptiste Say. He regarded this as something commendable, for "economic freedom is, as science acknowledges, the fountainhead of the wealth of nations" (Alberdi 1977, 4). The Constitution, enacted in 1853 and put into full force in 1860, establishes in Article 17 the inviolability of private property, thus providing for private property a protection clearer than the one afforded by the U.S. Constitution, which merely forbids the taking of property without due process of law. Article 14 guaranteed the rights to "work and exercise any legitimate trade," to "travel and engage in commerce," and to "use and dispose of property."

The Constitution established the bases of agrarian law, as Alberdi pointed out. Sale and leasing of national lands was one of the resources of the national treasury (Article 4), and congress had the power to use and sell those lands and to provide for the colonization of them (Article 67, paragraphs 4 and 16). Additionally, all foreigners enjoyed the right to own, purchase, and transfer real estate (Article 20) (Alberdi 1977, 124). However, the Constitution lacked a special provision guaranteeing contracts – in the style of the contract clause of the U.S. Constitution, it left this matter to civil legislation, with responsibility for enactment granted to the federal congress (Article 67, paragraph 11).

The Argentine Civil Code, like other civil codes in Europe and Latin America, regulated legal relations among private persons. Thus it contained rules governing obligations, torts, contracts, ownership, and inheritance. The civil law jurist and political leader Dalmacio Vélez Sarsfield was commissioned to draft the code (Cháneton 1938, 106–07). He did so from 1863 to 1869 and followed a great variety of sources. Karst and Rosenn (1975, 46) assert that almost none of the code's 4,051 articles are original. Relying on the estimations of Borchard and Eder, these authors mention the following sources: some 1200 articles were lifted from Teixeira de Freitas' draft code for Brazil (1856–65); 700 came from Aubry and Raw; 300 articles were taken from García Goyena, a Spanish author; 170 articles were taken from the Chilean Civil Code; 145 articles came directly from the French Civil Code; 78 articles came from Zacharie;

and 52 articles derived from Louisiana's Civil Code. Other articles were taken from different commentators and codes, including the Code of Prussia.

Despite its lack of originality, the Civil Code played a useful role in giving Argentine private law uniformity and stability. Prior to its enactment, the courts had to search for solutions in a complex array of Spanish and colonial provisions. The code, which congress enacted in 1869, mandates in Article 1197 that contracts have the same authority for parties as law. Since this provision cannot be abrogated by provincial legislatures, in practice Argentine law provided a strong protection against impairments of contracts. Unlike Andrés Bello, the draftsman of the Chilean Civil Code, Vélez Sarsfield rejected the doctrine of *lesión enorme*, which permits abrogation or modification of contracts that fix an extremely unfair price obtained by overreaching or unconscionable means. Vélez Sarsfield explained that rejection in the following terms: "We should cease to be responsible for our actions if the law should permit us to make amends for all errors or all our acts of imprudence. Free consent given without fraud, error or duress, and with the solemnities required by law, should make contracts irrevocable" (Karst and Rosenn 1975, 477). Nor did the code accept the theory of imprevision, which authorizes judicial termination or modification of the terms of a contract when the payment owed by one of the parties has become excessively onerous because of extraordinary and unforeseeable events. The doctrine of *lesión* and the theory of imprevision were only accepted by Argentine civil courts in the 1960s and eventually introduced in the Civil Code in the 1968 reform.

Alberdi pointed out that occupancy was the perfect mode of ownership acquisition in Roman law, and *traditio* the derivative mode. He emphasized that the contract, which was a remote cause of ownership for Romans, was sufficient to operate perfect and complete acquisition in the modern industrial economy (Alberdi 1977, 63). Given this doctrine on ownership acquisition, it is natural to find him some years later criticizing Vélez Sarsfield's code on the grounds that, unlike the French Civil Code, it subjects the emergence of real right to the transfer of possession of the sold good (Article 577). Alberdi contended that this requirement was anachronistic in the modern economy, where the greatest part of wealth was not land, but rather intangibles such as financial assets (Alberdi 1887, 94–5, 111–3). Although Vélez Sarsfield (1868) failed to address this issue in his reply, it is of little interest in view of the fact that public registries now play the informational role that transfer of possession had in old Rome. Moreover, just as in Rome, the chief factor of production in Argentina was land, which makes Alberdi's criticism difficult to understand. Be that as it may, the maintenance of this requirement for *in rem* protection did not affect the enormous economic growth that Argentina had in the years following the enactment of the Civil Code.

Though the Civil Code disregarded Alberdi's recommendation about the mode of property acquisition, it did establish the type of nonfragmented freehold that Alberdi advanced when he wrote:

> Any law depriving the present occupant or possessor of the incentives flowing from complete and absolute ownership renders her indolent, for nothing will spur her activity; lazy, because of the uncertainty in which it leaves its property or possession; and devastating and wasteful, giving her an interest to consume what she must seize from the imposed successor. (Alberdi 1977, 127)

Alberdi also recommended the rejection or repeal of any law that took away a land occupant's desire to sacrifice the present to the future and to improve the soil (Alberdi 1977, 126). He held that civil legislation should suppress various legal easements and testamentary privileges that came from Spanish feudal law, such as substitution and revocation rights.

Vélez Sarsfield introduced in his code various rules that limit an individual's capacity to break up property bundles. In particular, Article 2502 prohibits the creation of new types of estates (*numerus clausus*). In a footnote, Vélez Sarsfield wrote, "The multiplicity of real rights over the same goods is a fertile source of complications and conflicts, and can much damage the exploitation of those goods as well as the free circulation of real estate, perpetually embarrassed." Moreover, in the footnote to Article 2503 he justifies the suppression of *enfiteusis* and of the surface right, which he expressly prohibits in Article 2614, along with all kinds of prohibitions on alienation.[10]

The provisions of the Civil Code that guarantee the unity of ownership by preventing its voluntary disintegration have a clear economic foundation, recently systematized by Michael Heller in the course of his investigation of the causes of scarcity in Moscow's retail commerce during the transition from communism to capitalism. Heller studies the ways in which economic activities are affected by the decomposition of ownership rights into the hands of various holders. It is clear that Alberdi and Vélez Sarsfield were aware of the great hindrances to economic exploitation posed by the decomposition of property in medieval Europe, particularly in Spain. We suggest that in advancing complete, united

---

[10] During the late Middle Ages numerous prohibitions against alienation had become widely used in Spain to protect the privileges of nobility. The most popular were *mayorazgos* and *capellanías*. These prohibitions were also used in the viceroyalties of Peru and Nueva España, but were almost unknown in the Viceroyalty of Rio de la Plata (See Mariluz Urquijo 1978, 75–76). In Spain these restrictions were finally abrogated in 1820. In a recent effort to apply law-and-economic notions to Argentine property law, Kiper (1999, 222) says: "It may be observed that the spirit of our code is contrary to long or perpetual decompositions of property, which in practice deprived it of all its value and left it idle."

private ownership they tried to avoid inefficiencies associated with the so-called tragedy of the anticommons which occurs when transaction costs, strategic behavior, or cognitive deficiencies prevent the holders of several different property rights from coalescing the several back into a single bundle of rights. To be sure, Alberdi and Vélez Sarsfield did not articulate this modern notion, but they had a fine intuitive understanding of the underlying economic rationale of nonfragmented property. As we now know, the anticommons tragedy threatens the effective use and disposal of property, which was a great concern for both jurists. Heller holds that the tragedy of the anticommons manifested in the empty Moscow storefronts can be attributed to the incorrect design of property rights (Heller 1998).

Public land was privatized thorough bonds, rewards to the victorious military, and auctions (Muzlera 1943). Bernardino Rivadavia had attempted to establish during 1822–26 a system of public land tenure for a term of up to twenty years. The system, called *enfiteusis* after the Roman institution, was intended to serve both financial and economic goals and to avoid the inconveniences of large, perpetual land holdings (Lamas n.d.). After its demise during Rosas' dictatorship (Muzlera 1943), it would never be reestablished. It was common sentiment among political leaders in the 1860s that freehold property could provide greater security and certainty to titles and therefore encourage greater investments in the defense and improvement of the lands. As minister of government of the province of Buenos Aires, Nicolás Avellaneda promoted the enactment of the public lands law of 1867 that sought to produce a fair distribution of lands, respecting occupants and tenants. Avellaneda supported absolute ownership of fairly allocated and well-divided land. He abrogated *capellanías*, a prohibition against alienation that was definitively eliminated by the Civil Code (Cárcano 1972, 126–27). Avellaneda had a classical economic approach toward land property. For instance, he thought that "there are no truly normal prices, but only those that the market fixes, arising from spontaneous movement of transactions."[11] Once in the presidency, Avellaneda studied and passed in 1876 a federal law of public lands and colonization that tried to mobilize the economic potential of public lands and the rapid occupation of them by immigrants. Despite its laudable goals, the law allowed indirect colonization by companies, thus lending itself to abuses in the assignment of lands (Cárcano 1972, 152–63). In the province of Santa Fe, however, where colonizers did not have to compete with ranchers for land, the law gave rise to flourishing colonies (Adelman 1994, 65; Gallo 1983). In 1884, after completion of Roca's Desert

---

[11] Nicolás Avellaneda, from his *Escritos y Discursos* (Buenos Aires, 1910), quoted in (Cárcano 1972, 128).

Campaign, the government sanctioned a new Homestead Act modeled on the American counterpart. However, unlike the American act, in Argentina the law did not facilitate agrarian colonization, but rather enhanced the interests of *estancieros* who found in it a way to legitimize their occupation of vast extensions of Pampean land (Adelman 1994, 66–68; Cárcano 1972, 176–83).

In general, the way in which land legislation privatized public lands was inefficient, and gave insiders considerable advantage. This inefficiency probably had a larger impact than is usually suggested, given that the lands awarded in private ownership in the first years were more valuable than the ones privatized after 1880. However, there were no legal barriers to buying and selling or to leasing, and the land market was, at least during the period 1880–1913, generally competitive. The main hindrance to market allocation of land was the scarcity of long-term credit, although the size of landholdings varied efficiently with the prevalent type of economic activity, i.e., agriculture or cattle raising (Cortés Conde 1978; Díaz Alejandro 1970, 35–40; Gerchunoff and Llach 1998, 33; P. Lewis 1990, 21; Taylor 1997). However, there is still debate about which activity or combination of activities was most appropriate for the fertile lands of the province of Buenos Aires (Gibson 1997; Lobos 1997).

The first Argentine rural code was enacted by the legislature of Buenos Aires province in 1865.[12] Governor Mariano Saavedra assigned Valentín Alsina to draft the rural code in 1862. He had worked on the same issue in 1856, when he requested of the Committee of Landholders (*Comisión de Hacendados*) opinions on how to regulate agricultural activities. Instead of closely following Spanish and Indian sources, Alsina relied on the customs and practices of the country that he knew quite well (Storni 1997, 199–200). The code laid down, in Article 6, a regime of full private ownership in accordance with the Constitution, and regulated in a detailed way cattle trespass, cattle transportation, agricultural work, ownership and identification of livestock, the operation of beef-salting works, and many other matters. Although land was in those years unfenced, the code tried to solve the economic problem of lost cattle. Article 145 of the code read: "After eighteen months from the date when this code is promulgated, every rancher in possession of lost beef cattle will incur a fine of one hundred thousand pesos" (Sbarra 1964, 65).

The code also established a system of closed range to allocate losses provoked by marauding cattle. Thus, Article 9 prohibited the invasion of someone else's land and established a fine for this transgression. According to Article 11, the owner of the trespassed land had a right to a fee estimated according to the

---

[12] See *Código Rural* (1865). In 1868 the Argentine Rural Society asked the Buenos Aires government to prepare a reform of the code. The committee formed by the Rural Society finished its work in 1870. See *Código Rural* (1870).

number of herds that invaded his property. If cattle damaged groves, ditches, or fences, landowners could claim compensation before a judge (Article 13).

It can be safely assumed that Alsina developed the closed range regime based on rural practices and landholders' opinions and that he was aware of the economic implications of the regime. There are two arguments for this hypothesis. First, Richard Newton and Francisco Halbach, two pioneers of wire fencing in Argentina, were members of the Committee of Landholders that advised Alsina in the drafting of the code (Sbarra 1964, 41, 51). Second, the economic literature on rural law suggests that the gains (and costs) of shifting to a closed range policy are transparent to ranchers and farmers. In the United States, Ellickson (1991) shows that cattle trespass law in Shasta County, California evolved in the form of spontaneous social norms, and Kantor (1998) demonstrates that livestock enclosure in the postbellum South arose from political protest. We also know that Domingo Faustino Sarmiento advocated cattle fencing in the newspaper *El Nacional* (Sbarra 1964, 58–59). Wire fencing, which became widespread in the Pampas after 1875 (Sbarra 1964, 92), facilitated the expansion of cultivated land and increased the economic value of land in general.

In his recent analysis of the rule of law, Cooter (1997) holds that economic efficiency is well served when state law responds to social norms. By providing more certain and secure enforcement of social norms, state law diminishes enforcement costs while retaining the cooperation-promoting features of social norms. "State enforcement is more certain because a written law provides a canonical formulation of the underlying obligations and, in an ideal situation, courts apply the rule with impartiality. State enforcement is more secure because of the state's monopoly on official use of force" (Cooter 1997, 117). In our opinion, the rural code drafted by Alsina is an example of good state law, as it was designed following the opinions of its very addressees.

Since the eighteenth century the *Ordenanzas de Bilbao*, Spanish commercial norms that dated from the fifteenth century, regulated commercial activity in the River Plate. Though the guild (*Consulado*) was abolished in 1820, the guild's court, the *Tribunal de Comercio*, continued to apply *jus mercatorum* until the 1850s (Adelman 1999, 145–50). However, the sanction of French commercial code in 1808 and of Spanish commercial code in 1829, and the increasing discomfort with the Tribunal's uncertain, subjective way of handling disputes, created a strong climate of opinion in favor of shifting to a system of formal, codified commercial law. Finally in 1856 Vélez Sarsfield (then minister of government) decided to draft a commercial code for the Province of Buenos Aires and appointed Eduardo Acevedo, a Uruguayan jurist, to undertake the task. Vélez Sarsfield and Acevedo worked for ten months and eventually submitted the text to Domingo Faustino Sarmiento. The bill was passed by the

Buenos Aires legislature in 1859, and in 1862 the federal congress turned it into a national law (Aztiria 1971, 15; Malagarriga 1961, 25). In 1889 congress promulgated a general reform to the code, in great part to solve the problem of normative overlapping brought about by the promulgation of the Civil Code.

The commercial code reform in 1889 assigned the governance of corporations to a board of directors with the meeting of shareholders and a corporate officer (i.e., the *syndic*) to exercise supervisory functions over the board and the accounts. Although the code did not explicitly mention voting privileges, Article 352, which contemplated the case of shareholders lacking voting rights, was interpreted as allowing the creation of shares with multiple votes (Halperín 1958, 136–37). The possibility of having unissued but authorized stock in all corporations allowed the board to implement capital increases up to a certain limit without need of shareholders' prior approval. Despite Article 353, which gave all shareholders the privilege to declare null any unlawful decisions taken by directors or the meeting of shareholders, minorities were, in practice, unprotected in the system of the commercial code. The creation of corporations needed authorization by the executive branch (Article 318), but Article 342 only provided for government control of corporations managing public utilities. However, as soon as the inspection agency was created in 1893, the inspectors began to lobby to expand their jurisdiction over all corporations, regardless of their activities (Halperín 1958, 406–7). On the basis of favorable opinions of the attorney general, issued in 1891 and 1894, the executive branch prompted the sanction of a law creating the Inspección General de Justicia, an administrative agency controlling all corporations. The law was finally passed in 1897. The widening of the reach of the Inspección General and the correspondingly expansive interpretation of the Commercial Code accords perfectly with the economic theory of bureaucracy, which assumes that bureau heads try to systematically maximize their budget (Niskanen 1971).[13]

Another area of Argentine law that had great economic impact during the period was the currency and banking system. After many unsuccessful trials, monetary law 1130, passed on November 5, 1881, finally established the monetary unity of the country based on a bimetallic standard. The system was modeled on that of the Latin Monetary Union led by France (Difrieri 1967, 122–23; Piñero 1921, 20–21). However, the development of a system to regulate the power to issue paper money was a long and tortuous process. On May 30, 1836, Rosas decreed the dissolution of Banco Nacional and its replacement by the Casa de Moneda, which performed limited bank operations in the ensuing years (Difrieri 1967, 80; Piñero 1921, 142). In November 1853, after

---

[13] Authors are grateful to Héctor Mairal for his comments on this paragraph.

the fall of Rosas' government, Vélez Sarsfield (the drafter of the Civil Code) proposed a bill to the Buenos Aires legislature to grant to the Casa de Moneda depository functions (Piñero 1921, 163). In October 1854 the legislature passed a law organizing the Banco de la Provincia (Piñero 1921, 169). In the 1870s the country accelerated the design of its bank system. On November 25, 1871, Buenos Aires province established the first bank empowered to issue mortgage bonds (Quesada 1894, 173–207). And one year later, on November 5, 1872, during Sarmiento's presidency, the congress established the new Banco Nacional. Although the issue was debated in congress, there is little doubt that the creation of the bank was authorized by Article 67, section 5 of the Federal Constitution (Piñero 1921, 244–57).

Several years later, the National Law of Guaranteed Banks of 1887 and the decree of mobilization of metallic deposits approved on March 19, 1889 contributed to the financial crisis of 1890, which in turn devoured the Banco Nacional and the Banco de la Provincia (Cortés Conde 1989, 195–204; della Paolera and Taylor 2001, 55–60; Piñero 1921, 292–93). In 1891, once the crisis was surmounted, the government founded the Banco de la Nación Argentina to replace the old Banco Nacional, and in 1904 the Banco de la Nación Argentina was completely reorganized as a state-owned bank (Dieulefait 1970, 113–166; Piñero 1921, 344). As regards the Banco de la Provincia, it was only reestablished in 1906 and merged with the Banco de Comercio Hispano Argentino, a private bank (Difrieri 1967, 133; Piñero 1921, 355–60).

Unlike banks authorized to issue paper money, private deposit and discount banks were allowed to operate under the norms of the Code of Commerce as ordinary companies with no specific regulation. They were under no reserve requirements. Only in 1907 did law 5125 establish the requirement to submit monthly balances to the Inspección General de Justicia (Difrieri 1967, 149–50). This free legal environment, which allowed many private Argentine and foreign banks to flourish in a period of around half a century, would be completely changed with the bank reform of 1935. In that year various bank laws were passed, including the law creating the Central Bank (law 12155) and the law that regulated for the first time the operation of private banks in Argentina (law 12156) (Vilaseca 1988). The latter law laid down a reserve requirement of 16 percent for sight deposits and 8 percent for time deposits; it fixed, however, no capital requirements.

Constitutional judicial review by the Argentine Supreme Court accompanied the economic policy by implementing a model of limitations on government, which held sway from the 1880s until the 1930s. In 1903, when Dr. Antonio Bermejo assumed his office as Justice of the Court, this model was at its zenith. During this period, the Court protected private property from police power, struck down state legislation intervening in the economy, and grounded its holdings in Alberdi's ideas and the principles of free trade.

In two industrial sectors, sugar and wine, provincial governments tried market regulations that were annulled by the Court. In 1902, for the first time, Tucumán province attempted to solve the problem of falling sugar prices through regulation of supply (Rougés 1991, 8). Ernesto Tornquist asked Governor Lucas Córdoba to promote a law assigning shares and differentially taxing the production of sugar above a certain limit. The provincial law of June 14, 1902, known as *ley del machete*, established a quota system devised by Tornquist. It was widely opposed. The law benefited Tornquist and his friends, whose factories received 35 percent of the total sugar quota. According to the law each kilo of sugar produced over the specified limit would be taxed 40 centavos (80 times larger than the normal tax of one-half centavo) which could be reclaimed only if the sugar was exported (Guy 1980, 133–34).

Clodomiro Hileret and the Nougués brothers started legal actions and eventually brought their case to the federal Supreme Court (Zavalía 1920, 351–54).[14] Hileret argued that the quota and the tax violated the plaintiff's right to "work and exercise any legitimate trade" (Article 14 of the Constitution) and that the policy of establishing differential market shares encroached upon the principle of equal protection under the law (Article 16). The province argued that the law represented reasonable regulation of the plaintiff's rights and an attempt to further the economic interests of the entire province, including the plaintiff's.

The Court gave a restrictive interpretation of the state's police power in both cases, its ruling in *Hileret* being clearly grounded in classical political economy:

> If the regulation imposed on sugar production were acceptable, it could be rendered extensive to all industrial activities; then the economic life of the Nation, along with the liberties grounding it, would be placed in the hands of legislators or congresses who would usurp, by ingenious means, all individual rights. Governments would be empowered to set the quantity of grape the vine grower can lawfully produce; the quantity of grains the farmer can produce; the quantity of livestock the rancher can raise, and so on, until we sink into State communism, in which governments would rule industry and trade and manage capital and private property.[15]

In addition, the Court maintained that the impugned law rendered production above a given limit impossible, for the tax's amount surpassed the sale price of sugar, therefore violating the right to exercise any legitimate industry. In the face of the Court's decision, the Tucumán government repealed the law; however, in the meantime, more than a year and two harvests had passed. Many planters had

---

[14] *Hileret c/ Provincia de Tucumán*, CSJN 98 Fallos 20 (1903), and *Nogués Hermanos c/ Provincia de Tucumán*, CSJN 98 Fallos 52 (1903).

[15] CSJN 98 Fallos 51 (1903).

ceased cultivating cane, and although they started again after 1903, ripening of the stalks took several years (Guy 1980, 134). Tucumán passed new regulatory measures of sugar cane production in 1927, 1932, and 1937 (Rougés 1991, 10–15). Unlike the machete law, these measures were never challenged before the federal Supreme Court.

In *Hileret* and *Nougués* the Court adopted a very restrictive interpretation of state's police power. According to this interpretation, police power was confined to cases in which public order, morals, hygiene, and the provinces' well-being were likely to be seriously affected. In his erudite study on the Argentine Court, Jonathan Miller suggests that the Court took a laissez-faire economic philosophy for granted. It offered only minor citations of Alberdi and the Constitutional Convention of 1853, and made no reference to U.S. decisions. Clearly, a state-run cartel was inimical to that economic philosophy (J. Miller 1997, 137).

The Court embraced the same doctrine in three cases challenging laws passed by Mendoza to create a state-run cartel in the wine industry.[16] In *Grosso,* the Court struck down a law establishing a tax on wine production but offering a bounty to the members of the province's wine producers' cooperative. The cooperative was a cartel authorized to establish monthly sales quotas in accordance with market demand. The province reformed the law by creating a governmental agency authorized to regulate the wine market, but the Court also declared this law unconstitutional in *Passera* (J. Miller 1997, 138–39).

Ironically enough, the emergence of federal interventionist legislation in Argentina, and the Supreme Court's deference to it, appeared in the name of free competition. The first important measure was taken by the government in 1922 as a form of ameliorating the effects of monopoly and abuse in the commercial and residential rental market. After the war and amid a massive wave of immigration, housing prices had soared. The government tried to freeze rents through law 11157. The law was challenged in the case *Ercolano.* The plaintiff adduced that the regulation of rent prices is incompatible with the right to use and dispose of property, the principle of inviolability of property, and the prohibition on altering fundamental guarantees through regulatory provisions, respectively set forth in Articles 14, 17, and 28 of the Constitution. The Court held that the presence of both strong public interest and monopoly gives rise to "conflict between the right of an individual wishing to freely use his property and the interest in preventing major damage potentially caused upon society by the abuse of such freedom." It adds that ownership is subject to numerous

---

[16] *Grosso c/ Provincia de Mendoza*, CSJN 128 Fallos 435 (1918); *Laborde Hermanos c/ Provincia de Mendoza*, CSJN 131 Fallos 219 (1920); and *Passera c/Provincia de Mendoza*, CSJN 139 Fallos 358.

restrictions in the Civil Code, which are based on society's economic interest, and that the same rationale should apply to law 11157 given the housing crisis and speculation and rises in rent prices. Regarding the monopoly issue, it says, "maybe there has not been a real monopoly, but there is no doubt that there has been a prolonged situation of virtual monopoly with all its associated effects." In his famous dissidence, Dr. Bermejo warned about the possible dangers of adopting the Court's interpretation: "The economic life of the Nation, and the liberties promoting it, would be confiscated by legislatures or congresses using shrewd rulings to usurp all individual rights until a situation of State communism would be reached, where governments would control industry and commerce, and play the role of arbitrators of private capital and industry."

Ercolano can be viewed as a turning point in the Court's conception of police power. Although the Court protected vested rights stemming from contracts in *Horta c/ Harguindeguy* (1922), and declared the rent-control law unconstitutional in *Mango c/ Traba* (1925), deducing that the state of emergency had ceased, *Ercolano* was the first decision allowing serious statutory transgression of contractual liberty on grounds of public interest. The new conception of police power, more fully acknowledged in later decisions, was congenial to the new trend of judicial deference that was developing in the United States and that reached its final shape in New Deal jurisprudence (Dalla Via 1999, 382–83; De Jesús and Gonzales Biondo 1990; Lynch 1982).

In the 1930s and 1940s, regulatory legislation became widely accepted by the Court as consistent with Constitutional provisions. As Miller says, "the Argentine Supreme Court supported essentially all the changes favored by the economic elite" (J. Miller 1997, 144). Economic interventionism's most propitious soil was undoubtedly the beef industry, precisely the sector ruled by the most conservative wing of Argentine society. Unhampered free markets had been the firm position of stockmen and their British clients since 1880. But when American companies entered the sector, the specter of monopoly loomed.

Although the production of *tasajo* was known in the River Plate region from the beginning of the nineteenth century, the growth of fresh beef exports to Britain began in the 1880s when British companies erected meatpacking factories in Campana and Zárate. In 1900, Britain suspended the importation of live animals because Argentine livestock were infected with hoof-and-mouth disease. This provoked an expansion of the packers' business. In 1907 the growth of its home market led the United States to look for Argentine sources of chilled beef. This marked the beginning of U.S. investment in the flourishing Argentine meat packing industry (Crossley and Greenhill 1977, 290–94).

Meat packers established in Argentina were exposed to competition. Although meatpacking plants were more costly than beef-salting works and had economies of scale, the establishment of new factories was not outside local capital's possibilities, as the Sansinena plant exemplified. Even if packers' combinations were sometimes feasible, they were inherently unstable given the lack of government support. In strict accordance with the teachings of modern game theory, defection in the price agreements often occurred (Crossley and Greenhill 1977, 304–5). When Argentine cattle growers, allied with consumers, started advocating antitrust control in the late 1900s, they were most probably attempting to capture a part of the surplus available in the beef industry without the long-run investments needed to enter the meat packing business. The purchase of favorable legislation was less risky and also less expensive thanks to the nationalistic feelings that Argentine ideologues and writers, such as Adolfo Saldías and Juan Agustín García, were disseminating.

In 1909, deputies Carlos and Manuel Carlés, members of a cattle-owning family, introduced the first bill to prohibit any trust or joint action in the meat packing business. Far from being engaged in an anti-imperialist crusade, the Carlés brothers were defending British meatpackers and their allied local interests as the Chicago-based packing factories were already shipping around half of the chilled beef exported from Argentina (Smith 1969, 59). The attempt to pass the bill failed again in 1913, and the main argument against it was based on the convenience of maintaining the free market in the sector. Indeed, British consumers benefited from the arrival of the Americans in the Argentine meatpacking industry, which lowered the price of chilled beef, as seen in Figure 11.1 (Crossley and Greenhill 1977).

The outbreak of the war changed these circumstances. The price of beef soared during the war years, and toward the end of the war beef producers and consumers had become dissatisfied. These sentiments made an alliance of cattlemen and consumers possible. However, the passage of the antitrust law only occurred in 1923 (law 11110) when the effects of the reduction of beef exports and the fall of livestock prices that had started in 1919 became serious for livestock growers. This shows that they were the key players in the alliance (Smith 1969, 80). The meatpacking houses protected their profits by driving down the prices for livestock through the economic power of their pool (Smith 1969, 83–85). The emergence of a project to counteract meatpackers' bargaining power by a state-run cartel was only a matter of time. In 1923 the Congress passed a number of regulatory measures: governmental inspection and supervision of the beef trade (law 11226), a minimum price on the sale of cattle for export, and a maximum price on the local sale of meat (law 11227) and the sale of cattle on a live-weight basis (law 11228). The laws were not enforced, however, while the meatpackers pressured the government by suspending the purchase of steers. A new round of beef industry regulation would come as a

Fig. 11.1. Prices of Argentine mutton and beef at Smithfield, 1898–1926
Annual average, index 1913 = 100

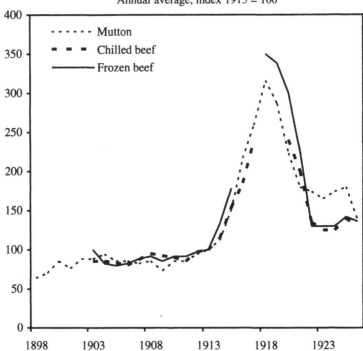

Notes: Broken line indicates accurate figures not available.
Source: From Weddell and Company's *Review of the Frozen Meat Trade,* quoted by Crossley and
Greenhill (1977).

response to the post-Depression cattle crisis in 1933, which caused a dramatic
fall in beef prices (see Figure 11.2). The institutional climate was at that moment
ripe for advancing rampant interventionist legislation. The so-called meat law
(law 11747), sanctioned in that year, established the National Meat Board (Junta
Nacional de Carnes) and the Argentine Meat Producers' Corporation (CAP) and
enforced former laws 11226 and 11228. The Meat Board, which was funded
through a compulsory fee extracted from cattle sellers, had powers to inspect the
accounting books of meatpacking companies and to fix minimum prices. The
national meatpacking house would compete with foreign meatpackers and thus
preempt a purchasing boycott such as the one seen in the 1920s. The meat law
would serve as the model for later interventionist legislation in Argentina. For
nationalist authors, the law represented the practical application of the British
plan to reestablish imperial dominion over Argentina (Puiggrós 1957, 128).

Fig. 11.2. Reaction to the depression: monthly prices for cattle bought on ranches, 1929–33

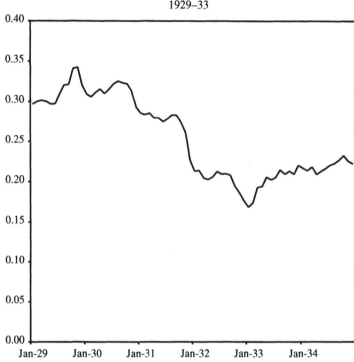

Notes and sources: Junta Nacional de Carnes (1937, 17–18). A similar graph is presented in Smith (1969, 139).

On the basis of the theoretical assumptions made at the outset of this paper, one might think that the meatpacking factories established in Argentina, given their smaller size, had advantages over cattlemen in lobbying for favorable governmental measures. Central to the meatpackers' agenda was preventing the government from establishing minimum prices for cattle. Cattle breeders and fatteners, on the contrary, constituted latent groups; as such, they could organize only if rural organizations provided selective incentives. From 1900 to 1946 the Argentine Rural Society (Sociedad Rural), the strongest rural organization existing at the time of the great government intervention of 1933, had between 2,000 and 5,000 members among whom only about 10 percent of stockmen were represented (Smith 1969, 50). This relatively small representation confirms the organizational difficulties of latent groups, but also suggests that the association managed to provide selective incentives, the identification of which requires specific research. Even granted that sufficient selective incentives were being generated, it remains to be explained why a small group (the packers), with fewer organizational costs, was unable to stop the legislative program of a larger group (the fatteners and breeders) that as yet was not fully organized.

One plausible hypothesis is that the organizational advantage of the packinghouses was outweighed by the political advantage of the stockmen. In fact, members of rural groups occupied key positions in the government and the congress (Smith, 1969, 48–49). We must also stick to our working assumption, made explicit at the outset of this paper, that litigation before the Supreme Court is an endogenous factor in explaining the emergence of interventionist legislation. Given the general climate of the time, favorable to economic interventionism, we can admit the hypothesis that the economic and commercial information supplied to the Argentine Supreme Court was directly or indirectly manipulated by organized groups.[17] In fact, we can speculate that public offices were one of the selective incentives provided by the Argentine Rural Society, although this observation would need further research. If this hypothesis were true, the rural sector was not only demanding but also supplying rural legislation, and we could conclue that the organizational variable plays a limited role in the business struggle for government support. However, the packers did not lose completely, as they acquired a seat in the Meat Board created by law 11747. On this point Smith remarks: "How the packers achieved this much remains something of a political mystery" (Smith 1969, 168). Our suggestion is that this mystery is actually the great organizational advantage of packers, which spared them from major economic failure.

Most of the regulatory legislation in the beef industry was challenged before the Supreme Court and succeeded. In the case *Compañías Swift De La Plata S.A., Frigorífico Armour De La Plata y Otras c/ Gobierno Nacional* a group of American meat packing houses argued that Article 11 of law 11226, which allows governmental inspection of all packinghouse accounting books and documents, violated the guarantees protected by Articles 14, 18, and 28 of the Constitution.[18] The Court said that, though the beef industry was born as a private industry, in time it became an industry that affects public interests and thus is worthy of state regulation. It added that Congress adopted this view in sanctioning law 11747, which created the Meat Board, and that this criterion was not subject to judicial review because it fell within the purview of legislators' jurisdiction to understand national reality and to give the country the most

---

[17] It is possible that the U.S. Supreme Court was more exposed to manipulation of information. Since the Argentine court used to follow American precedents, American business groups were indirectly influencing it! For a case study of how business groups have influenced the U.S. Supreme Court see G. Miller (1994).

[18] CSJN, 171 Fallos 348.

convenient norms possible in the face of such reality. The court made it explicit that its own criterion on the economic convenience of a certain norm could not be substituted for the congress' criterion. Moreover, it held that, as it met the requirement of a regulatory law required by Article 18 of the Constitution, the norm did not affect a privacy interest.

In the case *Inchauspe Hnos. c/ Junta Nacional de Carnes* the plaintiff attacked the constitutionality of the compulsory contributions to the National Meat Board established by law 11747. He alleged that the norm violated several guarantees laid down in the Constitution; to wit, the right to "work and exercise any legitimate trade" (Article 14), the freedom of association that entails the freedom not to associate (Article 14), the inviolability of private property (Articles 4 and 17), and the prohibition against the delegation of congress's tax powers (Articles 4, 17, and 67). The Court declared that the constitutionality of the challenged norm should be analyzed on the basis of two concepts: state of necessity and reasonable means. If there is a state of necessity, the Court reasoned, the measures addressed to resolve that state are presumed to pursue a legitimate goal. With respect to the state of necessity, the Court asserted that "by means of law 11747 the Congress sought to impede the monopoly and the arbitrary maneuvers and procedures of those companies that buy and process livestock, to create an instrument of struggle against the organization that dominated the beef trade, to increase internal and external consumption, to cheapen the latter by approaching producers to consumers, and to improve beef quality." As regards the reasonability of the measures adopted by Congress, the Court held that the plaintiff did not prove that the means adopted failed to bear relationship to the goals sought in defense of the national livestock industry, and cited as disproving evidence the fact that beef prices rose in the period 1935–37. It added that "...[liberty to contract and to exercise any legitimate industry] are not in any way hampered, and the law, far from preventing free competition, actually furthers it, since it was precisely enacted to fight against the monopoly and to enable cattle producers to compete with freedom."

In *Avico c/ de la Pesa*[19] the Court abandoned its commitment to protect vested rights expressed in *Horta*. By relying on decisions of the American Supreme Court, the Court backed the constitutionality of a law passed in 1933 that established a three year moratorium on mortgage payments, capped the rate of interest on mortgages at 6 percent, and halted executions and judicial sales (J. Miller 1997, 143–44). Other decisions taken in later years continued to back government interventions in markets. As Miller explains: "Almost no limits on state economic regulation survived after 1947, regardless of the political

[19] 172 Fallos 21 (1934).

philosophy of the government in power and the degree to which it tended to directly intrude on the Supreme Court's independence" (J. Miller 1997, 149).

The new interpretation of economic and commercial liberties meant, in practice, a new legal charter for economic activity. Instead of the Alberdian vision of constitutional review of regulatory laws, the Court established a weakened scrutiny confined to the reasonability of the means employed. In Argentina, whose majority parties amply support government control of the markets and whose Constitution very clearly precludes it, the view endorsed by the Court added to the constitutional alienation of politics and facilitated abuses that, over time, far exceeded the most aggressive regulations attempted in the United States. As one commentator recently said about Latin American politics, "Alberdi was not heeded outside of Argentina – and even there, his compatriots eventually threw away the enormous progress brought about by the triumph of his ideas in the previous century" (Vargas Llosa 1998, 38).

11.3 The infrastructural development of the Argentine state

This section discusses the expansion of the state apparatus in the 1930s. Our argument has unfolded as follows: a new role for the state was defined as a result of private interests' demands for rents and subsidies as well as of the capacity of state elites to capture public resources for certain strategic areas. Thus, a new public-private partnership was established despite (and to some extent, due to) political instability and the relative ineffectiveness of formal institutional mechanisms. This section discusses the steady expansion of the state apparatus as a consequence of this particular dynamic. Its relatively autonomous direction mainly was due to two factors: institutional inertia and the capacity to regulate and control (or even repress) social conflict. Also, by expanding the demand for goods and services, the state helped create new economic actors that were therefore *incorporated* into the economic and political system.[20]

Before analyzing the infrastructural development of the Argentine state, it is important to comprehend the political and institutional dynamic in which it unfolded. To that end, we first present a brief conceptual framework that stresses the entangling relationship between state and civil society. We will then analyze in more detail the characteristics of infrastructural development.

From the 1930s to the 1980s, Argentina developed the type of state that could collect and mobilize substantial economic resources, influence the implementation of development policies, and incorporate, shape, and even create social actors in the political arena who were able to centralize and control social and

---

[20] See Collier and Collier (1991), particularly with regard to their use of the concept incorporation and its impact on the formation and functioning of the party system.

political conflicts in diverse ways. Thus, the dominant economic, political, and social actors in such countries are closely associated with the state apparatus.

This particular kind of institutional configuration can be characterized as a state-centered matrix (SCM).[21] This concept emphasizes the relative importance of institutions, actors, and political processes related to the sphere of influence of the state as opposed to those associated with civil society, which perform a rather marginal role.[22] The concept of SCM certainly does not imply that the state monopolizes or rigidly controls the economic, political, and social environments. The relevant, though variable, role of civil society – such as urban and rural social actors, new social movements, and other autonomous groups – cannot be ignored. In Argentina, in fact, the expansion of the state created opportunities for rent-seeking strategies that had significant political and economic consequences.

Indeed, state-society relations were diverse and complex; while basically authoritarian, some democratic elements did prevail.[23] Interest representation was generally structured through corporatist arrangements.[24] The prevalence of these corporatist mechanisms explains the weakness of party systems in general and parties as organizations in particular. In this context, Argentine patterns of institutional development were very singular. The executive administered most of the material and political resources and therefore commanded the design and development of institutions, both political and economic. Such a concentration of power may have introduced a source of vulnerability and uncertainty in situations of crisis and political turmoil. Yet the otherwise strong executive branch contributed to the achievement of some sort of political order, partially because of the concentration and overlapping of powers and resources within, or close to, the presidency.

In addition, the state apparatus controlled a myriad of economic and political resources that helped coordinate economic, political, and social milieus as it established various regulatory mechanisms. A complex set of agencies and institutions, though often poorly differentiated with respect to design and location, empowered the central state to become the organizational cornerstone of

---

[21] See Cavarozzi (1992, 1997). The source of this concept stems from what Albert Hirshmann (1973) called the politico-economic matrix of inflation in Latin America.

[22] Following the Gramscian notion, civil society includes the market and other autonomous spheres of social interaction, which are totally or relatively isolated from the state.

[23] See Most (1980).

[24] In some cases, the state selectively accepted civil society actors, using the capacity of legal recognition as a disciplinary tool. In other cases, the state created social actors, even at the expense of destroying other, more independent organizations that competed for the same constituencies and resources. On the development of corporatist structures in Argentina see de Riz et al. (1987).

the political system. Also, the president, who was both chief of state and head of government, controlled a plethora of institutional, political, and symbolic resources. As the system of checks and balances never worked on a practical level, no consensual and legitimate means existed to counterbalance the hegemony of the executive power.

The resulting institutional arrangements tended to generate cycles of conflicts, including episodes of violence and instability. Moreover, those arrangements contained and nurtured the main causes of their eventual decadence and implosion. In particular, let us stress two main sources of conflict.

First, as in any presidential system, a crisis of governance could result in a lack of confidence and legitimacy in the presidency and eventually in a crisis of the state. In any event, the weakness of the executive power could disturb, and even halt, important parts of the governmental structure. There was no institutional buffer to prevent the executive from being punished in case of mismanagement or unexpected shocks. Consequently, as the president was held accountable for the (often impetuous) political course, the overlapping of state and political leadership turned out to be a source of uncertainty and instability for the whole political system.[25]

Second, the administrative apparatus of the state did not reach a level of adequate proficiency, nor did it achieve autonomy vis-à-vis politicians (whether elected or not). On the contrary, political elites (both authoritarian and democratic) had a tendency to actually colonize the state apparatus to build and strengthen clientelistic relationships, thus securing constituencies (electoral, political, or both). This, in turn, had at least two negative consequences. First, politics developed a strong dependency on the state: not only public financing, but also the spheres, mechanisms, and means for bargaining and interaction were all somehow related to, if not totally manipulated by, the state. Therefore, political actors found it difficult to develop autonomous organizations, as well as to establish independent links to civil society. Second, as the central state accumulated the bulk of the political resources, political actors oriented their strategies to maximize their control over those resources, thus downgrading other choices and spheres of influence such as local politics.

Having discussed the concept of a state-centered matrix and its main implications, we turn to analyze the infrastructural development of the state in Argentina. Table 11.1 shows one dimension of state enlargement – the creation of regulatory and consulting committees that included a myriad of economic activities. Note that most of them were created by decree. Tariffs or quotas provided for the financing of these agencies, which included representatives

---

[25] For a critical view of the presidential system, see Linz (1990) and Linz and Valenzuela (1994).

Table 11.1. *Juntas and regulatory/consulting commissions*

Office	Decreto or law	Date	Characteristic
Comisión Nacional de Azúcar	Decreto N 702	11/05/1928 Constitution 2/01/1931	
Comisión Nacional de Fomento Industrial	Decreto N 58	15/01/1931	
Comisión Nacional de Patatas	Ministerial Resolution	8/07/1931	
Comisión Nacional de Fibras Textiles	Decreto N 1401	14/11/1931	
Comisión Nacional de Extracto de quebracho	Decreto N 25092	15/10/1933	
Dirección Nacional de Elevadores de Granos	Decreto N 11742	7/10/1933	Transitory
Junta Nacional de Yerba Mate (Later Comisión Reguladora de la Producción y el Comercio de la Yerba Mate)	Decreto N 30854 / Decreto 12236	8/11/1933 / 4/10/1935	Autonomus and Permanent
Junta Reguladora de Granos	Decreto N 11742	28/11/1933	Transitory
Junta Reguladora de la Industria Lechera (later Dirección de la industria Lechera en el Ministerio de Agricultura)	Decreto N 40140	12/04/1934	
Comisión Nacional de la Industria Lechera con Comisión Consultiva Honoraria	Decreto N	5/08/1939	
Comisión Nacional de Aceite	Decreto N 42621	5/06/1934	
Comisión de Productos Alimenticios Nacionales	Decreto N 44423	30/06/1934	
Juntas para promover exportaciones de carne dissolved by	Decreto N 46299 / Decreto N119263	27/07/1934 / 30/10/1927	
Comisión Nacional de la Industria vitivin'cola	Decreto N46837	11/08/1934	
Junta Reguladora de Vinos con Comisión Asesora Honoraria	Law 12137	24/12/1934	Transitory
Junta Nacional para combatir la Desocupación	Law 11896	21/08/1934	Autonomus and Permanent
Comisión de harinas	Ministerial resolution	13/04/1935	
Comisión Nacional de Algodón	Decreto N 59802	27/04/1935	Autonomus and Permanent
Comisión Nacional de Granos y Elevadores	Law 12253	5/10/1935	Autonomus and Permanent
Comisión de Fruticultura	Ministerial Resolution	12/12/1935	
Comisión de Prestamos de Semillas	Decreto N 77114	22/02/1936	

Table 11.1. (Continued)

Office	Decreto or law	Date	Characteristic
Comisión de Petróleo y demás hidrocarburos	Decreto N 82162	8/05/1936	
Comisión Consultiva Nacional de bosques	Decreto N 83731	3/06/1936	
Comisión Nacional de Coordinación de transportes	Law 12346	5/01/1937	Autonomus and Permanent
Comisión Nacional del Carbón vegetal	Decreto N107529	12/06/1937	
Junta Consultiva de la Industria molinera	Decreto	14/05/1938	
Comité asesor de lanas	Decreto	24/05/1938	
Comisión de control de abastecimiento (later transfered to Dirección de Industria y Comercio del Ministerio de Agricultura	Decreto 40980	8/09/1939	
Consejo Agrario Nacional	Decreto N 53249	17/01/1940	
Junta Nacional de Carnes	Law N 12636	21/08/1940	Autonomus and permanent
	Law N 11747	7/10/1933	Autonomus and permanent

Source: Bunge (1940, 271–73).

from both government and the private sector and served as mechanisms for information sharing, lobbying, bargaining, and rent-seeking strategies.

The transformation of the business environment had dire effects on public finances as the tax structure was refurbished to meet the new realities of an increasingly inward-oriented economy. Table 11.2 shows how the sources of tax revenue changed during the 1930s. Taxes on income, sales, and inheritance were created to compensate for the diminishing collection of export-related levies. This suggests that the government also had a revenue-seeking goal in the expansion of the domestic economy.

Tables 11.3 and 11.4 present evidence on the expansion of public demand and expenditures during the 1930s. Public demand expanded by 50 percent between 1925–29 and 1935–39. While public consumption increased 32 percent, public investment increased 66 percent. Notice also that the main stimulus took place in the second part of the decade, that is, when the economy had already recovered from the 1930 shock. Table 11.4 shows the evolution of public expenditures, which increased by 36 percent between 1925–29 and 1935–39.

One obvious concern is the fiscal impact of this public sector expansion. Table 11.5 reveals interesting information in this regard. While the federal budget experienced substantial imbalances, both at the beginning and at the end of the decade, it was balanced by the mid-1930s – just when the acceleration of public demand started. National income grew around 57.7 percent during the decade as total expenditures expanded 60 percent.

The expansion of domestic investment can be attributed primarily to public works projects, in particular expenditures on roads and highways. As Table 11.6 shows, public investment represented less than 11 percent of the total investment during the 1925–29 period, while it was 25.3 percent for the 1935–39 term. The same tendency can be seen with regard to investment in construction. Construction represented 54.6 percent of total investment in 1925–29 and reached 67.8 percent in 1935–39. Table 11.6 also provides interesting data on investment by economic sector. Transport and communications received 21.5 percent of total investments during 1925–29 and attracted almost 35 percent by the 1935–39 period. The opposite trend can be seen in the rural sector, where investment declined to 4.8 percent per year. The industrial sector showed a decline of 3.9 percent per year, foreign investment fell by 12.7 percent per year, and the decrease in national investment was 2.7 percent during the 1930–39 period.

Table 11.7 illustrates the importance of public works using data on cement consumption and the construction industry. Between 1930 and 1938, the former increased by 66 percent. Cement was mainly used for paved roads and

Table 11.2. *Fiscal revenue as a percent of GDP*

Sources of Revenue	1930	1939
Customs and ports	56.7	29.6
Internal taxes	17.2	23.3
Land tax (*contribución territorial*), licenses, and stamps	11.1	10.7
Income	—	12.5
Sales	—	4.1
Inheritance tax	—	1.7
Post and telegraph	6.2	4.1
Others	8.8	14
Total	100	100

Sources: Memorias de la Contaduría General de la Nación; Memorias del Ministerio de Hacienda; Garcia Vizcaino (n.d.).

Table 11.3. *Public sector demand as a percent of GDP*

	Total	Public Consumption	Public Investment
1900–04	10.0	6.9	3.1
1905–09	11.8	6.2	5.6
1910–14	11	6.3	4.7
1915–19	9.7	8.0	1.7
1920–24	9.2	7.1	2.1
1925–29	10.5	6.9	3.6
1930–34	11.5	7.8	3.7
1935–39	15.1	9.1	6.0

Sources: 1925–34: CEPAL (1959); 1935–39: República Argentina (1955).

Table 11.4. *Total public expenditure as a percent of GDP*

	Total	Current expenditure	Capital expenditure
1925–29	15.6	10.9	4.7
1930–34	19.8	15.2	4.6
1935–39	21.3	14.8	6.5
1940–44	19.5	14.9	4.6

Source: CEPAL (1959).

Table 11.5. *Budget and fiscal deficit*
Millions of current pesos moneda nacional

Year	National income	Total expenditure	Surplus (Deficit)	Surplus/ expenditure
1914	250.1	419.6	-169.5	—
1915	237.2	399.8	-162.6	—
1916	240.5	374.6	-134.1	—
1917	241.0	389.6	-148.6	—
1918	308.3	421.1	-112.8	—
1919	389.6	427.9	-38.3	—
1920	493.9	459.8	34.1	—
1921	456.5	546.4	-89.9	—
1922	438.9	613.2	-174.3	—
1923	524.4	533.7	-9.3	—
1924	577.6	580.0	-2.4	—
1925	643.3	630.9	12.4	—
1926	619.3	652.3	-33.0	—
1927	658.4	884.5	-226.1	—
1928	702.9	695.8	7.1	—
1929	718.0	844.1	-126.1	—
1930	691.5	906.7	-328,4	36.22
1931	724.8	830.6	-106.4	12.81
1932	755.3	781.0	-25.7	3.29
1933	758.2	777.7	-19.5	2.50
1934	765.4	765.6	-0.2	0.02
1935	896.6	869.5	27.1	—
1936	1190.7	1166.3	24.4	—
1937	1994.7	2086.0	-91.3	4.37
1938	1175.2	1433.0	-257.9	18.00
1939	1570.9	1533.7	37.2	—
1940	1196.2	1491.9	-295.7	19.82

Sources: Memoria de la Contaduria General de la Nacion; Memoria del Ministerio de Hacienda; Garcia Vizcaino (n.d.).

streets, which increased by a factor of five during that period. Conversely, the construction industry suffered the consequences of recession. This is a significant trend in itself, but also because of the forward linkages that were created for other industries, particularly the auto industry. Table 11.8 reports on the development of the cement industry. Note that the number of firms and total capacity increased substantially, thus helping reduce imports.

It is worth elaborating on the development of the new road system. The government passed the Ley Nacional de Vialidad in 1932 with the goal of expanding the existing network from 2,000 to 30,000 kilometers. It was financed by new taxes on gas and oil, and by the appropriation of 1 million pesos from the treasury. This was a key initiative in the fortification of the infrastructual

Table 11.6. *Total gross fixed investment, components and changes*

	1920/1924 Share	Percent change	1925/1929 Share	Percent change	1930/1934 Share	Percent change	1935/1939 Share	Percent change	1930/1939 Share
Total	100.0	30.2	100.0	9.2	100.0	-11.8	100.0	5.1	-3.7
Public	7.8	27.2	10.8	20.1	16.7	-0.2	25.3	6.6	3.2
Private	92.2	30.4	89.2	8.0	83.3	-14.1	74.7	4.6	-5.2
Machines and equipment	37.5	24.1	45.4	11.3	37.0	-16.0	45.8	9.7	-4.0
Building	62.5	35.2	54.6	7.7	63.0	19.0	67.8	2.4	-3.5
National	86.5	34.9	85.5	8.7	85.4	-13.0	89.5	8.4	-2.9
Foreign	13.5	9.6	14.5	12.5	14.6	14.8	10.5	-19.9	-12.7
Agricultural	16.8	15.8	16.3	7.7	13.2	-25.6	14.1	7.5	-4.8
Industrial	15.4	26.4	16.0	7.9	15.4	-13.4	16.9	6.7	-3.9
Transports and communication	15.5	48.7	21.5	12.9	19.9	-8.2	34.8	7.0	-0.9
Other services	45.1	33.5	35.0	4.0	36.4	-12.6	24.3	2.1	-5.6
State	7.2	37.5	11.2	22.7	15.1	-9.9	9.9	4.0	-3.2

Source: CEPAL (1959).

Table 11.7. *Cement and construction*

	Consumption of cement[1]	Building in Buenos Aires	Building of paved streets[2]
1930	755.3	2523	1045
1931	744.7	1696	2847
1932	588.2	1195	2598
1933	530	1145	1765
1934	605.9	1484	1589
1935	752.4	1369	2611
1936	892.8	1245	3964
1937	1109.4	1647	4484
1938	1254.3	1781	5336

[1] In thousands of tons. [2] In thousand of square kms.
Source: Asociación de Fabricantes de Cemento Portland.

Table 11.8. *Evolution of the cement industry*

Year	Number of firms	Total capacity[1]	Production[1]	Imports[1]
1915	1	14	4	253
1920	3	166	79	125
1925	3	166	133	311
1930	3	511	412	343
1935	6	925	722	31
1936	6	1044	869	24
1937	8	1113	1010	99
1938	10	1361	1179	75
1939	11	1812	1135	20
1940	11	1904	1049	1
1941	11	1904	1160	—
1942	11	1904	1145	—
1943	11	1904	959	—
1944	11	1904	1080	—
1945	11	1904	1088	—

[1] In thousands of tons.
Source: Asociación de Fabricantes de Cemento Portland.

power of the state. Table 11.9 demonstrates the primitive state of the previous road system. Paved roads were very limited, as most of the network consisted of dirt or gravel roads. Also note that, as a result of the expansion of the new road system, the number of passengers using buses increased sevenfold between 1930 and 1939.

The development of a new road system served many purposes as the nation's territory gained better communication and became more integrated. Indeed, market transactions were facilitated by the improving infrastructure, which also invigorated the economy by expanding aggregate demand. As Table 11.10

Table 11.9. *Expansion of the road network*

	National network				Federal co-operation				Access roads to train stations (Law 5315)				Total
	Basic	Intermediate	Superior	Total	Basic	Intermediate	Superior	Total	Basic	Intermediate	Superior	Total	
1933	—	—	95	95	258	78	2	338	458	14		472	905
1934	568	165	134	867	2277	133	59	2469	874	5		879	4215
1935	856	182	71	1109	5211	282	56	5549	668	34	1	703	7361
1936	2166	771	392	3329	1965	331	48	2344	1289	35		1314	6987
1937	1612	529	678	2819	7402	265	81	4478	1069	59	4	1132	11699
1938	2117	617	297	3031	4708	367	107	5182	1325	100	3	1428	9641
1939	1899	969	243	3111	1466	523	77	2066	937	33	2	972	6149
1940	925	716	20	1661	772	319	53	1144	1222	60	4	1286	4091
1941	1616	1208	47	2871	958	628	31	1617	910	65	4	979	5467
1942	2517	777	95	3388	430	427	153	1010	798	36		834	5232
1943	1291	491	22	1804	810	488	10	1308	310	20	5	335	3477

Sources: Sanguinetti (1946, 195).

Table 11.10. *Oil production and derivatives*
Thousands of cubic meters

	Petroleum	Gas	Fuel	Diesel
1920	262.5		13.9	—
1925	952.2	41.4	255.6	—
1930	1431.0	90.8	1083.6	—
1935	2272.9	218.1	1110.9	
1936	2457.6	353.6	1227.4	123.7
1937	2600.1	273.0	1309.8	197.4
1938	2714.8	118.4	1319.8	296.5
1939	2959.2	117.0	1235.9	310.0
1940	3276.5	116.6	1417.3	349.2
1941	3409.8	111.2	1571.6	384.9
1942	3768.6	95.3	1616.7	359.5
1943	3948.4	76.5	1705.5	292.3
1944	3852.1	61.8	1657.3	266.2
1945	3637.5	58.9	1633.6	241.0
1946	3307.2	80.1	1578.3	329.3
1947	3473.3	81.9	1687.4	331.4
1948	3692.5	138.7	2052.8	440.7
1949	3591.4	197.9	2159.1	448.6
1950	3730.0	293.6	2708.2	583.5

Source: Estadística del Petróleo, Subsecretaría de Energía.

reports, the production of petroleum and gas roughly doubled between 1930 and 1939, and the production of diesel increased substantially in the second half of the decade.

Defense considerations were also at stake as the road system helped to complement, albeit not properly, the existing railroad infrastructure. This development allowed for an easier movement of troops and equipment. The Justo administration (1932–38) implemented other important programs to strengthen the armed forces; for example, the building of the Colegio Militar de Palomar, the Hospital Militar in Campo de Mayo, the Ministerio de Guerra, and the Ministerio de Marina. Table 11.11, which provides annual funding data, demonstrates the state's commitment to defense infrastructure during this period. By 1936, more than 24 percent of the National Budget was devoted to defense expenditures, including not only investments in construction but also generous pension programs. Table 11.12 includes information on arms procurement.

Table 11.13 shows data on industrial development. During the 1935–39 period, an expansion in the number of firms and white- and blue-collar workers, and an increase in value added and wages, reflect the impact of the new policies.

Table 11.14 includes information on population and employment. The num-

Table 11.11. *Cost of military constructions*
Millions of current pesos moneda nacional

1932	3.8
1933	5.1
1934	7.3
1935	9.5
1936	14.0
1937	27.0

Source: Rouquié (1978).

Table 11.12. *Cost of arms procurement*
Millions of current pesos moneda nacional

1928	42
1929	16.7
1930	27.9
1931	11.7
1932	8.9
1933	8.9
1934	9.8
1935	37.9
1936	46.8

Source: República Argentina (1938).

ber of government jobs increased around 37 percent during the 1930s. With regard to total employment, the percentage of governmental jobs increased from 6 percent in 1930 to 7.5 percent in 1939. As expected, nonrural jobs also increased in that period. They represented 55 percent of total employment in 1930 and 66 percent in 1939. Thus, these two sectors compensated for the loss of jobs in the rural sector.

In sum, the infrastructural development of the state had a profound impact on society as a whole. The expansion of public expenditures helped the economy recover from the 1930s crisis, but from 1935 it became a constant and ever more encompassing feature. Along with the previously analyzed changes in the orientation of the Supreme Court, the transformation of the state that took place in the 1930s should be understood as a turning point in Argentine history, particularly regarding the relationship between business and government.

Table 11.13. *Industrial development, 1935–54*

	1935	1937	1939	1941	1943	1946	1948	1950	1954
Number of firms	38456	46399	50361	53797	61712	86440	81937	83370	151828
Owners or directors	48822	52649	55915	61031	72002	115923	114969	121217	224956
Employees	49295	57403	63106	74086	87778	135484	136630	143523	166980
Workers	418020	496347	534605	633411	756222	938387	917265	923824	1055496
Owners' relatives employed	–	20342	21522	22234	25185	33958	28709	26244	50683
Wages and salaries paid in cash[1]	667.7	834.0	934.2	1075.1	1404.7	2635.2	4903.7	8068.7	14521.9
Value of elaborated products[1]	3251.4	4341.1	4668.8	5975.8	7997.2	15640.3	23138.6	37689.9	80899.9
Value added per industry*	1274.0	1512.3	1700.3	2008.6	2661.6	7662.5	11763.7	20123.5	41094.1

[1] In millions of pesos moneda nacional.
Source: Instituto Nacional de Estadísticas y Censos.

Table 11.14. *Population and employment*

Millions

Year	Total population	Total employment	Rural employment	Nonrural[1] employment	Government employment
1920	8.8610	3.4108	1.2807	1.9250	0.2052
1921	9.0920	3.5068	1.3798	1.9114	0.2125
1922	9.3680	3.0603	1.5035	1.8784	0.2208
1923	9.7070	3.7229	1.6537	1.8387	0.2305
1924	10.0540	3.8509	1.7572	1.8530	0.2407
1925	10.3580	3.9711	1.8290	1.8924	0.2497
1926	10.6520	4.0543	1.9664	1.9295	0.2585
1927	10.9650	4.1623	1.8109	2.0833	0.2680
1928	11.2820	4.2809	1.7901	2.2134	0.2774
1929	11.5920	4.4006	1.7246	2.3891	0.2868
1930	11.8960	4.4941	1.6828	2.5153	0.2960
1931	12.1670	4.5197	1.5971	2.6182	0.3045
1932	12.4020	4.4819	1.5419	2.6281	0.3118
1933	12.6230	4.5533	1.4773	2.7569	0.3190
1934	12.8340	4.7461	1.4038	3.0164	0.3259
1935	13.0440	4.8081	1.3576	3.1179	0.3326
1936	13.2600	4.9328	1.3505	3.2268	0.3556
1937	13.4900	5.0900	1.3389	3.3796	0.3714
1938	13.7240	5.2280	1.3548	3.4802	0.3930
1939	13.9480	5.3188	1.3892	3.5237	0.4060
1940	14.1690	5.4218	1.4253	3.5771	0.4194
1941	14.4010	5.5374	1.4666	3.6404	0.4304
1942	14.6370	5.6625	1.4615	3.7454	0.4557
1943	14.8770	5.7837	1.4597	3.8558	0.4682
1944	15.1300	5.8854	1.4717	3.8906	0.5231
1945	15.3900	5.9876	1.4867	3.9030	0.5978
1946	15.6540	6.1078	1.5061	3.9790	0.6227
1947	15.9290	6.2673	1.4914	4.0629	0.7129
1948	16.2640	6.0348	1.4866	3.7725	0.7757
1949	16.6680	6.1230	1.4446	3.8786	0.7999
1950	17.1500	6.2891	1.4797	3.9756	0.8338

[1] Excluding govenment.
Source: IEERAL (1986).

11.4 Conclusion

The widespread presence and burden of the state apparatus is one of the most distinctive features of contemporary Argentine history, permeating the relationships between business and government as well as the overall patterns of interaction between social and political actors. Indeed, these actors increasingly tended to look to the state for rents, subsidies, or other income distribution policies, given the concentration of power attained by the state apparatus. Moreover, state officials (be they elected ones, bureaucrats, or military cadres) became key players as they gained the authority to allocate (or refuse to allocate) a great quantity of resources. Thus, Argentina became a state-centered society.

We argued that, during the 1920s and 1930s, Argentina experienced a critical change in both doctrine and political dynamic. On the one hand, an inward-oriented, protectionist model emerged that created the foundations of corporatist and authoritarian schemes and policies. We understand the emergence of populism as a continuation of this process as the long-term expansion of the state apparatus bounded civil society's autonomy. Hence, strong incentives for a narrowed relationship between state and society had already been established.

After discussing the existing literature, we examined the role of law in shaping government and business relationships by focusing on legal changes introduced in response to group pressures arising during the economic turmoil of the 1930s. We showed how, from 1860 to the beginning of the 1920s, the Supreme Court struck down economic regulations issued by the federal government or the provinces, ruling instead in favor of laissez-faire economic doctrines. However, the *Ercolano* case of 1922 represented a turning point as the constitutional doctrine regarding commercial activity and property began to legitimize a vastly expanded state role in the economy. In particular, we studied legislative and judicial changes in the beef industry, which had enormous implications for the politics of regulatory policies, as a leading case for establishing precedence.

Finally, we examined the development and expansion of the state apparatus since the 1930s. Both political and economic actors were involved. The latter demanded rents and protections; the former multiplied their capacity to capture public resources. Firms, groups, and individuals developed strategies to take advantage of the opportunities this created, perpetuating the cycle of state interventionism. It is striking that the democratic experience that started in 1983 coincided with, and to some extent also provoked, the collapse of the state, which had become wracked by fiscal and political crises. The fragility and instability of the few democratic experiences that took place before 1983 can be understood in light of the framework proposed in this chapter, as can the events of the recent crisis of 2001, which showed that the development of a stable and credible legal-economic nexus remains a work in progress.

References

Acuña, Carlos H. et al. 1988. *Relación Estado-empresarios y políticas concertadas de ingresos: El caso argentino. (Política económica y actores sociales: La concentración de ingresos y empleo.)* Santiago: PREALC.

Adelman, Jeremy. 1994. *Frontier Development, Land, Labour, and Capital on the Wheatlands of Argentina and Canada, 1890–1914.* Oxford: Oxford University Press.

————. 1999. *Republic of Capital: Buenos Aires and the Legal Transformation of the Atlantic World*. Stanford: Stanford University Press.

Alberdi, Juan Bautista. 1887. El proyecto de código civil para la República Argentina. In *Obras Completas*. Buenos Aires: Imprenta de "La Tribuna Nacional."

————. 1977. *Sistema económico y rentístico de la Confederación Argentina según su Constitución de 1853*. Buenos Aires: Escuela de Educación Económica y Filosofía de la Libertad.

Alhadeff, Peter. 1985. Public Finance and the Economy in Argentina, Australia and Canada during the Depression of the 1930s. In *Argentina, Australia and Canada: Studies in Comparative Development, 1870–1965*, edited by G. Di Tella and D. C. M. Platt. London: Macmillan.

Aztiria, Enrique A. C. 1971. *Origen y evolución histórica del Derecho Comercial y antecedentes argentinos*. Buenos Aires: Cooperadora de Derecho y Ciencias Sociales.

Berensztein, Sergio. 1990. *Un partido para la Argentina moderna*. Buenos Aires: Cedes.

————. 1998. The Politics of Tax Reform in Argentina and Mexico. Ph.D. dissertation, University of North Carolina at Chapel Hill.

Bravo, María Celia. 1993. Cuestión regional: Azúcar y crisis cañera en Tucumán durante la primera presidencia de Yrigoyen. *Ruralia: Revista Argentina de Estudios Agrarios* (Buenos Aires: FLACSO, Ediciones Imago Mundi) 4 (Octubre): 45–60.

Buchrucker, Cristian. 1994. Pensamiento político militar argentino: El debate sobre las hipótesis de guerra y la geopolítica. *Estudios* 3 (Otoño): 137–53.

Bunge, Alejandro E. 1940. *Una nueva Argentina*. Buenos Aires: G. Kraft.

Cárcano, Miguel Angel. 1972. *Evolución histórica del régimen de la tierra pública 1810–1916*. Buenos Aires: EUDEBA.

Cavarozzi, Marcelo. 1992. Beyond Transitions to Democracy in Latin America. *Journal of Latin American Studies* 24 (3): 665–84.

————. 1995. Los partidos políticos argentinos durante el siglo XX. *Secuencia* (México City: Instituto Mora) 32 (2): 31–48.

CEPAL (United Nations, Economic Commission for Latin America). 1959. *Análisis y proyecciones del desarrollo económico, Vol. V: El desarrollo económico de la Argentina*. Mexico City: CEPAL.

Cháneton, Abel. 1938. *Historia de Vélez Sársfield*, vol. 2. Buenos Aires: Librería y Editorial "La Facultad" Bernabe y cía.

Cheresky, Isidoro 1981. Sindicatos y fuerzas políticas en la Argentina pre-peronista: 1930–1943. *Boletín de Estudios Latinoamericanos* (Amsterdam: Centro de Estudios y Documentación Latinoamericanos) 31 (Diciembre): 5–42.

Chiaramonte, José Carlos. 1962–63. La crisis de 1866 y el proteccionismo argentino de la década del 70. *Anuario del Instituto de Investigaciones Históricas* (Rosario, Argentina: Universidad Nacional del Litoral) 6: 213–62.

Ciria, Alberto. 1968. *Partidos y poder en la Argentina moderna, 1930–46*. 2d ed. Buenos Aires: Editorial Jorge Álvarez.

Código Rural de la Provincia de Buenos Aires. 1865. Buenos Aires: Imprenta Americana.

————. 1870. Buenos Aires: Imprenta Americana.

Collier, Ruth Berins, and David Collier. 1991. *Shaping the Political Arena: Critical Junctures, the Labor Movement, and Regime Dynamics in Latin America*. Princeton: Princeton University Press.

Cooter, Robert. 1997. The Rule of State Law versus the Rule-of-Law State: Economic Analysis of the Legal Foundations of Development. In *The Law and Economics of*

Development, edited by E. Buscaglia, R. Cooter, and W. Ratliff. Greenwich, Conn.: JAI Press.

Corradi, Juan E. 1985. *The Fitful Republic: Economy, Society, and Politics in Argentina.* Boulder, Colo.: Westview Press.

Cortés Conde, Roberto. 1978. *El mercado de tierras en Argentina 1880–1913.* Torino: Einaudi.

———. 1989. *Dinero, deuda y crisis: Evolución fiscal y monetaria en la Argentina, 1862–1890.* Buenos Aires: Editorial Sudamericana.

Crossley, J. Colin, and Robert Greenhill. 1977. The River Plate Beef Trade. In *Business Imperialism, 1840–1930: An Inquiry Based on British Experience in Latin America,* edited by D. C. M. Platt. Oxford: Clarendon Press.

Dalla Via, Alberto Ricardo. 1999. *Derecho constitucional económico.* Buenos Aires: Abeledo-Perrot.

della Paolera, Gerardo, and Alan M. Taylor. 2001. *Straining at the Anchor: The Argentine Currency Board and the Search for Macroeconomic Stability, 1880–1935.* NBER Series on Long-Term Factors in Economic Growth. Chicago: University of Chicago Press.

De Jesús, Marcelo Octavio, and Mónica González Biondo. 1990. *Análisis comparativo del poder de policía en la Argentina y en los Estados Unidos.* Cuadernos de la Fundación Carlos Pellegrini 12.

de Riz, Liliana. 1986. Política y partidos: Ejercicio de análisis comparado: Argentina, Chile, Brasil y Uruguay. *Desarrollo Económico* 25 (1): 659–82.

de Riz, Liliana, Marcelo Cavarozzi, and Jorge Feldman. 1987. *Concertación, estado y sindicatos en la Argentina contemporánea.* Buenos Aires: Centro de Estudios de Estado y Sociedad.

de Sagastizábal, Leandro, et al. 1990. *Argentina 1880–1943: Estado, economía y sociedad, aproximaciones a su estudio.* Buenos Aires: Editorial Biblos.

Díaz Alejandro, Carlos F. 1970. *Essays on the Economic History of the Argentine Republic.* New Haven, Conn.: Yale University Press.

Díaz Fuentes, Daniel. 1994. *Crisis y cambios estructurales en América Latina: Argentina, Brasil y México durante el periodo de entreguerras.* Mexico City: Fondo de Cultura Económica.

Dieulefait, Carlos E. 1970. *El Banco de la Nación Argentina en su 75° Aniversario, 1891–1966.* Buenos Aires: Banco de la Nación Argentina.

Difrieri, Jorge A. 1967. *Moneda y bancos en la República Argentina.* Buenos Aires: Abeledo-Perrot.

Elhauge, Einer R. 1991. Does Interest Group Theory Justify More Intrusive Judicial Review? *Yale Law Journal* 101 (1): 31–110.

Ellickson, Robert C. 1991. *Order Without Law: How Neighbors Settle Disputes.* Cambridge, Mass.: Harvard University Press.

Gallo, Ezequiel. 1983. *La Pampa gringa: La colonización agrícola en Santa Fe (1870–1895).* Buenos Aires: Editorial Sudamericana.

Garcia Vizcaino, José. N.d. El equilibrio del presupuesto: Un imperativo de politica economica. *Revista la Ley* 113: 971.

Gerchunoff, Pablo, and Lucas Llach. 1998. *El ciclo de la ilusión y el desencanto: Un siglo de políticas económicas argentinas.* Buenos Aires: Ariel.

Gibson, Heriberto. 1997. La agricultura en la provincia de Buenos Aires. In *De la República posible a la República verdadera (1880–1910),* edited by Natalio R. Botana and Ezequiel Gallo. Buenos Aires: Ariel.

Girbal de Blacha, Noemí M. 1988. Estado, modernización azucarera y comportamiento empresario en la Argentina, 1876–1914: Expansión y concentración de una economía regional. *Anuario de Estudios Americanos* (Sevilla, Spain: Consejo Superior de Investigaciones Científicas, Universidad de Sevilla, Escuela de Estudios Hispano-Americanos) 45: 383–417.

Guy, Donna J. 1976. Tucumán Sugar Politics and the Generation of Eighty. *The Americas* 32 (April): 566–84.

————. 1980. *Argentine Sugar Politics: Tucumán and the Generation of Eighty.* Tempe, Ariz.: Center for Latin American Studies, Arizona State University.

Halperín, Isaac. 1958. *Manual de sociedades anónimas.* Buenos Aires.

Heller, Michael A. 1998. The Tragedy of the Anticommons: Property in the Transition from Marx to Markets. *Harvard Law Review* 111 (3): 621–88.

Hirschman, Albert O. 1987. The Political Economy of Latin American Development: Seven Exercises in Retrospection. *Latin American Research Review* 22 (3): 7–36.

IEERAL (Instituto de Estudios Económicos sobre la Realidad Argentina y Latinoamericana). 1986. Estadísticas de la evolución económica de Argentina 1913–1984. *Estudios* 9 (39): 103–84.

Jones, Charles A. 1985. The Fiscal Motive for Monetary and Banking Legislation. In *Argentina, Australia and Canada: Studies in Comparative Development, 1870–1965,* edited by G. Di Tella and D. C. M. Platt. London: Macmillan.

Junta Nacional de Carnes. 1937. *Informe de la labor realizada desde el 1 de octubre de 1935 hasta el 30 de septiembre de 1937.* Buenos Aires: Junta Nacional de Carnes.

Kantor, Shawn Everett. 1998. *Politics and Property Rights: The Closing of the Open Range in the Postbellum South.* Chicago: University of Chicago Press.

Karst, Kenneth L., and Keith S. Rosenn. 1975. *Law and Development in Latin America: A Case Book.* Berkeley and Los Angeles: University of California Press.

Katz, Jorge M., and Bernardo Kosacoff. 1989. *El proceso de industrialización en la Argentina: Evolución, retroceso y prospectiva.* Buenos Aires: Centro Editor de América Latina, CEPAL.

Kiper, Claudio. 1999. El análisis económico del derecho y los derechos reales. *Revista de Derecho Privado y Comunitario* (Buenos Aires: Rubinzal-Culzoni Editores) 21: 215–45.

Lamas, Andrés. N.d. *Rivadavia y la legislación de las tierras públicas.* Buenos Aires: Ediciones Populares Bernardino Rivadavia.

Lattuada, Mario J. 1988. *Política agraria y partidos políticos, 1946–1983.* Buenos Aires: Centro Editor de América Latina.

Lewis, Colin M. 1985. Railways and Industrialization: Argentina and Brazil, 1870–1928. In *Latin America, Economic Imperialism and the State: The Political Economy of the External Connection from Independence to the Present,* edited by Christopher Able and Colin M. Lewis. London: Athlone.

Lewis, Paul H. 1990. *The Crisis of Argentine Capitalism.* Chapel Hill, N.C.: University of North Carolina Press.

Lobos, Eleodoro. 1997. Apuntes sobre legislación de tierras. In *De la República posible a la República verdadera (1880–1910),* edited by Natalio R. Botana and Ezequiel Gallo. Buenos Aires: Ariel.

López del Amo, Fernando. 1990. *Ferrocarril, ideología y política ferroviaria en el proyecto liberal argentino, 1852–1916.* Madrid: Centro Español de Estudios de América Latina.

Lucchini, Cristina. 1990. *Apoyo empresarial en los orígenes del peronismo.* Buenos Aires: Centro Editor de América Latina.

Lynch, Horacio M. 1982. Socialismo bajo una constitución liberal. *La Nación* (Buenos Aires), February 21.

Mainwaring, Scott. 1986. The State and the Industrial Bourgeoisie in Perón's Argentina, 1945–1955. *Studies in Comparative International Development* 21 (3): 3–31.

Malagarriga, Carlos C. 1961. *Reseña de la legislación comercial argentina (1810–1960)*. Buenos Aires: Depalma.

Mallon, Richard D., and Juan V. Sourrouille. 1975. *Economic Policymaking in a Conflict Society: The Argentine Case*. Cambridge, Mass.: Harvard University Press.

Mariluz Urquijo, José M. 1978. *El régimen de la tierra en el derecho indiano*. Buenos Aires: Perrot.

Mann, Michael. 1993. *The Sources of Social Power, Vol. II: The Rise of Classes and Nation States 1760–1914*. Cambridge: Cambridge University Press.

McGuire, James W. 1995. Political Parties and Democracy in Argentina. In *Building Democratic Institutions: Party Systems in Latin America*, edited by S. Mainwaring and T. R. Scully. Stanford: Stanford University Press.

Miller, Geoffrey. 1994. The True Story of Carolene Products. In *Law and Justice: Cases and Readings on the American Legal System*, edited by D. A. Nance. Durham, N.C.: Carolina Academic Press.

Miller, Jonathan M. 1997. Judicial Review and Constitutional Stability: A Sociology of the U.S. Model and its Collapse in Argentina. *Hastings International and Comparative Law Review* 21 (1): 77–176.

Most, Benjamin A. 1980. Authoritarianism and the Growth of the State in Latin America: An Assessment of their Impacts on Argentine Public Policy. *Comparative Political Studies* 13 (2): 173–203

———. 1991. *Changing Authoritarian Rule and Public Policy in Argentina, 1930–1970*. Boulder, Colo.: Lynn Rienner Publishers.

Munck, Ronaldo. 1987. Cycles of Class Struggle and the Making of the Working Class in Argentina, 1890–1920. *Journal of Latin American Studies* 19 (1):19–39.

Muzlera, Joaquín M., ed. 1943. *Recopilación de leyes, decretos y resoluciones de la Provincia de Buenos Aires sobre tierras públicas, desde 1810 a 1895*, vol. 1. La Plata: Isidro Solá Sans.

Niskanen, William A. 1971. *Bureaucracy and Representative Government*. New York: Aldine-Atherton.

O'Donnell, Guillermo A. 1976. *Estado y alianzas en la Argentina, 1956–1976*. Buenos Aires: Centro de Estudios de Estado y Sociedad.

Olson, Mancur. 1971. *The Logic of Collective Action*. Cambridge, Mass.: Harvard University Press.

Oszlak, Oscar. 1997. *La formación del estado argentino: Orden, progreso y organización nacional*. Buenos Aires: Planeta.

Peralta-Ramos, Mónica. 1992. *The Political Economy of Argentina: Power and Class Since 1930*. Boulder, Colo.: Westview Press.

Piñero, Norberto. 1921. *La moneda, el crédito y los bancos*. Buenos Aires: Jesús Menéndez.

Pomer, León. 1988. El Estado nacional argentino. *Revista de Historia de América* 105 (Enero–Junio): 53–88.

Puiggrós, Rodolfo. 1957. *Libre empresa o nacionalización en la industria de la carne*. Buenos Aires: Editorial Argumentos.

Quesada, Sixto J. 1894. *El Banco Hipotecario de la Provincia de Buenos Aires*. Buenos Aires: Martín Biedma.

Randall, Laura. 1978. *An Economic History of Argentina in the Twentieth Century*. New York: Columbia University Press.

Remmer, Karen L. 1976. Economic Dependency and Political Conflict: Chile and

Argentina, 1900–1925. *Studies in Comparative International Development* 9 (2): 3–24.

———. 1984. *Party Competition in Argentina and Chile: Political Recruitment and Public Policy, 1890–1930.* Lincoln, Nebr.: University of Nebraska Press.

República Argentina. 1938. *Ajuste de los resultados financieros de los ejercicios de 1928 a 1936.* Buenos Aires: Ministerio de Hacienda.

República Argentina. 1955. *Producto e ingreso de la República Argentina en el período 1935–54.* Buenos Aires: Secretaría de Asuntos Económicos.

Rougés, Pedro. 1991. *Sistemas regulatorios de los mercados azucareros.* Tucumán: Editorial Universidad de Tucumán.

Rouquié, Alain. 1978. *Pouvoir militaire et société politique en République Argentine.* Paris: Presses de la Fondation Nationale des Sciences Politiques.

Rosenzvaig, Eduardo. 1987. *Historia social de Tucumán y del azúcar: Del ayllú a la encomienda; de la hacienda al ingenio.* Tucumán, Argentina: Universidad Nacional de Tucumán.

Sanguinetti, Julio. 1946. *Nuestro potencial económico industrial y la defensa nacional.* Buenos Aires: Biblioteca del Oficial.

Sbarra, Noel H. 1964. *Historia del Alambrado en la Argentina.* Buenos Aires: EU-DEBA.

Schvarzer, Jorge. 1991. *Empresarios del pasado: La Unión Industrial Argentina.* 2d ed. Buenos Aires: CISEA, Imago Mundi.

Sikkink, Kathryn. 1993. Las capacidades y la autonomía del Estado en Brasil y la Argentina: Un enfoque neoinstitucionalista. *Desarrollo Económico* 32 (1): 543–74.

Smith, Peter H. 1969. *Politics and Beef in Argentina: Patterns of Conflict and Change.* New York: Columbia University Press.

———. 1974. *Argentina and the Failure of Democracy: Conflict Among Political Elites, 1904–1955.* Madison, Wis.: University of Wisconsin Press.

Storni, Carlos Mario. 1997. *Investigaciones sobre la historia del derecho rural argentino.* Buenos Aires: Instituto de Investigaciones de Historia del Derecho.

Taylor, Alan M. 1997. *Latifundia* as Malefactor in Economic Development? Scale, Tenancy, and Agriculture on the Pampas, 1880–1914. *Research in Economic History* 17: 261–300.

Vargas Llosa, Alvaro. 1998. A Capitalist Revolution in Latin America? *Critical Review* 12 (1–2): 35–48.

Vélez Sarsfield, Dalmacio. 1868. El folleto del Dr. Alberdi. *El Nacional,* June 25.

Viguera, Aníbal. 1995. Partidos y política en Argentina: Reflexiones sobre una relación compleja. *Secuencia* (México City: Instituto Mora) 32 (2): 49–55.

Vilarreal, Sofia, Mirta Palomino, and Victoria Itzcovitz. 1986. Les organisations patronales face au gouvernement démocratique. *Problèmes d'Amérique Latine* (Paris: La Documentation Française) 82: 57–78.

Vilaseca, Héctor J. 1988. Banco Central de la República Argentina: Sus primeros 50 años de vida, capítulo I: período 1935–1945. *Serie de Temas Institucionales y Bancarios* 7.

Waisman, Carlos H. 1987. *Reversal of Development in Argentina: Postwar Counter-revolutionary Policies and their Structural Consequences.* Princeton, N.J.: Princeton University Press.

Wynia, Gary W. 1978. *Argentina in the Postwar Era: Politics and Economic Policy Making in a Divided Society.* Albuquerque, N.M.: University of New Mexico Press.

Zavalía, Clodomiro. 1920. *Historia de la Corte Suprema de Justicia de la República Argentina en relación con su modelo norteamericano.* Buenos Aires: Jacobo Peuser.

12

Epilogue: The Argentine puzzle

GERARDO DELLA PAOLERA
American University of Paris and Fundación PENT

EZEQUIEL GALLO
Universidad Torcuato Di Tella

If one had undertaken the task of examining the economic history of Argentina in 1910 – the year in which Argentines greeted the centennial of their nation's independence – the outcome would have reflected a much more optimistic view of the country's legacy. Not only residents, but also foreign investors had bright prospects about the future. Some even thought that the Argentine nation would parallel the economic dynamism shown by the United States of America. As early as the 1910s, both the First Bank of Boston and the City of New York Bank (Citibank) opened their two major overseas branches in the capital Buenos Aires. They were drawn to bright economic prospects much as the British bankers and investors had been decades before. This is how powerful and inescapable the future of the Argentine economy and society then seemed. Today, influenced by the gloomy years from 2001 to 2003, the analytical task might be tainted by exactly the opposite force. Foreign and domestic investment is in the doldrums, political and societal leadership is badly needed, and the minimal institutional framework necessary to become a well-integrated dynamic capitalistic economy has been destroyed once again.

In those brilliant 1910s, the retrospective analysis would have been biased naturally to the explanation of the causes that contributed to the long-run cycle of Argentine prosperity that started in the 1880s. An 1860–1910 economic growth trend would easily suggest that Argentina was the main candidate to join, if not surpass, the ranks of the core and newly settled economies, as shown in the introductory chapter in this volume. Today, conversely, we are tempted to emphasize the factors that are contemporaneously present in the current profound crisis of Argentine economic life. However, the factors and causes that precipitated the crisis did not appear overnight: they have roots in the past, as was illustrated in many of the chapters in this volume. Cracks in the façade accompanied genuine economic promise throughout the late-nineteenth and early-twentieth centuries.

For all these reasons Argentina remains an essential object of study for those interested in long-run economic growth, institutional economics, and quantitative history, and it is interesting to note what one of the pioneers in the new economic history of Argentina, Professor Alec Ford, had to say on the topic: "You may be interested to hear how I came to work on Argentina. In 1951 after my PPE finals at Oxford I was awarded the Webb Medley Research Scholarship and intended to work on the pre-1914 Gold Standard. A casual conversation with John Hicks led me to Argentina. He suggested that I could well look at Argentine experiences in the period 1860–1914 – 'some strange things happened in that period' – so I did, and he was right!"[1]

The last sentiment is echoed by some observations by the historical actors of the time. For example, there is the recollection of the well-known Argentine writer and politician Lucio V. Mansilla (1889, 7): on the eve of the Baring crisis he had an encounter with a Uruguayan trader who advised him never to forget that in the River Plate "*nuestras costumbres son de curso forzoso. ¿Estamos?*" ("our uses are those of inconvertible money"). Or one can call to mind the later warning of Minister of Finance José María Rosa at one of the most successful moments in Argentine economic history (1910), when he addressed legislators about the perils of complacency in a community with fragile and unstable cultural patterns. His words bear repeating:

Nada es más difícil de gobernar, dice un economista contemporáneo, que la prosperidad. Un desarrollo rápido y extraordinario de riqueza es una de las mayores pruebas a que la Providencia somete la cordura y el buen sentido de un pueblo. Nos encontramos en este caso: el desarrollo del país, durante los últimos seis años, ha sido extraordinariamente febril y sorprendente. Ha llegado el momento de contener nuestros excesos, de adoptar una política financiera de recogimiento, de prudencia y de economía. Estamos a tiempo, y creo que la acción de los poderes públicos será muy eficiente sobre la economía nacional y las finanzas, dirigidas así hacia los rumbos indicados. Moderación hay que predicar y aplicar, y especialmente a los gastos públicos.[2]

These and other observations would be highly relevant if we applied the old, and sometimes discarded, proposal of Simon Kuznets for the writing of history in a backward-looking fashion. The problem of applying exclusively

---

[1] Private correspondence to Alan M. Taylor, 25 February 2002. Professor Ford is alluding to his famous work *The Gold Standard, 1880–1914: Britain and Argentina* (1962).

[2] Quoted in Botana and Gallo (1997, 477). Our translation is as follows: "Nothing is more difficult to govern, says a contemporary economist, than prosperity. Fast growth and extraordinary wealth are some of the greatest challenges for which Providence calls on the wise judgment and good sense of the people. We are in this position: the development of the country, during the last six years, has been extremely febrile and surprising. The moment has arrived to contain our excesses, to adopt an austere, prudent, and savvy financial policy. We are just in time to do it and I think that the action of the government will be very efficient over the national economy and finances. Moderation is what we have to predicate and to apply, especially on public expenditures."

this approach is that it violates the principles by which we can reconstruct the past, according to the formula of Leopold Von Ranke that we analyze "what really happened" (*"wie es eigentlich gewesen"*). In other words, historical interpretation should be congruent with the ideas and the social climate that formed the frame in which people and policymakers acted. This is exactly one aim of this volume, achieved by emphasizing a methodological harmony between economic and institutional theory and historical facts to reconstruct the most salient aspects of the economic history of Argentina.

In this approach, in almost every chapter there is an emphasis on pointing out peculiar political economy and legal aspects that led economic and political economy outcomes to deviate from what social scientists would call a "first best" societal equilibrium. And it transpires from the text that these idiosyncratic design failures emerged frequently and with strong persistence through time, even in the most promising and successful periods. In this respect, the lack of respect for institutional and political economy rules appeared in most of the chapters as an endemic variable that severely handicapped the economic behavior of the Argentine nation. This characteristic is, after all, present above in Mansilla's 1888 observation about the Argentine addiction to inconvertibility or in the exhortation of Minister Rosa in 1910 not to violate the limits imposed by the fiscal budget and approved by the Congress.

It was also the perception overseas that Argentine domestic institutions were immature, and observers were skeptical about the existence of a leadership class that could ensure the adoption of clear rules of the game and property rights. In 1891, W. H. Bishop writing for a new publication called *The Economic Journal* stated:

Investors here, with minds disorganized by the fate which has overtaken those concerned with reckless speculations and borrowings of the past years, seem to conclude that Argentina is ruined because they, themselves, have lost money because they carried their speculation to undue lengths; but the Argentine have profited and the country is profiting by the sowing broad-cast of capital in the country....A solid administration is required under an honest President....Some assistance in the formation of a bank upon sounds principles is needed, with improvement in the currency. It is possible that the system of taxation might be varied so as to provide for the provincial and municipal loans which were too readily granted; though probabilities disincline an observer to conclude that local taxation will be increased without great difficulty. Suggestions have been hazarded relative to foreign financial control. Foreign financial control may be needed, and may be possible in the case of a feeble or a decaying state.[3]

---

[3] Quoted in della Paolera and Taylor (2003). Interestingly enough, a recent recommendation to solve the present Argentine political economy mess by Dornbusch and Caballero (2002) suggested some technocratic external auditing and support to regain international credibility.

It is perhaps in the arena of macroeconomic monetary, financial, and fiscal affairs that one can identify early warnings about failures in institutional and legal design. This was true in Argentine economic history even during the heyday of a mostly laissez-faire legal framework, as shown by Berensztein and Spector's chapter, at least for the period that preceded the First World War. In fact, from as early as 1810 onward, the various "stop and go" cycles in money, banking, and public finances show clearly how the nation had a serious constitutional design problem. We like to exemplify the monetary issue because money is so close to the rule of law and property rights. Salvatore and Newland show the painful road of the young republic toward settling a credible monetary framework and a coherent set of commercial rules.

Notably, the first stable monetary framework, the monetary union, was established by the republic only as late as 1890, and really only by default after the Baring crash.[4] Only after a substantial fiscal war of attrition among the different elements of the Argentine republic, which ended in disaster, was serious consideration given to settling the monetary and seignioreage question.[5] The 1820–62 secession of the Province of Buenos Aires from the rest of the Confederation had exposed the unsustainable "entente" among the federal and provincial fiscal institutions, in which the inflation tax was always the soft option. In other words, the nineteenth currency question was the other side of the coin of an unachieved political pact that could share the benefits and costs of becoming a viable federal nation.

If one were to ask an international economic historian for the central difference between the Argentine development trajectory in the nineteenth century and that of other newly settled economies such as the United States, Canada, and Australia, the most likely answer would be inflation. The inflation tax was the typical mode of public finances. The steady presence of an inflationary scenario is thus central to an understanding of the relative failure of Argentina as a federal collection of provinces. Few things in economic life are as intimately related with the rule of law and a contractual culture as the money issue. This is sometimes not well understood and, frequently, the "monetary veil" seems innocuous in good times.

Once Argentine reunification took place, moral hazard about the conduct of monetary and fiscal policies was the norm and impeded the creation of solid domestic capital and financial markets.[6] Volatility in the monetary, financial,

---

[4] See della Paolera and Taylor (2001) and della Paolera, Irigoin, and Bózzoli in this volume.

[5] And here again, the Bank of England as the lender of last resort for Argentina during the Baring crash might have been extremely influential in the creation of the Conversion Office as the sole monetary authority. See della Paolera and Taylor (2001), especially chapter 5.

[6] See della Paolera, Irigoin, and Bózzoli in this volume.

and public finance regimes ("rules of the game") was something that particularly differentiated Argentina from, say, the United States of America (Bordo and Végh 2001). The recurrent violation of property rights was something that pervaded the money and bond markets and only the establishment of short-lived metallic regimes throughout the nineteenth and early-twentieth century produced a sense of calm and civility (Bordo and Rockoff 1996).

For example, after the reunification of 1862 the national government adopted a system of plural banks of issue. In 1865 the Bank of London and River Plate decided to become a bank of issue in the Province of Santa Fe under the national and provincial laws, only to see its rights to issue being repudiated by the Province within two years. There was worse to come. The provincial government sent a local militia that confiscated the gold deposited in the bank and jailed the manager of the branch, a German citizen. A tense diplomatic situation followed when the British government sent a gunboat to put pressure on the Provincial government. Even the national press was shocked (by the province, not the gunboat), as when the Buenos Aires newspaper *La Nación* of 25 June 1876 stated "estamos en los tiempos de los abusos, de la ilegitimidad, del fraude" (Gallo 1971).

Another case of unreliability was the 1889 partial default on an internal public bond denominated in hard currency that the government wanted to pay in depreciated paper currency, all the more remarkable since the trick was attempted at the height of a boom period. The default had a domino effect on the perceived risk of Argentine external bonds, both national and provincial, and the country hit an external debt ceiling later that same year. The Law of National Guaranteed Banks of 1887 was then violated in 1890 when the national government seized the gold reserves of the banks for fiscal purposes. This institutional meltdown in the late 1880s strongly resembles the 2001–03 fiscal war of attrition among several political actors that brought about the eventual alteration of financial and central bank institutions in 2001 and the demise of President de la Rua in December of that same year. In 2002 it could be said that

Argentina's economic crisis has strong similarities with crises stretching back to the nineteenth century. A common thread runs through all these crises: the interaction of a weak, undisciplined, or corruptible banking sector, and some other group of conspirators from the public or private sector that hasten its collapse. This pampean propensity for crony finance was dubbed gaucho banking more than one hundred years ago.[7]

Macroeconomic and microeconomic institutional failures thus permeate Argentine history in a recurring way. In the 1990s, as in the past, there were

---

[7] See della Paolera and Taylor (2003).

moments of fiscal and monetary stability, but always these were subject to the lobbying forces of different economic groups, which transformed a promising opportunity for prosperity into a rent-seeking game. In a populist setting it is always very hard (if not impossible) to get an economic "soft landing" after a successful take-off. The 1990s are a clear example yet again of these political economy dynamics – which, as we have learned from some of these chapters, were present in Argentina long before the uprising of even the best known populist movement, namely, Peronism.

The rent seeking aspects of Argentine society in relation to the real economy are clearly spelled out in economic policies with respect to international trade and investment, and this is particularly relevant to performance in most of the twentieth century. Here too there is an invariable tendency to prioritize income redistribution to the most forceful economic, political, and social groups, with a neglect of the efficiency considerations that would spur sustainable economic growth. Populism has to privilege immediate results just to survive, so these regimes encourage extremely volatile rules of the game. The long-run welfare effects have no place whatsoever in the incumbent policymaker's decisions. The negative effects of early populism in the process of capital accumulation and hence on economic growth are clearly established in Taylor's chapter and also are spelled out in the trade policies analyzed by Berlinski's chapter. Policy interventions after the 1930s resulted in a set of very high relative prices for investment goods impeding capital accumulation in the economy. At this time there appeared a definite divergence of Argentina from the rest of the world in terms of real wages and productivity, and hence per capita income and wealth.

In short, Argentina was, and is, a country with outstanding economic potential, but during the *Belle Époque* she missed the opportunity to design the right institutions that would secure sustainable growth and insulate the society from the voracity of politicians and rent seekers. Another way of saying this is that Argentina's *Belle Époque* was based on prosperity of incomes, not of institutions (della Paolera and Taylor 2001, 235), and this sentiment is borne out in the chapters presented in this volume. The Argentine economy has looked very resilient in the face of this perennial incapacity of its political and leadership class to forge durable and beneficial institutions. After one or another crisis, it is always the case that economic growth resumed and critical institutional and political economy reforms were always postponed because of a false sense of renewed well-being. Successful democracies with dynamic capitalistic economies may not achieve first-best economic growth, but they nonetheless manage the conflict between short-run societal impatience (third-best rent seeking with stop-and-go) and the long-run design of a feasible social contract (albeit only second best).

To understand Argentina is to acknowledge the recurrent and unresolved conflicts between the nation's short- and long-run political economy and institutional goals. We firmly believe this book carries important lessons on the nature of these conflicts in areas as diverse as international trade, investment, labor and capital markets, law and economics, and money. We expect that these essays will be fruitful for scholars and policymakers concerned with the complex dynamics of emerging economies in all parts of the world. For the Argentines and their economic puzzle, we hope that a clearer view of the past will prevent its recurrence.

References

Bordo, Michael D., and Hugh Rockoff. 1996. The Gold Standard as a "Good Housekeeping Seal of Approval." *Journal of Economic History* 56 (June): 389–428.

Bordo, Michael D., and Carlos A. Végh. 2002. What if Alexander Hamilton Had Been Argentinean? A Comparison of the Early Monetary Experiences of Argentina and the United States. *Journal of Monetary Economics* 49 (April): 459–94.

Botana, Natalio, and Ezequiel Gallo. 1997. *De la república posible a la república verdadera (1880–1910)*. Buenos Aires: Ariel.

della Paolera, Gerardo, and Alan M. Taylor. 2001. *Straining at the Anchor: The Argentine Currency Board and the Search for Macroeconomic Stability, 1880–1935*. NBER Series on Long-Term Factors in Economic Growth. Chicago: University of Chicago Press.

della Paolera, Gerardo, and Alan M. Taylor. 2003. Gaucho Banking Redux. *Economía*. In press.

Caballero, Ricardo, and Rudiger Dornbusch. 2002. The Battle for Argentina. Massachusetts Institute of Technology (April). Photocopy.

Ford, Alec G. 1962. *The Gold Standard, 1880–1914: Britain and Argentina*. Oxford: Clarendon Press.

Gallo, Ezequiel. 1971. El gobierno de Santa Fe vs. el Banco de Londres y Río de la Plata, 1876. *Revista Latinoamericana de Sociología* 7: 147–74.

Mansilla, Lucio Victorio. 1889. *Entre-nos: Causeries del jueves*. Buenos Aires: J. A. Alsina.

13

Historical statistics

GERARDO DELLA PAOLERA
American University of Paris and Fundación PENT

ALAN M. TAYLOR
University of California, Davis, NBER, and CEPR

CARLOS G. BÓZZOLI
Princeton University

This appendix and the accompanying CD-ROM present an up-to-date compilation of the established historical statistics for Argentina. Many of these data series were used by the contributors in this volume and we hope that this resource will assist future researchers seeking to build on the current state of knowledge in the field.

Still, as with all historical statistics, the data will often be found to be incomplete and are almost certainly subject to revision as future economic historians explore archival documents and unearth more information. Another hope is that once this compilation is available its shortcomings will inspire later generations of scholars to continue this important task.

Various sources are available for Argentine historical statistics. For the present we simply offer the data that exist, sometimes from competing sources. For precise details on the construction of these data, the reader is referred to the primary sources, where the robustness and comparability of the different data may be more accurately judged.

The most frequently used sources that we employ are abbreviated as follows.

A: Alvarez (1929);

BCRA: Banco Central de la República Argentina (official sources);

C: Cortés Conde (1997, 1998);

D: della Paolera and Ortiz (1995);

I: IEERAL (1986) and Mundlak, Cavallo, and Domenech (1989);

F: IMF (various years);

M: Ministerio de Economía de la República Argentina, *Informe Económico* (several issues), and the website http://www.mecon.gov.ar;

P: Penn World Table 6.0 (2001);

VP: Vázquez Presedo (1971,1976);

OT: Organización Techint (various years);

CO: Cottely (1981, 1990).

We use dollars to refer to U.S. dollars. When we refer to pesos, the reader should note that there have been several currency reforms in Argentina, and changes in currency units complicate the presentation of historical statistics. We use the same unit throughout for consistency. All nominal units are the "convertible peso" (i.e., the peso that was convertible into one dollar as of 2001 and is still the legal currency of the country at the time of writing). For reference:

1 convertible peso (January 1, 1992–present)

= 10,000 australes (June 15, 1985–end of 1991)

= 10,000,000 pesos argentinos (June 1, 1983–June 14, 1985)

= 100,000,000,000 pesos ley 18188 (January 1, 1970–May 31, 1983)

= 10,000,000,000,000 pesos moneda nacional (1881–end of 1969).

The data from Global Financial Data are reproduced by kind permission of Global Financial Data.

National income

Real

YZC: Gross domestic product, index, base 1900 = 100 (C).

YZD: Gross domestic product, constant 1986 prices (D).

YZI: Gross domestic product, market prices, constant 1960 prices (I).

XZI: Gross domestic product, factor cost, constant 1960 prices (I).

YZF: Gross domestic product, constant 1993 prices (F). Original data: before 1980, at 1980 prices; between 1980 and 1992, at 1986 prices; and from 1993 on, at 1993 prices. Conversions of old series (1980 and 1986) prices to 1993 prices were made given the ratios at 1993 and 1980.

YZH: Gross domestic product, Hofman estimate, constant 1980 domestic prices (Hofman).

YZHI: Gross domestic product, Hofman estimate, constant 1980 international prices (Hofman).

Nominal

YD: Gross domestic product, current prices (D).

YI: Gross domestic product, market prices, current prices (I). Computed as the product between YZI and PI (GDP deflator, see below).

XI: Gross domestic product, factor cost, current prices (I). Computed as the product between XZI and PI (GDP deflator, see below).

YF: Gross domestic product, current prices (F).

Real per capita

RGDPF: Real per capita GDP, constant 1993 prices (F). Calculated as the ratio of YZF to IMF population estimation (NF*1000000, see below).

RGDPCH: Real per capita GDP chain method, constant 1996 U.S. dollars (P).

RGDPL: Real per capita GDP Laspeyres method, constant 1996 U.S. dollars (P).

RGDPTT: Real per capita GDP terms of trade adjustment, constant 1996 U.S. dollars (P).

CGDP: Real per capita GDP in current U.S. dollars (P).

RGDPEA: Real GDP per equivalent adult, constant 1996 U.S. dollars (P).

RGDPW: Real GDP per worker, constant 1996 U.S. dollars (P).

Y: Current year per capita GDP relative to the United States (%, P).

YH: Real per capita GDP, constant 1980 international prices (Hofman).

Population

NV: Population, millions of inhabitants (VP).

NH: Population, millions of inhabitants (Hofman).

NI: Population, millions of inhabitants (I).

NF: Population, millions of inhabitants (F).

NP: Population, millions of inhabitants (P).

D2059: Population share age 20–59 (I).

D15: Population share age under 15 (Taylor and Williamson).

D1564: Population share age 15–64 (Taylor and Williamson).

Consumption

CZI: Private consumption, market prices, constant 1960 prices (I).

CI: Private consumption, market prices, current prices (I).

CF: Private consumption, current prices (F). Due to changes in National Accounts Definitions, the methodology varies over time. Private consumption is properly calculated only before 1980 and from 1993 onward, when, among other features, the decomposition between Public and Private Consumption is available.

GZI: Government expenditure, market prices, constant 1960 prices (I).

GI: Government expenditure, market prices, current prices (I).

GF: Government expenditure, current prices (F).

CYZ: Private consumption share of GDP (%), constant prices (P).

GYZ: Government expenditure share of GDP (%), constant prices (P).

CY: Private consumption share of GDP (%), current prices (P).

GY: Government expenditure share of GDP (%), current prices (P).

CGEM: Consolidated Government expenditures (all levels of government) constant 2001 prices (M).

Investment and the capital stock

IZI: Gross investment, market prices, constant 1960 prices (I).

I1ZI: Gross investment, agricultural sector, market prices, constant 1960 prices (I).

I2ZI: Gross investment, nonagricultural sector, market prices, constant 1960 prices (I).

I3ZI: Gross investment, government sector, market prices, constant 1960 prices (I).

II: Gross investment, market prices, current prices (I). Computed as IZI*PII.

I1I: Gross investment, agricultural sector, market prices, current prices (I). Computed as I1ZI*PII, see below.

I2I: Gross investment, nonagricultural sector, market prices, current prices (I). Computed as I2ZI*PII, see below.

I3I: Gross investment, government sector, market prices, current prices (I). Computed as I3ZI*PII, see below.

IF: Gross investment, current prices (F).

IYZ: Gross investment share of GDP, constant prices (%, P).

IY: Gross investment share of GDP, current prices (%, P).

KZI: Capital stock, constant 1960 prices (I).

K1ZI: Capital stock, agricultural sector, constant 1960 prices (I).

K2ZI: Capital stock, nonagricultural sector, constant 1960 prices (I).

K3ZI: Capital stock, government sector, constant 1960 prices (I).

KE: Capital stock, ECLAC estimate, constant 1950 prices (Hofman).

KYE: Capital-output ratio, ECLAC estimate, constant 1950 prices (Hofman).

KYI: Capital-output ratio (I). Computed as KZI/YZI.

KHG: Capital stock, gross, constant 1980 domestic prices (Hofman).

KHN: Capital stock, net, constant 1980 domestic prices (Hofman).

KHGI: Capital stock, gross, constant 1980 international prices (Hofman).

KHNI: Capital stock, net, constant 1980 international prices (Hofman).

KYHG: Capital-output ratio, gross, constant 1980 domestic prices (Hofman).

KYHN: Capital-output ratio, net, constant 1980 domestic prices (Hofman).

KYHGI: Capital-output ratio, gross, constant 1980 international prices (Hofman).

KYHNI: Capital-output ratio, net, constant 1980 international prices (Hofman).

Land

AI: Cultivated land, unweighted, thousands of hectares (I).

AAI: Cultivated land, weighted by the value of production, thousands of hectares (I).

Sectoral activity

X1ZI: Gross domestic product, agricultural sector, market prices, constant 1960 prices (I).

X2ZI: Gross domestic product, nonagricultural sector, market prices, constant 1960 prices (I).

X3ZI: Gross domestic product, government sector, market prices, constant 1960 prices (I).

X1I1: Gross domestic product, agricultural sector, market prices, current prices (I).

X2I1: Gross domestic product, nonagricultural sector, market prices, current prices (I).

X3I1: Gross domestic product, government sector, market prices, current prices (I).

IND1: Industrial Production, index 1900 = 100 (Cortés Conde,1997).

IND2: Industrial Production, constant 1950 prices. (BCRA).

IND3: Industrial Production, constant 1960 prices. (BCRA).

IND4: Industrial Production, constant 1970 prices. (BCRA).

IND5: Industrial Production, constant 1986 prices (M).

IND6: Industrial Production, constant 1993 prices (M).

Trade

EXZI: Exports, constant 1960 prices (I).

EXZF: Exports, millions of current U.S. Dollars (F).

EXI: Exports, current prices (I). Computed as EXZI*PEXI, see below.

EXF: Exports, current prices (F).

IMZI: Exports, constant 1960 prices (I).

IMZF: Imports, millions of current US Dollars (F).

IMI: Exports, current prices (I). Computed as IMZI*PIMI, see below.

IMF: Exports, current prices (F).

OPEN: Ratio of Export and Imports to GDP (%, P).

Saving, investment, and the current account

CAF: Current account, millions of current US Dollars (F).
   CAT: Current account , current prices (Taylor).
   IT: Gross domestic investment, current prices (Taylor).
   ST: Gross domestic saving, current prices (Taylor).

Prices

EUS: Exchange rate, pesos per U.S. dollar, free market, end of year (OT for the period 1935–1995 and DATAFIEL since 1995).
   EUSEX: Exchange rate, pesos per U.S. dollar, official export, end of year (OT for the period 1935–1975 and DATAFIEL since 1981).
   EUSIM: Exchange rate, pesos per U.S. dollar, official import, end of year (OT for the period 1935–1976 and DATAFIEL since 1976).
   WPID: Wholesale price index, annual average, base 1884 = 100 (D).
   CPII: Consumer price index, base 1960 = 1 (I).
   WPII: Wholesale price index, base 1960 = 1 (I).
   WPI1I: Wholesale price index, agricultural sector, base 1960 = 1 (I).
   WPI23I: Wholesale price index, nonagricultural sector, base 1960 = 1 (I).
   EXPI: Export price index, base 1960 = 1 (I).
   IMPI: Import price index, base 1960 = 1 (I).
   PAI: Land price index, base 1960 = 1 (I).
   PI: GDP deflator, base 1960 = 1 (I).
   P1I: GDP deflator, agricultural sector, base 1960 = 1 (I).
   P2I: GDP deflator, nonagricultural sector, base 1960 = 1 (I).
   P3I: GDP deflator, government sector, base 1960 = 1 (I).
   PCI: GDP deflator, private consumption, base 1960 = 1 (I).
   PGI: GDP deflator, government expenditure, base 1960 = 1 (I).
   PII: GDP deflator, gross investment, base 1960 = 1 (I).
   PIMI: GDP deflator, imports, base 1960 = 1 (I).
   PEXI: GDP deflator, exports, base 1960 = 1 (I).
   PCR: Price of crops, 1960 = 1, base 1960 = 1 (I)
   PLS: Price of livestock, 1960 = 1, base 1960 = 1 (I).
   REK1A: Rate of return on capital, agricultural sector (I).
   REK2: Rate of return on capital, nonagricultural sector excluding government (I).

REK1A2: Rate of return on capital, agricultural and nonagricultural sector excluding government (I).

REK23: Rate of return on capital, nonagricultural and government sectors (I).

PP: Price level of GDP with United States = 100 (P).

PCP: Consumption price level (PPP/Xrate, P)

PIP: Investment price level (PPP/Xrate, P).

PGP: Government price level (PPP/Xrate, P).

EUSP: Exchange rate relative to U.S. dollar (P).

EPFA: Exchange rate, pesos *papel* per peso *fuerte* (A).

EUST: Exchange rate, pesos per U.S. dollar, end of year (Taylor).

Wages and factor prices

WI: Nominal wage index (I).

WZI: Annual average wage, constant 1960 prices (deflated using CPII, see above, I).

W1ZI: Annual average wage, agricultural sector, constant 1960 prices (deflated using CPII, see above, I).

W2ZI: Annual average wage, nonagricultural sector, constant 1960 prices (deflated using CPII, see above, I).

W3ZI: Annual average wage, government sector, constant 1960 prices (deflated using CPII, see above, I).

WW: Nominal wage index (Williamson).

WZW: Real wage index (Williamson).

Employment

LI: Employment, millions (I).

L1I: Employment, agricultural sector, millions (I).

L2I: Employment, nonagricultural sector, millions (I).

L3I: Employment, government sector, millions (I).

U: Unemployment gap, millions (I).

Banking and finance

IGLONG: Yield on external long term government bonds (*titulos publicos*), annual average, percent (D and della Paolera 1988).

IUSLONG: Yield on long-term U.S. government bonds, percent (D).

IUKLONG: Yield on U.K. consols, percent (Mitchell).

IDISC: Discount rate of banks, percent (Baiocco).

PSTK1: Stock price index (Nakamura-Zarazaga).

PSTK2: Stock price index, Swan, Culbertson and Fritz (Global Financial Data).

PSTK3: Stock price index, BOLSA General Index (Global Financial Data).

PSTKBK: Stock price index of banks (Baiocco).

IGLONGC: Yield on external long term government bonds (*titulos publicos*), annual average, percent (C).

Monetary aggregates

M0D: Broad money or monetary base, M0, end of year (D).

M3D: Narrow money, M3, end of year (D).

M1I: Money supply, M1, end of year (I).

M3I: oferta monetaria, M3, end of year (I).

M3REAL: Real M3 (D).

M3VELO: Income velocity of M3 (D).

CURR: Currency in the hands of the public, end of year (D).

RES: Currency in banks (*Encajes*), end of year (D).

DEP: Bank deposits, end of year (D).

FIDCA: Fiduciary issue of Caja de Conversión (Baiocco).

REDCA: Rediscounts of Caja de Conversión (Baiocco).

GOLDCA: Gold reserve of Caja de Conversión, including legaciones, at official parity (Baiocco).

FIDBC: Fiduciary issue of Banco Central (BCRA).

RESBC: International reserves of Banco Central, at official parity (BCRA).

RESI: International reserves of Banco Central, millions of U.S. dollars (I).

M0CC: Monetary base, M0, (CC).

M3CC: Money supply, M3, (CC).

MSCC: Money supply, millons of *paper* pesos (CC).

Fiscal aggregates

GREV: Federal government revenue (CO). Original data denominated in pesos oro between 1864 and 1864. Conversion from pesos oro to pesos based on Alvarez average exchange rates for each year between 1864 and 1884.

GEXP: Federal government expenditures (CO). Original data denominated in pesos oro between 1864 and 1864. Conversion from pesos oro to pesos based on Alvarez average exchange rates for each year between 1864 and 1884.

GDEF: Federal government deficit (CO). Original data denominated in pesos oro between 1864 and 1864. Conversion from pesos oro to pesos based on Alvarez average exchange rates for each year between 1864 and 1884.

IPUDV: Change in internal public debt (I).

EPUDV: Change in external public debt, millions of U.S. dollars (I).

EPRDV: Change in external private debt, millions of U.S. dollars (I).

PSE: Consolidated government expenditures (I).

GE: Federal government expenditures (I).

GR: Federal government revenue (I).

INGCC: Fiscal Revenues of National Treasury (1810–20) and Provincia de Buenos Aires (1820–62, C). The assumed parity between the peso moneda nacional and the peso *papel* is 25:1.

EGCC: Fiscal Expenditures of National Treasury (1810–20) and Provincia de Buenos Aires (1820–62, C) The assumed parity between the peso moneda nacional and the peso *papel* is 25:1.

DEFCC: Fiscal deficit of National Treasury (1810–20) and Provincia de Buenos Aires (1820–62, C). The assumed parity between the peso moneda nacional and the peso *papel* is 25:1.

FGEM: Federal Government expenditures, constant 2001 prices (M).

Commercial policy

TEXP: Export tax revenues (I).

TIMP: Import tax revenues (I).

RETCO: Ad valorem tax rate (*Retenciones*) on wheat exports, percent (CO)

RERC: Real Exchange Rate Index (1937 = 100) with the U.S. dollar, free market (CO).

RER2: Real Exchange Rate Index (Jan 1970 = 100) with the U.S. dollar, free market (own calculations using CPI and WPI of Argentina and U.S.).

MRER: Multilateral Real Exchange Index (1991 = 100), Centro de Economia Internacional (CEI), Secretariat of Trade, International Economic Relations and Consular Affairs, http://cei.mrecic.gov.ar.

References

Álvarez, Juan. 1929. *Temas de historia económica argentina*. Buenos Aires: El Ateneo.

Baiocco, Pedro J. 1937. *La economía bancaria argentina*. Buenos Aires: Universidad de Buenos Aires.

Cortés Conde, Roberto. 1997 *La economía argentina en el largo plazo*. Buenos Aires: Sudamericana

Cortés Conde, Roberto. 1998. Fiscal Crisis and Inflation in XIX Century Argentina. Universidad de San Andrés. Photocopy.

Cottely, Esteban. 1981. Características básicas de la gestión fiscal en la Argentina. *Boletin Techint* 223: 42–76.

Cottely, Esteban. 1990. Enigmas de la política cambiaria. *Boletin Techint* 262: 29–78.

della Paolera, Gerardo. 1988. How the Argentine Economy Performed During the International Gold Standard: A Reexamination. Ph.D. dissertation, University of Chicago.

della Paolera, Gerardo, and Javier Ortiz. 1995. *Dinero, intermediación financiera y nivel de actividad en 110 años de historia económica argentina.* Documentos de Trabajo Universidad Torcuato Di Tella (December).

Heston, Alan, Robert Summers, and Bettina Aten. 2001. Penn World Table Version 6.0 Center for International Comparisons at the University of Pennsylvania (CICUP). http://pwt.econ.upenn.edu/.

Hofman, André A. 2000. The Economic Development of Latin America in the Twentieth Century. Northampton, Mass.: Edward Elgar.

IEERAL (Instituto de Estudios Económicos sobre la Realidad Argentina y Latinoamericana). 1986. Estadísticas de la evolución económica de Argentina 1913–1984. *Estudios* 9 (July/September): 103–84.

International Monetary Fund. Various years. *International Financial Statistics.* Washington, D.C.: International Monetary Fund.

Mitchell, Brian R. 1971. *Abstract of British Historical Statistics.* Cambridge: Cambridge University Press.

Mundlak, Yair, Domingo Cavallo, and Roberto Domenech. 1989. Agriculture and Economic Growth in Argentina, 1913–1984. Research Report no. 76, International Food Policy Research Institute (November).

Nakamura, Leonard I., and Carlos E. J. M. Zarazaga. 1999. Economic Growth in Argentina in the Period 1905–1930: Some Evidence from Stock Returns. In *Latin America and the World Economy Since 1800,* edited by John H. Coatsworth and Alan M. Taylor. Cambridge, Mass.: Harvard University Press.

Organización Techint, *Boletín informativo,* several issues.

Taylor, Alan M. 1998. Argentina and the World Capital Market: Saving, Investment, and International Capital Mobility in the Twentieth Century. *Journal of Development Economics* 57 (October): 147–84.

Taylor, Alan M., and Jeffrey G. Williamson. 1994. Capital Flows to the New World as an Intergenerational Transfer. *Journal of Political Economy* 102 (April): 348–71.

Vázquez-Presedo, Vicente. 1971–76. *Estadísticas historicas argentinas.* 2 vols. Buenos Aires: Ediciones Macchi.

Williamson, Jeffrey G. 1999. Real Wages, Inequality, and Globalization in Latin America Before 1940. *Revista de Historia Economica* 17: 101–42.

Index

Abramovitz, Moses, 170
Acevedo, Eduardo, 337
Adelman, Jeremy, 37–8
aforos, and industrial production, 272
age groups, and labor force
    participation, 145–6
aggregate demand, and cyclical
    behavior of GDP, 99–103, *115t*
Agote, Pedro, 81
agriculture: and banks, 185–6; and
    crop failure of 1913–14, 317; and
    economic history of Argentina,
    24–7, 233–59; labor market and
    expansion of, 125–6; livestock
    exports and survival of
    self-sufficient, 42. *See also*
    frontier; land and land ownership
Alberdi, Juan Bautista, 331, 332,
    333–4, 335, 341
Albert, Bill, 271n18
Alesina, Alberto, 47n2
Alfonsín, Raúl, 60
Alsina, Adolfo, 55, 57, 67, 71
Alsina, Valentín, 336, 337
Amaral, Samuel, 22n3, 24, 25, 26, 29
analytic narrative, and style of
    economic writing, 1
anarchism, and trade unions, 131
antitrust law, and meat packing and
    livestock industries, 343
Anuario Estadístico (INDEC), 81
Anuario Pillado, 304
Argentina: agriculture and economic
    growth in, 233–59; and capital
    accumulation, 170–94;
    development of economy in period
between 1810 and 1870, 19–44;
and economic cycles, 87–112;
evolution and performance of
industrial sector, 261–90;
international trade and commercial
policies of, 197–230; and labor law,
127, 160–5; literature on economic
history of, 1–2, 8–10; monetary and
fiscal policies in macroeconomic
history of, 46–76; puzzle of
economic growth in, 2–5, 369–75;
role of banking and finance in
economic growth of, 295–322;
scope of study of economic growth
in, 10–16; state apparatus and
economic growth, 324–63; and
timing controversy, 5–8;
transformation in labor market
during nineteenth century, 122–60
Argentine Meat Producers'
    Corporation, 344
Argentine Rural Society (Sociedad
    Rural), 345, 346
Argentine Yearbook, 304
Armour Research Foundation, 278
Ashenfelter, Orley, 134
automobile industry, and industrial
    growth, 284, *285t*
Avellaneda, Nicolás, 55, 65, 67, 68,
    70, 335
Avramovic, Dragoslav, 80

Backus, David K., 96, 98, 99, 103,
    107
Bagehot, Walter, 297
Baiocco, Pedro J., 300

A New Economic History of Argentina

Scholars, policymakers, and laymen alike have been struck by the Argentine puzzle: why has this country of recent European settlement and rich endowments stagnated economically for so long? The melancholy is more acute after one recalls the brief *Belle Époque* almost one hundred years ago, when this country was considered to have joined the club of developed economies; but putting this nostalgia aside, economic performance has been for the most part a disappointing mix of inflation, crises, default, and financial turmoil, with an occasional boom thrown in to raise false hopes. Social and political structures have varied during this malaise, but none has yet reversed the dismal trend. A reasonable constitution exists on paper and the populace has always been relatively well educated. Demographic trends have not been unfavorable and the country was spared the great wars of the last century. Colonial ties are almost two centuries old, with ample time having passed to overcome the legacy at independence. There appear to be no simple answers. The advent of another crisis in 2001, perhaps the most severe of all time, only forces the question yet again: what has gone wrong? The answers will not arrive from an examination of the last week's newspapers, the last year's policy choices, or the last decade's economic trends. A longer view is needed, and these essays present a state-of-the-art examination of the development record by today's leading specialists in Argentine economic history. The authors expose the historic dimension of the Argentine puzzle – and, it is hoped, provide some of the answers.

GERARDO DELLA PAOLERA is President and Professor of Economics at the American University of Paris and Senior Visiting Fellow at Fundación PENT, Argentina. He received his Licenciado in economics from Universidad Católica, Argentina, and his Ph.D. in economics from the University of Chicago. From 1991 to 2001 he served as the founding Rector and Professor of Economics at Universidad Torcuato Di Tella in Buenos Aires. He co-authored *Straining at the Anchor: The Argentine Currency Board and the Search for Macroeconomic Stability, 1880–1935* (with Alan M. Taylor, 2001) and he has published numerous articles in journals such as *Revista de Historia Económica, Explorations in Economic History*, and *Economía*. He has served as a Visiting Fellow or Professor at many institutions including the Hoover Institution at Stanford University, the London School of Economics, Oxford University, Doshisha University, and the University of Chicago.

ALAN M. TAYLOR is Professor of Economics at the University of California, Davis, Research Associate at the National Bureau of Economic Research, and Research Fellow at the Centre for Economic Policy Research. He read the Mathematical Tripos at King's College, Cambridge, and received his Ph.D. in economics from Harvard University, with a dissertation that won the Alexander Gerschenkron Prize. He has written or edited six books, and his papers have appeared in various journals including *Journal of Political Economy, Quarterly Journal of Economics, American Economic Review*, and *Econometrica*. He co-authored "Economic Recovery from the Argentine Great Depression: Institutions, Expectations, and the Change of Macroeconomic Regime" in the *Journal of Economic History* (with Gerardo della Paolera, 1999), which won the Arthur H. Cole Prize. He was an Academy Scholar at the Harvard Institute for International and Area Studies and a National Fellow at the Hoover Institution. He currently holds a Chancellor's Fellowship at the University of California, Davis.

Lightning Source UK Ltd.
Milton Keynes UK
UKHW01f1833130918
328808UK00001B/83/P